Brazillionaires

Brazillionaires

WEALTH,
POWER,
DECADENCE,
AND HOPE
IN AN
AMERICAN
COUNTRY

Alex Cuadros

SPIEGEL & GRAU
NEW YORK

Published in the United States by Spiegel & Grau,
an imprint of Random House,
a division of Penguin Random House LLC, New York.

SPIEGEL & GRAU and design are registered trademarks of
Penguin Random House LLC.

LIBRARY OF CONGRESS CATALOGING-IN-PUBLICATION DATA
Names: Cuadros, Alex.
Title: Brazillionaires : wealth, power, decadence, and hope in an American country /
by Alex Cuadros. Description: New York : Spiegel & Grau [2016] |
Includes bibliographical references.
Identifiers: LCCN 2015037361 | ISBN 9780812996760 (hardcover) |
ISBN 9780812996777 (ebook)
Subjects: LCSH: Billionaires—Brazil. | Wealth—Brazil—History—21st century. |
Finance—Brazil—History—21st century. | Economic development—Brazil—
History—21st century. | Brazil—Economic conditions—21st century.
Classification: LCC HC190.W4 C83 2016 | DDC 305.5/2340981—
dc23 LC record available at http://lccn.loc.gov/2015037361

International edition ISBN: 9780399589539

Printed in the United States of America on acid-free paper

randomhousebooks.com
spiegelandgrau.com

246897531

First Edition

Frontispiece by istock
Book design by Barbara M. Bachman

To the memory of my godfather,
DAVID SULLIVAN

Why deny it? I had a passion for showiness, for billboards, for pyro-
technics. Perhaps the modest will reproach me for this defect; I trust,
however, that people of discernment will acknowledge my talent.
Thus my idea, like a medal, had two sides, one turned towards the
public, the other towards me. On one side, altruism and profit; on
the other, thirst for fame. Or rather, let us say, love of glory.

—MACHADO DE ASSIS,
Memórias Póstumas de Brás Cubas
(trans. William Grossman)

Contents

THE CRASH

On a stretch of highway not far from Rio de Janeiro, a silver SLR McLaren idled on the shoulder, its futuristic door hinged open at the top like a wing extended toward the evening sky. The warning lights blinked yellow. In the driver's seat, a twenty-year-old kid named Thor sat spattered with blood. The windshield sagged inward, weirdly limp, spiderwebbed with cracks, half-detached from the roof, and in the car's nose, a perfect round hole gaped where the Mercedes-Benz symbol had been dislodged. Along the hood, a zigzag of thin, dusty tread marks traced the improbable dance of a bicycle tire.

Thor and his passenger had been driving back from a steakhouse in Petrópolis, the old summer retreat of Pedro II, the Brazilian emperor. They were on a highway that winds south toward Rio from mountains blanketed in rain forest so dense the trees look heaped on one another. Coming into the lowlands, shacks of dull red cinderblock cluster along the road. Landslides during the summer rains sometimes carry these homes away; once the ground hardens, their residents rebuild them.

Wanderson Pereira dos Santos was from here. He unloaded trucks for a living. His bicycle lay in a gully by the road, the red frame bent up, back tire curled in on itself like a wilted flower. He'd been pedaling from the store, on his way home to celebrate his wife's birthday, when Thor's car struck him. The impact tossed his body two hundred feet down the road. His left foot was torn off, his left arm too. His chest split open; police would later find his heart inside the McLaren.

As Thor and his friend sat dazed in their seats, a med student in a Ford pulled up alongside them and said, "You just killed that guy back there." He had no idea then that Thor's dad was Eike Batista, the richest man in Brazil. The McLaren's license plate read EIK-0063; sixty-three was Eike's lucky number.

Other drivers stopped at the scene. Someone called an ambulance. Thor felt steady enough to emerge from the McLaren, and his bodyguards, who'd lagged behind in their pickup truck, took him and his friend to a first aid station a couple of miles down the road. There a nurse looked at Thor and sent him on his way—apart from some nicks from broken glass, the blood on him wasn't his. But he didn't go back to the crash site just yet. Instead he went thirty miles into Rio proper and stopped at home before returning to the highway with his dad's lawyer Flávio Godinho. A bodyguard drove them now.

Two miles from the crash site, Thor stopped at a roadside police station where the lights of emergency vehicles flashed. He blew zero on a Breathalyzer and gave a written statement—he'd been rounding a curve down an unlit hill when all of a sudden in the middle of the road this cyclist appeared, dragging his left foot inexplicably on the ground; Thor braked right away, but it was too late. The officers asked him to go downtown for questioning, but Godinho wanted to avoid the circus of reporters who would show up. They relented. Though they'd spent just a couple of hours examining the McLaren, Godinho even persuaded them to let him tow it away on the condition he wouldn't alter or destroy any evidence. Wanderson's body was removed from the scene just as quickly. His widow's lawyer later said, "I've never seen the state work so fast."

That was March 17, 2012. The next day the crash was all over the Brazilian press.

———

THIS EVERYDAY TRAFFIC DEATH became national news because Eike Batista, Thor's father, was more than just a major businessman. When he wasn't making headlines for some new venture—and he always had new ones in those days, whether in oil and gas or microchips or gold—then you found him in the gossip pages. One day he'd host the president at his Manhattan-size port project, the next he'd be on TV talking about the thirty-five-thousand-dollar treatment that restored hair to his balding head. His ex-wife, Luma de Oliveira, was a *carnaval* queen and *Playboy* cover girl. He was so big that Brazilians knew him just by his first name: Eike. He seemed at times everywhere at once in his bright pink tie. Paparazzi would shoot him jogging, flanked by bodyguards, around Rio's Rodrigo de Freitas Lagoon—which he'd paid to depollute—not far from the mansion where, before passing it on to Thor, he'd kept that silver McLaren in one of his living rooms. One of a dozen of its kind in Brazil, the car cost him 1.2 million euros.

In a deposition a few days after the crash, Thor insisted he'd obeyed the 110-kilometer-an-hour speed limit—about 68 miles an hour. Thor's lawyers touted an autopsy revealing alcohol in Wanderson's blood. But the med student who'd been driving behind Thor told investigators the McLaren had zigzagged past him like in a police chase. Reporters discovered that Thor had racked up eleven traffic violations in the previous eighteen months, most for speeding, and enough that his license should have been taken away, if not for Brazil's sluggish bureaucracy. Even more damning, it turned out that Thor had driven his Audi into an eighty-six-year-old cyclist on a Rio street a year earlier, breaking his hip. Eike had paid the medical bills and the family had kept quiet until now. One of the old man's children said, "We were just worried about saving our father, who didn't want any *confusão*." In Portuguese the word means "confusion," also "trouble."

Eike paid four thousand dollars for Wanderson's funeral. The burial took place on a gray day in the cemetery in the village of Xerém, not far from the length of asphalt where Wanderson had died. A half-dozen friends, none wearing suits, some in shorts and flip-flops, carried the lacquered casket up a concrete walkway, past proper stone tombs, to an empty grave on a muddy slope. A throng of reporters followed them snapping pictures. Wanderson's aunt gave interviews. She'd raised him. He'd never met his dad, and his mom, a drunk, had abandoned him when he was a kid. A mortician, the aunt said, had reconstructed his face for the funeral. News stories often ran two photos together: Thor, with fair skin and a high-lighted flop of hair, and Wanderson, skinny and black, his shaved head sometimes covered by a baseball cap.

To many people, the way things went down embodied some of Brazil's deepest problems: not just the gulf between rich and poor but also the special treatment reserved for the powerful and the well connected. Why did police let Eike's lawyer tow away the McLaren? One TV presenter shouted, "Just because he's a billionaire doesn't mean you don't need a proper examination! Just because he's a bil-lionaire doesn't mean justice shouldn't work the same way!" But Thor was soon back on the road. Less than two months after the crash, he competed in a drag race near São Paulo, driving a bright red Ferrari 458 Italia.

"Thor symbolizes the new rich Brazil," a blogger wrote. "Wan-derson made me think: poor, old Brazil."

Two months after the crash, the police came out with a forensic report calculating the McLaren's speed at the moment of impact: 83 miles an hour, well above the legal limit on that twisty mountain road. That same day, inspiring a mix of surprise and skepticism across Brazil, prosecutors indicted Thor for manslaughter.

AT THE TIME OF THE CRASH, Eike Batista was worth thirty billion dollars, and this made him the eighth-richest person in the world. He was a symbol of his country's dramatic transformation. Just a generation ago, Brazil was an impoverished dictatorship mostly famous for samba, poetic soccer, and the violence of its slums. It had since become a stable democracy with the world's seventh-largest economy. Though its rise would soon screech to a halt, Brazil remains the top exporter of coffee and sugar, soybeans and beef; it also produces more oil than Norway. Four icons of American consumer culture—Budweiser, Burger King, Heinz, and Kraft—now belong to a trio of billionaires from Rio. And in a country of two hundred million people, forty million have risen from extreme poverty since the turn of the twenty-first century.

I moved to Brazil in 2010, at the peak of its rise. Like many foreigners, I was drawn at first by an aura of romance and adventure, but I ended up discovering a place with many more layers to it. And when Bloomberg News invited me to cover billionaires as a full time job, I found myself in the middle of two great stories. One was about the Brazilian boom, a story of national ambition. The other was about the accumulation of wealth, and this story went well beyond Brazil.

I hadn't given billionaires much thought before, but as I immersed myself in their world, they took up more and more space in my head, and I found myself obsessed with them. Of course I had practical questions: how they put their fortunes together, how they shaped the economy, how they influenced the government, and how all that changed life for everyone else. I also had squishier questions about how their minds worked and how they justified their wealth to themselves and the world. I was fascinated too by the general fascination with billionaires. They're celebrities who change the world: symbols of meritocracy and progress for some, a cabal of monopolists to others. At times I admired what they built; at other times I wondered whether it was just plain wrong to be so rich in a country this poor—or in any country. I wondered which extreme was closer to the truth: Did the ultrarich take a society forward or hold it back? Could billionaires create progress at all, or did progress simply create billionaires?

Eike fascinated me most of all, and I came to see him as a bridge between two traditions that define the billionaires of Brazil and the world. In the American style, he was a salesman with a nose for a trend and vast ambition. He got rich by selling the new Brazil. His goal was to be the world's richest man by 2015, and his startups raised billions of dollars from private investors all over the world. At the same time he followed a script common in emerging economies under heavy state influence: He won the favor of people in government to secure massive transfers of public money.

And yet Eike didn't want just to get rich. With his plan to build the greatest industrial empire Brazil had ever seen—from scratch— he hoped to remake his country as a modern power. He was self-conscious in his symbolism, and he eagerly played role model to ordinary Brazilians aspiring for a better life. But things didn't go as planned. He failed to deliver what he'd promised. Before it ever got off the ground, Eike's empire collapsed under the weight of its debts, and he went broke. His net worth of thirty billion dollars evaporated in just a year and a half. Of the few people ever to amass a fortune that size, no one had ever lost it all in such a short span. Plenty of Brazilians lost their savings too.

This book is about Brazil and about billionaires—but more than that, it's about how wealth is accumulated in the modern world and the stories we tell ourselves to explain this process. The first part, "Roots of Wealth," is at once a panorama of Brazil—a vast, vibrant country perennially on the cusp of a brilliant future—and of a new world of billionaires that transcends national borders. I show how Brazil's billionaires get rich and stay rich, how they shape Brazil and reflect it. I also show how ordinary Brazilians interact with the empires built by their richest citizens and how more American ideas of wealth reverberate throughout.

Part Two, "The Brazilian Dream," mostly follows the epic rise and fall of Eike—and with him, the changing fortunes of Brazil, whose dreams of prosperity approached and then grew distant just as Eike's empire began to crumble. First the economy began to sputter; then came a corruption scandal of unprecedented proportions. On the eve of the 2016 Olympic Games in Rio, the country sank into crisis—a familiar predicament, but one that many, including Eike, had believed to be a thing of the past.

What I found in Eike wasn't just a story of fantastic wealth creation and destruction and a man of almost pathological charisma. Eike also seemed to embody all the tensions and contradictions in the way we think about the role of wealth in society. Like people in a lot of countries, Brazilians are trying to figure out the right balance between economic growth and equality, between government action and private initiative. They're grappling with ideas about prosperity, how to achieve it, and what to do with it. I saw these ideas come into conflict in the lives of the billionaires I trailed. Between the lines of their stories, a drama about a country's dreams for itself played out.

PART ONE

ROOTS OF WEALTH

CHAPTER 1

GOD IS BRAZILIAN

THE NEW BRAZIL, MIAMI,
AND HIDDEN WEALTH

"I follow the rules that I built for myself."
—ABILIO DINIZ ($4 BILLION)

A HELICOPTER DESCENDED FROM THE SKY, ITS GLOSSY BODY catching the oblique winter light. As it drew closer to me, a machine hiss overwhelmed that familiar deep faraway chop. Its little wheels perched gingerly on the roof of the São Paulo Sheraton. A pilot wearing wraparound sunglasses and pilot's headphones hopped out, slid open the back door, and set up a three-step ladder for us to board. He clasped his hands in front of him, waiting for us to get in, a chunky metallic watch on his right hand. It was 4:25 P.M. His punctuality was English, as Brazilians like to say.

The helicopter wasn't for me. It was for a top editor visiting from New York, whose time Bloomberg News judged more valuable than the fifteen hundred dollars an hour it cost to hire a chopper to ferry him around. I was a twenty-nine-year-old reporter tagging along to meet a big newsmaker. I climbed aboard with three other colleagues, my knees touching theirs in the backseat. Everyone put on a pair of those headphones.

As we rose into the air, the helipad retreated, São Paulo shrank. The Pinheiros River dwindled to a dark stripe, tiny cars filling up six lanes of freeway on either side. We left behind the Octávio Frias de Oliveira Bridge, a concrete X intersected by yellow cables supporting two crescents of road. We passed over office towers of gleaming dark blue glass, luxury condos of imitation granite, new buildings copying many architectural styles at once. I took photos on my Black-Berry, craning to see a city whose chaos seemed from this height to reorder itself in neat rows. The Bloomberg editor also sneaked a shot or two. Then, almost as soon as it had begun, the trip was over.

From the helipad we tromped downstairs into an office of many beiges—the carpets, the desks, the filing cabinets. We were in the headquarters of a company known as Brasil Foods, BRF for short. It was surprisingly quiet given that BRF was Brazil's biggest producer of packaged foods and the world's biggest exporter of poultry, feeding millions of Russians and Arabs and Chinese. We settled into a conference room to wait for the company's new chairman, Abilio Diniz, one of Brazil's richest men. He owed his four-billion-dollar fortune to his family's supermarket chain, Brazil's largest—another superlative. It was called Pão de Açúcar, Sugarloaf, after the iconic mountain in Rio.

Abilio Diniz famously worked out several hours a day, running, lifting weights, boxing, and playing squash, even at seventy-six years old. He ate like a stereotypical Californian, avoiding the Brazilian staples of rice and beans and red meat. I'd seen a picture of him in a tank top doing the pectoral fly, and his face, lined and tan as a leather shoe, looked Photoshopped onto the body of a much younger man. Now here he was, bounding over to shake our hands, wearing khakis and a simple white button-up shirt, no tie. He sat down, and the Bloomberg editor jumped straight into the interview. This was a mistake. In Brazil, you can't cut straight to the chase. You need to ease into business, glide through some small talk, something about soccer, the weather, traffic. The other mistake was hitting him with the most obvious and least comfortable question first: How can you possibly be chairman of two public companies that do business with each other? Pão de Açúcar bought BRF's TV dinners and yogurts and smoked turkey. "In all my time as a journalist, I don't think I've ever seen such a thing," the editor told Abilio.

Abilio wasn't just chairman of both companies, he owned stock in them. This had led to a clash between him and his French partner at Pão de Açúcar, Jean-Charles Naouri. Alleging that Abilio's dual roles made for a glaring conflict of interest, Naouri had filed for international arbitration. The dispute permeated the business press. For Abilio, though, it was just his latest messy public battle. In the early eighties, his father had decided to hand out shares in Pão de Açúcar based on his children's performance in the company. Abilio got a sixteen percent stake while each of his two brothers got eight percent and their three sisters got just two percent each. Fights ensued, and as the alliances shifted, the siblings spilled their woes to a series of delighted journalists. In 1993 Abilio finally persuaded most of his family to sell their shares to him, cementing his control.

Abilio spoke halting English as he explained to us that the legal issues existed exclusively in Naouri's head. There was no conflict of interest because Abilio *felt* there was none. "I follow the rules that I built for myself," he said. He bounced in his chair, looking from one to another of us as though being interrogated. Now and then he squinted at his PR people with a look of pained incomprehension, and they helped him explain what his English couldn't. Pressed on his dual roles, he snapped at last, in Portuguese: "Did you come to interview me, or did you come to provoke me?"

The conversation kept on like this for twenty minutes, until Abilio glanced around and asked, "Okay?"—indicating our time was up. This was a man with a hierarchy of attentions. Journalists ranked low, though possibly above his press people. These he addressed without ever quite meeting their eyes, making offhand orders—"I'll take a water"; "You'll send me that article later?"—in the way of someone who rarely repeats himself.

But there was more to Abilio than conflict. In recent years he'd become a champion of healthy living. He wrote a best-selling self-help book, translated into English as *Smart Choices for a Successful*

Life, and created a sports research center to advise Brazil's Olympic athletes (and himself). Prepping before the chopper ride, I'd explained this to the Bloomberg editor. And so as Abilio began to hover from his seat, the editor's last question was "What about health?"

Abilio settled into place again. His demeanor shifted entirely, his voice growing soft, quiet. His wife was forty-one, younger than all four children from his first marriage. With her he had a six-year-old daughter and a three-year-old son. He believed these were signs he'd been blessed, literally, with special vitality, and his duty as a Catholic was to share this gift with the world. "The thing inside Abilio is my faith in God," he said. "Okay?" Then he stood up, thanked us, and hurried off to other battles.

The helicopter returned to whisk the Bloomberg editor to the airport, an eleven-minute flight that could take three hours by car during rush hour. I didn't get to join him this time. Instead I walked to the nearest bus stop, an island in the middle of six lanes of frenzied traffic. There was an aerial walkway, but a half-dozen people stood by the side of the road waiting to leap through a gap in the oncoming cars. They wore jeans, springy old running shoes, and puffy jackets whose color had faded in the strong sun of subtropical winter. In erratic dashes a few at a time, they surged across. Brazil was booming, but people still risked their lives just to get to work and back.

BRAZIL SOUNDED MORE IDYLLIC when I was growing up in Albuquerque, New Mexico. My parents told me stories about coming to Brazil in 1980. They had met by chance while traveling in Guatemala earlier that year, and made their way to Rio de Janeiro together. They went to a party with Jorge Ben Jor, the funk musician, and my dad first told my mom he loved her at a café in Copacabana. In their yellowing snapshots, they have long hair.

I heard another kind of story from my godfather, a private investigator named David Sullivan. He lived in Brazil off and on in the seventies and eighties and married a Brazilian who became my sister's godmother. They later divorced, but he went on visiting the country up until his death in 2013. He used to tell me wild tales that ended with him greeting the morning sun on the beach, bleary-eyed after a night of adventure. Once he told me how, when he first arrived in Brazil as a twenty-something quasi-drifter, he met a woman on the street hawking apartments for rent. He made as though he had more than a few dollars to his name, a fiction she didn't even believe, he said, and she agreed to show him one of the units. Within moments, they were making love on the bare floor. Samba implicitly played in the soundtrack to these stories.

David dismissed São Paulo as a secondary attraction, a place you go to work, so I skipped it the first time I came to Brazil. It was 2005, and David had invited me to the house he'd built on an island near Paraty, down the coast from Rio. I'd just graduated from a small liberal arts college, and I decided to spend a month down there with my college girlfriend. Since I already knew Spanish, I figured three hours of Portuguese lessons would be enough to prepare me. I was wrong. The taxi driver at the airport seemed to speak solely in nasal vowels, breaking here and there into a theatrical falsetto. I could barely understand a word.

David received us in Rio. In Copacabana we walked the *calçadão*, the promenade whose white limestone and black basalt sidewalk forms geometric waves mirroring the waves offshore. Bronzed dudes in Speedos on the beach passed a soccer ball from head to chest to foot to knee without ever letting it drop to the sand. We passed the Copacabana Palace hotel where Brigitte Bardot stayed, and then we passed a nightclub called Help, and David told us stories about the prostitutes there. In the street, a ragged minivan burped along with the sliding door ajar and a dark-skinned kid hanging out, shouting out destinations to potential fares. Past the city, from the top of Corcovado Mountain, Christ the Redeemer spread his white stone arms to us. East was Pão de Açúcar, Sugarloaf, a giant thumb of rock poking up from the sea, with tiny tramcars creeping up and down distant threads of tramline. Corner shops offered the juice of dozens of fruits we'd never heard of, delicious flavors that just can't be compared to anything up north: *jabuticaba, acerola, caju.* Of course we couldn't help but notice the favelas. They crawled up the hills jutting from touristy neighborhoods, dull red cinderblock shacks stacked upon one another, crawling upward till they couldn't crawl farther.

Along the way I meandered into Portuguese. I learned words with no English equivalent, like *saudade,* a nostalgic longing, and *cafuné,* the act of lovingly stroking someone's hair. *Malandros* are tramps who live off the occasional swindle—a category that, by consensus, includes most Brazilian politicians. But the *malandro* can also be a kind of antihero, because he gets what he wants in a country where most people struggle just to get by. My godfather told me about a *malandro* nicknamed O Cagão—The Big Turd—who seduced a whole town's married women yet always skirted retaliation from their husbands. The *malandro*'s talent is *jeitinho.* If *jeito* means "way," then *jeitinho* is the "little way" around society's rules. A word like that suggested a culture very different from the one I'd grown up with. I was hooked; I wanted to learn more.

In 2008 I quit my job at a publishing house in New York. My girlfriend had broken up with me, and I decided to take off backpacking around South America. I meant it as a salmon-like repeat of my parents' trip, except that I hoped to stay somewhere along the way and try my hand at journalism. I spent a month and a half in Brazil but ultimately settled in Colombia, which was much cheaper for a fledgling reporter.

I'd been freelancing for a year in Bogotá when someone from Bloomberg called me up and offered me a gig in the bureau there. My idea of the company was so vague that I didn't even connect it to Michael Bloomberg, its billionaire owner and then the mayor of New York. Bloomberg News turned out to be the media appendage of Bloomberg L.P., which makes most of its billions by renting out financial-data terminals to bankers and investors for twenty-four thousand dollars a year. I knew nothing about finance and next to nothing about economics, and I was way more interested in writing about the poor. But I imagined the job would give me good reporting experience. More urgently, my savings had run out. So I accepted. With a few embarrassing errors along the way, I figured out the basics of quarterly profits, stock prices, bond yields. Surprising myself, I ended up fascinated by what I learned. Since I'd picked up some Portuguese while traveling, Bloomberg eventually offered me a job in São Paulo, Brazil's financial capital. I took it for a simple reason—I wanted to live in Brazil.

Bloomberg was one of scores of foreign companies expanding in Brazil. Commodity prices were soaring, and the economy had just about doubled in size in a decade. In the wake of 2008's global financial crash, the GDP had stalled only briefly before revving up again. Some analysts predicted that, any day now, Brazil would surpass France and the UK to become the world's fifth-largest economy. The Brazil my godfather had seen in the eighties and early nineties, when prices at shops could double in a single month and forty million people barely earned enough to eat, seemed distant now. In a sign of its newfound credibility, Brazil had won its first-ever investment-grade credit rating from Standard & Poor's. *The Economist* summed up the mood with a cover that showed Rio's Christ the Redeemer statue rocketing skyward with the headline BRAZIL TAKES OFF.

I moved to Brazil in April 2010, American spring, São Paulo fall. Bloomberg put me up at first in a hotel near the company's offices in Brooklin (sic). It seemed history-less here, all brand-new offices, cranes slanting against the skyline. The Pinheiros River cut through, black and deadly still, its surface reflecting the rows of corporate towers whose dark glass reflected back their jagged rows in the river. Every morning as I passed through the lobby of Brooklin's World Trade Center, which housed Bloomberg's offices, my nostrils filled with the river's ever-shifting bouquet of sewage and industrial run-off. From my desk on the twenty-first floor, I heard the constant brap of helicopters. I watched executives being deposited on a nearby helipad, neckties spiraling in the chopper wind. Five hundred helicopters swarmed around São Paulo, more than in any other city in the world.

One day I went to the top of the forty-six-story Edifício Itália. I looked out at the sea of high-rises that ended beyond the limits of the city's beige haze. Here were twenty million people, all jammed up against one another and yet simultaneously sprawling. São Paulo is what would happen if New York threw up on L.A., is one analogy I heard.

Like L.A., the city is ruled by traffic. A thousand new cars hit the streets of São Paulo each day. Each week rush hour seemed to start a bit earlier and end a bit later. Taxi drivers kept miniature TV sets on their dashboards so they could watch telenovelas or soccer matches while waiting for the stopped-up flow to inch forward. Fridays at the Bloomberg office, when six P.M. approached, one of the salesmen would sometimes go to the window, spreading the shades to peek at the riverside freeway. "It's ugly," he'd say. Or he'd just groan, withdrawing his hand in frustration to let the shades clap shut again. Some days you could get home faster walking than driving. It was even worse for the cleaning ladies and doormen who lived two hours from the city center. At rush hour commuters can line the subway platform ten people deep, and when the train pulls in, spitting out a few passengers, the crowd outside will do its best to ram its way into the crowd inside. You'll see people half-emerging from the doors, and still someone will run up and press herself against them, seeking to enter by osmosis. Station attendants wedge people in so the doors can close. The bus experience is similar, except without air conditioning; bad shocks lurch you into sweaty strangers.

In São Paulo, in Brazil in general, it's a battle just to achieve the basics in life. Signing up for any service—a phone, a bank account—requires a perplexing amount of paperwork. The price will surreptitiously jump at random intervals, and canceling the service can bring worse hassles than signing up. Just to switch my Internet provider, I once had to make an official complaint with the government's telecom agency. That's normal. Notaries are another hassle. I'd never needed a notary in the United States, but in Brazil I spent hours waiting for some ten-*real* stamp of approval alongside dozens of other people barely containing their despair. Whatever you submit to the government must be notarized. Paperwork begets paperwork. Sometimes the demands of the bureaucracy are literally impossible or just rude. To register children born at home, notaries have been known to ask for photos or video of the birth. Red tape entangles the whole economy. Your average Brazilian company spends twenty-six hundred man-hours just to prepare its taxes. There's even a profession, *despachante,* dedicated to navigating the bureaucracy, mostly by making friends with the right bureaucrats.

"Brazil is not for beginners," Tom Jobim, the bossa nova composer, famously said. São Paulo is especially hard. But it's got energy. Reading the history, I learned it's long been a magnet for ambitious types. Migrants from all over started showing up in the late nineteenth century, first to work in the coffee fields and later in the factories built with coffee profits. "It is a consortium of languages, a little Babel," one observer wrote back in 1905. Today the world's largest colonies of Japanese and Lebanese and Italians all live here; at lunch buffets you'll see people put sushi and kibbeh and cannelloni all on the same plate. After 2008 a fresh wave of Portuguese and Italians and Spaniards came over, fleeing recession back home. I knew Americans who slogged through the bureaucracy to found startups here. The University of São Paulo brings students from every country in Latin America. The city must be like New York was in the eighties, I thought—gritty, creative, highly charged.

São Paulo wasn't romantic like Rio. Vinícius de Moraes, the poet, called it "samba's tomb." But I liked the people of São Paulo, *paulistanos,* ever since I'd backpacked through in '08. A Brazilian journalist I'd met glancingly in New York invited me to a birthday at her place. The crowd was worldly and intellectual and also refreshing, because they lacked New Yorkers' default sarcasm and detachment. They genuinely wanted to know about me, where I came from, what

I thought of Brazil; they excessively complimented my Spanish-inflected Portuguese. As the night advanced, we made plans for a variety of outings that would never occur. A Brazilian will invite you to dinner at her mother's house within an hour of meeting you. She'll make this invitation with utmost sincerity even though she has no intention of following through. Brazilians are false, some expats will say. But they'll also tell you how easy it is to make friends here. And every now and then these plans really do materialize.

MY JOB AT FIRST was to cover the stock market. With four screens of ever-changing tickers in front of me at all times in my office, I didn't technically need to visit the exchange, but I found excuses because I got antsy reporting on intangibles from a desk. The exchange was in a stately old building downtown. On the cobblestone streets surrounding it, men in ill-fitting suits and once-white shirts took espresso at tiny bar-cum-restaurants with one wall open to passersby. Just steps away from a place where billions of dollars traded hands each day, I saw the poverty you could forget still existed in Brazil if you just read the financial headlines. Between the pillars of century-old buildings that had gone up during São Paulo's coffee boom, breathing heaps of blankets spread over cardboard indicated sleeping humans. Crack addicts with their zombie gait roamed about; I could smell the tangy concentration of urine as I passed them. Heading back to Brooklin by taxi, I'd see kids with brown skin and blondish hair at traffic lights peddling candies among Mercedes-Benzes with darkened windows. Shirtless, muscular men pulled rickshaws piled high with recyclables that reflected the light from the sun.

In the seventies, an economist named Edmar Bacha came up with the term *Belíndia* to describe what he thought Brazil was becoming then: Belgium-like bubbles of wealth surrounded by destitution worthy of India. The reverse could also be true. Favelas, the poor, informal neighborhoods built ramshackle by their own residents, are a feature of every Brazilian city. In São Paulo, most of them sprawl across the *periferia,* the outskirts. But people also set up shacks wherever they could find empty space. Across the river from the Bloomberg office, past luxury condos with balconies webbed in to keep cats from committing suicide, a favela had wedged itself between the riverside freeway and a big-box home improvement store's parking lot. Once in the Faria Lima financial district I saw a mini-slum tucked into an alley between two skyscrapers. Curious, I walked in, pretending I belonged there, though it seemed obvious I didn't. I saw a guy hosing off his car, kids playing with well-worn plastic toys in a narrow passage through homes of cinderblock, men in tank tops shooting the shit in a plywood doorway: life on open display.

Working at Bloomberg, I sponged up an arcane Portuguese that allowed me to describe market operations in exact terms but left me at a loss at a hardware store. I compensated by exploring the city's nightlife. Many expats flocked to sleek bars with suited bouncers where the door might cost a hundred dollars and a single drink another twenty-five. I tried those places but preferred the dingy fluorescent-lit establishments known as *botecos* where locals—mostly working class, but really any class—will buy a *cafezinho* and a deep-fried snack or a shot of *cachaça.* On most blocks you'll find one or two whose folding tables spill onto the sidewalk. I learned a lot at *botecos.* While we drank frigid, nearly tasteless beer, Brazilians—from newspapers and ad agencies, universities and corporate offices—eagerly shared their country with me, the good and the bad. They lamented how the same old problems—the same old overloaded roads, crappy schools, hospitals that you can leave worse off than when you arrived, prisons that are basically medieval, politics that thrive on patronage, companies that thrive on government ties, the corruption tax inflating the value of public works, all executed with truly astonishing . . . slowness—how all this held them back. I learned the clichés that surface in any Brazilian debate about the national progress. A Viennese writer named Stefan Zweig coined one favorite cliché in a book he published in 1941. Agog at the wealth of natural resources here, he touted Brazil as "the country of the future." Brazilians appended a joke—"and it always will be."

Screwy as it was, though, no one could think of a time when Brazil had it this good. Some of the old clichés were changing, and I noticed this as much in *boteco* conversation as in the world of finance I got to know through Bloomberg. The unlikeliest thing about Brazil's popularity with investors was the man at the center of the country's transformations: Luiz Inácio Lula da Silva, known to all just as Lula. He was the first Brazilian president who grew up poor. In a country of patrician elites, Lula didn't learn to read till he was ten, and in speeches still mangled his grammar. He lisped. He was squat and bearded, with the barrel torso of a manual laborer who ate beans and rice. The industrialist Antônio Ermírio de Moraes, one of Brazil's first billionaires, said of him back in 2002, "He's no statesman, for the love of God."

Lula came from the northeast. The region was the economic heart of the Portuguese colony back when sugar plantations made big profits, but it fell into decline in the eighteenth century and has been the poorest part of Brazil ever since. Lula's hometown was in the backlands known as *sertão,* drought-ridden cattle country that is poor even by northeastern standards. Over the course of the twentieth century, millions of Brazilians migrated from the northeast to the factories springing up along the southeastern coast. Lula made this journey with his family as a seven-year-old in 1952, traveling for thirteen days in the back of a flatbed truck to reach Santos, a port city near São Paulo. To help support the family, he quit school early and sold oranges and peanuts on the docks. When he was nine, he and his mother and some of his seven siblings moved in to the back room of a bar on São Paulo's outskirts, and he worked at a dry cleaner's and shined shoes. Then at fourteen he got a job in an auto parts factory. Foreign carmakers then were churning out cars. He made a decent living, but it was hard work under bad conditions, and by his own admission he sometimes swigged *cachaça* on breaks. Working late one night, he got his left pinky caught in one of the machines, and at the hospital a doctor amputated it. Lula went on to become a union leader and got famous in the late seventies for heading up the first major strikes under the military dictatorship.

Brazil had been through booms in the past—sugar in the seventeenth century, gold in the eighteenth, coffee in the nineteenth, the industrial awakening of the twentieth—but the one now unfolding under Lula looked different, broader than any that had come before. Depending on the political leanings of my *boteco* companion, I would hear two versions of Brazil's economic success story. Simplifying a bit, one version held that Lula just followed the orthodox policies of his predecessor and surfed the rising tide of commodities prices. In the other, Lula stimulated the economy by pumping more cash into welfare than any other president before him, uniting underfunded programs into something called Bolsa Família, or Family Allowance. Both versions were actually true, and they complemented each other, but the second was the more interesting story, because it pointed to a new set of priorities in Brazil, long one of the world's most unequal countries. Through Bolsa Família, Brazilians making less than a dollar a day got modest cash payments each month for vaccinating their kids and sending them to school. Malnutrition would fall by half during Lula's presidency.

Lula had dabbled with socialism as cofounder of the Workers Party in the eighties, but now he spoke the language of consumerism. "I worked my whole life and could never afford a car," he said once. "What I want is for people to have cars, I want people to buy motorcycles, I want people to buy televisions, I want people to buy fridges, washing machines." As he raised the minimum wage each year, he also expanded credit to people who'd never had it before, and the working class started looking something like a middle class in its American ideal. Millions of new consumers emerged. One lefty political scientist, André Singer, believed Brazil was on its way to fulfilling a "Rooseveltian dream" of widespread material well-being. And then the state oil company found fifty, possibly a hundred bil-

lion barrels of offshore oil, enough to put Brazil in a league with
Kuwait. "Petrobras's discovery proves once and for all," Lula said,
"that God is Brazilian."

Lula approached rock star status. First he won the right to hold
the World Cup in Brazil in 2014; then he got the 2016 Olympics for
Rio. At a summit in London, Barack Obama shook his hand and
declared, "This is my man right here. Love this guy. He's the most
popular politician on earth."

This was like historic retribution for something Charles de Gaulle
had supposedly said in the sixties, that *Brazil is not a serious country*. Though apocryphal, the phrase flourished in the popular imagination. God might be Brazilian, but Brazil seemed never to get
anything right, always falling short of its potential. It was like a fun-
house mirror-image of American exceptionalism. The writer Nelson
Rodrigues called this feeling of inferiority *complexo de vira-lata*, literally "mutt complex"—another essential cliché. The phrase suggests
a stray dog begging for scraps. Rodrigues coined it in 1950, after Brazil lost the World Cup to Uruguay in Rio de Janeiro. That had been a
national tragedy. Now Brazil had a lot more going for it than soccer.

At Bloomberg in those days I covered a frothy stock market. If I
had put a hundred dollars in at the beginning of 2009, I would have
earned another hundred in just a year. With foreign money streaming
in, dozens of companies went public. As soon as I arrived in São
Paulo, I started hearing about a businessman named Eike Batista.
He'd just held his fourth IPO in as many years, raising more than a
billion dollars for a startup to build oil platforms. In its list of billionaires that year, *Forbes* named him the world's eighth-richest person, worth twenty-seven billion dollars. No Brazilian had ever ranked
that high. Seventeen other Brazilians joined him on the list, most of
them also relative newcomers.

Brazil's showing on the *Forbes* list was another sign of just how far the country had come. And yet the phenomenom went well beyond its borders. Billionaires were rising all over, even in developed countries hit hard by the Great Recession. In 2006 *Forbes* had named some eight hundred billionaires across the world. Five years later there were twelve hundred.

When Bloomberg started putting together a team of journalists to cover the ultra-rich, the timing was apt, if unintentionally so. It was the fall of 2011, and protesters had just set up tents in Manhattan's Zuccotti Park, calling their movement Occupy Wall Street. They had a lot of messages, but the one that resonated was the simplest: *We are the 99 percent.* The movement divided America into the ninety-nine percent of people who took the brunt of the financial crash and the richest one percent—the bankers involved in the crash, especially—who seemed to suffer no consequences. The one percent, though, covered a lot of people. Most were professionals and managers who lacked much power on their own. Bloomberg's new "billionaires team" would focus only on the top 0.0001 percent, a thin slice of humanity whose combined wealth, at four and a half trillion dollars, could pay off the entire public debt of Germany and the UK combined.

The head of Bloomberg's billionaires team, Matt Miller, a former *Forbes* guy, asked me to join up and track the ultrarich of Latin America. My title would be "billionaires reporter." The team's main goal was to create something called the Bloomberg Billionaires Index, a *Forbes*-like ranking that would be updated once a day rather than once or twice a year. On the Bloomberg terminal, it would be accessible by typing RICH<GO>. I was wary at first, because the *Forbes* list had always struck me as a billionaire pissing contest. Matt helped me see it another way: "Billionaires control swaths of the economy." They influence our lives far more than your average senator but receive only a fraction of the public scrutiny. I took the job, again for a simple reason—billionaires seemed like interesting characters.

———

I SOON FOUND MYSELF getting to know a parallel world, previously invisible to me. I was surprised to learn that the wealth capital of Latin America was located back in my home country. My new job meant getting to know Miami, but a Miami different from the one most Americans see. On one trip I went to a party thrown by Paulo Bacchi, a Brazilian who owns a chain of furniture stores called Artefacto. His store in Miami caters to rich Brazilians buying luxury Miami apartments. This had become a big industry; the financial crisis actually gave it a boost. When the housing bubble popped, Miami condo prices fell by more than half. Meanwhile, with interest rates near zero in the United States, investors hungry for returns funneled their dollars into emerging markets with higher rates like Brazil. This caused the local currency, the *real,* to soar in value, which in turn made it cheaper for Brazilians to buy stuff abroad. In 2012 Brazilians accounted for one in seven Miami home purchases.

The occasion for the party was Miami Swim Week, a fashion-industry swimsuit event. A taxi dropped me off at Artefacto's Aventura location, a big-box store glowing white in the night. A light rain fell as bow-tied valets jogged to receive well-polished cars—Escalades, Bentleys. Past a three-pillared entryway, photographers snapped shots of the guests coming in. The paparazzi seemed to know who everyone important was; they did not take my picture. I asked them where I could find Paulo Bacchi and they pointed out a tan, full-chested man dressed all in black, gripping the hands of men he knew, kissing the cheeks of the women.

Electronic music pulsed from a DJ booth in the mezzanine. Waiters weaved through balancing trays of fusion hors d'oeuvres. The bar offered three drinks: champagne, pink champagne, and *caipiroska,* a take on the *caipirinha* that switches low-class *cachaça* for Stoli. Long white sofas with zebra-print throw pillows sliced up the place. A chandelier of large glass droplets hung down from the ceiling. Some guests sat in white love seats set too far apart to have a conversation without shouting, orbiting coffee tables too distant to put down your drink. Artefacto liked to arrange everything in such a way as to make life feel luxuriantly and unrealistically spacious.

I heard Portuguese all around me, as well as Spanish, some Spanglish, and also Portunglish. Men favored dress shirts tucked into jeans, unbuttoned low enough to show off their chest hair. Many wore blazers despite the sticky heat undercutting the A/C. Lots of women wore cocktail dresses. Paulo Bacchi's wife's dress was cream-colored and rhinestone-covered. The median age might have been forty-five, but many guests flashed the unnatural smile of a face made artificially to look younger. One of the Real Housewives of Miami, Alexia Echevarría, posed for a photo. Her tanned cleavage rose out of a bright red dress; her hair rose from her scalp into a tight blond bun.

I made small talk with an American woman who introduced herself as a luxury real estate broker for Sotheby's. I asked her how business was; it was better than ever. In the bubble days people often put down just a tenth of a condo's value, intending to flip it. Now she couldn't remember the last time she'd dealt with a mortgage. Foreign buyers had changed the market with their habit of paying cash for second homes. For Brazilians this was a legacy of hyperinflation and double-digit interest rates that made buying on credit prohibitive. Venezuelans and Russians wanted somewhere safe and discreet to park their money. For all of them, Miami real estate was a hedge and an investment—but also more than that. I'd heard about this party from a Brazilian broker named Cristiano Piquet. He told me, "The idea is that you're not just buying an apartment, you're buying a lifestyle."

The way Cristiano describes Brazil, it's chaotic, it's dirty, it's dangerous. He's not alone. Every day on the news you hear stories of a new carjacking or *arrastão*. An *arrastão*—literally "trawling"—is a mass robbery at a restaurant, on a beach, or on a traffic-choked road. A group of *bandidos* will round everyone up at gunpoint and flee with the loot before the police arrive. In May 2006 a gang known as the PCC basically took São Paulo hostage for a week. Its members torched buses and banks and shot down police officers while coordinated uprisings broke out in prisons around the state. A few dozen cops and prison guards died. The cops in turn killed at least a hundred suspected PCCers, probably more.

A young heir to a paper fortune once told me that when he set foot outside his apartment in São Paulo, he felt as if he was leaving Baghdad's Green Zone. This isn't totally paranoid. There have been a few high-profile kidnappings over the years. Abilio Diniz, the old supermarket tycoon, always hired bodyguards for his children but used to drive around alone, believing he could fend for himself. He knew judo and karate. He carried a gun in his car and trained at a shooting range. And so in São Paulo one morning in 1989, when an ambulance cut him off and blocked the way forward, he grabbed for his pistol—but another car slammed into his from behind. A man dressed as a police officer approached the driver's side, distracting Abilio while another man opened the passenger door and snatched his gun away. The men tied him up, hooded him, and took him to a safe house. There they enclosed him in a brightly lit space barely large enough for him to fully extend his body. They cranked *sertanejo*—Brazilian country music—to full blast. They turned it down only to ask him a question: *How much do you think you're worth?*

The gang set his ransom at thirty-two million dollars, but police found the safe house after six days. Abilio's captors let him out of his box to shout to the officers outside that he was alive. In the standoff, he would act as the gang's human shield. They carried assault rifles and shotguns. Former leftist guerrillas, mostly Chileans and Argentines, they told him they'd rather die than go to prison. Some had undergone torture at the hands of various governments. Abilio tried to persuade them to lay down their arms and surrender, but he made it out only thanks to the archbishop of São Paulo, who guaranteed the kidnappers' safety in police custody. (Despite his efforts, they were beaten.) When Abilio emerged from the house, newspapers ran photos of the famously fit man looking gaunt, his tan washed out,

wearing a week's graying beard and sweatpants and a too-long T
shirt, unsmiling as he walked with the aid of a friend who took his
arm. Other kidnapping victims lost ears, fingers, their lives.

Miami in the American imagination might conjure *Miami Vice,*
but rich Brazilians live in a Miami of security and order—Brickell
Avenue, Miami Beach, certain beachy suburbs. The women I saw at
Artefacto wore jewelry with diamonds and gold, and some of the
men did too. In Miami they can roll down the windows of their Bentleys and Escalades and let the balmy air in without fear that some
nervous kid with a giant pistol will hold them up. In Brazil these
people live in homes like fortresses. I visited Abilio's mansion once,
and it had high walls and an imposing metal door manned by armed
guards. Some São Paulo execs move their families to Alphaville, a
gated suburban compound with a private security force where from
multiple helipads they can essentially teleport to work. You can't
spend your whole life at home, though, which is why malls exist.
Brazilians call them *shoppings.* Measured in square feet, São Paulo
has more *shoppings* than parks. They've been called the *praia dos
paulistanos,* São Paulo's beach—an air conditioned fluorescent-lit
beach, where guards monitor the entrance for suspicious characters,
where you have luxury stores and fancy restaurants to take dates to,
a bubble of Belgium inside São Paulo.

The Miami of rich Brazilians is a *shopping* swollen into a city.
Many visit just to buy stuff. Brazil has always been expensive. There's
a name for the country's inflated prices—*o custo Brasil,* the Brazil
cost. Partly it's the decrepit roads and scant railroads and overloaded
ports that raise freight costs, and partly it's the high import tariffs
that shield local industry. Partly it's the labor laws that make formal
jobs in Brazil some of the most protected in the world but also make
it expensive to fire anyone. Partly it's Brazil's chronic inflation problem, those double-digit interest rates, and the odd fact that you can
buy almost anything *parcelado,* in installments of several months—
even your toothpaste and ibuprofen. Partly it's just unexplainable. In
any case, when the *real* was near its peak, you could buy iPhones and

Hermèses in Miami for half the price in Rio or São Paulo. It was easily worth the plane ticket and a few nights' hotel to load up on consumer goods. Miami shops hired Portuguese-speaking staff to meet demand from moneyed Brazilians. At airport duty-free stores, I'd see them filling their baskets with Johnnie Walker Black Label and Grey Goose and improbable amounts of chocolate. To accommodate the extra shopping ballast, Tam Airlines had to fill its planes with more fuel for return flights.

Brazilians weren't the only nouveaux riches from emerging economies showing off. A new class of wealthy Chinese were making similar displays on their trips abroad. The difference is that there's a tradition of wealth in Brazil. In nineteenth-century Rio, I learned, travelers from Europe chuckled at the locals who gauchely flaunted Parisian fashions in the tropical heat.

France used to be the inspiration for Brazil's elite. By the late twentieth century, though, America had taken France's place. The English term *high society* was Brazilianized as *soçaite*. In the marketing world, the English language came to suggest all the qualities of a Brickell Avenue condo—newness, cleanness, modernness—that Brazil lacked. In São Paulo you see fancy apartment complexes with names like Upscale and Urban Solution. I myself lived in a building called Duplex Top Tower. From the French, Brazilians hold on to the word *chic*—pronounced "sheeky" in Portuguese and surely uttered more in Brazil than in France. Once when I told a woman where I was from, she replied, *"Estados Unidos, que chique."*

MIAMI IS A MAJOR private banking hub. Private bankers tend to avoid press, but having Bloomberg on my business card opened doors. Some considered me a fellow traveler in the world of wealth, I sensed. Others probably just wanted intel on this index where their clients could show up. On my first trip to Miami, I met Santiago Ulloa, a Spaniard who works for several rich families from Latin America and Europe. Santiago spoke in heavily accented English and listened with a smile that conveyed goodwill and calm. He dressed immaculately, in a well-tailored navy blue suit, crisp tie, and fashionable rimmed glasses. We drank espresso at a conference table overlooking Brickell Avenue's shining new office buildings, vacant for years in the wake of the crash but now filling up again.

Santiago runs a "multifamily office." His job is to help UHNW families maintain their money from generation to generation—I had to learn acronyms like this: ultra-high-net-worth. His company created games to teach young heirs to deal with the burdens of wealth. For five-year-olds, he has a sectioned piggy bank with slots labeled SAVE, SPEND, DONATE, and INVEST. For ages eight and up, he has a Monopoly-like game called "Shirtsleeves to Shirtsleeves"—a reference to how fortunes built in the first generation tend to dissipate in the third. The board game's cover asks *How Long Will Your Money Last?*

"The biggest thing that upsets these people is if money is going to be good or bad for their kids," Santiago told me. He gives his clients a deck of cards titled "Keeps Me Up at Night," which works as a brainstorming exercise for family patriarchs who need help giving voice to their concerns. Each card carries a theme like "Trust" or "Second Home" and questions like "How will the age difference between me and my spouse affect my wealth planning?" or "How can I make sure that my values live on after I'm gone?"

Santiago also arranges kidnapping insurance and prenup lawyers. He hooks his clients up with the best investment people too. You can't just let all that money sit there. Bloomberg built a calculator to estimate the growth of a billionaire's investment portfolio over time. Even with a basket of generic index funds, it amazed me to see how fast a billion dollars could become two billion. This was especially true in Brazil. As in Balzac's France, the government sustains a class of rentiers, paying high interest rates on its Treasury bonds. This helps explain why so many Brazilian names on the *Forbes* list—the Setubals, the Moreira Salleses, the Aguiars—belong to banking heirs.

Calculating someone's net worth, I learned, involves a mixture of reporting, math, intuition, and unwritten tradition. It means digging through securities filings, learning to read a balance sheet, and interviewing analysts who know how to put a dollar value on opaque assets. Helping out with calculations on billionaires in other countries, I saw tax policy in action. Billionaires in the United States, where capital gains taxes are low and dividends are taxed as regular income, tend to sell their shares bit by bit to raise cash. In Brazil, where dividends are untaxed, billionaires tend to hold on to their shares, instead paying themselves juicy dividends. In either case, they skirt all the taxes they legally (and sometimes not so legally) can. They put their assets in a variety of exotic structures in a variety of exotic locales—Uruguay, Liechtenstein, the South Pacific island of Niué.

The problem becomes taking care of your stuff. With a hundred million dollars, you might have bodyguards and assistants and a permanent staff to care for your homes. With a billion, you need someone like Santiago. With a few billion, you need a family office of your own, a whole company to manage your assets and affairs. Abilio Diniz's occupies multiple floors of an office building in São Paulo. Sometimes not even that's enough. I met a former management consultant named Natasha Pearl who tends to the trickier aspects of life for the ultra-rich. She knows what numbers to call if you want to buy a racehorse or sell a diamond necklace. She knows discreet psychiatrists for troubled heirs and heiresses. She can ensure that every one of a billionaire's homes stocks the exact same outfits, so that he never has to pack much when traveling.

EXPLORING THE BILLIONAIRE WORLD, every time I thought I'd seen the peak of luxury, I discovered a higher level. I used to feel special just because Bloomberg flew me around in business class. One day I got bumped up to first class, and business class struck me as almost proletarian. Then in São Paulo I visited an "executive aviation" fair, where large-bellied executives still in suit and tie after work sipped champagne and smoked cigars among helicopters and jets and scantily clad promo girls, laughing over European techno. I walked up an airstair into a hundred-foot Bombardier Global 6000, which cost fifty million dollars and could fly from São Paulo to Paris without refueling. The interior was spacious in a way airplanes aren't supposed to be. A few wide cushiony seats lined one side; toward the back was a double bed. The bathroom had a shower and a leather-covered toilet, wide and thronelike, as if for an obese king.

Once I took a date to D.O.M., the best restaurant in São Paulo, or at least the priciest, which is sometimes made out to be the same thing. We both ordered the tasting menu and the "wine harmoniza-tion." Over three and a half hours, we consumed ten small dishes, each of whose artfully clashing ingredients was explained to us in minute detail. One course was just two ants plucked from the deep-est Amazonian jungle. Served raw, they tasted like citrusy flowers; I needed a gulp of wine to wash down their prickly legs. Inevitably the bill had to arrive. Even though I told myself this was research, I was spending my own money and I felt kind of dirty dropping 1,889.52 *reais*—nearly a thousand dollars then—on dinner for two. That was three times Brazil's monthly minimum wage. I looked around the dim, hushed room, and if anyone else had a heavy conscience, their faces didn't show it. At one table all six guests played with their iPhones, as if to broadcast that eating at D.O.M. was totally banal to them by now. And they were probably just millionaires. It wasn't long before I heard myself using the word *just* like this. *So-and-so is worth "just" a hundred million dollars.*

On a trip to Rio, I asked a luxury real estate broker to show me his finest property. We met in front of a nondescript six-story build-ing on Ipanema beach and took the elevator to the penthouse, a sixty-five-hundred-square-foot duplex. The owner was away, but the *mordomo,* the butler, let us in. (A beach butler, he wore shorts.) In the kitchen, copper pots and pans hung above a continental island where I could imagine Alex Atala, D.O.M.'s chef, preparing an inti-mate meal. From low-slung modernist chairs in the high-ceilinged living room, we beheld panoramic sea. In the master bedroom, the butler pressed a panic button, and metal shutters lowered over the doors and bulletproof windows. The windowless *quarto de empregada,* the maid's room, could have fit into the master bathroom's shower.

The butler led us into a sitting room with wavy bands of bright color emblazoned on the walls. It struck me as tacky and garish next to the understated elegance of everything else. But he told me to look closer. Leaning in, I could see that the rich purple or orange in each stripe derived from the wings of thousands of exotic butterflies. "Don't worry," the butler told me. "They've all been certified by Ibama"—Brazil's environmental protection agency. The apartment's asking price was $13.4 million. A similar space in Manhattan might cost three times that.

I was coming to grasp what it means to be a billionaire, at least in material terms. It's a lot different from having a hundred million. With a hundred million, you can't buy a fifty-million-dollar jet and a forty-million-dollar penthouse and a twenty-million-dollar yacht— you have to choose one. With a billion, not only can you have all these things but they're sensible investments. When the waiting list for new jets grows, used ones can rise in value. And as the population of billionaires expands, so the price of superluxury apartments climbs, regardless of what's happening in the economy of the masses. I heard them called "crisis proof."

Between a ten-digit billionaire and an eleven-digit billionaire is an order of magnitude. At those reaches, it's impossible to spend all your money on beachfront villas and superyachts and such toys. That's when you get into vanity projects, like when Jeff Bezos, the founder of Amazon, put down a quarter-billion dollars for *The Washington Post.* That was still just one percent of his wealth. You can burn through far more with philanthropy. Bill Gates has the Gates Foundation, Warren Buffett has the Giving Pledge. Mike Bloomberg has given more than a billion dollars to Johns Hopkins University.

In the ladder of luxuries, art occupies a rung up near philanthropy. Purchasing art confers a patina of status and culture for money made in unsexy sectors like cement or packaged foods. Anyone with a little bit of money can buy a Louis Vuitton handbag, of which thousands are manufactured each year. Very few people can buy the new Jeff Koons, even if they do have the tens of millions of dollars required. But art is an investment too, a must in any billionaire's portfolio. Art, like any other product, follows the laws of supply and demand. The canonical works (Picasso, Cézanne) tend to appreciate faster than the S&P 500—but unlike stocks, blue-chip art is as crisis proof as a penthouse on Central Park West.

THE ART INDUSTRY NOTICED the rise of the Latin rich early on. In 2002 the people behind Art Basel in Switzerland started an offshoot of the fair in Miami. For a week each December, Miami Basel fills the half-million-square-foot Miami Beach Convention Center with a few billion dollars' worth of paintings, photos, and found objects cleverly arranged. The fair is open to the public, but serious buyers attend the day before the general opening. Even among the VIPs, though, there are gradations of very importance. The lowest level of VIPs can attend the *vernissage* from six to nine P.M. on the eve of the general launch. There's a more exclusive showing from three to six, and before that you have something called First Choice.

Journalists aren't invited to First Choice, but a gallery friend got me in one year. Inside, white walls divided the gallery spaces in honeycomb fashion. At Gagosian's nook, a little Picasso hung; at Luciana Brito's, photos of Marina Abramović swimming naked. I saw a stack of wooden chairs going for thirty-five thousand dollars, and then at a different gallery I saw another stack of chairs by another artist priced higher. Art world people milled around—men with facial hair of perfect length and tightly tailored suits strutted with bright pocket squares; clusters of tall women made taller by their heels poked above the crowd as a forest of bare elegant necks. Flowing between them were money people. I saw an old lady in a red dress and red-dyed hair snapping an iPhone picture of a gold-encased succulent on the floor. I saw Lorenzo Mendoza, Venezuela's third-richest man, just standing around casually chatting with an acquaintance, because at least in this room, he was not the center of attention. Gradually, little red dots appeared stickered below artworks that had sold.

To call your VIP lounge by its name would be crass, so the fair had a Collectors' Lounge. Crates of Miami Basel's official champagne were arrayed in a kind of rainbow shape at one side. The champagne brand, Ruinart, was not a conceptual artist's joke. Past the bar I could see a booth for NetJets, the private-plane time-share company. Toward the back of the lounge was another, smaller lounge administered by UBS, the Swiss bank. You could only enter with some higher-level credential I hadn't heard of. The fair was organized like Russian nesting dolls of exclusivity.

I stopped by my friend's gallery space for a chat. She told me she'd seen Alfredo Setubal, an heir to Latin America's largest private-sector bank, Itaú Unibanco. Abilio Diniz's wife, Geyze, whose purchases cluttered their mansion in São Paulo—she was strolling around too. Walking away without watching where I was going, I kicked an object that flopped into the air and back down again, loudly smacking the floor. It looked like a long leather doormat and probably cost one year of my salary at Bloomberg. My friend's eyebrows contorted with horror; she waved at me to get out of there before her boss noticed.

MIAMI WAS A LITTLE UTOPIA for the new rich of Brazil, but some of the richest Brazilians wouldn't be caught dead there. The country's top art buyer, Bernardo Paz, never attends Miami Basel; he sends an emissary. He built the world's largest open-air art museum, Inhotim, on a 240-acre estate he owns in southeastern Brazil. He feels no affinity with his fellow billionaires. He once referred to the moneyed global elite as *bundas-moles*—soft-asses—who don't get Inhotim like its working-class visitors do.

Though his money was new, Paz's discretion placed him in an older tradition of wealth in Brazil. He made his fortune quietly, over the course of many years, mining iron ore. Few had heard of him until Inhotim opened its doors in 2006. He poured seventy million dollars into the place each year but was still nowhere to be found on the *Forbes* list. The number of Brazilians on the list had jumped from six in 2002 to thirty-six a decade later, and yet there were plenty of billionaires *Forbes* hadn't found. My editors gave these people the fancy name "hidden billionaires" and told me to dig them up. Unlike most of the Brazilians on the list, they usually ran private companies that didn't release any financial information. They gave few interviews. They might own half of Miami, but they didn't publicize it. I felt at first like I was looking for leprechauns.

One of my editors, Pete Newcomb, an old *Forbes* hand, gave me a tip. Visiting São Paulo, he took me to dinner at the rooftop restaurant of Hotel Unique, which looks like a giant watermelon slice of polished stone. "Who owns this building, anyway?" he asked me. I had no idea. So I dug a bit. Turns out a guy named Jonas Siaulys owns it. Jonas's late father helped found Brazil's largest pharmaceuticals maker, Aché. I'd bought Aché's ibuprofen tons of times without absorbing the brand name or wondering who might be behind it. And Aché products filled the shelves of the Pague Menos pharmacy near my house. Pague Menos, I learned, is Brazil's largest pharmacy chain. It belongs to a guy named Francisco Deusmar de Queirós. Jonas might be a billionaire; Deusmar definitely was.

I started looking at everything around me in terms of its owner. Some were obvious, like the Pão de Açúcar supermarkets of Abilio Diniz. But at Pão de Açúcar, I bought Vigor brand yogurt made by the meatpacking giant JBS, owned by an old country boy named José Batista Sobrinho. On the way to work each day, I passed two gleaming *shoppings,* Iguatemi and JK, both owned by Carlos Jereissati, scion of a northeastern political clan. Here were two more billionaires, neither on the *Forbes* list yet.

Suddenly billionaires seemed to be everywhere. I couldn't believe how many ultrarich people lurked all around me. For someone hunting billionaires as if they were rare animals, it brought a kind of gold-rush feeling. At times it was exhausting. Arriving at my apartment one day, I paused before shutting the door. On the lock's strike plate, I could read the name La Fonte—another company owned by the Jereissatis. Even at the bar I couldn't get away from them. I drank Brahma beer made by Anheuser-Busch InBev, a company controlled by three well-known *Forbes* listers, Jorge Paulo Lemann, Marcel Telles, and Carlos Alberto Sicupira. But what about beers like Itaipava and Devassa? The first brand belonged to Walter Faria, the second to the Schincariol brothers—some of the first hidden billionaires I uncovered. It wasn't long before billionaires started showing up in my dreams.

Eventually I looked beyond consumer brands. In a downtown subway station, a plaque announced the contractor who had laid the subway line: Camargo Corrêa. In Rio I'd seen a building that resembles grayscale Rubik's cubes arranged in Jenga stacks midplay. It's the headquarters of Petrobras, the state oil company, but it was built by a private company known as Odebrecht. Camargo and Odebrecht both were family-owned—and huge, raking in many billions of dollars in revenues each year. I realized I was looking at two of Brazil's richest families. They made way more money than Eike Batista but were nowhere on the *Forbes* list. That's how they liked it. They didn't want to draw attention to themselves. Soon I would realize that this wasn't just press-shyness. Behind their fortunes lay a dark history.

CHAPTER 2

THE PRICE OF PROGRESS

**BRIBES, DICTATORSHIP,
AND PUBLIC WORKS**

———

"It's been forty-six years of arduous work."

—PAULO MALUF ($1 BILLION?)

"I'm always here. It's you gentlemen who change."

—SEBASTIÃO CAMARGO ($13 BILLION)

OR A FEW MONTHS I LIVED A BLOCK FROM A FREEWAY KNOWN AS
the Minhocão, which means Big Worm. People came up with the
name because of the way it writhes for two miles through the city
center, carving a path through exhaust-stained high-rises. Whole
rows of windows are level with the traffic, close enough to spit on it,
so residents keep shutters closed against the noise and the eyes of
drivers. At six P.M. all four lanes are thick with lurching cars. *Moto-
boys* on their motorcycles cling to the fading paint lines, emitting
brief honks that add up to an uninterrupted hum. Anywhere they can
reach, in places it's hard to figure out how they reach, kids paint the
black runic-looking graffiti of *pichação*. There's no neon, no billboards, because a few years back São Paulo banned most ads in public
spaces. They called the law Cidade Limpa, "clean city."

For a long time I just took the Big Worm for granted, another
piece of São Paulo's landscape of gray. As I learned the names behind

the concrete, though, I came to see it as a symbol of something else: wealth. In Brazil, two of the oldest ways of getting rich are politics and public contracts. It's an essential symbiosis, and to understand how construction giants like Camargo Corrêa and Odebrecht got so powerful, I also had to learn about the men who made government into a business opportunity. Progress never came unencumbered here. Mixed up in the quest for national development, I would find a history of accumulation through exorbitant transfers of taxpayer money, outright theft, and even torture. It's a contradiction at the heart of Brazil's ambitions.

Paulo Maluf likes to take credit for the Big Worm. Twice as São Paulo's mayor, once as state transportation secretary, and once as governor, Maluf oversaw the construction of hundreds of miles of tunnels and roads and overpasses. Every day from the windows of the Bloomberg office, I would see the many pulsing lanes of freeway— Maluf's freeway—that ran along both sides of the Pinheiros River. The river was crisscrossed by three Maluf bridges. Eventually Bloomberg would move its office to Faria Lima Avenue—Maluf's avenue. In his authorized biography—*Him: Maluf, a Path of Daring*—he declares, "No one can go a kilometer in São Paulo without running into one of my projects." Some of his projects even helped speed up traffic—for a while.

I started looking into Maluf because I thought he could be a hidden billionaire. After half a century in government, Maluf has been accused of spectacular feats of corruption. In agreeing to try a case against him in 2011, one of Brazil's Supreme Court justices cited evidence that Maluf may have skimmed a billion dollars from public works in just the four years he spent as mayor in the nineties. Maluf is wanted by Interpol, the international police organization. On Interpol's website you can see a low-quality JPEG of his plump octogenarian face, with big rimless eyeglasses and a receding crown of slicked-back gray hair, his half-smile revealing a row of white teeth. He looks like a nice old uncle trying to hide his debauched side. He made it on Interpol's list after the New York district attorney indicted him on charges of laundering $11.7 million through the city's banks. He's got tendrils of cash snaking through bank accounts all over the world, allegedly.

Maluf has always denied it all. He denies ever even having owned an account abroad. And in Brazil he's a free man. Brazil doesn't allow its citizens to be extradited, and in 2007, when he got elected to Congress, he won constitutional immunity from criminal prosecution by any court except the Supreme Court. At the time he faced four different indictments for corruption, money laundering, conspiracy, and falsifying documents. Because the statute of limitations is halved when you turn seventy, the court found Maluf too old to stand trial for the last two charges. Maluf's lawyers argue he can't be tried for money laundering because it became a crime in Brazil only in 1998, after the alleged crimes were allegedly committed. That's their defense. But the Supreme Court justices agreed to try him— someday. It could take a while, considering their backlog. Dozens of other congressmen face corruption charges too.

The corruption in Congress is a joke, literally. In 2010 Brazilians elected a clown named Tiririca—Grumpy—to the Chamber of Deputies. Tiririca's slogan was "It Can't Get Any Worse." In campaign ads he said, "What does a federal congressman do? The truth is I don't know—but if you vote for me, I'll find out for you." And "Elect me so I can help the neediest—especially my own family." He received 1.3 million votes, the second-highest count of any congressman in Brazil's history.

Comedians love Maluf. The presenters of a television comedy show called CQC will approach him at a São Paulo gala, and with good humor he'll deflect their gags about his alleged corruption. For one bit they meet him at his home in São Paulo, a thirty-three-thousand-square-foot mansion half-obscured by sculpted trees, flawless hedgerows, and tall walls topped by electric wire. Maluf is passionate about cars—on weekends he'll take a spin in his Porsche 996, the engine humming with horsepower jacked up to double the factory level—but he lets CQC take him around town in a minivan.

He waits hidden inside as a comedian asks people on the street what they think of Brazilian politicians. "There's a lot of *malandragem*," one guy says. "They steal a ton, and they don't care about the country." What about Maluf specifically? "He's bad." And would the guy say this to Maluf's face? "Definitely." Then Maluf emerges from the minivan and approaches with arms outstretched and that goofy smile. The guy is freaking out, but he accepts the hug, and Maluf makes his pitch about all the roads he built, Faria Lima, and so on. Of the allegations against him, Maluf asks, poking his finger in the air, "Have you ever seen one bit of proof? One bit?"

"No one ever finds anything," the guy concedes with a chagrined smile. He says this because most people don't read court documents for fun. But one case from the British island of Jersey shows in detail how Maluf works. Jersey is a notorious tax haven, but like Switzerland in recent years, it's bowed to international pressure for better transparency and cooperation with outside investigators. So its courts moved quickly when Brazilian prosecutors brought a civil suit in 2009 seeking to recover ten million dollars Maluf had stashed there. The suit centered on a road that gained fame as the most expensive in the world, mile for mile: Roberto Marinho Avenue. Completed in the nineties, it spans three miles and cost four hundred million dollars. Maluf claimed it was simply a very high quality road. But the project hid what I'd come to recognize as a typical Brazilian slush fund. The construction firms in charge, Mendes Júnior and OAS, presented inflated costs to the city government, a practice known as *superfaturamento*—charging an artificial markup on an order of cement, say, or billing for cement that was never even purchased. As mayor, Maluf signed off on the price increases. In the case of Mendes Júnior, the firm would transfer the extra money to a subcontractor, which kept ten percent as its take and wrote checks for the rest. Once they'd cashed the checks, Mendes Júnior employees would hide stacks of hard currency in boxes of chocolate and cases of Johnnie Walker Red Label. An intermediary would deliver the packages to Maluf or his deputies. Maluf's typical cut was twenty percent, according to prosecutors.

To move ill-gotten funds out of Brazil, you turn to a *doleiro* (the word comes from "dollar"). He'll open an account for you abroad, usually in the name of a front man. You give the *doleiro* cash in Brazil, and undeclared dollars land in your new anonymous account. As part of a plea bargain, a *doleiro* who'd received cash from Mendes Júnior testified to having deposited the amounts in a secret Maluf account at New York's Safra National Bank. With the help of authorities in New York, Brazilian investigators discovered that Maluf had used this account for personal expenses, once withdrawing $56,385 to buy two gold watches from Sotheby's. But usually the funds didn't sit there long before he transferred them to two accounts with Deutsche Bank across the ocean in Jersey. The authorities in Jersey found that the accounts were held by Maluf-controlled companies registered in the British Virgin Islands.

Maluf comes from a wealthy family of Lebanese immigrants, but by the late nineties the family business, Eucatex, a publicly traded wood products manufacturer, had reached the brink of bankruptcy. According to prosecutors, Maluf used his offshore shell companies to inject cash into Eucatex by purchasing convertible bonds—debt securities that can be converted into shares. In other words, he lent the family enterprise stolen money that it never had to repay.

Maluf's lawyers held to the refrain that he'd never owned an account abroad, but the judge on the case in Jersey declared that "no evidence of any kind, documentary or oral, was adduced by the defendants to support their pleaded case." In his ruling in 2012, the judge found that Maluf had orchestrated the Roberto Marinho Avenue scheme. He ordered Maluf to return the money he'd stolen to the city of São Paulo, plus interest and legal fees, a total of twenty-eight million dollars.

It took the Jersey court three years to try the case. Justice in Brazil doesn't move that fast. In the late nineties, investigators uncovered *superfaturamento* in a Maluf project built by a subsidiary of Ode-brecht, the construction giant, along with a smaller firm. Originally budgeted at seventy-five million dollars, the not-very-long tunnel under Ibirapuera Park ended up costing five times that amount. Maluf paid for it in part by cutting the city's budget for health and education. It took until 2001, four years after he'd stepped down as mayor, for prosecutors to indict him on the watery charge of "administrative improbity." It took a judge until 2009 to reach a conviction. It took until 2013 for another judge to uphold the conviction, fining Maluf the equivalent of around twenty million dollars. The case went through at all only because it's not a criminal case, which would be subject to his parliamentary immunity. And he's still appealing. Odebrecht got a slap on the wrist too: a fine for a few million dollars and a five-year ban from working with the government, applicable only to the subsidiary.

Even for Brazilians, it's hard to understand how justice can go so slow. And the slowness doesn't benefit everyone equally. Petty thieves and marijuana dealers often await trial in jail, and when convicted, they tend to go straight to prison. As long as you can afford to appeal, and your lawyer can submit arcane requests to bog down the process, convictions don't mean much because your sentence is usually suspended during the appeal process. The longest Maluf ever spent in jail was forty days in 2005. The police had tapped his family's phones and overheard his son Flávio trying to intimidate the *doleiro* who'd ratted on them, so a judge ordered Maluf and his son arrested to keep them from interfering with the investigation. Paulo Maluf turned himself in at a São Paulo police station, but when the police arrived at their country home to arrest his son, Flávio offered to take the officers to São Paulo in his private helicopter. They accepted. Once in jail, father and son were placed in a special cell, because under Brazil's penal code, university graduates are held separate from common prisoners. A different judge soon ordered the two Malufs' release.

The press calls Maluf the Teflon man, since nothing ever sticks to him. This probably explains Maluf's good humor about his fame for graft. After his name became a verb for misappropriating public funds—*malufar*—someone from the comedy show *CQC* asked him how he felt about it. Without losing his cool Maluf replied, "This is all in your head. *Malufar*, in my mind, is to work, to build. . . . It's been forty-six years of arduous work." In the bit with the minivan, one woman on the street rejects Maluf's hug and asks how he thinks God will judge him in the end. Maluf replies, "When I tell God what I did, after a while—seriously—he'll say, 'Stop stop stop stop stop. I've heard enough. You're going straight to heaven without passing through purgatory.'" In his authorized biography, Maluf compares the legacy of his public works to the glory of the ancient Romans' Colosseum.

There's a saying in Brazil: *"Rouba mas faz"*—He steals, but he gets things done. In a poll from 2013, twelve percent of *paulistanos* called Maluf the best mayor the city ever had. Once I heard an older gentleman say of Maluf, "Well, all politicians steal. And everyone deserves a second chance." And Maluf visibly got things done: all those roads.

WHEN THE BIG WORM went up in 1971, it plunged a wide tree-lined avenue into darkness. I used to cross under the freeway on my way to meet friends for drinks downtown, and in the cavernous spaces between pillars, I'd see clumps of people sharing crack pipes on soiled mattresses. Prostitutes populated the corners, some of them tall and broad-shouldered, with stubble on their faces, in miniskirts and heels. On a Sunday afternoon I saw a fat man inserting a syringe between his toes.

One night, riding under the Big Worm in a taxi, my gray-haired driver said you'd never see this stuff in the good old days. I asked what he meant, and he responded by talking about the military dictatorship that lasted from 1964 to 1985. Maluf rose to prominence during the dictatorship. He first became mayor not because anyone

voted for him but because he was appointed by General Artur da
Costa e Silva. That's how things worked then. The Big Worm's official name, given by Maluf, is the President Costa e Silva Freeway.
Across the country, schools and roads carry the names of the military men who kept citizens in line by censoring the press, cracking
down on protests, and torturing and disappearing dissidents.

As an outsider, it's easy to be fooled by Brazil's image of liber-
tinism. I was at first. But Maluf represents a conservative strain in
the country that goes deeper than the sultry images of *carnaval*
might lead you to believe. A devout Catholic, Maluf says he follows
the Ten Commandments. He believes men shouldn't marry other
men. To crack down on crime, he wants to change the constitution
so that sixteen-year-old muggers can be tried as adults. This is a popular position. In a recent survey, half of Brazilians agreed with the
statement "a good criminal is a dead criminal."

Another gray-haired taxi driver told me once that the only way to
end corruption was with another coup. (I heard a lot of strange ideas
from taxi drivers.) This idea grew from a common myth: that the
military regime, at least for a while, stamped out corruption in Brazil. According to this logic, corruption sprouts organically from a
democratic system, like tropical mold. This may explain why, despite
Maluf's high-profile corruption cases, so many see him as a symbol
of "Order and Progress," that positivist slogan stamped on the Brazilian flag.

This myth of a clean regime is based on a bad correlation. After
their coup in 1964, the generals announced a crusade to cleanse Brazil of corruption, but the kickbacks never stopped. They just flowed
to different hands. Anytime an investigation touched someone dear
to the regime, the generals squelched it. Censorship created the illusion of clean government.

Maluf's alleged stealing didn't start in the nineties. It goes back to
the regime years—and even involves some of the same construction
firms. Recently an eighty-two-year-old accountant named João Paulo
dos Santos decided to tell the press about his role as bag man for

Sebastião Camargo, the late construction tycoon behind Camargo Corrêa. Immune to prosecution thanks to an expired statute of limitations, Santos confessed to paying three hundred million dollars in bribes over his four-decade career. As late as 1993, he claimed to have bribed Maluf to increase the price on a tunnel to São Paulo's Jockey Club. But he also said he'd started paying off Maluf way back during the dictatorship. Though he didn't specify the project, Camargo Corrêa built one of São Paulo's first stretches of subway under Maluf in the early seventies. Sometimes, Santos said, he delivered bribes by hand. He described how Maluf would rise from his seat, open a secret compartment in his chair, drop the package in, then sit back down again.

As usual in such cases, Camargo Corrêa denied the claims. Anyway, they're too old to prosecute.

THAT LINE FROM BALZAC—"The secret of great fortunes without apparent cause is a crime forgotten, for it was properly done"— resonates in Brazil. But people tend to misremember it, omitting the words "without apparent cause," as if all wealth were tainted. There's ample reason for this. Maluf got into politics by engaging in the ultimate form of campaign finance. As head of the family business, he donated money to a think tank known as Ipês before the 1964 coup. Ipês's function was to unite business leaders and military officers in a conspiracy to take down João Goulart, the left-wing president, while designing a kind of shadow government that could step in afterward. It coordinated with the American ambassador and the CIA. Comparing the *Forbes* list with one of Ipês's backers, I saw some of the most powerful families in Brazil today—Klabin, Gerdau, Ermírio de Moraes—on both. It dawned on me that many of Brazil's great fortunes contained the traces of crimes committed in the name of keeping the economy free.

At the height of the Cold War, with the Cubans trying to export revolution across Latin America, it wasn't crazy to think communism might spread to Brazil. But Ipês trumped up the communist threat. A wealthy cattle rancher from down south, Goulart was no commie, even if he did have radical proposals like redistributing land and capping rents. He also had less radical proposals like giving formal workers an extra month's pay each December, today a beloved institution known as the thirteenth salary. Ipês framed this as a step toward a "unionist republic." Radio stations ran Ipês propaganda claiming the Soviets had infiltrated Goulart's government, and workers at Ipês-affiliated companies were made to watch short films on their lunch breaks that warned, over images of interminable bread lines, that Brazil could go the way of East Germany.

Once in power, the generals put Ipês economists in policy positions. One of them, a fat man with thick, blocky glasses named Antônio Delfim Netto, suggested Maluf to run a state bank, his first public post. Maluf did a good job modernizing the hulking old lender, and this is what got him named mayor of São Paulo in 1969.

Many businessmen had expected the military to bow out after the coup, and grew disillusioned as the regime dug in and hardened. Many others, though, went further in their support. In July 1969 the generals created a secret unit in São Paulo known as Operação Bandeirante, Oban for short. The *bandeirantes* were colonial-era folk heroes who searched for gold and precious stones, captured Indians, and crushed rebellions by black slaves. Oban's *bandeirantes* hunted subversives. The regime kept the operation off budget at first, so the officers in charge had to raise outside money to fund it. Delfim Netto rallied bankers to pledge payments of around one hundred thousand dollars. Some industrialists provided equipment on top of cash; Oban's agents drove trucks lent by Ultragaz, a fuel distributor. Ultragaz's president, a Danish expat named Henning Boilesen, even liked to watch the violent interrogations of subversives real and imagined. He's said to have donated a device known as the Pianola Boilesen, an electric piano used to administer shocks to detainees. Maluf was mayor by then, and when he raised funds for Oban, he gave it "the tone of a civic project," in the words of one historian.

Four decades before she would become Brazil's first woman president, Dilma Rousseff was forced to endure Oban's interrogations.
At nineteen she had joined an underground organization, one of
many that emerged as the regime cracked down on protests, student
groups, any legal kind of opposition. Dilma and her fellow guerrillas, largely middle-class kids inspired by Che Guevara, wanted to
overthrow the government and replace it with Cuban-style socialism.
This was a fantasy; their ranks were thin. But they had a romantic
idea of their mission and pursued it ruthlessly. They robbed banks,
planted bombs, and killed more than a hundred people, many of
them soldiers and police but many civilians too. One group kid-
napped the American ambassador for four days in 1969.

Though Dilma never participated in violent actions, she did help
organize some, and when she was arrested in São Paulo in 1970, she
was carrying a gun. Government agents took her to Oban's headquarters in a middle-class neighborhood near Paulista Avenue. "The
first time I had a hemorrhage was at Oban," Dilma would say many
years later. "It was a uterine hemorrhage. They gave me an injection
and said not to hit me that day." During three years in multiple prisons, she became very familiar with the agents' techniques: "If it's a
long interrogation, with an experienced interrogator, he'll put you
on the parrot's perch for a little while, and then he'll move on to the
shocks—pain that doesn't leave a trace, it just wears you down."
Known in Portuguese as the *pau de arara,* the parrot's perch dates to
Brazil's slave days. It's a horizontal pole, where detainees were made
to hang by the backs of their knees, their hands tied together at their
shins, the crooks of their elbows pressed against the other side of the
pole so they couldn't slip off. It strains joints and muscles and causes
all the blood to rush into the head, and it's most useful in combina-
tion with other devices, like the Pianola Boilesen or the *palmatória*—
one of those spanking paddles with air holes for quicker whacks.

There's a photo of Dilma appearing before a military tribunal
that year. Slim with close-cropped hair, she wears a look of cold de-
termination while two military judges cover their faces in the back-

ground. The repression in Brazil pales next to the dirty wars of Argentina and Chile, where tens of thousands of dissidents were disappeared, but several thousand Brazilians underwent what Dilma described, and worse. More than four hundred suspected rebels were killed.

Ultragaz's trucks still deliver cooking gas in cities across Brazil. To announce their arrival, they play a jolly Muzak xylophone tune overlaid with an eerie flute. Each time one rolled through my neighborhood, I couldn't help but think of Boilesen's device. The family that founded Ultragaz is now worth two billion dollars.

How do you justify collaborating with torture? Businessmen said they feared for their lives. "It was either us or them," as one banker later put it. Boilesen himself was ultimately shot to death in the street by left-wing guerrillas. But that's only part of the story. Everyone knew the example of Mário Wallace Simonsen, a wealthy businessman who owned coffee plantations, a bank, a supermarket chain, a TV station known as Excelsior, and what was then the largest airline in the country. A supporter of President Goulart, he refused to allow Excelsior to air news of the coup the day after it came off. Sometimes his station just ignored military censors. Other times it put up a screen showing its two cartoon mascots with their mouths and ears covered and the legend CENSURADO. In retaliation the generals opened a corruption probe, and Simonsen lost his license to export coffee. His airline's license was suspended too, then passed to a friend of the regime. In exile in Paris, watching his empire disintegrate from afar, Simonsen died of a heart attack in 1965.

One civilian in the military government later said that pretty much everyone in São Paulo's business elite ponied up. Foreign companies too. Still there were those who stood out. A truth commission launched during Dilma's presidency would name Sebastião Camargo, owner of the construction firm Camargo Corrêa, as one of Oban's top sponsors. Through a joint venture with Ultragaz, he even provided frozen meals for Oban's agents. It was here, supporting an off-the-books torture unit, that Maluf's and Camargo's destinies apparently first crossed.

Sebastião Camargo was tight with the generals. In 1967 the military's High College of War awarded him an honorary diploma. Camargo Corrêa still keeps a black and white photo of the event on its website. A little man with a mottled bald head, Sebastião stands smiling in an auditorium of besuited men. For his squinty eyes, he earned the nickname China.

He was a typical figure in the little business world of those years. He owned a mansion in the tree-canopied neighborhood of Jardins, not far from Maluf's. He liked to be called *doutor,* a Latin American term of respect (which implies no medical training or formal education at all). He wore a gold tie clip and was almost always smoking a pipe filled with Dunhill 965 tobacco. He had extravagant tastes. At his office he had paintings of lions devouring zebras and elephants mired in mud, and he would show visitors photo albums from his big-game hunting trips to Africa and the Arctic. At one of his ranches he raised Arabian horses from Egypt and pureblood Nelore cattle.

Sebastião kept an intense pace; his butler brought him eight espressos a day. On the rare occasions he gave interviews, though, he spoke so blandly that it was hard to quote much. People called him "closed off"; even a friend described him as "mysterious, enigmatic." Still, when he threw parties for his three daughters—sweet fifteens, then engagements—social columnists came to write about the movers and shakers in attendance. Officials from the military government always showed.

Contributing to Oban kept you in good standing with the men who ran things in Brazil. This carried special weight in a country where capital was scarce and the government offered cheap credit. If Sebastião stood out among Oban's backers, as a public works man he also had more to gain. And indeed, his support came back to him in the form of public contracts assigned to Camargo Corrêa. General Costa e Silva had launched a massive public works drive—

highways and bridges and dams—when he assumed the presidency in '67. He wanted to fulfill the nation's long-postponed potential for greatness, he wanted to do it with Brazilian companies, and he had the money. Having won the confidence of foreign creditors scared off by President Goulart, the regime was flush with loans from the American government and the World Bank.

The Ipês economist Delfim Netto, who was named finance minister, became a legendary figure in these years. To raise up Brazil's construction industry, he banned foreign contractors from bidding on infrastructure projects, gave tax breaks to local firms, and sometimes even guaranteed profit margins. "We needed the builders to be strong and completely loyal to Brazil," he said later. He embodied a philosophy known as *desenvolvimentismo*, literally "developmentalism," according to which a strong state fosters local industries.

Camargo Corrêa wasn't the only contractor to acquire power in those years. A few others leaned on regime friendships to grow their businesses—including Odebrecht, which would collude with Maluf in the nineties to inflate the price of that infamous tunnel. But Delfim Netto sent some of the best contracts to Sebastião, his fellow *paulista* and Oban collaborator. One was the eight-mile bridge between Rio and the town of Niterói. A project on the drawing board since the nineteenth century, it would be one of the longest bridges in the world once completed. Like the Big Worm, it was named after Costa e Silva.

ONE UNCOMFORTABLE FACT OF the dictatorship is that its most brutal period of repression, *os anos de chumbo*—the years of lead—overlapped with what Milton Friedman called an economic miracle. In the late sixties and early seventies, GDP expanded at an average rate of ten percent a year. Brazil's economy, nineteenth largest in the world before the coup, grew into the eighth largest (for a while). Jobs abounded, and the regime then was actually popular. But censorship disguised the government's failures. *Veja,* a popular news magazine, ran special editions on the regime's public works while papering over delays, cost overruns, and accidents. Catching up to the developed world, the regime wouldn't let worker safety, which had always been a joke anyway, impede its advance. You didn't hear about the thousands of Camargo men who, while building the Rio-Niterói Bridge, suffered from decompression sickness and bone necrosis after working in pressurized retaining structures. Nor about the eight men who died all at once when a platform at the bridge collapsed.

"May the rich get richer so that, thanks to them, the poor may in turn become less poor," Costa e Silva said. But inequality, already extreme, only deepened. The miracle was lopsided; it depended in part on keeping wages down. Company managers pointed out rabble-rousers as potential communists to the intelligence services, so you could forget about agitating for a raise. Despite the surge in the GDP, life for many remained precarious. Migrant workers from the northeast often slept at construction sites. One in five Brazilians couldn't always get enough to eat. One in three kids didn't attend school. One of the official slogans of those years was *"Ame-o ou Deixe-o"*—Love It or Leave It. The poor had no choice but to stay.

THE RIGHT WING HAS its myths about the dictatorship. One is that the generals cleaned up corruption. Another is that they managed the economy brilliantly. In fact, the miracle was great while it lasted, but when oil prices shot up in the seventies, fuel imports gobbled up the government's budget. Refusing to scale back their quest for economic glory, the generals borrowed with abandon to finance ever-more-grandiose projects. Camargo got to work on what is today the world's second-largest hydroelectric dam, Itaipu, on the border with Paraguay. Odebrecht received the contract to build Brazil's first nuclear power plants; the generals liked the idea of one day having the bomb. By the time the projects came online in the eighties, Brazil had piled up the world's largest foreign debt. Inflation hit surreal numbers, and the government verged on default.

The left has its myths too. It's popular to say that the construction giants owe their wealth to the military regime. On the surface this appears to be true. In reality, it confuses a condition with a cause. If being chummy with the generals was enough to be successful, the company that built the Big Worm, Construtora Rabello, would have done as well as Camargo. Its founder, Marco Paulo Rabello, had helped to finance Ipês, the anti-Goulart think tank. But while Camargo Corrêa is now a giant conglomerate, Construtora Rabello no longer exists.

What separated Rabello from Camargo was probably a mix of luck and talent. In his memoirs, a longtime Camargo Corrêa CEO admiringly called Sebastião *"o homem dos relacionamentos,"* the man who made the right friendships. But Sebastião was also a man with an eye for opportunity and a strategist with an aggressive, occasionally reckless drive for expansion. The only way to understand the full extent of his ingenuity is to rewind past the dictatorship years.

Sebastião spent so much time rich, it's hard to think of him any other way, but he grew up poor. One of ten children, he was born in 1909 to a couple of farmers in a small town in São Paulo state, of which São Paulo is the capital. When he was six, he quit school to help support his family. He worked at a coffee warehouse and then as a laborer for a small construction firm, where he rose to overseer. He was still a young man when he started his own business, hauling sand for a road project with a small fleet of donkey-pulled carts. He wanted to expand, to win road projects as the main contractor, but wit and hard work could take him only so far. Luckily he met a lawyer named Sylvio Corrêa, who'd married the sister of an up-and-coming politician, Adhemar de Barros, and had money to invest. In 1939 they founded Camargo Corrêa. Adhemar had become the governor of São Paulo, and with him as their *padrinho político*— political godfather—the two partners won highway contracts around the state.

It was for Adhemar that people came up with *rouba mas faz,* the expression later applied to Paulo Maluf. As early as the forties, Camargo Corrêa was accused in the press of conspiring with its political patron to siphon off public money. When he died, Adhemar reportedly left eight safes full of ill-gotten cash hidden around Brazil. During the military dictatorship, the biggest score ever made by the left-wing underground came when Dilma's group robbed one of those safes containing nearly three million dollars.

With a friendship like Adhemar's, another businessman might have been content to receive a slow but steady flow of contracts. For Sebastião, it was the lever that launched him into projects all over the country. He built highways and airports as far west as Mato Grosso do Sul, on the border with Paraguay.

In a rare interview in 1990, Sebastião was asked his favorite project. He told the reporter about a dam from the fifties, Limoeiro, the first Camargo Corrêa tackled on its own, without a foreign partner. He bought a new bulldozer to dig the foundation, but the machine burrowed twenty feet deep and still didn't hit solid rock as expected. It went another five, another ten, and still nothing. The engineers worried the hole might collapse, burying the bulldozer and killing its driver. An official from the public works department showed up at the site and told Sebastião, "Any old contractor would remove his tractor. But a real dam-builder would persevere and reach solid rock." Though Sebastião himself wasn't an engineer, he decided to risk it. He was lucky. After another three feet, the bulldozer hit rock.

Sebastião's big leap came later in the fifties, during the construction of Brasília. To take on as many projects as possible—several roads, a major dam—he marshaled all his equipment from less urgent projects across the country. In the process he grew close to President Juscelino Kubitschek, who had campaigned on the promise to build the new national capital in five years from scratch in the middle of the desert. Kubitschek would end up exiled by the military regime after the coup, but Sebastião's job was to be friendly with whoever was in power; he even worked well with João Goulart, who would be overthrown in 1964. Once, at the inauguration of a new governor of

São Paulo, an official remarked, "Hello, Mr. Sebastião, you're here too?" And Sebastião said, "I'm always here. It's you gentlemen who change."

His chameleon-like nature served him well in the democratic transition. Public investment dried up for a while in the eighties, but during the privatizations of the nineties, he snapped up cheap state holdings in electricity and toll roads. In postcommunist Russia, privatizations created a new class of oligarchs; Brazil already had its oligarchs.

Sebastião Camargo never tired of scaring up new business, opening new fronts. He was one of three Brazilians on *Forbes*'s first list of the world's billionaires in 1987, and at eighty years old he tried to retire and failed. It was pancreatic cancer that stopped him. On his death in 1994, eulogies from his fellow businessmen filled the newspapers. The soy magnate Olacyr de Moraes called him a "fighter," a nationalist symbol in an economy long dominated by foreigners. Antônio Ermírio de Moraes, a fellow *Forbes* lister, declared, "He was a man who brought progress to Brazil."

AS AN OUTSIDER, I had a hard time at first understanding the Brazilian version of entrepreneurship. Characters like Paulo Maluf and Sebastião Camargo didn't fit the American ideal of the brilliant innovator who achieves greatness without any help from the government or powerful friends and family. But then I started dating a PhD student in history from the south of Brazil, and she recommended a great book from 1936, *Roots of Brazil,* which explained a lot. The author was Sérgio Buarque de Holanda; I'd already heard of his son Chico Buarque, the popular musician.

Buarque, a sociologist, wanted to explain Brazilians to themselves. He defined the archetypal Brazilian as "the cordial man." In the word *cordial,* what mattered most for him was its Latin root: "of the heart." In a society moved by the heart, you prize personal ties over impersonal institutions. Buarque believed that the national

THE PRICE OF PROGRESS 49

habit of calling everyone by their first name, even figures from politics and business you've never met, grew from the desire to see everyone as part of the same family. Brazilians' innate friendliness fits into this idea. But the flip side of cordiality isn't friendly at all. If a cop pulls over someone important, a judge or a politician, she's likely to hear the phrase *"Cê sabe com quem cê tá falando?"*—You know who you're dealing with here?—and will just as likely let him go unmolested.

There's an old saying: "For my friends, anything. For my enemies, the law." It's an attitude that goes back to Brazil's earliest days, when the Portuguese crown awarded a few well-placed men "hereditary captaincies," land grants that encompassed vast stretches of the country. The captains in turn doled out parcels for sugar plantations and cattle ranches. Unlike the freewheeling colonies of North America, power here worked strictly top-down. Bureaucracy was one of the few career paths for would-be self-made men. One of the richest Brazilians of the sixteenth century built his fortune doling out favors as an assistant to the colony's governor-general. Above all, government meant patronage, the power to distribute posts and favors to family and friends.

Brazil's first real business elite got rich breaking the rules. It was made up of slave traffickers who greased palms to skirt Lisbon's ban on international trade by native-born colonists. The slavers' wealth was an open secret, but it got an official stamp of approval when João VI brought the Portuguese royal family to Rio in 1808. Strapped after his narrow escape from Napoleon's forces in Europe, he offered them titles of nobility in return for cash. Even after the slave trade was banned under pressure from England, local authorities looked the other way when shipments of slaves pulled into port. This gave rise to the expression *"para inglês ver"*—for the English to see—still employed whenever the rules are broken and everyone kind of knows it, but nobody says anything.

The system of patronage didn't change much after independence in 1822, the weirdest independence in the Americas, in which a son of the Portuguese monarch declared Brazil its own empire. Industry had been forbidden in Brazil's colonial days, and when it began to bloom, the imperial government assigned the contracts and the capital. Your ability to snuggle up to power mattered more than your business acumen. It was a meritocracy of schmooze. Another historian, Raymundo Faoro, defined Brazil's early economy not as feudal or capitalist but as "patrimonialist," with a business class that attached itself, barnacle-like, to the state.

Brazilians never drew a clear line between public and private. This is one reason corruption in Brazil is so entrenched. Corruption is part of the culture, even the language here. So many people secretly hold assets in others' names that there exist at least two slang terms for front man: *testa de ferro* (figurehead) and *laranja* (literally "orange," an etymological mystery). *Rabo preso* (tied tail) refers to the gentlemen's agreements that keep corrupt politicians from outing each other (imagine two rats with their tails entangled). When a scandal dies smothered by the judicial bureaucracy, you say it ends in *pizza* (because of a famous dispute among managers of a soccer club, finally resolved over an order of eighteen pizzas). Lots of words refer to tricks and cheats: *trambique, negociata, mamata, maracutaia, falcatrua*. Remember the *malandro*, the slick individual who lives off the odd swindle? And his special talent, *jeitinho*, the "little way" to dodge the rules? Researchers estimate that between fifty and ninety percent of all political campaign spending is funded by *caixa dois*, the undeclared "second cash register" companies keep for bribes and under-the-table donations. They fill their *caixa dois* through *superfaturamento*, overbilling on public contracts.

I've often heard Brazilians say they wish their country was like mine, where corrupt officials actually go to jail. But corruption in Brazil goes beyond the rich and powerful. Returning from Miami, Brazilians will bring Lacoste perfumes and iPads undeclared in their luggage to avoid paying import tariffs. In any Brazilian city, the owner of the corner bar will buy his cigarettes from Paraguay to avoid same. And the cashier may not issue you a receipt, to hide his revenue from the taxman. Paying a small bribe to pass your driver's license test is so normal, officials don't even lower their voice when presenting you with the option. In the favela, people will illegally siphon off the essentials—electricity, water—but also less essential services like cable TV.

People talk a lot about the *custo Brasil,* the mysterious high price of everything here, but not as much about the *lucro Brasil,* the profits to be reaped from this system. According to one estimate, corruption shaves more than a percentage point from Brazil's GDP. That's around twenty billion dollars. From a cold economic perspective, once corruption is the norm, you risk a competitive disadvantage if you fail to keep up. In the early nineties a journalist asked Emílio Odebrecht, son of the founder of the construction giant, whether his company had bribed a minister. He denied it but said he'd bribed other public officials, sure. In Brazil, he argued, you're practically obliged to pay special favors to get things done. "I'm not going to say we're an innocent company," he said. "No company can survive if it's innocent."

Emílio's statement helped me understand that Brazil's bureaucracy has a purpose. It favors those willing to bribe their way through, creating a kind of cartel of lax ethics. Once at a Brazilian conglomerate an executive told me he would love to get into public works but the market's impossible to crack. "There's more than enough work to go around, but the big players don't want to share," he said. "They're like some fat guy alone at a feast who's completely stuffed himself and still doesn't want anyone else at the table." Later, in an investigation known as Carwash, police would at last identify a *formal* cartel—in which Camargo, Odebrecht, and a few other top firms allegedly divvied up all the major contracts from Petrobras, the state oil company. Decades of muffled misconduct would finally burst into the open, shaking the foundations of the political establishment. But it's not time for that yet.

———

IN MY SEARCH FOR "hidden billionaires," I ran into a wall trying to put a number on Paulo Maluf's net worth. It was a matter of public record that he and his family owned shares in Eucatex, their wood products company, worth around eighty million dollars—but beyond that, his fortune was the subject of ongoing criminal cases. The most I could say for now was that it *allegedly* passed the one-billion-dollar mark. So I gave up on trying to out him. Camargo Corrêa, on the other hand, was (mostly) a legitimate business. By the time I started looking into the firm, it had swollen into a conglomerate with twelve billion dollars in revenue and operations in twenty-one countries. It had recently taken over the largest maker of cement in Portugal. It even controlled the company that makes Havaianas flip-flops. (So there were billionaires on my feet too.) And the boom years had revived its construction business at home: As president, Lula announced a quarter-trillion dollars in public works.

Despite its reach, the Camargo family kept a low profile. Sebastião's widow, Dirce, had dropped off the *Forbes* list during an economic crisis in the late nineties, and the local press seemed to have forgotten about her. She had three daughters, Regina, Rosana, and Renata, who apart from occasional charity events avoided publicity. It was their husbands who took places on the company board, and one of the husbands had recently died in a plane crash. A magazine story from 2009 called Camargo Corrêa a "giant without a face." Except that old Dirce was still kicking, I learned. She was a hundred years old and, it turned out, still controlled the family fortune. At Bloomberg we calculated her net worth at thirteen billion dollars. She was a hidden billionaire who happened to be Brazil's third-richest person.

When I said I was planning a story about the family fortune, Camargo Corrêa didn't react well. "You're an American, so you probably don't know this, but Brazil is a dangerous place," the company's head PR guy told me. "If you run this story," he said, "you'll be putting the family at risk." This idea left me queasy at first. But as I mulled it over, it didn't hold up to scrutiny. During the dictatorship, the same left-wing militants who killed Henning Boilesen had also put Sebastião Camargo on their hit list, and yet he invited social columnists to cover parties at his home. In more recent years, each of the daughters' husbands had built his own golf course outside São Paulo, two with nine holes and one with eighteen: ostentation on a grand scale. I suspected that their real fear was bad publicity.

Camargo's PR guy called my higher-ups and tried to get the story killed. I wondered how often that worked with the local press; it didn't work with Bloomberg. When the story went live, all the major local outlets picked it up: BRAZIL'S RICHEST WOMAN REVEALED. It was big news, the biggest scoop so far in my short career, despite being kind of obvious. Anyone who took the subway in São Paulo could see Camargo Corrêa's name engraved in grimy plaques at downtown stations. Every day thousands of people commuting from Niterói to Rio crossed a bridge built by Camargo, paying a toll to a company part-owned by Camargo. If the family's wealth was hidden, it was hidden in plain sight.

I UNDERSTOOD WHY THE Camargo family got along with whoever was in power. It was good for business. I had a harder time understanding what was in it for Lula and his chosen successor, Dilma Rousseff. Both had resisted the dictatorship, Lula as a unionist, Dilma as a guerrilla. Both had dabbled with socialism. Lula used to advocate defaulting on Brazil's debt, nationalizing the banks, redistributing land. But he lost three presidential elections this way, so he moved to the center. His running mate in 2002 was a textile magnate. He promised to respect Brazil's financial obligations, at home and abroad. He once called himself a "walking metamorphosis."

The markets tanked at first when Lula surged in the polls, but businessmen came around in the end. After he'd won the election, they gladly helped pay off his campaign debts. The biggest donations, as usual, came from companies that depended on the state for their income. Soon a quarter to half of all donations to the Workers Party would come from the construction industry. In Lula's 2006 campaign for reelection, Camargo Corrêa alone accounted for four percent of the total. (And that's only what was declared.) Like old Sebastião, though, today's construction giants didn't play favorites. They gave to the opposition too.

With his unionist history, Lula might look like an idealist, but even back in the seventies he was willing to bargain with factory owners in hopes of striking a deal. Above all, he's a pragmatist. He set aside the old Workers Party plank calling for an end to corporate campaign donations, because elections are expensive. He welcomed old allies of the regime to join his coalition in Congress, because he wanted to get things done. They were after patronage, so for them ideology came second if at all. Lula used to promise to break with the corrupt old elite; instead he worked with it. This became painfully clear when a massive bribery scandal erupted in 2005. The press dubbed it the *mensalão*, or big monthly payment. Lula was never directly implicated, but some of his top deputies were later convicted of paying millions to congressmen to vote for his projects.

My girlfriend, the PhD student, had been a Workers Party stalwart for as long as she could remember. Her parents were middleclass lefties who'd supported the party since Lula helped found it in 1980. She told me the party had no choice but to grease the gears if they wanted to get their agenda through and lift up the poor. In her view, the *mensalão* was the Faustian bargain that made Brazil a more equitable country. Buying votes was nothing new in Brazilian politics, she said, accurately. And she didn't see why Lula's deputies should go to prison before, say, Paulo Maluf.

I had a hard time accepting this, but her pragmatic take turned out to be common. I sometimes chatted with an economist at the BNDES, Brazil's state development bank, which lent billions to the construction industry. His name is Marcelo Miterhof and he's a lefty who admires Franklin Delano Roosevelt. When I asked him about

THE PRICE OF PROGRESS 55

the government's decision to fund companies that had backed the military regime, he told me, "You can't develop the country just with the kind of people you'd invite home for dinner." In the nineteenth-century United States, after all, railroad tycoons laid tens of thousands of miles of track not out of selfless civic interest but for profit, engaging in a crony capitalism that would be very familiar to Brazil's "cordial man."

Like the leaders of the military regime in the sixties and seventies, Lula wanted to build highways and dams and ports, to get Brazil caught up with the developed world. He wanted to build huge refineries to process Petrobras's oil discoveries, and he wanted Brazilian companies employing Brazilian workers to do the job. If he'd gotten hung up on who collaborated with the dictatorship, he'd have few people to work with whether in business or politics. He even brought on Delfim Netto as an economic adviser, and Camargo Corrêa and Odebrecht won the usual incentives: generous contracts and low-interest government loans. These policies became the models of what Lula framed as a win-win for business and labor. Before leaving office he said, "If you look at the banks' balance sheets this year, you will see that the banks have never made so much money in Brazil as they have during my government. The big companies have never sold as many cars as they have during my government. But the workers have also made money."

Dilma continued this line. When she served as Lula's cabinet chief, he called her the "mother of the PAC," as his public works program was known. As president, she claimed to govern for the poor but put the same amount of money into Bolsa Família, the welfare program, as into what some called *bolsa empresário*—the subsidy in state loans for businessmen. She didn't disturb the truce with the old elite. She ignored the old Workers Party call for a tax on large fortunes. She started a truth commission to investigate the crimes of the dictatorship but agreed not to touch the amnesty that shields military torturers from prosecution. She became a pragmatist too. One afternoon at the presidential palace in Brasília, she'd just announced a plan to lend money to small farmers when Paulo Maluf approached her among a huddle of people. He took her hand, leaned over, and kissed it.

Maluf may be corruption's poster boy. He may have raised funds for Oban, where Dilma was tortured. But he commanded a lot of votes, and the Workers Party wanted his support for São Paulo's mayoral election that year.

Dilma looked matronly in her burgundy power suit. Her face had filled out since the lean years she spent in secret prisons. As Maluf's lips left her knuckles, she smiled graciously at him.

THE MORE I LEARNED about Brazil, the hazier the boundaries looked between people who, on the surface, should have been antagonists. Some have called Brazil *"república das empreiteiras"*—republic of the construction firms—and rather than upset this system, Dilma and Lula slipped inside it. Pragmatic, conciliatory, they proved that even those who see politics as more than a way to enrich themselves tend to act like cordial men (and women). Implicitly they accepted the idea that corruption is just the price of progress here, that in the phrase *rouba mas faz* what matters is not the stealing but the getting things done.

This idea was convenient for their allies in the private sector. Sérgio Bourroul, a spokesman for Odebrecht, told me his company only wants what's best for the nation: infrastructure to help the economy grow. "Odebrecht's interests," he said, "are Brazil's interests." I was reminded of the old American saying "What's good for General Motors is good for the country," and I told him so. "That's exactly it," Sérgio replied. There's actually something to this. When Lula got the World Cup for Brazil, he pitched it as an excuse to build modern airports, better buses and roads, more subways. All of this would serve ordinary Brazilians. But what about the stadiums? There would be twelve, every one of them financed by public money, many in far-flung cities with no major league soccer team. Here, the interests of tycoons and the interests of citizens might diverge.

Lula's own interests got mixed up in there too. After he left office, he followed in the footsteps of American ex-presidents like Bill Clinton and started earning millions giving talks for private companies. Odebrecht and Camargo Corrêa paid him to speak in countries where they hoped to win business. Though "influence peddling" is illegal under Brazilian law, Lula often promoted the firms with foreign leaders on his trips. When he came under fire for these activities, his foundation released a statement calling it "natural" for a former head of state to "defend national interests abroad."

When a politician spends a lot of time with the people who give him money, he tends to absorb their views. What's stranger is when the views trickle down to the bottom tiers of power and wealth. The person who cleaned my apartment every couple of weeks, Maria, took an hour and a half on multiple buses to reach my house from her favela, Brasilândia. I asked her once which politicians she admired, and she named Lula first. That made sense, because Lula had brought her Bolsa Família. Then she named Maluf. She'd heard about the accusations of corruption, but *weren't they all corrupt*? Which other mayor had gotten so much done for São Paulo? Of course, what he'd done mostly benefited those who could afford a car, but this was not a problem for Maria. It took me a while to realize that Brazil's poor don't dream of a city with better public transit. They dream of earning enough money to buy a car of their own.

CHAPTER 3

MANIFEST DESTINY

SOY BARONS, THE AMAZON, AND A MEGA-DAM

"The people who criticize me are antidevelopment."
—BLAIRO MAGGI ($1.8 BILLION)

"Belo Monte is very important for the country."
—MARCELO ODEBRECHT ($6 BILLION)

BRAZIL HAS A LOT OF OLD MONEY. BUT NEW FORTUNES WERE forming far from the traditional centers of wealth along the southeastern coast, São Paulo and Rio. So I decided to take my search for billionaires inland. This also gave me an excuse to explore parts of the country where even most Brazilians rarely traveled. The national territory is vast, larger than the contiguous United States, but the westward push came late here, and one half of the country remains sparsely populated and for the most part desperately poor. On the frontier of development, I would find stories of accumulation where wealth and political power were almost indistinguishable. Some of the protagonists were new, some familiar, but in both cases the stakes looked even higher than before.

I flew first to a spot smack in Brazil's geographic center, Cuiabá, capital of Mato Grosso state, way closer to Bolivia than to the sea. Inside Mato Grosso you could fit Texas with room left over for Nebraska. Half a million people lived in Cuiabá, but I couldn't tell from the airport. I had to walk along radiating tarmac from the only landing strip to the only luggage belt. Driving away in a taxi, I saw workers erecting a new terminal to receive World Cup tourists in 2014.

When I told people I planned to take a bus from Cuiabá to Lucas do Rio Verde, they laughed. No one who could afford a car would subject himself to that. And indeed, the trip took much longer than the four hours advertised. Speeding along the two-lane highway, my bus would heave to a near-halt to negotiate potholes that moved my gut suddenly higher. Once we stopped outright, and I realized we'd hit a traffic jam, even though we were a hundred miles from any major city. My fellow passengers spoke in a mix of accents from around Brazil—Portuguese divorced from the written word, with consonants swallowed, syllables slurred: the Portuguese of someone who didn't do much school. They'd come to work on the *fazendas* that patchwork the state. On either side of me, under a sky of cloudless rich blue, rows of soybeans and corn stretched to the horizon.

Lucas, I'd heard, might be home to freshly minted billionaires. Across Mato Grosso, backwater farmers had gotten very rich very quickly. Land that fetched a hundred dollars an acre in the sixties now might sell for a few thousand. Soy prices had soared thanks to demand from China, and as Brazil overtook the United States as the world's top soy exporter, Mato Grosso's economy quadrupled in size in a decade. For the western half of Brazil, this was the first real boom since the late nineteenth century, when rubber barons built grand opera houses in remote Amazon river ports. Before the price of rubber collapsed on the eve of World War I, the tycoons had so much money that they sent their laundry to Lisbon and dentists capped their teeth in gold. Today's soy men were more discreet.

My top hidden billionaire suspect in Lucas was the mayor, Otaviano Pivetta. In a country where one percent of the population owns half the land, his company—Vanguarda Agro—alone controlled some eight hundred thousand acres. I went to see him at Lucas's city hall, recently constructed, its white paint crisp against the afternoon sky. I'd never seen such an orderly, outwardly prosperous rural town in Brazil. Except for grain silos here and there, Lucas resembled a Florida suburb, with wide, freshly paved avenues lined by palm trees and uniform houses in neat rows. Every neighborhood I passed had a park with a green lawn and a brightly colored playground.

Pivetta received me wearing khaki pants, an untucked blue button-up shirt, and well-used leather loafers. His gray hair was receding, his smile kind; his eyes peered from deep concentric wrinkle-circles. A taxi driver had told me that Pivetta owned my hotel, and when I mentioned this, he chuckled. "Ah, that. Lucas didn't use to have a good hotel, and I had a hard time bringing businessmen to town because they didn't want to spend the night here. So I put in a good hotel. But it could be better, no?" He said this in the same apologetic tone of a friend who offers you her pull-out couch.

Like most Mato-grossense growers, Pivetta had started small. Born in the southern state of Rio Grande do Sul, he raised hogs and planted rice on thirty-seven acres he'd inherited down there from his dad. He showed me photos of the old farm—of him and his brother, also a farmer; of him and his dad, still working as a trucker at eighty-three years old; and of him and his grandfather, who taught him to love the earth. In 1982 he followed his uncle north to this deserted stretch of Mato Grosso, and with the money he made selling his land down south, he bought a thousand acres from the government here. The land was cheap because no one wanted it. The topography might be nice and flat, but the soil was inhospitable, twelve hundred miles from the nearest port, linked by one mostly dirt road to the rest of Brazil. Thousands of southerners like him migrated anyway. Pivetta grew what he knew how to grow, rice. Electricity didn't arrive in Lucas till 1988, and only intermittently at first. Amid droughts in the eighties, many newcomers gave up and left. Many stayed only because they had nowhere else to go. "In my case, it was shame that kept me from returning home," he said. "I didn't want to be considered a failure."

An American evangelical pastor is believed to have brought soy to Brazil a century ago, but few Brazilian farmers grew it until the sixties and seventies, when global demand picked up. Pivetta and his fellow pioneers experimented with the bean, but the crops turned out poorly until a government research body bred a variety that could thrive in Mato Grosso's acidic soil. Soon this desolate earth became some of the richest in the world, allowing farmers two soybean harvests a year. In the nineties, as the government started offering incentives to buy farm equipment, global trading companies advanced cash to Mato-grossenses to grow soybeans. Pivetta and his fellow farmers expanded their fields, hired more workers. They grew corn and cotton and raised pigs and chickens too. Lucas's population went from seven thousand in the early nineties to sixty thousand by the time I showed up two decades later.

Still just that one sad road, the BR-163, connected Lucas to the rest of the country. Plentiful in the United States, railroads in Brazil are scarce, so two-thirds of the country's soy must make it to port by truck on such highways. As a result, it costs more to get the soy to port than to ship it from there to China. "We receive a lot of committees of European and especially American growers, and they don't understand how we survive here," Pivetta said. "The agriculture around the 163 is the most efficient in the world. It wouldn't be viable otherwise. But just imagine if we had a railroad to the north"—deep into the rain forest, where cargo could be shipped via Amazon tributaries to the sea.

I COULDN'T HELP ADMIRING Pivetta's perseverance. Yet his rise pointed to another conflict at the heart of Brazil's ambitions—a conflict that affects the world beyond Brazil's national borders. *Mato Grosso* literally means "dense forest," so named because the north of the state used to be jungle untouched by anyone but scattered Indians. Most of the rest was covered by savanna known as *cerrado*. Since 1970, a fifth of Brazil's Amazon rain forest has been slashed and burned, an area nearly equal to that of France and Germany combined. It's thanks to deforestation that Brazil ranks fourth in the world in carbon emissions.

One reason the cutting continues is that agribusiness is powerful in Brazilian politics. It has a caucus, the *bancada ruralista,* which controls a third of the votes in Congress. One of its most prominent members is a friend of Pivetta, Blairo Maggi, a recent addition to *Forbes*'s list of billionaires with a family fortune of $1.8 billion. He and his father founded Amaggi, a soy producer with operations across Mato Grosso. As one of the world's top growers, Blairo was called *o rei da soja,* the soy king, until a cousin of his took the title. His family got its start much as Pivetta did but branched out broader. Under Blairo's leadership, they started an export business to sell crops from fellow growers, bypassing global trading firms like Bunge and Cargill. They also got into river transport, hydroelectric mini-dams, and even rubber, that old boom crop. Pivetta told me he used to invite Blairo to Lucas and encourage him to get into politics. When Blairo ran for governor of Mato Grosso in 2002, his platform was to raise up agribusiness and build thousands of miles of roads to connect far-flung farms. He won by a landslide.

Less than a year into his first term, Blairo upset people all over the world when he told *The New York Times,* "To me, a forty percent increase in deforestation doesn't mean anything at all, and I don't feel the slightest guilt over what we are doing here. We're talking about an area larger than Europe that has barely been touched, so there is nothing at all to get worried about." At the time, Mato Grosso was losing more trees than anywhere else in Brazil. In the year following his declaration, a Connecticut-size stretch of forest disappeared from Mato Grosso—a record. The next year Greenpeace bestowed him with a Golden Chainsaw Award for his role in promoting deforestation. Mato-grossenses didn't care. Blairo won reelection as governor in 2006 and was elected senator in 2010 in another landslide. Then, with the support of the *bancada ruralista,* he became head of the Senate's environmental committee.

Some industries tried to sway officials with campaign donations, but Blairo seemed to have cut out the intermediary, becoming both the industry and the official. I wanted to know how he navigated this conflict, so I flew to Brasília to meet with him.

BRASÍLIA SITS ON A HIGH PLAIN, the Planalto, some six hundred miles east of Cuiabá, eight hundred miles from the sea. As my airplane descended, I saw the plane's shape echoed in the city plan below. It's known as the Plano Piloto. A nose of city points east into an arcing squiggle of lake, urban wings extending north and south along the lake's edges.

A taxi took me from the Juscelino Kubitschek Airport, which was also under renovation for the World Cup. Along a freeway bordered by wide green lawns, residential buildings flitted by. With their uniformity and the empty spaces dividing them, they resembled New York public housing projects—except that this was some of the priciest real estate in the world. Approaching the Plano Piloto's fuselage, the Central Bank thrust up at my right, a tall obelisk of beige concrete and dark glass reflecting clouds. Some of these roads had been build by Camargo Corrêa. We made our way onto a fuselage avenue, and on both sides identical squat buildings held Brazil's three dozen government ministries. Their windows, patternless shades of pastel green, gave them a pixelated look. All were designed by Oscar Niemeyer, the legendary Brazilian architect.

Dated as it looks now, Brasília sprouted from a futuristic vision. Politicians had dreamed of building a new inland capital since the eighteenth century. When President Kubitschek finally began construction in 1957, promising to advance the country fifty years in five, he hired Niemeyer and his former boss, Lucio Costa, to design the new city. Costa, in charge of the city plan, imagined a little utopia—except in his utopia, everyone would own a car. Sprawling, full of green spaces, the Plano Piloto is wonderful for the bureaucrats and lobbyists who can afford to live there. Costa never worried much about the workers who came to build Brasília. They settled in favelas on the outskirts, now plagued by violence, a long commute from the city center.

I headed for Congress, past a square of murky water at the end of the Esplanade of Ministries. The Brazilian Senate building resembles a soup bowl facedown, the Chamber of Deputies a soup bowl face up, with twin towers of congressional offices in between. I took an elevator to the nineteenth floor, and an aide brought me to Blairo Maggi's office. Blairo received me in a black suit with overlong sleeves and a Brazilian flag pinned to his lapel. He was pale and freckled, and the knot of his burgundy tie pushed against a neck hanging loosely around the suggestion of a chin. On one wall he'd hung a painting of a Pocahontas-looking woman peeking out from a gap in some Amazonian greenery; he told me his daughter had painted it. When I explained my interest in speaking to him, Blairo didn't meet my eyes but squinted through heavy lids at a TV screen showing the news behind me. Multitasking, he absorbed it all nonetheless.

Blairo knew that activists saw him as a fox in the henhouse. But he'd changed his ways, he said. Global outrage over the *New York Times* interview actually spurred him to work with Greenpeace to fight deforestation. "Everything you produce has to match up with what the consumer wants," he told me—and customers in Europe didn't like buying from environmental pariahs. Green sells.

Following this logic, Blairo helped persuade his fellow growers to adopt sustainable methods and lobbied soy buyers to boycott plantations in illegally deforested areas. His most important initiative was to offer amnesty and credit lines to landowners who agreed to replant trees in such areas. It appeared to work. Deforestation rates were falling across the Amazon, but they fell most in Mato Grosso—by more than ninety percent during his time as governor. To celebrate his turnaround, some Greenpeace people gifted Blairo with sweets made from *cupuaçu*, a delicious Amazonian fruit. Perhaps most impressive of all, soy yields kept on breaking records thanks to more efficient growing methods.

Blairo's strategy pleased both sides of the debate for a while. When he became a senator, his program in Mato Grosso provided the basis for a set of nationwide regulations known as the Forest Code. With the backing of the *bancada ruralista,* though, the amnesty went much further than Mato Grosso's had. Even as it ordered landowners to preserve eighty percent of their rain forest properties, it freed them from the obligation to restore areas they'd illegally cut clear. Many interpreted this as a green light to slash and burn again, since another amnesty might come at a later date, absolving them of any fresh violations. The year after the code was signed into law, deforestation would rise in Brazil for the first time in five years. Activists again pointed to Blairo as an environmental villain. But he thought Brazil was doing more than enough to protect the Amazon without hamstringing business. "The people who criticize me are antidevelopment," he told me. "The United States is a world power today because it became an agricultural power first. And it's still an agricultural power."

REPORTING ON BILLIONAIRES COULD feel like celebrity journalism because I spent most of my time breathing on the glass. What with all the layers of press people and assistants who meted out access, I often reported around my billionaires, measuring them by the marks they left on the country. With Blairo, I now had a confirmed *Forbes* lister in front of me, and I wanted to know more than how he'd acquired his wealth. I wanted to know how it felt.

I asked him what he thought about having his net worth published in a magazine for all to see. He responded defensively at first: He had nothing to hide, everything was declared. When I said that in the United States being on the list was usually considered a good thing, this seemed to put him at ease. "I don't have to be ashamed of having capital," he said. "I worked for it, and I didn't steal from anyone, I didn't do anything wrong. So if Americans are proud of being on there, then so am I."

What about being a billionaire in a country as poor as Brazil? I asked. How did he feel about that? Without hesitating he said, "The truth is that when you own a company of this size, it belongs to society. You have a lot of obligations, a lot of taxes, thousands of people who depend on how you run it—if it goes poorly, they do poorly. So the truth is that being part of a family that owns a big company actually gives you big responsibilities, both social and environmental."

I wasn't sure I'd heard his Portuguese right. Did he mean to say Amaggi belonged more to society than to his family?

"The family controls it," he said. "We're responsible for indicating the company's direction. But the company's results belong much more to Brazilian society than to us, because it generates progress, development, opportunity."

When I asked Blairo if he'd ever run into a conflict between his roles as environmental policy maker and agribusiness tycoon, his response was "Absolutely not." A conflict was impossible, he said, because the interests of farmers like him lined up with those of Brazilian society as a whole. It was another variation on the "What's good for General Motors is good for the country" mantra. I began to suspect that every billionaire saw his industry as the main engine of progress.

An aide came in. A Senate vote was about to start. Blairo apologized and said he'd have to cut short our interview. I followed him out into the hall, and a special senators-only elevator whisked him down to the open session.

BLAIRO'S IRRITATION WITH ENVIRONMENTALISTS is common in Brazil. Al Gore stirred up a furor here when he said, "Contrary to what Brazilians think, the Amazon is not their property; it belongs to all of us." Imagine if a Brazilian politician said the same about Alaska. Lula once declared, "I don't want any gringo coming here asking us to let an *amazonense* die of hunger under a tree." But Lula's complaint reflected more than a feeling of wounded sovereignty.

It reflected the belief expressed by Blairo, an ally of his, that protecting the environment is at best less urgent than economic growth—and at worst a barrier to it.

This trade-off went far beyond the soy industry. Before she became Lula's cabinet chief, Dilma had served as his energy minister, and she enthusiastically backed a drive to build mega-dams across the Amazon region. The most expensive among them, Belo Monte, was slated to be the fourth-largest hydroelectric dam in the world. Budgeted at fifteen billion dollars, it was a symbol of the ambitions of the Workers Party years—and one of the most ambitious public works under way anywhere. Twenty more mega-dams were planned. The idea was to harness all the potential of a country that holds one-eighth of the world's fresh water, securing energy for a growing economy and creating tens of thousands of jobs along the way. With these projects, Lula and Dilma also got to extend their political influence by doling out pork to regional power brokers. The biggest winners, though, may be a handful of top campaign donors: Camargo Corrêa, Odebrecht, and the eight other firms building the dam.

For all Belo Monte's apparent benefits, activists were worried it would devastate the rain forest and displace the indigenous tribes who live in it. The dam seemed to revive one of the oldest conflicts in the New World, where government-backed expansion has often come at the expense of the land's original inhabitants. At the same time, Belo Monte embodied very new tensions faced by just about every country in the world. I saw parallels with the United States. As the U.S. economy struggled to recover from the crash of '08, politicians on both sides of the aisle embraced the advent of shale gas extraction through a method known as fracking. All at once, this new technology seemed to offer jobs in depressed rural areas, fresh revenues for American companies, and the prospect of independence in the nation's energy supply. But serious debate over the environmental fallout was postponed.

Belo Monte is being built near a city called Altamira, deep in the state of Pará. You can fly there, but I decided to take the long way to get a fuller sense of the changes on the Amazonian frontier. From São Luís, a port on the northern coast, I took a fourteen-hour train southwest to the city of Marabá. In the standing space at the train car's end, hot air wafted through open windows, and I traded pleasantries with passengers—an evangelical pastor, a worker at an iron ore mine—as they got off and on at little towns like Açailândia, named for the delicious Amazonian berry *açaí*.

The landscape was more desolate than the one I'd seen heading to Lucas. Brazil has two hundred million head of cattle, the largest commercial herd in the world, and in mile after mile of clear-cut pasture, humpbacked zebus grazed among the odd lonely tree with high foliage hinting at the jungle it once belonged to. The only uninterrupted forest I saw was the neat rows of uniform-height eucalyptus grown for paper mills. Here and there tumbledown shacks with thatched roofs flitted by, their wooden walls sometimes painted with the faded slogan of a local politician. At each stop, villagers in the punishing sun approached the train to sell corn on the cob, ice-cold water, or tasteless beige puff rings, the local Cheetos. Part of the Workers Party dream was to lift these people up with megaprojects like Belo Monte. And yet Lula and Dilma were also picking up where the military regime had left off amid the economic crises of the eighties.

From Marabá I went deeper inland, taking a twelve-hour bus ride along a highway known as the Transamazônica. This was the backbone of the Amazon's first major colonization effort, launched by General Emílio Médici after he assumed the presidency in 1969. Built in part by Camargo Corrêa, the Transamazônica pierces from Brazil's northeastern tip twenty-five hundred miles west into jungle reachable only by river before. Médici's hope was to open up a "land without people for people without land," sending the rural poor of Bahia to turn Amazonian rain forest into farm country. Despite some modest subsidies, though, the pioneers failed to overcome the jungle's poor soil. Even with two billion dollars invested in it, the highway remained completely unpaved for years, becoming impassable swamp in the rainy season. Locals came to call it the Transmiséria. Four decades later it's still mostly dirt; the road to Lucas felt first-world by comparison.

The dreary scenery I'd seen coming from the north continued along the Transamazônica. This devastation, I learned, was the result of a policy that handed over huge tracts of the country for private businessmen to develop with scant controls. One of Médici's initiatives gave generous tax rebates for big investors to put their money in the region, but the system was nepotistic, riddled with fraud, and poorly thought out. With few official standards for the projects and little expertise, investors such as Sebastião Camargo put the money into cattle ranches because they were simple and low-cost. Migrant workers slashed and burned thousands of acres of jungle whose soils were quickly exhausted by overgrazing. As the cattle herds multiplied, the frontier advanced. But far from providing a base for permanent settlement, the ranches created precarious, temporary jobs. They paid a pittance when they didn't resort to debt bondage and even displaced subsistence farmers, who were branded squatters and evicted. If the farmers refused to leave, gunmen would intimidate and sometimes murder them. The government turned a blind eye.

The region's earliest inhabitants fared even worse. General Médici's phrase about a "land without people" was telling. Going back centuries, Brazil's elite had seen Indians as foreign elements, stubborn obstacles to progress. During the dictatorship, the agency ostensibly meant to protect them—the National Foundation of the Indian, known as Funai—worked hand in hand with the armed forces to move tribes out of the way of development projects. When Funai's coaxing failed, soldiers went in. During the construction of one Amazon highway in the seventies, the armed forces tried to scare off the Waimiri-Atroari tribe by firing machine guns into the forest, setting off grenades and dynamite. Thirty-three members of the tribe allegedly died when a military aircraft dropped a toxic powder on their village.

Antônio Delfim Netto, then the finance minister, compared the westward ranching push to the conquest of America's frontier the previous century. "First comes the Wild West stage," he said. "It's only later that the sheriff arrives." The sheriff still hasn't arrived, though. In the town of Anapu in 2005, *fazendeiros* ordered a hit on an American-born nun named Dorothy Stang to keep her from speaking out about human rights and environmental abuses. She was shot to death in broad daylight, and the only person in prison today is a gunman who went on to commit another homicide. Despite the projects of Lula and Dilma, impunity still reigns in these parts.

APPROACHING ALTAMIRA EARLY IN the morning, my bus came to a halt at a lazy brown waterway, the Xingu (pronounced sheen-GOO). This is the Amazon tributary that serves as Belo Monte's power source. Its headwaters lie a thousand miles south, not far from the soy fields of Lucas do Rio Verde. We inched onto a barge along with a dozen motorcyclists and a few trucks and then drifted across. Once at the other side, we glided along one of the Transamazônica's few paved stretches. If the government's plans are fulfilled, one day it will all be paved.

After stopping at my hotel, I went for a walk around town. Founded by Jesuits in the eighteenth century, Altamira became a regional hub after the Transamazônica arrived in the 1970s but remained fairly sleepy until Belo Monte started up. Now it felt stuck between boomtown and backwater. A rush of people had come to work on the dam, and in just a few years, the population went from a hundred thousand to a hundred and fifty thousand. Property prices tripled and quadrupled just as quickly. Downtown shops offered cheap clothes and electronics, with disreputable hotels on the floors above, but I also saw a store for fancy kitchen remodels, with a bored-looking sales attendant resting his elbows on sleek granite countertop. A billboard advertised a planned neighborhood with illustrations of expansive green lawns and the slogan INVESTMENT OPPORTUNITY.

It was a hundred degrees by midmorning. At street corners, vultures scavenged the overflow from trash cans. Pickup trucks and mule-drawn carts and bicycles and motorcycles vied for space on dusty streets with scant traffic lights. The traffic bottlenecked at half-blocked-off streets where bulldozers tore into the earth. Norte Energia, the state-owned enterprise that controls Belo Monte, was supposed to install water and sanitation lines for the influx of people but only started two years after the dam's construction had begun. Raw sewage trickled along the sidewalks.

At one point I took a taxi whose driver went by the nickname Ceará, for his native state. He'd lived in Altamira for the past decade. He used to walk around at night unconcerned, but violent crime had spiked, and now he feared getting held up. Belo Monte employed twenty-five thousand people at the peak of construction but far fewer in the rainy season when daily downpours slowed the work. Brazil has what appears to be a permanent cloud of rootless workers, and many drawn by the scent of a job failed to find one. Some got into drugs. Crack-cocaine seizures by the police soared. Ceará went home to visit family one weekend, and when he came back, burglars had cleaned out his apartment. But what he found most absurd was the city's frequent power outages. In the future home of one of the world's great energy projects, the supply of electricity couldn't keep up with demand.

Belo Monte is an odd hybrid between public and private, and in this way it embodies the "patrimonialist" style of business in Brazil. Almost all of Norte Energia's stock belongs to the government, but construction was outsourced to Camargo Corrêa, Odebrecht, and their peers. This arrangement guaranteed their revenues while sparing them from losses if the dam turns out to be a boondoggle. Taxpayers will be on the hook for that, even though it was the construction giants who came up with Belo Monte to begin with.

Belo Monte dates to the seventies, when the military government asked Camargo Corrêa to draw up studies for dams along the Xingu. The way Belo Monte was first designed, it would flood a New Jersey–size expanse of forest. For a sense of the devastation this would have caused, consider a smaller Amazon project, Tucuruí, built by Camargo in the early eighties and today the world's fifth-largest dam. Hydropower is championed as clean energy, but the government failed to clear-cut the reservoir area, and the flooded trees released huge amounts of carbon dioxide and methane into the atmosphere. As they rotted, they also produced poisonous acids that killed fish and corroded the dam's turbines. There was a human toll too: Thousands of Indians were forced from their homes.

Belo Monte was controversial from the start. When planning geared up in the eighties, the newly democratic government invited the tribes of the Xingu to weigh in. They knew what had happened with Tucuruí, and in a televised hearing, a chieftainess named Tuira Kayapó approached a government energy official, José Antonio Muniz Lopes. Her face painted, her breasts naked, she brandished a machete and shouted at him in her language. She pressed the machete once against his right cheek, once against his left, as he sat immobile, petrified. With the help of celebrity activists such as Sting, the Indians pressured the World Bank to back out of financing Belo Monte, and the dam was shelved. But Lopes, with the help of the construction industry, helped keep it alive.

In the early 2000s, Lopes left his post at a division of Eletrobras, the state electricity concern, and went to work for a group of contractors led by Camargo Corrêa and Odebrecht. He lobbied the government for a more palatable version of the dam. The new Belo Monte wouldn't flood any Indian territories. Its reservoir would take up a fifth of the area of the Tucuruí dam while generating about the same amount of electricity each year, enough to supply all of Rio de Janeiro state. At first it was supposed to cost just three and a half billion dollars, and in the euphoria of the Lula years, that was nothing. Of course, some optimism probably owed to the fact that Lopes's old employer, Eletrobras, outsourced the viability studies to his current employers, Camargo and Odebrecht, rather than independent analysts. Lopes ended up returning to government and now holds a high executive position at Eletrobras.

Businessmen in Brazil often blame environmental regulations for slowing down public works. But there was so much political pressure behind Belo Monte now that two successive heads of Ibama, the environmental agency, had to resign before one was willing to sign off on the start of construction. Tribal leaders of the Xingu Basin complained that the government had failed to properly consult with them and took to protesting the dam. Wearing a mix of Western clothes and traditional body paint, they would travel to Altamira from distant reservations, blocking the road to Belo Monte and occupying the construction site. In one statement signed by members of several tribes, they declared, "You're putting a gun to our heads. We're dying, and every dam kills us off a bit more."

For all its disruption, Belo Monte is a far cry from China's Three Gorges Dam, which displaced more than a million people. Yet its main environmental virtue—that it floods a very small area—is also a defect. With such a small reservoir, Belo Monte can run at full speed only during the rainy months, when the Xingu fills to its fullest. Averaging in the dry months, it will run at less than half its capacity throughout the year. Célio Bermann, a professor of energy studies at the University of São Paulo, says the only way to make Belo Monte worth the money is to build another dam upriver to produce a steadier flow of water. The government promised the Indians it won't do that, but Bermann's skeptical.

Bermann is one of a group of forty experts who issued a report in 2009, before construction began, saying that Belo Monte would do more harm than good. The government ignored it, preferring to listen to those who had the most to gain from its construction. Norte Energia had drawn up a billion-dollar plan to protect the environment and the local population, and Lula and Dilma seemed to feel that this was enough.

Based on Camargo and Odebrecht's studies, Norte Energia's plan called for schools, homes, and first-aid stations to indemnify the Indians of the Xingu Basin. Since the dam would draw thousands of migrant workers, it also called for security posts to prevent incursions into tribal lands. But as with renovations for the city of Altamira, execution of the plan fell short even as dam construction charged ahead. Late on everything it had promised, Norte Energia just handed out cash for a couple of years, fifteen thousand dollars a month for each village. A Funai official in Altamira, Francisco Brasil, told me how the sudden gush of money had remade Indian life. Some villages split in two to double their payments. Others abandoned farming and fishing in favor of packaged goods from regional supermarkets. With all the Coca-Cola and sweets, cases of diabetes and hypertension spiked. One group from the Arara tribe had come into contact with modern civilization only in 1982—and now they were buying freezers and motorbikes and pricey sound systems. "You'll see a thatch hut with a TV screen this big," Francisco said, pointing to a white markerboard spanning the wall of his cramped office.

Many Indians in the Xingu Basin now depend on the Bolsa Família welfare program. This is increasingly common among the half a million indigenous living on reservations that cover more than one-eighth of the national territory. Their lands are home to some of Brazil's best-conserved rain forest, but development keeps encroaching. One morning I passed by a reservation north of Altamira that the highway sliced in half. On my right side I saw a high metal-wire fence and a sign that read TERRA INDÍGENA. On the left was another fence, where I saw a half-open gate. I asked my taxi driver to go in, and we made our way onto a bumpy unpaved path overhung by light tree cover. When I reached a clearing, I got out and approached a few people hanging out in a wooden shack with a dirt floor. A few women in simple faded flower-print dresses washed dishes while a couple of men in board shorts and tank tops, the uniform of poor Brazilians anywhere, chatted to one side. I asked if I could speak to them about the dam. Some chickens clucked around. They told me I needed authorization from Funai even to be there. The scene was bleaker than any Indian reservation I'd seen back home in New Mexico.

The reservation I'd stumbled into belonged to members of the Juruna tribe. Many Jurunas made a living catching *acari,* a rare little multicolored fish that sells for a few hundred dollars apiece to big-city collectors. The Jurunas feared the dam would screw up the Xingu's ecosystem, depriving them of their best source of income. Tribes also fished the Xingu to eat. Norte Energia touted the fish ladder that would allow native species to make their normal migrations, but with construction under way and the river partially blocked, fishermen had already seen their yields drop. Soon one long meandering bend of the Xingu would be reduced to a trickle.

I wondered what would happen when the dam was finished, and tens of thousands of unskilled workers were marooned with their families in an area with little in the way of economic opportunity. Some might pick up and move on to the next dam project, whenever it came. But many would stay. Francisco Brasil feared they'd turn to reliable old jobs in logging and ranching, pushing deeper into the surrounding forest, invading Indian lands to cull valuable mahogany, clear-cutting the rest for cattle. This is one of the greatest dangers of Brazil's dam drive.

Despite all this, the indigenous aren't unanimous on Belo Monte. There are twenty tribes in the Xingu Basin, and they have more than twenty opinions. Tooling around Altamira, I struck up conversation with an Indian in Western clothes who betrayed no tribal affinity when he speculated that Belo Monte would bring progress to the region.

NORTE ENERGIA HAD A weekly tour for locals to see Belo Monte firsthand as it went up. The press department let me tag along. The bus left from a parking lot in Altamira every Saturday morning, and when I arrived, a handful of guides were handing out baseball caps and T-shirts that read GET TO KNOW BELO MONTE in Portuguese. People changed into the T-shirts in the bus bathroom. After a roll call, we headed north on the highway as a video detailed the virtues of the project. Thanks to Norte Energia's prevention efforts, malaria in the region had dropped eighty percent. As part of its training program,

Norte Energia taught illiterate workers to read. Norte Energia had built twenty-seven schools, with another seventeen planned. (Never mind that a civil complaint found one of these schools had "shipping-container walls, beaten-earth floors, windows of rusty iron bars sticking out, unpainted door, no space for recreation, and not a single tree in the middle of the Amazon.")

The guides handed a microphone around so we could all introduce ourselves and explain our interest in the dam. When I said I was an American journalist, a PR person held this up as a sign of Norte Energia's commitment to transparency. There was a group from Altamira's secretariat for the environment and tourism. The secretary spoke of his excitement over the economic development that Belo Monte would bring. "People are against Belo Monte only because they don't know enough about it," he said. A colleague of his added, "I'm sad about the environmental destruction, but Brazil needs energy." Then she added grandiosely, "Belo Monte represents humankind's ability to shape nature."

Belo Monte is actually two dams, one small and one large. The first, small dam will divert most of the Xingu's flow into a twelve-mile canal and then into a reservoir feeding a second, large dam. The scale of the whole thing exhausts superlatives. According to a pamphlet they handed out, with all the concrete being poured into Belo Monte, you could build forty-eight soccer stadiums like the giant Maracanã in Rio. With Belo Monte's steel, you could erect sixteen Eiffel Towers. If you took all the earth excavated at Belo Monte and put it in dump trucks and lined them up end to end, they would circle the planet twice. But this all remained abstract till I saw it up close.

We arrived at a wide-open pit where water would one day rush from the second dam's turbines back into the Xingu. The pit had been carved out of rock. At the far end, stairs of smooth cement, too large for any mortal to climb, emerged from the rock's jagged edges and rose high above. At the top of the stairs, a series of turrets took shape. Once completed, each turret would guide the water into a stainless steel turbine some thirty feet in diameter, allowing the water to drop forty-five stories before flowing out the turbine's end. When flashes of soldering hit my retinas, I noticed microscopic workers crawling around in the turrets' bristle of iron rods. Cranes overhung them at obtuse angles.

We got out at the top of a hill that offered a profile view of the work in progress. Everyone had donned yellow hard hats, and while our guides took pictures of the group, I stared out over the guardrail. The steps echoed the steps of an Aztec temple. The eighteen turrets, evenly repeating, conjured an air of ritual. The journalist Elio Gaspari defined the archetypal public works man as "the guy who convinced the pharaoh to stack stones in the desert." I imagined the structure before me now as a modern-day pyramid in the time before its decay.

MARCELO ODEBRECHT, A GRANDSON of the construction giant's founder, served as CEO of the family business in those days. He oversaw a fortune of six billion dollars. Young-looking for a forty-something, with the build of a runner, he tended to smirk when speaking in public. At a conference once, he said cleaner energy sources like wind simply couldn't keep up with Brazil's growth the way Amazonian dams could. "Belo Monte is very important for the country," he said, shrugging with an air of nonchalant faith in his words.

It's true that the economy needs energy to grow. But Brazil's love of megaprojects reflects the influence of money—and the lure of power—as much as any objective logic of development. According to Professor Bermann, a lot of energy goes to waste in Brazil. The ethanol industry throws out enough sugarcane dregs to generate two or three Belo Montes' worth of energy, and fifteen percent of the nation's electricity is lost to crappy old power lines. It would be cheaper than building mega-dams, Bermann says, to address these problems. But the revenues would be diffuse, with less value as patronage. Brazil's construction giants are already specialized in dam building. And new power lines don't make much of an impression in campaign ads.

Toward the end of her first term as president, Dilma would visit Belo Monte for a reelection photo op. When a reporter asked her about the dam's potential for environmental fallout, she replied, dripping with sarcasm, "Would you prefer to go without electricity? And pay high energy bills too?"

Dilma's response betrays a Manichean concept of progress in which growth and the environment are fundamentally at odds. This idea may already be proving shortsighted. Even as Dilma visited Belo Monte, São Paulo was sinking into its worst drought in eighty years. Scientists put some of the blame on deforestation, because the Amazon's vapors turn into rain clouds that make their way southeast. As I stocked up on bottled water, it struck me that Dilma's attitude about the environment belongs to the same brand of pragmatism that led her and Lula to ally themselves with corrupt politicians and dubious companies, believing it was for the good of the country. Later, when the construction giants' schemes finally erupted into scandal, Brazilians would get an idea of how much had been skimmed off Belo Monte for bribes.

Flying out of Altamira, I scanned the Amazon from my window seat. Cow pasture abutted patches of jungle at geometric angles with arteries of dirt road crawling between—that same barren landscape I'd seen on the Transamazônica. But then the bald patches petered out, and I found myself thirty thousand feet above an endless sea of green. I felt my chest fill with relief that there still existed so much untouched rain forest. This gave way to a nervous feeling. The Amazon's bigness struck me as a threat to its own existence—a tempting illusion of infinitude. I wondered if it was the same sort of illusion that led crooked politicians and businessmen to take their cut of public money, to grab something that belonged to everyone and make it their own.

CHAPTER 4

NATION BUILDING

THE MEDIA TYCOON, INHERITANCE, AND RACE

"We would like to have the power to fix everything that
doesn't work in Brazil."

—ROBERTO MARINHO ($25 BILLION)

THERE'S AN IMAGE I OFTEN REMEMBER FROM MY TRIP TO AL-
tamira. At one point I visited the *baixões,* or lowlands, a district of
faded wooden shacks on stilts in a floodplain by the highway leading
into town. Kids ran around in dirty clothes on uneven walkways
spanning trash-strewn, murky water. It was the worst poverty I've
ever seen in Brazil, but up on the sagging roofs above, I noticed pris-
tine satellite dishes. As far as they were from the centers of wealth,
the people there were connected through television to some version
of Brazil's shared story.

I'd been missing out on this story by failing to keep a TV in my
apartment. I realized my mistake hanging out in my ninth-floor living room one night, when from outside I heard shouts of *"Chupa,
Carminha!"* Living in São Paulo, I was used to hearing my neighbors
shout insults at one another. It happened whenever two São Paulo
soccer teams faced off. After a goal, first would come the incredulous
shrieks resolving into joy or despair in stereo around me, then fire-
works: that rapid-fire *crack-crack-crack-crack-crack,* pause—then a

deep *boom*—and then a fan in a shiny jersey would lean out his balcony and yell *"Chupa, Palmeiras!"*—Suck it, Palmeiras! Later I knew the score was tied when another fan shouted *"Chupa, Corinthians!"* This was different.

Carminha turned out to be a character in a telenovela called *Avenida Brasil,* and that night was the finale. A shrieking conniver, she'd just taken a slap to the face. In a country of two hundred million people, eighty million were tuned in. Novela finales often drew huge audiences but this was the biggest in years. The only other time Brazilians dropped everything else to plant themselves in front of the TV like this was when the national team played in the World Cup, and the divisions between Palmeiras and Corinthians disappeared.

I didn't get telenovelas. I'd seen *Avenida Brasil* on at the gym, but whatever was special about it was lost on me. When I asked a Brazilian colleague in the Bloomberg newsroom what was so good about it, he said it was just *good*. As far as I could tell, it had little to do with the actual plot. Like all novelas, this one was written as it aired, adapting to the hopes and complaints of viewers six nights a week, and the twists were as endless and hard to swallow as always.

Media critics latched on to two reasons for *Avenida Brasil*'s success. One was that it set a new standard for production values, with smoky cinematic shots, say, of the garbage heap where one of the characters was abandoned as a little girl. The other was that its characters hailed to an unprecedented degree from the emerging middle class. Until recently, novelas had mostly stuck to a thin slice of Ipanema privilege where chesty, perfectly bestubbled men in crisp white blazers break the hearts of gorgeous blond ladies in palatial homes decorated in the style of Artefacto, complete with fireplaces, however impractical in balmy Rio. These days, though, formerly poor Brazilians had money to buy stuff: washing machines, smartphones, plane tickets, cars. What with the growing economy and social policies of the Workers Party years, half the population now fit into what economists called *classe C,* with household incomes that went from a few hundred to a few thousand dollars a month. Advertisers were willing to pay to reach them. And like anyone, these new consumers wanted to see people like themselves onscreen.

People translate the word *telenovela* as "soap opera," but that understates its place in the culture. Novelas have been wildly popular since before the *tele* was tacked on, as a staple of radio in a country where cinema came late. On TV they play during prime time, and everyone watches them, men and women alike. Even on an average night, *Avenida Brasil* drew three-quarters of the national viewership. "If I can make something that is watched every night by seventy million people," the director of *Avenida Brasil* said, "why in the world would I want to go to Hollywood?"

In the seven months that it ran, *Avenida Brasil* reportedly raked in a billion dollars in ad revenue. It may be the highest-grossing novela in Brazil's history. But Rede Globo, the network that produced it, is used to dominating the market like this. Globo's programming was at the center of an old Brazilian routine: You watch the nightly news on *Jornal Nacional,* you watch Globo's nine o'clock novela, and if there's a soccer game that night, it starts when the novela's over. In recent years the network has lost ground to the Internet and cable TV, but more than half of all money spent on TV ads in Brazil still goes to Globo. By 2012, when I started looking into its finances, the group brought in six billion dollars a year in revenues.

As usual, the ownership of Globo left traces in the city around me. Paulo Maluf's infamous four-hundred-million-dollar avenue was named after Globo's founder, Roberto Marinho. Today Marinho's sons run the conglomerate, which encompasses TV, newspapers, magazines, and radio stations. Outside politics, no other family has wielded as much influence in Brazil's national affairs. A former president, Fernando Henrique Cardoso, once referred to Globo as an "institution of power" in Brazil. It's shaped the debate on wealth, sex, and race for the past half-century. If Camargo Corrêa was a barnacle on power, Globo looked more like a whale. The Marinhos' example shows what happens when you take the accumulation of wealth to its logical end: monopoly.

———

WHEN I SAID WHAT I did for a living, Brazilians sometimes named their favorite billionaires: the Syrian-Jewish Safra brothers, Count Francesco Matarazzo, the film director Walter Salles. Just as often, though, Brazilians listed off their chosen villains. Paulo Maluf was one. Roberto Marinho was another. He's a bogeyman of the left, and with good reason. Marinho helped bring the military regime to power, running anti-Goulart propaganda on Radio Globo and in-flammatory editorials in his newspaper to drum up support for the coup in 1964. His most infamous distortion came in 1984, in the twilight of the regime, when hundreds of thousands of protesters took to the streets of São Paulo to demand free elections, and a TV Globo anchor surreally claimed they were out there celebrating the city's birthday. I could fill another book recounting Marinho's controversies. There's one for almost every inflection point in twentieth-century Brazil.

To much of the business class, Marinho is a symbol of entrepreneurship. Even though he was born into the media biz, he made the most of it. His father, a Rio de Janeiro newspaper tycoon, founded *O Globo* in 1925 but died of a heart attack three weeks later. Roberto was left in control at just twenty-one years old. He'd already worked as his father's secretary, but he wisely took the backseat at first. He watched and learned how to do the news before taking over as publisher six years later. Eventually his younger brothers joined the business, but Roberto was the one with the instinct for expansion. Over the next couple of decades he started a radio network and additional newspapers to serve different niches.

As in many other parts of the world, the press in Brazil back then was openly partisan—sometimes sponsored outright by political parties—and willing to squelch bad news about companies that paid for ads. Roberto Marinho was early in championing the twentieth-century American press ideals of objectivity and neutrality. He liked to cite Arthur Miller: "A good newspaper, I suppose, is a nation talking to itself." He imagined he spoke not for himself but for Brazilians in general, channeling what he called public opinion. Except Marinho's idea of public opinion reflected his own convictions: anticommunist, pro-business, pro-democracy, but also sympathetic to the military. Marinho inherited his dad's friendships among the *tenentes,* a cohort of young military officers who rebelled against the corrupt politics of the decades-old republic, and when they brought Getúlio Vargas to power in a coup in 1930, he at first supported the new government.

Getúlio is a legendary figure in Brazil. He was one part ruthless dictator—he idolized Mussolini—and another part "father of the poor," as his propaganda department put it. Even as he rounded up and tortured communists, he enfranchised the working man. He instituted a minimum wage, paid vacation, social security, and state-sponsored unions. "He took a whole nation up from a state of semi-slavery and turned us into citizens with rights," Lula later said. Under Getúlio, the country came to manufacture products it had only ever imported before, and Lula admired this too. It was during the hard-line phase of Getúlio's dictatorship, which he gave the utopian name New State, that Stefan Zweig wrote his book *Land of the Future,* expressing the hopeful national feeling of those years. But Getúlio overstayed his welcome, and as World War II drew to a close, Marinho and others in the press agitated for free elections. Some of the same officers who'd brought him to power now deposed him.

Lefties still blame Marinho for 1954. Getúlio had returned to the presidency through the ballot box, and as he drifted further into the left-wing labor camp, he and Marinho became open enemies. He blocked Marinho's first bid for a TV license, and Marinho railed against the inflation and the corruption of his government, lending editorial pages and ample radio time to his detractors. When the usual officers demanded Getúlio step down once again, this time, rather than acquiesce, he shot himself in the heart. It was a national tragedy. Hundreds of thousands of mourners filled the streets of Rio. Some set fire to *Globo* trucks and threw rocks at the newspaper's headquarters.

There's a myth that Marinho received his TV-broadcasting licenses as gifts from the military regime that took power in 1964. In reality, he bought most of his licenses from other businessmen. The only two he ever got from the government came from Juscelino Kubitschek and João Goulart, Getúlio's political heirs. As with Sebastião Camargo, business came before ideology, and at times *O Globo* actually lent its support to Goulart, even though Marinho would ultimately work to overthrow him. Marinho's authorized biography shows a photo of him in a pin-striped double-breasted suit, his mustache neatly trimmed and his head mostly bald, standing between Goulart and Kubitschek in 1961. All three men have pocket squares, and all three are laughing, though only Marinho's eyes remain wide open, looking into the camera.

Marinho arrived late to the TV game. By the time Globo started airing in 1965, the leading network, TV Tupi, had been in operation for fifteen years. The fact that Globo would soon rise to number one is proof to Marinho's critics that he owed his wealth to the generals. But this is another case of confusing a condition for success with a cause. A handful of media outlets went out of business because of their owners' political leanings, but TV Tupi, for one, was just as loyal to the regime as Globo.

A few things set Globo apart. One was a loophole Marinho found in the constitution, which banned foreigners from investing in local broadcasters. Since it was vague on profit-sharing arrangements, he struck a deal with the American firm Time-Life to inject several million dollars into his enterprise. This allowed him to buy the best equipment and hire the best talent. (It also brought an investigation led by a congressman who happened to be a Tupi exec, but this ended in *pizza*, with Marinho suffering no legal consequences.)

Another thing was Marinho's management style, which had no apparent logic but worked just the same. Despite Time-Life's money,

TV Globo started as a shoestring operation, and yet Marinho hardly read financial statements, focusing instead on the big picture. He was reserved but authoritarian; his brother Rogério once said, "When he lowered his voice, it was terrible." He expected people to trust his intuitions, often without any explanation other than, "You see the world as an ocean, noticing only the bubbles. What's going on down below, only I know." After a year on air, discouraged by the network's slow takeoff, Marinho's brothers sold their shares to him. Time-Life got out in 1969, frustrated by the lack of profits. Still Marinho was so sure about Globo's future that when he bought out his American partner, he put up his own house as collateral for a loan. The network didn't turn a profit till 1971.

Probably the most important ingredient to Marinho's success was his gift for delegating responsibility, despite his love of control. In the mid-sixties he brought on two brilliant execs from Brazil's fledgling TV industry, Walter Clark and a guy everyone knows as Boni, and offered them a share in the earnings. With their shirts buttoned down to show off their chest hair and large pointy collars askew, they clashed with the suit-and-tie style Marinho favored. They were three decades his junior, but he trusted them with rich budgets, and with their instincts for smart programming, they played a key role in making Globo profitable. One important break came in 1966, when torrential rains hit Rio, and Clark canceled the whole TV schedule for wall-to-wall coverage of what turned out to be some of the worst flooding in the city's history. The public was riveted. Anchors announced an initiative called SOS Globo, asking viewers to send in clothes and food for flood victims, and this also won points for the network. Almost overnight, the little-known station earned a big reputation.

Rare for an entrepreneur, Marinho was already past sixty when he started TV Globo, the business that would define him. At times he could seem immortal. Even in his eighties, he would joke about Globo's future, saying "*if* I'm no longer around one day . . ." rather than *when*. He kept working till dementia hit in his final years.

When Marinho died, his butler counted 5,328 ties in his wardrobe. He had a vain streak. He wore discreet elevator shoes to lift him above his natural five feet four and a half inches. A competitive show jumper, he would force the producers of *Jornal Nacional* to run long clips of his victorious circuits. He invited Globo photographers to document cocktail parties for artists and businessmen at his mansion in Rio. It was the kind of home you might see on one of Globo's novelas. Tucked into the base of Corcovado Mountain, he modeled it after the estate of a seventeenth-century sugar baron and hired the famous landscape architect Roberto Burle Marx to design its gardens. He filled it with fine paintings and a twenty-by-twenty-foot tapestry by Jean Lurçat.

Marinho also had a temper. In the early days of the military regime, he declined to support the political ambitions of a firebrand journalist named Carlos Lacerda, who had been named governor of Rio. Previously an ally in the fight against Getúlio, Lacerda took to publicly attacking Marinho and his deal with Time-Life. Marinho's own official biography reveals how one day he put a revolver in his waistband and went to Lacerda's residence to kill him. The guards, recognizing Marinho, let him through. But Lacerda had been tipped off and fled before Marinho arrived.

SEBASTIÃO CAMARGO MIGHT HAVE adhered to the military regime mainly out of self-interest, but Roberto Marinho believed in the Revolution of 1964, as he called it. He believed enough to bend his definition of democracy. The day after the coup he praised the generals in a front-page editorial titled RESSURGE A DEMOCRACIA!—as if the overthrow of a popularly elected head of state had unstoppered a geyser of political freedom. A year later, concerned that the public might not vote the right way, he helped persuade the first military president to postpone elections. Even after the right to habeas corpus was suspended in '68, Marinho trumpeted the generals' democratic intentions on front page after front page. His bent was obvious. While giving patriotic coverage to events like the Military Olympics, Globo labeled all left-wing militants as terrorists whether they'd been proven guilty of a crime or not. Ironically, when terrorists targeted Marinho himself in '76, planting a small bomb at his mansion, they turned out to be right-wing paramilitaries bent on stalling the democratic opening then just barely taking root.

Marinho sometimes played the fool even though he knew better. Attending a soccer game once with General Médici, he asked, "President, can you assure me that, contrary to what people say, there is no torture in Brazil?" Médici, who was well aware of what went on in dungeons like Oban, gave Marinho his word, and Marinho would repeat the anecdote as if it were a vaccine for his conscience. Just the same, when suspected communists at Globo were taken for questioning, he made a point of accompanying them to ensure their safety. "Nobody messes with my communists," he would say. Despite Marinho's anticommunist convictions, many of Brazil's best artists were lefties, and as he did with Goulart, he was willing to compromise for the sake of his business. "If the communists win," he joked, "please have me hung with a silk rope. A fine silk rope."

Boni and other Globo execs from those years talk about how limited they were by military censors. But Marinho didn't do much to test the limits. A minister in charge of censorship in the seventies would later say, "Roberto Marinho never caused me any kind of problem." One São Paulo newspaper, the Mesquita family's *O Estado de S. Paulo,* stayed loyal to the regime but took a far more combative approach in its coverage. To make censorship obvious, it published old Portuguese poems in place of banned stories.

Still, Marinho did stand up to the regime now and then. In 1975 he ordered a *Jornal Nacional* anchor to denounce censorship on live TV. Why? Censors had approved one of Globo's first novelas shot in color, *Roque Santeiro,* and Boni had already filmed the first thirty-six episodes when they found out the writer was a communist and had adapted his script from an old antimilitary play. Before it aired, the censors asked for cuts so broad there was little novela left over. Marinho had no choice but to cancel it. He swallowed a loss of half a million dollars, a lot of money for Globo then, and this infuriated him. Boni cites this episode as a proud moment in the network's history. And yet it's telling that Marinho didn't protest the censorship of anyone's torture or disappearance, just censorship that hurt his bottom line.

Marinho framed disputes as political when the real issue seemed to be money. In the late seventies, when the communications minister refused to award him a TV license in northeastern Brazil, saying it would strengthen what was already becoming a monopoly, Marinho held up his support for the regime and declared that Globo "deserved attention and special favors from the government." Globo needed to keep growing, he said, because any organization that stops growing will begin to decline. His logic failed to convince the minister. The regime did, though, repay his support by buying lots of ads, an old government tradition.

Brazil became a TV nation watching Globo. By the seventies, destitute families might not have running water but they usually had a TV set, like the poor families in today's *baixões*. Joe Wallach, an American exec Marinho hired away from Time-Life, explained what this meant: "For the first time—it was incredible—a kid in Copacabana saw the buffalo off in the Amazon, and he didn't know that existed in the country. And over in Belém too, the Indians could see the buildings of Rio de Janeiro." This was a big deal in a country where, for much of its history, the major cities had kept more contact with Portugal than with one another. I did wonder whether Marinho deserved the credit for this, as his official biography implies. None of it would have been possible if the government hadn't created Brazil's first national telecommunications network, which went into operation in 1969. Without Globo, on the other hand, Marinho's competitors would probably have filled the gap.

IT WAS IN THE eighties that Marinho's monopoly reached its peak. Globo averaged ratings of eighty percent, and in a country where a quarter of the population still couldn't read, a fact was not truly a fact until it appeared on *Jornal Nacional*. As the military regime wobbled and prepared to bow out, this gave Marinho a power to shape the political narrative that would be unusual in the history of any country. There's a saying, probably born in those years: "In Brazil, television isn't a concession of the state; the state is a concession of television."

Marinho's influence helps explain why the transition from the dictatorship back to democracy was more of a glide than a rupture. He helped to moderate the contesting interests—and he was proud of his role. To justify his cover-up of the free-election protests of '84, he said he feared they could incite unrest and lead the military to crack down again. One of his sons remembers a military helicopter hovering outside TV Globo's windows one day, an implicit threat. And yet Marinho turned against the status quo the following year, after the free-election movement failed, as Congress was set to vote on the first civilian president in two decades. Snubbing Paulo Maluf, the candidate favored by the generals, Marinho instead backed Tancredo Neves from the opposition. It was this that gave many regime-allied lawmakers the courage to defect.

Most would agree that by shooting down Maluf—he of *rouba mas faz*—Marinho did a favor to the people of Brazil. But he also reaped lucrative favors for himself. Tancredo knew he stood no chance of putting the country back together without Globo's support, so he presented his cabinet picks one by one for Marinho's approval. To lead the communications ministry, which would oversee TV Globo, Marinho suggested a friend of his—Antonio Carlos Magalhães, known as ACM. Much to the displeasure of his party, the PMDB, Tancredo accepted. "I'll fight with the pope, I'll fight with the Catholic Church, I'll fight with the PMDB, with anyone," Tancredo explained. "I just won't fight with Dr. Roberto." Like Sebastião Camargo, Marinho liked to be called *doutor* (though he too never went to college, much less medical school).

Tancredo died before taking office, but José Sarney, the vice president who took Tancredo's place, did Marinho the same courtesy. And with Sarney's backing, ACM would intervene in a dispute between the partners of a telecom-equipment maker, allowing Roberto Marinho to buy a stake at a bargain price.

The favors were repaid. While ACM was still minister, Marinho gave his family the contract to run a Globo affiliate in his home state of Bahia. After Sarney stepped down, the ex-president got the same deal in Maranhão. These contracts were not only highly profitable but a powerful platform to win votes for their ongoing political careers. Marinho also distributed these contracts to congressmen, giving him sway in the legislature. These partnerships may explain why, even though the new democratic constitution called for a ban on media monopolies and oligopolies—like Marinho's—Congress never drew up the legislation to implement it. Today these TV stations still serve as pillars of power for the regional bosses Brazilians call *coronéis* or "colonels."

MARINHO WAS ONE OF the three Brazilians on that first global *Forbes* list in 1987. But he was much bigger than the other two, Sebastião Camargo and Antônio Ermírio de Moraes. In an interview with *The New York Times* that year, Marinho acknowledged his status as a kind of unelected branch of government in the new democracy. "I use this power," he said. But he added, "I always do so patriotically, trying to correct things, looking for the best paths for the country. We would like to have the power to fix everything that doesn't work in Brazil. We dedicate all our power to this."

Walter Clark, the former Globo exec, compared Roberto Marinho to *Citizen Kane*'s Charles Foster Kane, only without a Rosebud. But he wasn't as cold in his cunning as some believed. His responsibility weighed on him. He used to say that if he ever wrote his memoirs, he would title them *Condemned to Success*. He suffered from anxiety and scraped at his own flesh with his fingernails, leaving blood on his papers. He took pills to get to sleep; once he overdosed and nearly died. And he was troubled by the times he chose the wrong path.

In 1989 Marinho threw his weight behind a politician who promised to modernize the nation but ended up making Brazil look like a banana republic. It was the first free presidential election in three decades, and the country was in turmoil. Lula was running and talked about breaking up Globo if elected, so Marinho understandably backed his opponent, a handsome young politician named Fernando Collor de Mello. An ally of the defunct military regime, Collor hailed from a northeastern political clan that controlled a Globo affiliate in their home state of Alagoas. As mayor and then governor, he'd treated public office in the way of a typical "cordial man," hiring dozens of relatives for public posts and putting more of the budget into personal expenses than into education. Just the same, with Globo's help, he framed himself as a political outsider who would slim down a bloated state and sweep the corrupt "maharajas" of Brasília from power. On TV and in his newspapers, Marinho gave a lot of space to Collor's warnings that Lula would bring "disorder, fanaticism, and insanity." Globo also ran a novela that year titled *Que Rei Sou Eu?* (What King Am I?)—in which all the politicians of a mystical Kingdom of Avilan are corrupt save for a young prince who takes power in the end. Collor actually referred to the novela once in a speech, saying that he was fighting against a real-life Kingdom of Avilan in Brazil.

Brazilian elections have two rounds, and Lula and Collor made it to the runoff. A few days before the vote, the race was neck and neck. For the final debate, Marinho sent his top exec, Boni, to advise Collor. He probably didn't need to. After trouncing Collor in the previous debate, this time Lula appeared tired and sweaty. He spoke poorly, and most observers agreed he'd lost. Still, when Marinho saw

TV Globo's post-lunch recap the next day, he said it made Lula look too good. And so on *Jornal Nacional* that night, the producers cut together all of Lula's worst moments and all of Collor's best, and as Boni himself would later phrase it, Collor's 3–2 victory became a 3–0. Official campaigning had come to an end by then, so Globo's was the last word on the race before the vote. It's hard to say how much that swung the result, but Collor won.

Collor was a disaster. The first thing he did was freeze everyone's savings accounts in a half-baked plan to fight hyperinflation. This traumatized a whole generation of Brazilians. My godfather told me he lent dollars to his retired Brazilian in-laws so they could buy food and gas. Others without such connections fared worse. Unemployment shot up, and a wave of suicides swept the country. Meanwhile Collor's wealthy allies won exceptions to the rule. In the end all the Collor Plan accomplished was to lead Brazil into the worst recession in its history.

Then things got worse. Halfway into his term, Collor's own brother Pedro denounced a wide-reaching bribery scheme run by Collor's former campaign treasurer. Pedro also told the press that the president had induced him to snort cocaine in the seventies. Though Collor denied it, the allegation further tainted the president's image. Already outraged over their frozen savings, hundreds of thousands of Brazilians took to the streets to demand the president step down. Marinho distanced himself from Collor, not that he had much to worry about. Even while protesting Globo's candidate, students sang a song from a Globo miniseries—*Anos Rebeldes*—about youths who'd stood up to the dictatorship.

Collor resigned, but Congress impeached him anyway. In typical Brazilian fashion, though, he was never convicted and everyone ended up friends. Elected a senator years later, he joined Lula's coalition in Congress.

Lula never was the kind to hold a grudge. Ever the pragmatist, he also saw the value in making up with Globo. And so when Dr. Roberto died in 2003 at ninety-eight years old, Lula declared three days of official mourning. More to the point, he kept up the government ad budget, funneling hundreds of millions of dollars to Globo each year, much as the military regime had done.

I GOT TO MEET one of the Globo heirs not long after the finale of *Avenida Brasil,* the billion-dollar novela. Marinho's three sons each own an equal slice of the empire and do their part to maintain it. The oldest takes care of the business side, the youngest heads up the Roberto Marinho Foundation, and the middle son—João Roberto, who agreed to speak with me—runs the news operation. They've done well. Even though it has lost market share in recent years, Globo is more profitable than ever. Dr. Roberto was worth a billion dollars when he died; nine years later, when we added up the family fortune at Bloomberg, we arrived at a total of twenty-five billion dollars. Individually, each brother was almost as rich as Rupert Murdoch, the Australian media magnate who owns Fox and *The Wall Street Journal.*

I went to see João Roberto with a Bloomberg editor from New York who didn't rank high enough for helicopter service. We took a taxi to a narrow, nondescript building on a quiet street in Jardim Botânico, a wealthy neighborhood in Rio. I saw none of the glamour I expected from a company with so many celebrities on its payroll. From a dingy lobby, a receptionist led us through a turnstile, down an elevator, across an underground parking garage, and into a separate building where we passed through another set of turnstiles. We were handed off to another receptionist and she led us up a dark stairwell, through a hallway and another set of doors. Here and there guards manned our roundabout route, which suggested complex security precautions, a power that needed hiding.

We arrived at last at a door that swung open to reveal the billionaire heir we'd come to see. He extended his hand and introduced himself, as if it were necessary: "João Marinho." Wiry and tall, sixty years old but youthful-looking, João wore thick-rimmed tortoiseshell eyeglasses, a dark blue blazer rumpled in back, slacks of a subtly different dark blue, a white shirt, and no tie. He was less formal than his dad had been. His office was spacious but not extravagant, except for the view through the floor-to-ceiling glass walls on two sides: lush green Rio hills, a shimmering Guanabara Bay, Sugarloaf Mountain. I guessed the glass was bulletproof.

The Bloomberg editor started the conversation tactfully with small talk. He remarked on the beauty of Rio, also on the terrible traffic. For a moment João looked mystified before politely nodding. I gathered he was a helicopter man. I knew the Marinhos had installed a helipad at their fourteen-thousand-square-foot mansion near Paraty, down the coast from Rio. Built in the middle of an ecological reserve, in apparent breach of environmental laws, the home had won the Wallpaper Design Award for its sleek concrete-and-glass architecture.

João spoke carefully, quietly, properly—in English, for the benefit of the editor. The family rarely talks to the press, perhaps since they own so much of it, but João said they admire Bloomberg. This gave me a funny sense of being a piece in some imaginary game of Risk among global billionaires. *Bloomberg Markets* magazine's "World's Richest People" issue had just come out, so at one point I pulled a copy out of my bag and asked him what he thought of it.

"Yes, I've seen it," João said. "But we don't like to be on this list. We don't want to be known for *that*"—by which I understood *money*. "We want to be known for what we *do*."

When João talked about his family, he conveyed a sense of time much broader than mine. He showed us a photo on the wall of his father at a desk in O *Globo*'s newsroom in the fifties, and said he looked at it every day to remind himself where he came from. Though he'd inherited his fortune, João conveyed the idea that he'd earned it too. He told us how he'd worked his way up as a Globo journalist before becoming news chief in the mid-nineties. It's a version of meritocracy that makes sense if João sees himself not merely as an individual but as the standard-bearer of a long-term project, a lineage, a dynasty. The way João described it, he and his brothers are like stewards of Brazil. They seek to guide the nation as their father did. "To have a presence like we do in society gives us a permanent sense of responsibility," he said. In this he seemed to echo Blairo Maggi, only he didn't pretend that Globo belonged to anyone but the Marinhos.

Planning for the next generations of Globo shareholders, João and his brothers have already drawn up rules for their children and grandchildren. To join the family business, heirs have to get MBAs. Enter religion or politics, and they'll forfeit their shares' voting rights. The Marinhos are trying to change Globo's image of bias. They need to now, if they want to stay on top of an increasingly competitive market. In a section on Globo's website titled "Errors," they now acknowledge two, their most famous ones: the cover-up of free-election protests in '84 and the editing of Lula's debate with Collor in '89. There's a much longer section on the website titled "False Accusations."

Hoping to straighten the historical record, the brothers have distanced themselves from their dad's politics, sort of. When they repudiated O Globo's support for the 1964 coup, a Jornal Nacional anchor read the editorial live. They lamented the regime's human rights abuses, but they also praised its economic advances. It was a curious balancing act: a concession to public opinion on the one hand, a defense of their family's convictions on the other.

What are their convictions? João mentioned two: better education and small government, both old banners of Roberto Marinho. The first is hard to argue with. The second is complex. In the editorial pages of O Globo, the Marinhos will declare that a wealth tax like the one proposed by the French economist Thomas Piketty is simply unworkable, without hinting that they might have a stake in the issue. They'll deplore how the state has grown under the Workers Party. They just don't mention the government's massive Globo ad buys. Possibly to protect this subsidy, João told me they restrict their opinions to the editorial pages of O Globo and keep the TV network, with all its power to influence the debate, nonpartisan.

The opinions seep through anyway. Sometimes it's a question of focus. Though cases of fraud are rare among the fifty million Brazilians who depend on Bolsa Família, the Workers Party welfare program, they're frequent on the Globo network. Meanwhile tax evasion estimated in the hundreds of billions of dollars a year gets relatively short shrift (perhaps because Globo itself is fighting charges it evaded taxes). Other times complex national debates are resolved before they ever reach the viewer. To weigh in on Brazil's labor laws, producers will invite an orthodox economist to explain how they raise the cost of doing business but rarely a unionist to speak about the protections they provide. This dispute is similar to the one Marinho had with Getúlio Vargas more than half a century ago. One of Lula's advisers once told me he believed that the two most powerful institutions in Brazil were the Workers Party and Globo.

As a piece on the global-billionaire Risk board, I couldn't help thinking about how my employer presented the news. As one arm of a financial information provider, Bloomberg News reports on the people who pay its bills—bankers, investors, billionaires. Our editor in chief then, Matt Winkler, called our readers "those with the most at stake," which is to say, with the most money. Despite the "Chinese wall" between news and the business side, a member of the sales team once said I should avoid quoting sources who didn't own Bloomberg terminals. I never heard this from my editors, but the fact remains that Bloomberg News not only reports on its customers but uses them as sources. It can feel like an echo chamber at times. Bloomberg published stories critical of big clients like Goldman Sachs, but many other stories presented the views of the financial industry as if they were objective values. I remember one story whose opening sentence called Dilma Rousseff "a nightmare"—for the bond market.

As a journalist, obsessively reading the papers each day, I could forget that most people don't care too much about politics. Voting is obligatory here, but informing yourself is not, and in surveys just weeks after elections, a third of Brazilians can't remember which congressman they voted for. As many as one in ten will show up at the polling station and vote for no one—you can do that. Partly this reflects the old fatalism here about politicians, *all corrupt.*

Even apolitical Brazilians, though, watch telenovelas. This is where much of Globo's influence lies. João knew his family's power to set the cultural agenda. He told me about Globo's tradition of inserting "social messaging" in novelas to make a difference in society. This works. A Globo novela with poignant stories of romantic separation helped move Congress to approve the first legal framework for divorce in 1977. Since they ran for just one season, novelas could be cultural milestones. *Avenida Brasil* was a milestone in part because it put the emerging middle class onscreen in a big way. Still, I noticed something off about Globo's portrait of *classe C*. Though the novela took place on Rio's heavily black north side, the top black role was that of a maid.

This is an old tradition. From early on in Globo novelas, a black actress in her maid's outfit might dust off a candelabra as a blonde teared up about her husband's infidelity in the foreground. For most black actresses, the best they could hope for was to play a maid who got involved in the story somehow. When Globo adapted *Uncle Tom's Cabin* into a novela in 1969, the producers cast a white actor as Uncle Tom. He wore blackface, with little corks in his nostrils to widen his nose and cotton balls in his mouth to slum down his Portuguese. The same actor also played Abraham Lincoln, who'd been written into the plot line. Blacks did get to play the slaves. In one novela a white actor says of a maid he's fallen in love with, "What does it matter if she's colored, if her soul is white and pure?"

In an interview once, a Globo novela director explained that putting blacks on TV was just bad for business, since the people who had money then, the people advertisers wanted to reach, were almost all white. Blacks started to get more space in Globo story lines in the eighties, but even now they play few leading roles. Watching Globo, you could be forgiven for thinking that the vast majority of Brazilians are white. This even though slightly more than half of the population identifies as *pardo* (mixed race, literally "brown") or *preto* (truly black).

It's hard to blame Roberto Marinho for all this. While he loved the news, he left novelas in the hands of his deputies. He did, though, seem to harbor unresolved racial anxieties: All his life he put rice powder on his face to disguise his dark complexion. In this way, he was a creature of his country's traditions.

Over more than three centuries, Brazil imported four and a half million African slaves—ten times as many as the United States—and in 1888, when it became the last country in the Americas to abolish slavery, one major rationale was that it dirtied the racial mix. Here was *complexo de vira-lata,* "mutt complex," before the term had ever been coined. Brazil's tiny elite believed the best way to catch up to the club of serious countries was by "whitening" the population with immigrants from Europe. One reason a third of the people living in São Paulo state today have Italian blood is that the government paid ocean passage and set them up with jobs on coffee plantations. The hope was that they'd intermarry with blacks and mulattos and produce lighter-skinned children. Race has always been fluid in Brazil, never binary like in the United States. Partly this was because of a history of miscegenation that stretched back to cosmopolitan Portugal. Partly, since Portugal had so few inhabitants, racial mixing was a necessity in populating the colony. With so few native-born Brazilians of pure white ancestry, some mulattos in Brazil managed to rise through the ranks of business and politics. Some ex-slaves even bought their own slaves. There's an old expression here, "money whitens"—though the blacker you were to begin with, the harder it was to rise. And most didn't. As in most countries with a slave past, being born black puts you at a disadvantage in Brazil.

I remember one of my first conversations with the PhD student I dated from the south (who was white). Innocently I said São Paulo struck me as segregated, because I rode the bus with brown people, I rode the train with brown people, but I worked in an office with white people, and I rarely saw brown people in fancy restaurants or in bars where twenty-somethings with money hung out. She snapped at me, "You're the ones who segregate. You're the ones who had Jim Crow." Even many socially progressive Brazilians like her cling to the idea that theirs is a postracial paradise. Some critics trace this wishful thinking to an iconic book from 1933, *Casa-Grande & Senzala (The Masters and the Slaves)*. In it the historian Gilberto Freyre championed Brazil's mixed racial heritage, so long a source of shame. At times, though, he presented a violent history in an improbably harmonious light. Even today, many Brazilians like to imagine that their slavery was friendlier than the U.S. version.

Some activists blame the "myth of racial democracy" for the fact that Brazil never had a black civil rights movement. A rapper from São Paulo, Emicida, gave an interview a couple of years ago where he said, "It's fucked up to have to fight a *cordial* kind of racism, one that doesn't show itself. You don't know who the enemy is, because he never declares himself." The sociologist Florestan Fernandes called it *"preconceito de ter preconceito"*—prejudice against being prejudiced. It's a fantasy of Brazil that glides over the fact that apartment buildings, mine included, still maintain "service elevators" for maids who just happen to be overwhelmingly black, with "social elevators" for everyone else. A black friend told me how, riding the social elevator in her building once, an old lady asked her suspiciously which apartment she worked in.

As an outsider, I sometimes missed the codes. Not long after I moved to São Paulo, I went to a party at a penthouse in my neighborhood. I walked in and saw a middle-aged woman in the kitchen. Assuming she was someone's mom, I introduced myself and gave her the customary kiss on the cheek. She made an awkward face as if I'd done something wrong. I looked around and realized she was the only dark-skinned person in the apartment. She was a domestic employee, there to help serve drinks and clean up.

Even today, one in six women in Brazil's labor market works as a maid. During Dilma's presidency, they would finally win rights as formal laborers: the minimum wage, overtime, a lunch break, social security, severance pay. The law caused a backlash among middle-class Brazilians who, because of low unemployment and higher wages, already found it increasingly difficult to afford a full-time servant. Some took to social media to voice their displeasure. With the anonymity of the Internet, the cordiality peeled back. There's a Twitter account, @AMinhaEmpregada (My Maid), that retweets comments about cleaning ladies. A typical find: "The only black person whose complaining I can stand is my maid because she washes my underwear."

Still, Brazilians would tell me that inequality here is a matter strictly of class, not race. It's true that there are whites in the favelas too. But how many blacks do you ever see in the financial world? When I did interviews at banks, the only blacks I saw wore the hokey outfits of old-fashioned maids and butlers as they brought coffee to us on a silver tray. The divide starts early. The average poor white kid gets better schooling than the average poor black kid. Brazil's best universities are state-run and cost nothing but are so competitive that, given the crappiness of basic public education, it's very hard to get in unless you can afford private school or private tutoring. When public universities adopted affirmative action starting in the early 2000s, many white Brazilians were outraged. TV Globo's news chief, Ali Kamel, wrote a book titled *Não Somos Racistas* (We Are Not Racists) in which he complained that the quotas undermined the principle of meritocracy. It's a curious position for the employee of a company whose current owners were born into their places at the top of the pyramid.

Of the hundred and fifty Brazilians worth at least a billion *reais*— around a quarter million dollars—none is black.

A NOVELA TITLED *SALVE JORGE* had recently debuted when I met with João Marinho. It was the first to be shot largely on location in a favela. If it had a message, it was to promote a new program to install UPPs—Police Pacification Units—in Rio's one thousand favelas. João spoke enthusiastically about the program, how it could transform the city. It was a big deal because favelas had become the semisovereign fiefdoms of drug gangs. The idea of the UPPs, hatched as Rio campaigned for the 2016 Olympics, was for police to sweep out the gangs with an overwhelming assault and then establish a permanent force that would, for the first time ever, build a relationship with the community. Public services would follow: sewage lines, garbage pickup, public transport, proper housing. The program started with the favelas bordering nice, rich, touristy areas like Copacabana and Ipanema. Eventually it reached the location for *Salve Jorge:* Complexo do Alemão, an infamous stronghold for a gang known as the Red Command. This isn't one of the favelas I'd seen on my first trip to Rio. It's in the city's working-class *subúrbio,* a long way north from the beach.

Complexo do Alemão ("The German's Compound") is so named because the land once belonged to a Pole, close enough. Migrant families filled its hills starting in the fifties, and in the eighties the drug gangs took over. Usually the only state presence residents ever saw was when police stormed the alleyways hunting down *bandidos* in gun battles whose stray bullets ended plenty of innocent lives. Politicians cared about favelas only when elections came around. They would come and negotiate votes in return for the promise to build a daycare center or a first aid post. Favelas not under the control of drug traffickers might be ruled by cops who formed paramilitary gangs known as *milícias.*

The pacification of Alemão came in response to a wave of attacks across Rio in November 2010. Hoping to disrupt the Red Command's communication networks, the authorities had transferred imprisoned gang members to penitentiaries far from Rio, and the Red Command decided to show its power by coordinating high-profile hit-and-run robberies. At one point half a dozen armed men—apparently from Alemão—carried out an *arrastão,* blocking the Washington Luís Freeway to rob drivers. They set two cars on fire, and when a military vehicle happened on the scene, they tossed a grenade at it. Brazil's drug gangs are alarmingly well armed. Over the next few days, gang members ambushed police posts and clashed with security forces. I remember everyone in the Bloomberg newsroom watching the flaming carcasses of city buses on TV. The scale of the attacks frightened Brasília so much that the defense minister agreed to send in the military to take over Alemão.

Salve Jorge's first episode splices archival footage with dramatized scenes of the takeover. On the fourth and final day of the offensive, twenty-seven hundred men secured the perimeter in early morning darkness. Cannons thrusting forward, a line of tanks rolled up the street, their brown and green camouflage meant for jungle combat. Soldiers manning machine-gun turrets peered from under battle helmets while snipers claimed positions on rooftops.

Sixty thousand people live in the complex of favelas that make up Alemão. As the invasion commenced, residents looked curiously from their windows. Others heaped furniture in front of their windows to shield against stray bullets. Gang members flushed out of an adjacent favela, Vila Cruzeiro, had taken refuge in Alemão and were also expected to put up their final resistance here.

At eight A.M., two military helicopters lifted into the sky. The government forces began their advance up narrow, steep roads overhung by clusters of DIY electric lines. Embedded with them, reporters and cameramen in flak jackets relayed it all live. Bulldozers pushed makeshift barricades out of the way, and as the troops ascended the hill, taking cover behind armored assault vehicles, *bandidos* took potshots from the back of a fleeing motorcycle or a notch in an unfinished cinderblock wall. The Red Command was well armed but poorly trained, and despite their constant fire, they didn't cause a single casualty. They retreated, melting into the favela. By ten A.M., the troops had reached the top of a hill where a cable car station would soon go into operation. A soldier set off a green smoke flare to signal that official forces had secured the area. Everyone had expected bloodshed, but the mission was accomplished, just like that. The government had taken Alemão. Residents waved white flags from their windows, held up babies for the cameras. One group hoisted a banner that read PAZ—peace—with a backward z.

Up on the hill, an army captain stabbed a flagpole into a patch of earth. The wind caught the flag, and the green and yellow and blue of Brazil flapped proudly in the wind. All that actually happened. In the *Salve Jorge* version, the captain thrusts his helmet into the air, whooping in triumph, smiling wide with his handsome strong jaw. And in the next scene, of the favela the next day, Tim Maia is in the background singing "Rio de Janeiro is still beautiful. . . ."

I PAID A VISIT TO ALEMÃO to find out what its residents thought about Globo's take on their home. I got in touch with a local newspaper called *Voz da Comunidade* (Voice of the Community), and a twenty-four-year-old journalist named Daiene Mendes volunteered to be my guide. We arranged to meet one evening at the Bonsucesso train station, which connected to the cable car that would take us up into Alemão's hills. I felt a bit nervous visiting at night. Gang members who had lain low for a while after the pacification now were making noise again. There had been a shootout every day in recent weeks. Not long before my visit, the cable car had temporarily shut down because of stray bullets. But I didn't have long in Rio, and this was the time that Daiene could meet. I texted her to look for the guy with the nerdy glasses, and she replied, "I have nerdy glasses too!"

Daiene showed up in a puffy jacket against the mild Rio winter, and we took the cable car up with men and women returning from work in the city center. Daiene was born and raised in Alemão. She told me about a youth in which school came second to playing *futebol* in the alleyways with her friends. That changed when she was fifteen and her dad, a painter, heard about a class that *paid* students forty dollars a month. So she decided to attend. In the afternoons after school, she trained to work as a *monitor* at one of Rio's museums, which meant greeting visitors and guiding them around. After working at a science museum not far from Alemão, she grew close to the administrators, and they recommended her for a museum job in the city center—a long way from home. "My horizons weren't just widened, they were stretched out," she said. Before encountering the museum world, she'd never read a book, but when I met her, she was working toward a degree in journalism. Her exposure to a different Rio made her realize how much Alemão limited you. Most of her friends hadn't seen much outside the favela—except, she said, for what they watched on Globo.

On weekends, Daiene said, middle-class Brazilians now rode the cable car to observe favela life below. From the cables suspended above Alemão, they could see the chaotic texture of a self-built town, kids piloting kites from rooftops here, girls in bikinis suntanning on rooftops there, rebar protruding from all the rooftops because homes were never quite finished in the favela; you could always add another level. The residents didn't necessarily see the tourists as gawkers or invaders. Mostly they were pleased that outsiders wanted to visit for once.

At the first station, we got out and beheld the view. The sky was dark by now. With cheap white and yellow fluorescent bulbs making pricks of light in every direction, the complex of favelas resembled a night sky laid out carpet-like onto the contours of a craterous valley. "It's prettier from here than up close," Daiene said.

As we walked down a freshly paved road leading from the cable car into the favela, I could see why the politically correct word for favela was *comunidade*. Everywhere we went—along narrow roads where little sedans barely squeezed past one another, through narrower pathways where old guys sat on steps shooting the shit, past the tight tented stalls of a market where vendors sold fresh fruit or cellphone chargers, all of it thrumming with activity—everywhere we went, people shouted *Oi, Daiene!* and she shouted *Oi!* back. I felt safe with her.

After the government takeover, services really did arrive. The local utility came in and fixed up the power network. Lula's low-income housing program funded new apartment complexes to re-place old, sloping shacks. "These were the first public works I had ever seen here," Daiene told me, pointing out a housing project with bright fresh-looking paint.

Still, she said, the occupation didn't make all the problems go away. Other problems emerged. The soldiers occupying Alemão would kick down doors ostensibly looking for gang members, toss people's homes, and sometimes steal their valuables. In the favela, some say the military dictatorship never ended. During informal in-terrogations by police, torture is commonplace. Summary execu-tions are framed as "resistance killings." The victims are disproportionately black, young, and male—though in Rio at least, the cops are often black young men too. Daiene, who's black herself, put it like this: "It's poor black *favelados* killing poor black *favela-dos*, as usual."

The pacification program was supposed to turn a relationship of violence into one of trust. That's a tricky task. The police clamped down on *baile funk* parties financed by drug gangs where kids dance to beats inherited from Miami Bass, melodies sampled from every-where, and homespun raps. Working families appreciated their newly peaceful Saturday nights, but to many residents it felt like an imposition from above. *Favelados* have a complex relationship with the gangs. When the state is absent, they can act like an informal government, subsidizing food for needy neighbors, charging for ac-cess to pilfered electricity and cable TV, preventing petty crime, and dispensing primitive justice. Daiene said, "I've been stopped by the police, but I never had any problems with the *tráfico*"—the drug gangs. "They saw me grow up. They know my whole family. The police don't." This dynamic goes way back. In the early twentieth century, a bandit known as Lampião became a kind of folk hero. In his mythified exploits, he plundered his armaments from the police and robbed the ranches of northeastern cattle barons.

The government had sold a utopia, Daiene said—something like

Order and Progress. After soldiers planted the flag at the top of the hill, the national anthem blared from a sound truck. "Lots of people cried from the emotion of it all," she said. "I cried." As far as she could see, though, the government had failed to deliver its utopia. Money meant to integrate favelas with the rest of the city dried up while projects for the 2016 Olympics plowed ahead. Ipanema and Copacabana got a fancy bike-share system even as pacification police found themselves overextended, backsliding into their old role fighting *bandidos*. Daiene introduced me to the owner of a clothing shop that sold T-shirts reading FAVELA: FAÇO PARTE DELA, "Favela: I'm a part of it." Sales had surged after the UPPs came, as kids with money from the beachy south side felt safe enough to visit for the first time ever. But now the violence had scared them off again. Some residents preferred the old days with the Red Command in control. The drug trade brought in money that recirculated at bars and restaurants and shops in the favela. This fatalism frustrated Daiene.

I asked Daiene why she thought Globo wanted to film a novela at Alemão. "There's this favela aesthetic," she said. It's not just the cable car; foreign tourists now go on favela tours. She also knew that, for the first time since favelas began cropping up more than a century ago as northeastern migrants flocked south to big cities, they were valuable to the national economy as more than a source of cheap labor. Eleven million Brazilians live in favelas, and their homes now have flat-screen TVs and laptops hooked up to Facebook—ordinary trappings of modern life that are nonetheless something new here.

Daiene introduced me to the founder of *Voz de Comunidade*, Rene Silva. He'd gained some fame live-tweeting the military takeover, publishing firsthand information that even the embedded journalists couldn't get. Globo made him into a character on *Salve Jorge*. The head writer would sometimes call him up for advice. Globo never paid him for this, but it got his name out. He was one of those people born with an entrepreneurial instinct. He'd founded the paper when he was eleven, and while it never made any money, it kept him afloat. Roberto Marinho probably had this instinct, but I wondered, if his sons had been born in Alemão, whether they would have clawed out their own little media business as Rene Silva has.

I met Rene at the *Voz*'s offices, a cramped apartment where Daiene used to live, now filled with teenagers engrossed in vaguely productive chaos. Rene had an unruly Afro that he vanished into a beanie before standing up to chat with me. I asked him what he thought of *Salve Jorge*. He thought it was shallow. Apart from the occasional shootout for dramatic tension, all the social issues got smoothed over—like police abuse. The police in the novela were all heroes. He talked about the favela's resistance to state authority, its nostalgia for gangsters, and wished Globo had explored these contradictions. "It's a huge missed opportunity to help people understand why things are the way they are here," he said. "The novela was like, 'People are poor but they're happy.'"

And yet they do seem happy, despite everything. In one survey, ninety-four percent of *favelados* said they considered themselves happy. They embody a very Brazilian contradiction: pessimistic about the system that surrounds them, optimistic about their own lives. Perhaps strangest of all, most people from Alemão didn't mind being packaged and pandered to. They loved *Salve Jorge*. They loved seeing so-and-so's bakery where they bought their loaves of bread. So what if the black characters on the show were just sidekicks to lighter-skinned protagonists? Everyone watched. And this pride emerged. In the past you'd be embarrassed to say you were from Alemão. The name conjured some kind of postapocalyptic zone, so you'd say you were from a neighboring area. That had changed now, not because of the UPPs but because of Globo. People started announcing it: *I'm from Alemão—you know, like the novela.*

CHAPTER 5

PROSPERITY GOSPEL

**THE BISHOP, HIS NETWORK, AND
THE OUTSIDER TRADITION**

---

*"From the point of view of my faith in the Lord Jesus,
I am the richest man on the planet."*
—EDIR MACEDO ($1.2 BILLION)

IF GLOBO ISN'T AS POWERFUL AS IT USED TO BE, ONE REASON IS a Pentecostal pastor named Edir Macedo, founder of the Universal Church of the Kingdom of God. He has two million followers in Brazil, many of them in favelas like Alemão. As the owner of the country's number-two TV network, he had a net worth of $1.2 billion—but was unlike any other billionaire I'd studied up to now. He didn't come from the traditional elites. He was an enemy of Globo. In the end, he would expand my sense of what a billionaire could be.

Macedo preaches the prosperity gospel, which is the idea that your faith in God will bring you financial success. The message never really changes from one sermon to the next, but the way he tells it is always captivating. He's a bald little man but his charisma transforms him into a giant. One day in the inland city of Belo Horizonte, at one of the ten thousand churches he has across Brazil, he asked, "Which is the largest country in the world, economically speaking?" Five thousand people were in the church listening to him, and you could hear a murmur of answers rising from the crowd as he leaned his cuff-linked white sleeve on a lacquered podium. Rising high behind him, a TV screen framed by stained glass blew up his image so even the back rows could make out the bright red knot of his tie. "It's America, the United States. Do you know why?" Silence. "Because way back during the colonization of the United States— this is history, you can look it up on the Internet—the colonization was done by men who believed in the word of God. And they were tithers. That's why you see on the dollar bill: 'In God we trust.'"

His paunch pressed against a microphone transmitter holstered to his belt. He used a headset to keep both hands free to thrust into the air. He doesn't hide his fingers, which are congenitally deformed, gnarly, and attached by a hint of webbing to thin, pointy, unbending thumbs. He listed off American companies founded by good Protestants who, he said, had regularly donated money to their churches. "Have you ever heard of Quaker Oats? He was a tither. Have you ever heard of Caterpillar? Tither. Have you ever heard of Ford? Tither." What held Brazil back, he said, was that Brazilians always worshiped Our Lady and the saints rather than worshiping God unadulterated. Brazil's problem was its Catholicism, in other words. His voice rose: "Our culture is retrograde, a stingy culture, a culture with no vision of the future." And then quieted again: "Only you can change this situation. When you start tithing faithfully, you're changing your situation. Amen?" He looked over his glasses at the crowd, raising his eyebrows expectantly.

"Amen!" came the choral reply.

This sermon went far beyond the Belo Horizonte megachurch. Wherever he's speaking, Macedo's words are heard all over Brazil on computers and smartphones and on TV channels (not just his own) where the Universal Church buys hours of airtime each day. They're heard in Portugal and Angola, where Macedo has several hundred thousand followers, and also in the United States, where he has sixty thousand more, mostly Latin American immigrants and poor African Americans. When he launched the first volume of his memoirs in New York, the line stretched for blocks from the McNally Jackson bookstore in SoHo. There's even a Universal Church in my home-town of Albuquerque, New Mexico. When Macedo visits his congre-gations abroad, he goes by private jet, traveling on a diplomatic passport, a perk once reserved for Catholic cardinals. He's not the only Pentecostal leader in Brazil—a quarter of the population now declares itself evangelical—but he's the biggest by far.

Smart alecks will ask why God needs your money. Macedo has an answer: "Tithes symbolize your faithfulness to God." It's a sacrifice: "Tithing is you on God's altar, just as Jesus was God's tithe for hu-manity." He'll cite Malachi 3:10, where to those who tithe, God promises to "pour out so much blessing that there will not be room enough to store it." The standard tithe is one-tenth of your income, but that just zeroes your debt with God. Offerings above and beyond will return to you multiplied. Don't believe it? "Do the test!" Macedo shouted in Belo Horizonte that day. "I did the test. I said to God, 'Enough! I want to see a change in my life.' And it happened."

If Macedo paints his financial success as miraculous, it's proba-bly because the real explanation isn't fit for sermonizing. The short version is that he took his followers' donations, called them interest-free loans from the church, and used the money to take over a televi-sion network called TV Record back in 1989. The acquisition cost him forty-five million dollars. That sounds like a lot of money, but the Universal Church now pulls in far more. In 2006, the last year the number was made public, it declared donations of three-quarters of a billion dollars.

It was the scent of dirty money that led me to Macedo. He's as reviled by outsiders as he is beloved by the Universal Church faithful. A *carnaval* procession in Salvador poked fun at him once with signs reading CHRIST IS THE WAY. EDIR MACEDO IS THE TOLLBOOTH. He's controversial even among other evangelicals, who criticize TV Re-cord for putting on lewd reality shows. The thing is that Record is a for-profit, entertainment-based television network. The only time slots it sells to the Universal Church are in the wee hours shunned by advertisers (and allegedly at inflated prices).

I heard lots of opinions about billionaires, but only when Macedo came up was there consensus. The Brazilians I knew didn't belong to his church, and almost without fail they called him a thief who exploited the poor. In a case that's dragged on since 2009, Macedo is accused of conspiring to launder his followers' donations through offshore accounts. All this just made me want to learn more about his appeal. So even while I dug into court papers and corporate records, I also visited what was then the main Universal Church in São Paulo to try to understand his world. What I found felt like a new thread pulling through the story of Brazil.

MACEDO CALLS HIMSELF O *Bispo*, which means "The Bishop." But he's much more playful than his title suggests. The one time I saw him live, he started off his sermon yelling, *"Sua vida está um cocô!"*— Your life is a piece of poop! Swinging his arms from side to side, he said, "I want to smack you all in the face!" and everyone chuckled. He knows how to level with his people, even when he asks them to make sacrifices that amount to secular blasphemy in Brazil: Boycott *carnaval*! Don't watch the World Cup!

Despite these anti-Brazilianisms, he grew up as a lot of his followers did, though with some mystical touches. As he tells it, he was born in a tiny town in 1945, prematurely, when an explosion at a nearby dairy caused his mother to go into early labor. She had sixteen other children, ten of whom died while still infants. When Macedo was small, the family moved a hundred miles south to the big city, Rio. Growing up, his home didn't have a TV or a refrigerator. He quit school at eleven to work in his father's bar. At sixteen he got a job at the Rio de Janeiro State Lottery, pushing a coffee cart.

In his memoirs, Macedo calls himself the ugly duckling of his family. He was short and scrawny, and he had those deformed fingers. His dad sometimes beat him. He lost his virginity in a brothel, but despite his ungainly looks, he went on to pursue romances he describes as "spicy, heated, full of lasciviousness." Still, he couldn't shake an empty feeling. He found no solace in the loose religion of his family, Catholics who began attending a spiritist center when he was a teenager. Widely practiced in Brazil, spiritism is a century-old mystical philosophy invented by the Frenchman Allan Kardec. One day, when Macedo found himself covered from head to toe in warts, he sought out a spiritist healer, who asked him to point out the largest wart, penned a cross on it, and promised that in a week the malady would disappear. It did. But then the warts came back, with a vengeance. Macedo came to doubt the family religion.

His sister Elcy suffered from asthma, and spiritist healers couldn't help her either. Her asthma improved only when she started listening to the radio show of a Canadian preacher named Roberto McAlister, who ran a Pentecostal church in downtown Rio. It was one of the many evangelical churches cropping up in those days to serve the flood of economic migrants in the cities of the southeast. When he was eighteen, Macedo attended his first service there and felt an immediate connection. He baptized himself not once but three times. He felt the Holy Spirit enter him; he danced, sang, and spoke in tongues. "I would leave the service walking in the clouds," Macedo writes. "The feeling is indescribable. Peace, security, confidence, cheer . . . as if a light turned on inside of me, illuminating my whole body."

Still, he was restless. He thought of all the souls in the world yet to be saved. In his twenties, as a low-level bureaucrat with one job at the lottery and another at the national census, he spent his free time spreading the gospel with his future brother-in-law. They would pass out pamphlets in the favelas of Rio's hills and rent derelict movie theaters—once, a theater that used to show porn—to play films by the American preacher T. L. Osborn, a televangelist in the tradition of Oral Roberts. (At his peak in the eighties, Oral Roberts would pull in $110 million a year, a fraction of the Universal Church's revenues.)

Macedo met his wife, Ester, at McAlister's church, and they had two daughters. When the second was born with a cleft lip and palate,

Macedo fell into despair. That was the moment he decided to dedicate himself full time to Jesus. At thirty-two, he quit work with its cushy government benefits and joined his brother-in-law and another friend in starting a ministry. He hauled sound equipment to a gazebo at a public park. When the crowds were small, his fellow pastors balked at leading services, but Macedo was willing to preach for just one person. He built up a following. A picture from those days shows Macedo in a pin-striped blazer and white slacks. People called him the bossa nova pastor because of his passionate gestures and then-voluminous hair. Macedo's congregation swelled, so he rented space in an old funeral parlor to hold sermons. Eventually he split with his partners. In 1977 the Universal Church was born.

Macedo's services were as eclectic as the religious history of Brazil. When Catholicism arrived here, it already reflected the Moorish influence in Portugal. Then Africans arriving on slave ships brought over deities who disguised themselves in the pantheon of Catholic saints. Macedo took the Catholics' solemn ritualism and livened it up with the ecstatic gospel of American Pentecostals. And rather than reject Afro-Brazilian religions as superstition, he rebranded the spirits of Candomblé as biblical demons—then banished them with the power of Jesus Christ. He performed exorcisms and miracle cures and bought a plastic kiddie pool for baptisms. Once enough money was rolling in, he followed McAlister's example and purchased airtime on local radio stations. Hopeful listeners flocked to his little funeral parlor, fifteen hundred people on some days, well past capacity. It could get so hot that condensed sweat dripped from the ceiling.

As the donations grew, he opened more churches. He acquired his own radio station in Rio and started renting slots on local TV channels in cities where he'd started new branches. Even then he talked about one day owning his own TV network. He built churches on the poor outskirts, reaching out to poor strivers distant from the Catholic cathedrals downtown. Sensing unmet demand, he kept his doors open from dawn till past midnight, with services four or five or six times a day, seven days a week. By the eighties he was opening two

churches a month. He started gathering the faithful in Rio's Maracanã stadium, packing it way past full, two hundred thousand faithful in the stands. From the center of the field, he announced, "Forget
everything you did up until nine o'clock this morning. Starting now,
you have the chance to start a new life. . . . Don't think God is up
there distant from your misery, your accursed pain. No! He's here
right now."

One secret to Macedo's expansion was that he knew how to turn
his church into an organization. He delegated. He made the most
fervent of his followers into *obreiros*—pastor's assistants—and the
most fervent *obreiros* into pastors. The best pastors in turn became
bishops (though there was only one Bishop). He moved to New York
for a while and let his bishops run the show in Rio, São Paulo, Ma-
puto, London, and other cities across the world.

IN THOSE DAYS, the main Universal Church in São Paulo took up
most of a city block in a working-class neighborhood. It was only
three miles south of the Bloomberg office, but it looked like another
city, with run-down auto parts stores and tune-up shops, none of the
high corporate glass of the Brooklin business district. The constant
was the stench of the Pinheiros River. With stained-glass windows
two stories tall, lit from inside by powerful fluorescent bulbs, the
temple glowed like a beacon at night.

Every church follows a franchise pattern, with a set theme each
day of the week. The first time I went was a Thursday, when the
theme is Love Therapy. It's meant for the lovelorn who might otherwise call the phone numbers you see printed on signs all over São
Paulo that offer the services of *pais e mães de santo*—priests and
priestesses of Candomblé who cast love spells. Macedo, unusually
for an evangelical, takes an open-minded view of sex. He supports
the use of condoms and birth control and even the right to have an
abortion, which is illegal in Brazil. He encourages his pastors to have
vasectomies and adopt. He celebrates sex—in marriage—as a gift

from God. "When I have sex," he says, "I go stronger to the altar." In other matters, he hews to the line of the evangelical caucus that has dozens of seats in Congress—several of them held by Macedo's bishops. He says the Universal Church can cure homosexuality. Once he wrote a blog post decrying anal sex, whether gay or straight, as unnatural.

During the Love Therapy service, assistant pastors sold copies of a book titled *Bulletproof Marriage* by Macedo's daughter Cristiane and her husband, a Universal Church bishop. A typical line: "Men will always be motivated by career achievements and women will always be motivated by the desire to have all of a man's attention." They also present a couples therapy program on TV Record. Following Brazilian tradition, Macedo's operation was a family affair. His other daughter, Viviane, is also married to a bishop; his son, Moysés, has sung vocals for Record's telenovela songs.

I often saw synergies between the branches of Macedo's empire. His books were bestsellers in part because the church bought so many copies to resell to his followers. One evening the bishop leading services played a segment that had aired on Record. One of the network's news choppers had witnessed a robbery, reported it to police, and kept its camera on the suspect until the police caught him. "Was it chance that Record was there to solve this crime?" asked the bishop, Jadson Santos. Universal Church pastors never leave rhetorical questions open to doubt, so he answered himself: "No, it was the hand of God." He then said he'd be wrapping up the service early so that everyone could get home in time to watch Record's new biblical miniseries, *Joseph of Egypt*.

Fridays at the church are for cures and liberation. The day I went, as everyone settled into their seats, pastors passed through the pews with a dropper to add holy water to plastic bottles that congregants knew to bring. When Jadson Santos came out on stage, he wore a white T-shirt with bold black letters reading A HORA DO MILAGRE— The Miracle Hour. A handful of congregants gave testimonials, stepping up one by one to a microphone. One woman had overcome cancer her doctors believed incurable. Another, told she was infertile, had given birth to a son. All thanks to prayer and faithful tithing.

Jadson orchestrated the energy in the room just as the Bishop did. This was another secret to Macedo's success: His delegates copied his orating style. And so Jadson started with jokes before all of a sudden getting serious. He called everyone to the front. He closed his eyes tight; everyone did the same. He spoke Macedo-style constructions about suffering, about God's mercy, which an accompanist repeated in song through a microphone as he played soaring piano licks. People bounced on the balls of their feet, making their own private prayers, whispering to themselves, their whispers forming a collective hiss all around me. I couldn't always recognize the words as language. We held hands. Pastors wove through the crowd, grabbed congregants' heads, and shook them, releasing them from ailments and hang-ups, speaking blessings that came out with the harshness of curses into their ears. A stained-glass cross, lit from inside by fluorescent bulbs, spanned the length of the ceiling fifty feet above.

I went to the service with an open mind, ready to experience something, but I couldn't get swept up in it. I grew up without religion, without the day-to-day mysticism that defines life for many Brazilians. A pastor walked by me, and I bowed toward him, hoping for the head-shaking he'd administered to others. He seemed to know I wasn't for real; he clutched my head weakly, performing a quick perfunctory prayer.

And then from the back of the church, shrieks erupted. I looked and saw a heavyset middle-aged woman curling her hands behind her, craning her neck to one side, gnashing her teeth. Two pastors grabbed hold of her and led her to the stage. Bishop Jadson held a microphone to her face and demanded she identify herself. In a low growl she spoke as the demon possessing her, an *orixá* from Candomblé, torturing its host, making her do things that didn't make sense, petty self-destructive vengeful acts, screwing up her life. The woman's body writhed, trying to escape from the pastors' grasp. Jadson led the hall in prayer as one pastor grappled with her head, shaking it vigorously. Six thousand faithful stomped their feet and called for Jesus's help. The prayers crescendoed, and a tense humming energy filled the church. Eventually the woman's arms slackened, she relaxed in the pastor's arms, and the demon left her.

THE UNIVERSAL CHURCH'S MOST popular service is the one that best captures the aspirations of the up-and-coming classes who form Macedo's base. It's called the Congress of Winners, and it's all about financial success. The crowd when I went was a bit better dressed than at other services. I saw lots of neckties and office blouses and shiny watches. The woman in front of me held a smartphone whose rhinestone-studded case flicked light at me. This service also began with testimonials. A lineup of congregants described how poor they used to be. They described a litany of humiliations—sliding under the turnstile, eating others' leftovers, failing to provide milk for their children. Some spoke of debts that had piled up to a hundred thousand dollars or more. So what did they do? They took what little they had left and gave it to Jesus, by way of the Universal Church. And things got better. Shanilda, a dark-skinned woman with dyed-blond hair, said she'd arrived in São Paulo from the northeast with nothing but the clothes on her back and at first took abuse as a dishwasher at a local bar. Now, she said, she owns the bar. Some testimonials came with a slide show. Three tall TV screens at the front showed photos of a shiny new SUV, the playground at a brand-new home.

In these testimonials, donating money to the church was the only step between rock bottom and prosperity. Much as Macedo simplified the story of his own rise, his followers smoothed over the details as they narrated theirs. Divine agency was at work here. "An offering is an investment," Macedo writes. "He who gives everything receives everything from God. It's inevitable. It's *toma lá, dá cá*"—a give-and-take with the Lord. If your life didn't improve, pastors would say your faith wasn't strong enough, your sacrifices not painful enough.

From early on Macedo ran campaigns known as Fogueiras Santas, or Holy Bonfires. Typically there's one in December, when Brazilians with formal jobs receive an extra month's pay, the so-called thirteenth salary. During these campaigns, Universal Church pastors exhorted the faithful to make bolder donations than they'd ever made before, to *surprise* God—and surprise themselves—and congregants ended up handing over the keys to their cars and the titles to their houses. The Holy Bonfires proved so successful that it became too hard to deal with all the vehicles and properties, and pastors asked congregants to sell them and just turn over the proceeds. Some people made unusual sacrifices. One day in the mid-eighties, Macedo was preaching in Rio when a woman arrived with her two-week-old baby in her arms. She offered the child to Macedo and his wife, who legally adopted him, giving him the biblical name Moysés.

For pastors who met revenue targets during Holy Bonfires—say, half a million dollars in a single day—Macedo would offer bonuses of ten thousand dollars or more. He would offer brand-new cars. I spoke to a former bishop who remembered getting the first Peugeot 406 that arrived in Brazil—a luxury for someone like him from a humble background. On top of these bonuses, the church paid his rent and expenses and an annual salary of around fifty thousand dollars, which in Brazil in the nineties was a lot of money (and still is). The bishop described a culture where money became the measure of success. Directing the expansion in Brazil's poor northeast, part of his job was to shut down "unprofitable" churches that spent more than they took in.

Macedo's approach to soliciting money from his followers is at the heart of the controversy around him. In the nineties an ex-bishop leaked a video from a pastors' retreat at the beach in Salvador. In it you see pastors riding Jet Skis and playing pick-up soccer on the beach. At one point Macedo addresses some pastors sitting around him in the sand. Wearing swim trunks and a tank top, he suggests that followers who don't pony up will go to hell, and the pastors chuckle. "You have to impose yourself," Macedo says, gesturing passionately. "You have to be a superhero for them. You can never be ashamed, never be shy. Demand, demand, demand."

The pressure to give money can ruin people. I found a New York bankruptcy case in which a woman named Darnelle had given $78,977 to the Universal Church over the course of three years. In Brazil, reporters found a mentally disabled man who turned over his entire salary as a building superintendent in the hope that his disability might be cured. At his pastor's urging, he even stopped taking his meds. He donated thirty thousand dollars before his mother, who took care of him, put a stop to it.

Arriving at the church one day, I saw a caution-yellow armored car pull into the parking lot. I guessed it was there either to pick up donations or to refill the ATM in the parking lot, maybe both. The pressure I saw was constant. In a typical service, the lead pastor would call on the faithful three times in an hour and a half to "honor God." This was the cue to give money. As congregants lined up, pastor's assistants in brightly colored ties took cash donations in large velvet sacks. Others carried portable credit card machines so you could charge your offering. The Workers Party years have been good to the Universal Church. Addressing a gathering of pastors once, Macedo's nephew Marcelo Crivella, a bishop who also serves as senator in Brasília, praised the former president for raising up the poor with the Bolsa Família welfare program. "When they have more cash on hand," Crivella said, "they attend church more, because they can afford the subway and the train. They give more offerings, more tithes."

WHEN MACEDO LAUNCHED THE takeover of TV Record in 1989, the church didn't have forty-five million dollars in the bank, so he ordered his bishops to push their most aggressive campaign yet. Macedo said Record would be Brazil's first evangelical network, and that's how the campaign was pitched to his followers. The Bishop, though, was acquiring the shares in his name. The constitution bars religious institutions from owning for-profit channels.

The acquisition of Record is a dividing line both for Macedo's relationship with his own power and wealth and for how he got along with the establishment. Up until that point Macedo had been a harmless curiosity to the old elites. Now he was a threat. Roberto Marinho led something of a crusade against him. TV Globo played the pastors' retreat video endlessly. O Globo cited religious experts who called Macedo's brand of preaching a "spectacle of manipulation." That quote is from a story with the headline SUREFIRE PROFIT IN THE KINGDOM OF THE UNIVERSAL CHURCH, which noted that Macedo lived in an eight-hundred-thousand-dollar house in the suburban New York area of Westchester. The accompanying photo showed church staff during a stadium event shouldering sacks supposedly full of cash. (Macedo later said they held handwritten prayers.) TV Globo also ran a fictional miniseries called Decadência, about a corrupt church leader modeled after Macedo. The fictional pastor repeated some of Macedo's orations verbatim.

Revelations of small luxuries popped up in the press. It turned out that Record had purchased thirteen thousand dollars' worth of fancy Italian shoes for the Bishop. This wasn't illegal, since Record was a private company owned by Macedo, but it didn't look good. When police found him driving a BMW that had been imported irregularly to avoid tariffs, he claimed he was just test-driving it. Macedo usually had an explanation. When Veja magazine reported that Macedo and his wife had bought two multimillion-dollar apartments on Miami's chic Collins Avenue, he said he'd funded the purchases with book royalties and later donated both properties to the church. Of course, it's the church that often buys his books in the first place.

That Balzac line about "great fortunes without apparent cause" has limits even in Brazil. It was just too glaringly impossible for a pastor of humble beginnings to afford a forty-five-million-dollar takeover. Prosecutors started looking into the transaction, but the meatiest bits of their probe would take years to go anywhere. In 1992 they indicted him instead on charges of fraud, charlatanism, and *curandeirismo,* which translates roughly as "witch doctoring" and, according to a little-used article of Brazil's penal code, applies to those who offer cures without a medical license. An overzealous judge ordered his arrest, and Macedo spent eleven days in jail, the only time he's ever served. For a half-million-dollar fee, a big-time criminal lawyer got the charges dropped. They were hard to prove in a court of law. To decide whether Macedo had defrauded his followers would be to decide questions of faith.

It was also in 1992 that Record began its transformation into a commercial network. That year Macedo brought on a bishop named João Batista to take over as CEO. One of the church's earliest members, Batista had been an economist in his former life, and Macedo tasked him with making Record profitable. Batista is most famous for an episode that came later, in 2005, while he was serving as a congressman. One day he landed in Brasília aboard a private church plane, and police demanded to search it. They seized suitcases stuffed with the equivalent of around five million dollars in hard currency. In his defense, he said he was transporting donations from churches in far-flung cities where banks balk at taking so much cash. That episode didn't lead to charges, but Batista is now fighting money-laundering accusations in the same 2009 case as Macedo.

I met Batista at his office in São Bernardo do Campo, a São Paulo suburb where he now serves as city councilman. He was a little man like Macedo, with white hair and a button-down shirt tucked into his jeans. He told me how he'd fought at first with his fellow bishops at Record. The network was teetering on the brink of bankruptcy, and yet it ran sermons during profitable time slots and refused to show ads for booze or cigarettes. "They could only think of God's work, but my vision had to be broader," Batista said. With Macedo's blessing, he lifted the prohibition on sinful ads. He banned Bible orations at company meetings. He replaced pastors with professionals and invested in a news operation that could rival Globo's. With fresh ad revenue augmenting the Universal Church's late-night airtime buys, he hired away top talent to compete with Globo's telenovelas.

After Batista stepped down, the reality shows got so fleshly they surprised even him. "But they need money," he said, "and television is a very expensive little toy." By the time I arrived in Brazil, Record was tied for second place in the ratings—though Globo was still by far the top player.

When Macedo's commercial ambitions became clear, many pastors and bishops left the church in disgust. In his writings, though, he justifies running content "incompatible with our faith" as a necessary evil in the fight against Globo's media monopoly. Record's news chief, Douglas Tavolaro, told me Macedo aims to surpass Globo one day. Already Macedo has enough influence to keep Globo from targeting him as before. In 2009 a Globo newsmagazine published a Universal Church exposé titled "I Learned How to Extort the People," and the church's free newspaper responded with a special edition titled "How the Marinho Family Destroys Brazil," printing an extra-large run. Then TV Record followed up with a segment alleging that, among other sketchy dealings, Globo had improperly obtained government loans.

Batista told me he never would have spoken with me if I worked for Globo. And yet since their clash a few years ago, Macedo and the Marinhos now keep an implicit truce. Instead Macedo has chosen battles for market share—in TV and religion both. A few years ago the network accused a dissident pastor who was luring away Universal Church faithful of enriching himself at his followers' expense. If Macedo fails to see the irony in this, it's likely because he deems his movement specially sanctioned by the Lord. "God made the Universal stand out among all other evangelical churches," he writes.

As a commercial network with a wide audience, Record is far more useful to the Universal Church than as a religious niche channel. Like so many of Brazil's movers and shakers, Macedo was pragmatic about his power. Batista told me they got into politics not so much to sway issues like gay marriage but to "exert pressure" when the church's own interests came under threat—from the taxman, legislators, or prosecutors. Batista referred to their politicians as a "battalion" and to Record as the church's "cannon." In his description, the Universal Church is a kind of conglomerate with a spiritual arm, a media arm, and a political arm. "It's a company for saving souls," Batista said—with Macedo as its CEO.

BY THE BISHOP'S OWN count, he's beaten more than two dozen investigations, whether for lack of evidence or because the cases moved so slowly that they exceeded the statute of limitations. After his brief spell in jail, his worst punishment came in the form of tax fines for using his followers' donations to acquire his network.

That Edir Macedo enjoys the same impunity as Paulo Maluf seems to show that, wherever you come from in Brazil, money talks. I saw other similarities, as in the structure of their alleged schemes. According to the 2009 case against Macedo, pastors would deliver undeclared cash donations in garbage sacks to *doleiros*—black-market money changers—who spirited the funds to bank accounts in New York and then to shell companies in offshore tax havens. To bring the now-anonymous money back into Brazil, the shell companies made loans to pastors to invest in a slew of private businesses: security firms, accounting firms, travel agencies, an air-taxi business, even a health insurance provider. To expand Record's national network, they also used the money to acquire regional TV stations. They bought radio stations to form Rede Aleluia, the Hallelujah Network. And they continue to fund it all by selling airtime and services to the Universal Church.

At João Batista's office, I noticed a sun-faded certificate commemorating a pilgrimage he took to Jerusalem. From digging into company registries, I knew Batista had teamed up with another bishop to invest in Monte Sinai Turismo, a travel agency that takes Universal Church faithful to Israel. Was this opportunism? No, he said, it made the church stronger. "Why pay outside people to do something that we could put together?" He saw the church's wealth not as a contradiction but as a tool. "In the twenty-first century, if Jesus were here today, he'd be wearing fine leather shoes," he said. "He'd have a shirt of French silk, perhaps, or Japanese, with a suit of the best quality, a Pierre Cardin or whatever. And he'd travel by helicopter or private jet. And all of this—for what?" he asked. "To better preach the word of God."

Despite his growing influence in Brazil's establishment, Macedo's outsider cred remains an important part of his narrative. In his memoirs he compares his persecution to that suffered by Jesus. The cover of his authorized biography, *O Bispo,* shows him reading the Bible behind bars. None of the accusations put a dent in his following. For many evangelical Christians, to call Macedo a charlatan, to say his followers had been brainwashed—this was an insult to their faith and to their intelligence. As Macedo puts it, "If so many people arrive in dire straits and are tricked and exploited by me, why do they remain in the Church?"

So why do they? Attending services, I accumulated materials handed out by pastors, props for various rituals: faux-old scrolls with quotes from the Book of Revelation, black felt pouches embossed with gold birds, little Dixie cups to carry holy olive oil. At the prosperity meeting, I got a Congress of Winners booklet with ten pages to write down your goals; each Monday you tear off a page and include it with your donation. This all piled up on my desk at home. Maria, the person who cleaned my apartment every couple of weeks, saw it one morning and excitedly asked, "So you go to the prosperity meetings too?"

Originally from a small town in the northeast, Maria moved to São Paulo when she was young. She went to public school, where poorly paid teachers often can't pass the tests they're preparing students for. No one ever asked her to articulate what she wanted from life, to talk about goals and possible futures, but that's what happens at the Congress of Winners. Pastors tell you to put your goals in material terms—to save up for a car, say, that will allow you to forgo the sweaty marathon-commute of multiple buses and trains. And you'll work for it. The new car will require a new job, a promotion. You'll have to give up little guilty pleasures. You'll organize your life. I talked to a professor of religion, Andrew Chesnut from Virginia Commonwealth University, who spent a few years in Brazil studying the Pentecostals. He calls Macedo's brand of instruction "bootstrap preaching." Universal Church pastors dole out commonsense advice, becoming the guidance counselors you never had. If you want to start a business, the church also provides a network of coreligionists as a customer base. After one service I met a guy named Saporeto trying to get his start as a real estate broker. He was passing out flyers advertising a new apartment complex built by Camargo Corrêa.

Through a friend, I met a young woman who joined the church as a teenager in rural São Paulo state. She felt lost before, but here she found something she could belong to. While still in school, she got a job teaching English on the side. "There's a certain pride in being *able* to give that much," she told me. "I didn't feel any pressure to make offerings because I was getting so much from it—I thought, 'Of course you give.' It was almost like paying in." She went on to attend an American Ivy League school. After a while she began to doubt what her pastors told her and left the church, but she's not bitter. Much of her family is still *universalista*. (She asked me not to use her name to avoid alienating them, so I'll call her Neide.)

Even handing over ten or twenty or thirty percent of their paycheck to the church, a lot of people save money because they overcome vices—drinking, gambling, whoring, worse—that cost far more. The Universal Church actively reaches out to addicts, organizing trips to the Cracklands of São Paulo and Rio to bring food and the word of God. Drug addicts who turn their lives around will give themselves over to the work with rare passion. Many become pastors, bishops. "The Universal Church is made up of rejects, the dregs of society, but now they're being raised up by God," Macedo says. In 2014 Dilma Rousseff attended the inauguration of Macedo's biggest single project yet: a three-hundred-million-dollar replica of Solomon's Temple in São Paulo, with pillars taller than Rio's Christ the Redeemer statue and stones imported from Israel. In one speech a pastor said he used to sniff glue and chloroform, drink mushroom tea, snort lines of coke a meter long, and smoke eighty or a hundred rocks of crack in a night. The Universal Church rescued him.

Macedo says he fills in where the Brazilian state falls short. The Universal Church is big in prisons, where the state has basically failed. Brazil's prison population has increased more than sixfold since 1990, but facilities haven't kept pace. Six hundred thousand people live in prisons meant to hold half that number. A hundred and forty thousand are there on drug charges. Two hundred thousand are just awaiting trial. Inside, the law of the jungle applies. Inmates shed their prison uniforms for casual clothes brought from outside. Until the nightly lockdown, they can roam the premises as they please. Some run little businesses from their cells, taking cigarettes as currency for TVs, pornography, and drugs brought in by corrupt prison guards. Guards also bring in knives, revolvers. Medical services are a joke. Rather than work to prevent murders, guards will encourage prisoners to make the murders look like suicides. That's how the "Gatorade of Death" was born—a cocktail of water, cocaine, and Viagra that victims are forced to swallow.

When Macedo released the first volume of his memoirs in Brazil, the only launch he attended personally took place inside a detention center in São Paulo. TV Record covered the event. You can see Macedo addressing a loose crowd of men in uniform khaki pants and white T-shirts—a scene more orderly than the one in most Brazilian jails. He leads a prayer, and the men bow their heads. "You can be sure that work won't be lacking for you on the outside," Macedo says. "If on the outside nobody wants you, we do." The Universal Church donated thousands of copies of his memoirs to prisons around the country.

Globo made Macedo into a caricature, a telenovela version of the crooked pastor, but once I saw what the Universal Church meant to some people, his alleged thievery was a lot less black and white. The poor have always been fleeced in Brazil, and they know it. At the Universal Church, at least they get something, albeit tenuous, in return—community or a spiritual connection or a structure for self-improvement.

Macedo represents a counterculture in Brazil, not just because he welcomes felons and addicts. The Brazil of TV Globo might be rigidly hierarchical, but the Bishop advocates *revolta*. He loves this word, which literally means "revolt" but implies dissatisfaction with the hand you're dealt. The idea is that you don't have to wait passively for heaven. Life on earth can be better. You can stop suffering—*pare de sofrer!*—right now. Macedo's followers know about the money. They like the fact he lives well. He himself talks about his closet full of Italian silk ties, his fondness for fine wines. Private jets? "The feeling was 'Good for him,'" Neide told me. He's living what he preaches, prosperity.

EDIR MACEDO MAY BE the first outsider ever to acquire this kind of power here. There's a classic work of journalism from 1902, *Rebellion in the Backlands,* that describes the outsider tradition in Brazil. Written by Euclides da Cunha, it tells the story of a man who called himself Antônio Conselheiro—the Counselor—one of a string of self-styled prophets who flourished in the drought-ridden backlands of northeastern Brazil. Dressed in a blue robe, with long hair and a tangled beard, the Counselor shunned food beyond what was absolutely necessary and hiked with the aid of a staff. He wandered from town to town, and the inhabitants would abandon their tasks to listen rapt to sermons that spoke to the hopelessness of life on earth. He railed against the new republic and its "law of the dog," and he incited people to burn public notices of new taxes. He drew a following among the mystical-minded backlanders who drifted between minifamines and fleeting periods of fertility. *Jagunços*—bandits—joined up with him too.

One day the Counselor led his followers deep inland to the abandoned village of Canudos. Word spread, and the settlement grew. Herdsmen brought their families; bandits brought their muskets. In a packed church, the Counselor would intone, "In 1899, the waters shall turn to blood, and the planet shall appear in the east with the sun's ray, the bough shall find itself on the earth, and the earth some place shall find itself in heaven. There shall be a great rain of stars, and that will be the end of the world. In 1900 the lights shall be put out." Each of his sermons brought his congregation to ecstasy, everyone speaking in tongues, taking turns clutching images of saints that they covered with frenetic kisses.

Canudos was left alone until the Counselor got into a dispute with the mayor of a nearby town and threatened him. In response, the governor of Bahia assembled soldiers to put his movement down. Though the government forces carried modern rifles against their one-shot muskets and scraping knives, the *jagunços* repelled first a detachment of a hundred men and then a detachment of five hundred. Scores of *jagunços* lost their lives, but the official retreat looked like victory, and fresh converts streamed into Canudos. "Blessed are they that suffer," the Counselor said. In the government's next assault, thirteen hundred men made it into Canudos but lost themselves in the tight maze of alleyways and suffered heavy casualties in hand-to-hand combat. Again they retreated, only this time the *jagunços* attacked as they fled, killing dozens more. Afterward they cut off the soldiers' heads to display as warnings for the next expedition.

In the newspapers of Rio, this third defeat became a national emergency. It left rifles, artillery, and hundreds of thousands of rounds of ammunition in the Counselor's control. With this rebellion inside the national borders, the very integrity of the republic was at stake. The conflict inspired a patriotic fervor unusual in a country where regional identities had mattered most. Men from all over Brazil enlisted, and the government amassed two new columns totaling some five thousand soldiers. Foolishly they marched to Canudos on half-rations, certain of victory. Imagining a classic European battlefield, their commanders were unprepared for the *jagunços*' guerrilla tactics. When the first government column entered a narrow valley, the *jagunços* opened fire from trenches hidden in the hills. "It was a mass slaughter," Euclides reported: five hundred down.

Finally the secretary of state for the affairs of war was sent to take charge of the campaign. He saw that the war's problem was logistical and set up regular supply lines before mounting a final assault with an additional brigade. Properly reinforced, they pushed the *jagunços* back to Canudos. They bombarded the city daily with heavy artillery. House by house, they tightened their perimeter. One day the troops used ninety bundles of dynamite to blast the *jagunços* and their wives and children indiscriminately to pieces. Though cut off from outside food and water, the *jagunços* refused to surrender. The siege went on for weeks. The last half-dozen fighters dug their own mass grave inside the church and fell dead into it firing their final rounds. Arriving back in Salvador, the soldiers paraded the Counselor's partly decomposed head before cheering multitudes.

The Counselor was a fanatic and his rebellion was pointless, but I couldn't help but root for him as I read Euclides's account. He was the underdog, for one thing. Also, his followers might be fanatics, but where were they coming from? When the republic was proclaimed in 1889, they experienced little of its fancy rhetoric of Order and Progress. They lived in a Brazil totally estranged from the official one that existed in Rio. Then as now, Europe was more familiar to the elite than backwaters like this one. "It was not an ocean which separated us from them but three whole centuries," Euclides wrote. Canudos was an ancient tumor, a foreign body in the body of the nation. The soldiers excised Canudos but not the contradiction it represented. The contradiction still festers. In the country of Belíndia, where islands of Belgium persist inside seas of India, bubbles from the past still rise to the surface. You see them in Brazil's prisons. You see it in the Amazon where children still work as slaves. When people in the favelas say the regime of 1964 never ended for them, they're talking about a system that goes back much further.

Between the Counselor and Edir Macedo are far more differences than similarities. But both disrupted the official narrative of Brazil. They offered a place to belong in a country whose elite turned up their nose at the poor. It's meaningful that the word *favela* was born in Canudos. The site of the *jagunços'* valley ambush, where they cut down five hundred soldiers in a matter of hours, was known as Mount Favela. Long before the word meant "slum," a *favela* was a species of spiny shrub that dotted the mountain's slopes. After the Canudos campaign, soldiers arrived in Rio to wait for land grants the army had promised but would never deliver. They pitched tents on a hill along with ex-slaves, and the tents gradually gave way to wooden shacks. The place came to be called Morro da Favela, Favela Hill. As jumbled settlements like this one spread across Rio, the name caught on.

GIVEN HOW MACEDO CHAFED with the old establishment, I wasn't surprised that his press people stonewalled me when I asked for an interview. *Forbes* had recently run a story on him, outing him as a billionaire, and this made them especially wary. Toward the end of my reporting, though, they forwarded me his answers to some questions I'd sent by email. Most of it was pretty ordinary, repeating lines from his sermons and writings. He said he planned to donate all his earthly belongings to the church on his death. I asked what he thought of *Forbes*'s story, and he replied, "From the point of view of my faith in the Lord Jesus, I am the richest man on the planet."

It was in his answer to a standard throwaway journalistic question that he provided the missing piece to my puzzle of him. I asked what else he hoped to achieve, having achieved so much. "My only goal in life is to bring the word of God to every corner of the planet," he wrote. "An American multimillionaire stated that he always wants to earn one more dollar. The difference between us is that I always want to win one more soul for my Lord."

Macedo's comparison seemed banal on the surface. But he ended up deepening my understanding of what it means to be a billionaire. Despite the little luxuries that enthrall the press, money for Macedo truly seems to be a means to an end. He says his end is spiritual, but I suspect that word is a cover for his real ambition, and it's the same one that animated his rival Roberto Marinho—power. For all these people, I realized, the yachts and jets and big houses in nature reserves were just the by-products of accumulation, not its purpose. Marinho's son João didn't like to put a number on his wealth at all, and he had a point. You can measure how much revenue a novela brings in, but can you put a number on how *Salve Jorge* influenced Alemão?

I thought about the line that divided the people I covered at Bloomberg from the rest of the world's rich: one billion dollars. It's an arbitrary line, but in the end it makes sense, because to get there, unless you inherit it, you need something special, possibly genetic, not just wit and hard work and luck but a drive for accumulation that's as much instinct as addiction. There's a reason we refer to their businesses as empires. I started reading about the original tycoons from my own country too. When J. Pierpont Morgan died in 1913, *The Economist* called him the "Napoleon of Wall Street." Billionaires are after conquest. They want to leave a mark on the world. And Macedo isn't the only one who whiffs of messianism. John D. Rockefeller, himself an evangelical Christian, believed that his fortune was the product of divine will. "God gave me my money," he said.

In the Brazil of the Workers Party years, meanwhile, the prosperity gospel had an even greater preacher than Edir Macedo. He was a secular prophet, with a son named after the Norse god of thunder.

PART TWO

THE BRAZILIAN DREAM

CHAPTER 6

VISIONARY

THE RISE OF BRAZIL'S RICHEST MAN

"Brazil is the country of the present."
—EIKE BATISTA ($30 BILLION)

THE SAME WEEK I MOVED TO SÃO PAULO, IN APRIL 2010, EIKE
Batista recorded a Web video for a local brokerage. He had just been
named the richest man in Brazil, and he wanted to let mom-and-pop
investors in on the potential of his oil company, OGX Petróleo &
Gas. "I consider these exploration blocks maybe the best in the
world," he said. "I'm going to repeat it: in the world. There's a trillion dollars in value there." Trillion with a T. He spoke of the low
costs involved in extracting all this oil and calculated that the total
profits would add up to a hundred billion dollars. "That's more than
three times the value of the company today," he said. "One of the
reasons I'm here is that I don't want Brazilians to miss out on the
chance to make money with this. . . . Don't miss the chance to buy
this stock."

Eike wore a black suit and a black T-shirt that brought out his
pale white skin. Atop his gray sideburns sat a thatch of dark hair.
Sitting across from two analysts from the brokerage, he gesticulated
with both hands to emphasize his points. Screens of different sizes
on the wall behind them showed freeze-frame images of an oil rig,
giant construction cranes, concrete pillars rising from the sea—all

ostensibly part of his empire. The way they all talked, you might forget that OGX had yet to pump a single drop of oil. It was a startup. It was worth thirty billion dollars on the stock market because investors expected lots of oil one day to gush forth from its wells. In just a few years, Eike said, it would be producing a million barrels a day, more than the entire nation of Oman.

I called Eike by his first name because everyone in Brazil did. Only foreigners called him Batista. Partly that's because Batista is a common last name here, but mostly it's because he was so often in the news that you felt like you knew him. In Brazil's little business universe, he was a planet around which many moons revolved. At any given moment in the Bloomberg newsroom, at least one reporter would be writing about him, and often more than one, depending on how many beats he was churning that day—energy, mining, finance. I started covering him early on, when I was still writing about stocks. The market moved constantly on something he'd said or done.

Even as I investigated the Camargos, the Marinhos, and the Bishop, Eike occupied space at the front of my head. My job required it. On the Bloomberg terminal, I had alerts set for all Eike-related news and all Eike-related regulatory filings. At least once a week, often more than once, I had to tweak our Eike net-worth estimate to account for some new deal he'd closed, some rejiggering in the layout of his empire. But my fixation went further than the financial. I read all his interviews, all his tweets, every gossip-rag blurb. Now and then he showed up in my dreams, and we were pals, and he had an exclusive scoop to share with me.

His wealth was always increasing in my dreams. Awake, I wondered how anyone could possibly get so rich so fast. His rise was all the more startling since, up until recently, few outside Brazil had ever heard of him. Few inside Brazil knew him as anything but the ex-husband of Luma de Oliveira, a *carnaval* queen and *Playboy* cover girl. Or maybe as the son of Eliezer Batista, the renowned former CEO of Vale, the world's top producer of iron ore. Eike didn't even show up on the *Forbes* list in 2007. A year later he debuted with a fortune of $6.6 billion, then in 2009 he edged up to $7.5 billion, and suddenly in 2010 he was worth $27 billion.

But when he made nation-size revenue predictions for his start-ups, why did people believe him?

EIKE'S SECRET WAS TO offer up the best of the Brazilian boom, fast. In the early 2000s, iron ore prices went crazy because of all the demand from China's steel factories. So he bought the rights to some iron ore deposits, put them into a company with the bland name MMX Mineração & Metálicos, and decided to hold an IPO—an initial public offering of stock. When he went to the bankers at Credit Suisse and Pactual, a local investment house, they had two good reasons to listen to him. One, investors were all excited over the BRICs. A Goldman Sachs economist had come up with this acronym to describe the four countries—Brazil, Russia, India, and China—that he saw as the new motors of the world economy. But few Brazilian companies had shares listed on an exchange, so there was a lot of unmet demand for vehicles to invest in the country. The other reason to listen to Eike was that he put his famous dad on MMX's board. And with Eliezer's help, he hired away some of Vale's best engineers.

When you take a company public, you must first go on a "road show," explaining your project to people who manage large quantities of money—mutual funds in London, wealthy heirs in New York, pension funds in Toronto—so that they'll order shares in the offering. I spoke to a few who witnessed the Eike Batista pitch. He was nothing like the staid Brazilian billionaires who came before him. His reputation preceded him: Before he even showed up, you knew about the Playmate ex. Just the other day he'd broken the world record for fastest speedboat trip from Santos to Rio. And then he would burst into the air-conditioned quiet of your conference room, forty-nine but fit, pink-tied and bright-green-eyed, talking big, in five languages—he punctuated his English with *"voilà!"*—as he pitched an ideal version of his country and its natural resources. He hinted that he had a special role to play in this new Brazil. In an interview once he said, "God blessed Brazil with these things, and maybe He blesses those willing to take the risk to develop them."

To dispel the impression he'd beamed into the Brazilian boom from nowhere, Eike would talk about how he got his start. It was a narrative he repeated often, for investors and journalists alike; in 2011 he even set it down in book form. The second of seven children, he was born in 1957 in Governador Valadares, a town in the state of Minas Gerais—literally General Mines, the heart of the eighteenth-century gold rush. In the sixties his dad served as minister of mines and energy and then president of Vale, the state mining concern, in Rio. When Eike was twelve, Eliezer took the family to Europe. After a spell in the private sector, Batista *pai* worked to expand Vale abroad, and they spent time in Geneva, Düsseldorf, and Brussels. Eike was twenty when his parents moved back to Brazil and he enrolled at Aachen University, in the German town of the same name, to study metallurgy.

Eike liked to live well, even in college. His allowance would run short halfway through the month, so he began peddling insurance policies door to door. He had a knack for it; somehow he just knew how to connect to uptight German ladies in their homes. He got a taste for selling things. On vacation in Rio, friends introduced him to diamond miners who wanted to sell their product in Europe. He mediated the deals, carrying diamonds to Antwerp and Portugal. Then he happened on a magazine article about a gold rush in the Amazon, and in 1979, at twenty-two years old, he decided to drop out of school and join the rush. He moved back to Rio and convinced two jewelers to front him half a million dollars to buy gold out there and resell it in the big city.

The gold rush photos coming out of the Amazon showed a chaos of muddy half-clothed men scrambling up and down steep paths into open-pit mines. For any normal kid of privilege, this scene would hardly be inviting, but Eike was different. He took a plane to Belém, then another, smaller plane to Itaituba, three hundred miles west of Altamira on the Transamazônica. Itaituba was a tiny riverside boomtown where wildcatters brought gold by Cessna from hundreds of nearby mines to sell to intermediaries. His book has a picture of him then. It's black and white, but his complexion looks ruddier. He has a full head of wavy hair, his sleeves are rolled up, his top few buttons are undone, and a shiny amulet dangles from his neck. He compared himself to Indiana Jones. "What most drew me to mining was adventure," he wrote, "running after something that everyone was chasing, the conquest of the unseen." In one story he often repeated, he got into an argument with a wildcatter who owed him money. He lost his temper and called the miner *filho da puta* as he left. Drunk, the miner shot him in the back, but he had a crappy pistol and Eike wasn't seriously hurt. Eike's bodyguards shot back and killed him.

Buying and selling gold, Eike made six million dollars by the time he was twenty-three. One of the first things he bought was a black Porsche 928, paid in cash. He could have just chucked it all and relaxed on the beach, he said, but he wanted more. So he reinvested the profits in a mine of his own in the north of Mato Grosso, teaming up with his brother Werner and a friend to develop it. While miners in the Amazon just hacked at the earth with picks and shovels or panned for gold in the rivers, Eike wanted to do something first world. He ordered proper studies and bought modern equipment to set up what he claimed to be Brazil's first mechanized alluvial mine, which used water to separate gold from worthless earth and gravel. It was an ambitious project. To transport tractors and bulldozers to the remote site, he had to disassemble them in a city some sixty miles away, load them onto a DC-3 airplane, and reassemble them on location. "This is not to say I was always brilliant," he said. The operation was costly. Malaria struck. "I underestimated the weather, technical conditions, diseases, logistics, but ultimately the mine was so rich it was idiot-proof, because it survived all my mistakes." Eike held this up as his great talent: to locate assets so rich, even an idiot could turn a profit on them. He found "diamonds in the rough" and polished them up for investors.

It's a truism of the venture capital world that you don't invest in projects, you invest in people. On his road show now, for his audience of middle-aged money managers, Eike came off as a swashbuckler, a playboy with a gift for sniffing out profit, something from the id of capitalism. He said he planned to make MMX into the next Vale, the mining giant his dad used to run. He just didn't want to take a half-century to do it. That's why he needed your money.

Eike laid out the future, perfect, in PowerPoint slides. He was famous for these. On a map you'd see three abundant iron ore deposits and the infrastructure he would build to support them: rail or slurry pipeline connecting mines to ports and pig iron furnaces hundreds of miles away. Swooping arrows showed output ramping up to thirty-eight million tons annually in just a few years—enough to supply the iron ore needs of China for a month. The venture had no track record to pick apart, only promise, and the money managers ate it up. In July 2006, MMX raised four hundred million dollars, valuing Eike's stake in the company at nearly a billion. At the time it was the largest IPO Brazil had ever seen.

IT TOOK A WHILE, still, for Eike's reputation in business to eclipse his reputation in gossip columns. His celebrity in Brazil traced back to Luma de Oliveira. Baby sister of a Globo actress, she'd started modeling at sixteen and made a splash nationally in 1987, when she paraded through Rio's Sambadrome, the bleacher-lined avenue where samba schools perform during *carnaval*. She stole the show. She flicked a little cape of white feathers as she moved, wearing a tiara and the platonic *carnaval*-queen smile of unperturbable joy and nothing else but thin straps of silvery plastic, her breasts naked for all to see. One commentator said she danced "like the *mulatas,*" even though she's white. Afterward *Playboy* put her on the cover; newsstands sold out across the country. She was twenty-two.

When Eike met her in 1990, he'd just won a speedboat championship, and she was the pretty lady handing him an oversize check for the prize money. He fell in love—plummeted—even though he'd just gotten married to a Rio high-society girl. With the civil ceremony still a few days away, he called it off and eloped with Luma. The little *carioca* elite was scandalized, but he didn't care. He got the wedding annulled. Four months later he married Luma, by then pregnant with their first son, Thor.

Eike enjoyed being married to one of the most desired women in Brazil. He used to introduce himself, good-humoredly, as "the husband of Luma." She embodied a contradictory ideal of femininity in Brazil: beautiful, fiercely loyal—up to a point; sensual but maternal. In 1998, by then the mother of two children, she made her most famous *carnaval* appearance, parading in a Catwoman-like getup and a kitty collar with rhinestones that spelled out EIKE. "It's to show I have an owner," she explained. She caused a scandal; even years later feminists would say things like "Luma is harmful to democracy in marriage and to feminism" (though most reactions were closer to "Folks, *carnaval* is just for fun"). That was the moment when most Brazilians heard Eike's name for the first time.

Eike loved Luma's homage to him. But after a while he cooled to her exhibitions. In her late thirties she was still in demand, and he grew jealous of her image. Once he gave her a diamond ring to persuade her to cancel a nude shoot. He brought her Ferrero Rocher chocolates and double milkshakes to throw off her diet. He tried to get her interested in business, his passion, and started a cosmetics company for her to run. After a while, she would say in interviews, she got sick of his prohibitions. She got sick of his single-minded drive to work. After posing for a firemen's calendar, she got entangled with a studly young *bombeiro* she'd met at the shoot. Luma and Eike divorced in 2004, but the separation was friendly. Eike bought her the mansion next door to his so that their two sons would grow up nearby.

MORE THAN ANY BUSINESSMAN before him in Brazil, Eike exposed his life to the world. His life was part of his pitch. He invited reporters to his thirty-seven-thousand-square-foot mansion in Jardim Botânico, not far from the Globo office where I interviewed João Marinho. The mansion sits a couple hundred yards behind high, vine-covered walls on fifteen acres of land abutting the mountain atop which Christ the Redeemer stands, spreading his white stone arms to the people of Rio. In the entryway of his home, Eike kept a sixteen-hundred-horsepower speedboat engine of the sort that burns out after a single race. It cost seven hundred thousand dollars. On the walls were landscape paintings of Rio by Lelli de Orleans e Bragança, a descendant of Brazil's old royal family. A large glass door allowed Eike to drive a car straight into one of his six living rooms. In those days he displayed his Mercedes-Benz SLR McLaren, its silver paint job looking spit polished. He had fourteen other cars in the garage, Porsches and Beemers and his preferred day-to-day ride, an armored Toyota pickup truck. Sitting by a fountain in his yard, he liked to take his breakfast of fresh fruit and look out on the Rodrigo de Freitas Lagoon, past which lay Ipanema, Leblon, and the sea. A staff of seventeen tended to his needs.

The longer I reported on billionaires, the more the trappings of luxury felt repetitive. But Eike breathed new life into luxurious ostentation. Balding in his forties, he'd covered his scalp with the thin spongy cover of hair transplants. Then one night in 2010 he showed up at a charity auction in São Paulo with this thick brown mop atop his gray sideburns. Flicking the voluminous mass about as he beamed for the paparazzi, he looked like someone out of a shampoo commercial, like Samson's spiritual heir. In a TV interview afterward, a journalist asked him about "the new toupee." But it was not a toupee. "Tricosalus," Eike told her. "It's a capillary treatment—

extraordinary—from here in São Paulo." He leaned over, tipping his head. "Want to touch it?" (She didn't.)

I wrote a story about Eike's hair. I visited the Tricosalus clinic and spoke to the owner, an Italian named Alessandro Corona. He explained the process he called "ire restoration," which I understood to mean hair restoration. First he uses a computer to map and analyze your scalp. Then he sends the specs to Cesare Ragazzi, a company in Milan that will make a breathable "second scalp" of hand-sewn human hair—only the finest European hair—designed to match the natural direction and consistency of your remaining growth. Depending on the size of the area you need to cover, the thing costs anywhere between $3,500 and $35,000. Alessandro vehemently rejected the word *wig*. Whatever it is, you can shower with it, you can go windsurfing in it; it won't come off. You just have to visit Tricosalus once a month for a cleaning, or bacteria will build up.

Eike liked the treatment so much that he and Alessandro became friends. On his smartphone, Alessandro showed me texts from Eike to prove it. Eike even introduced him to Silvio Berlusconi, the billionaire and former prime minister of Italy. Best of all, Eike's endorsement brought a flood of new business to Tricosalus.

In those days of fantastic wealth creation, Eike was the gold standard for Brazil's *novos ricos*. *Veja* magazine ran a cover with his face on Deng Xiaoping's body and the tagline "To Get Rich Is Glorious"—as if Eike had brought capitalism to a communist country. The story was all about the entrepreneurs he'd inspired. Eike got the cover blown up and framed for his office.

I got a feel for Eike's resonance at a cocktail party I went to in São Paulo. Cristiano Piquet, a real estate broker I'd met while learning about the Miami scene, had organized it to promote fancy property developments in South Florida. One of the developments was called the Porsche Design Tower. The main draw is that owners can drive from the street straight into an elevator of panoramic glass which whisks them and their vehicles to their floor. The owner pulls directly into the apartment, and the car sits behind a wall of glass in the living room so he can admire it while relaxing at home, just like Eike. Except that in this development, you could maybe outdo Eike. The seventeen-thousand-square-foot penthouse, a quadruplex that starts on the fifty-sixth floor, is designed to exhibit *four* cars.

The Porsche Design Tower pointed to another Eikean phenomenon. Priced at $32.5 million, it was cheaper per square foot than the Ipanema penthouse I'd seen with walls covered in butterfly wings. The market in Brazil had gotten expensive. Property prices in São Paulo had tripled in less than a decade, and some investors were actually getting out. I heard about one ultrarich Brazilian family selling off a billion dollars of real estate back home and putting the money in Miami and New York. People started whispering about a bubble in Brazil. It seemed the economy might be overheating.

BY EARLY 2010, EIKE had taken five companies public in as many years: MMX Mineração (mining), LLX Logística (ports), MPX Energia (power plants), OGX Petróleo (oil), and OSX Brasil (oil platforms). He called his group EBX—his initials plus the indispensable X. He said it stood for wealth multiplication. And indeed, as his share prices rose, each offering added billions of dollars to his fortune.

Whatever investors wished for, Eike came up with an answer. With the rise of the BRICs, people talked about the potential for "South-South trade." The problem was that Brazil's infrastructure lagged way behind the needs of a first-rate economy. At the port of Santos, where Lula had sold peanuts on the docks as a kid, container ships idled for hours waiting for a berth. Truck drivers delivering Mato Grosso soy could line up so long that they set up hammocks between their rigs. So Eike decided to build the port of Açu (pronounced ah-SOOH), which means "grand" in the indigenous Tupi-Guarani language. He said it would be a future "Rotterdam of the tropics," fit to accommodate the largest boats in the world, four-hundred-thousand-ton Chinamaxes. Encompassing an area the size of Manhattan, it would also host factories to make cement and steel and the first-ever Brazilian-branded cars. Eike called it a "mega-logistics complex." He loved this prefix. He called himself "a mega-arbitrageur of Brazil's inefficiencies."

Of all the natural wealth in the country, it was oil that excited investors most. Brazil's state oil giant, Petrobras, now produced more than the entire nation of Norway. Such was the demand for its shares that, as oil prices climbed past a hundred dollars a barrel, the company ranked as one of the ten largest in the world by market value. The problem for investors was that Petrobras was majority-owned by the government and didn't always keep shareholders first in mind, putting employment above profits, for example. So Eike decided to pitch a kind of private Petrobras. That's how OGX, the centerpiece of his empire, was born.

To create OGX, much as he'd done to create MMX, Eike hired away dozens of Petrobras engineers. This was a bold move. Ever since its founding in 1953—under the slogan "The oil is ours!"—Petrobras had been a nationalist symbol. And while its monopoly on oil production had ended in the late nineties, it remained by far the largest player in the local market. So Eike was taking two risks: looking as if he'd raided the national patrimony, and making a very powerful enemy. But he had good reasons to take those risks. Petrobras's oil engineers were some of the best in the world, and they brought information that Eike's competitors lacked.

In November 2007, the government planned to auction exploration rights off Brazil's southeastern coast. The country had already carried out eight such auctions since the end of Petrobras's oil monopoly, but this one was different because it offered drilling rights in the pre-salt area, so named because its deposits lay deep below the sea under a mile-thick layer of salty crust. No one outside Petrobras knew then that these fields held great uninterrupted reservoirs of sweet, light crude. Except Eike, thanks to his Petrobras hires. To bid for the rights, he raised a billion dollars from a handful of investors.

The richness of the pre-salt reserves became public knowledge only on the eve of the auction, when Petrobras announced that it had discovered a "province of oil" that contained as many as a hundred billion barrels—Kuwait-size reserves. Petrobras's stock price jumped, and Eike's backers probably felt very smart. But President Lula and Dilma Rousseff, then his cabinet chief, feared that by selling the fields, they would be handing over a "winning lottery ticket" to former government insiders. They wanted Petrobras to control the bonanza. So they withdrew the pre-salt blocks from the auction, replacing them with fields in shallow waters that Petrobras had discarded years earlier.

The last-minute shakeup threw the auction into disarray. Chevron and Exxon backed out. But Eike framed the switch as a blessing in disguise. Extracting the pre-salt oil would be expensive and time-consuming; drilling in shallow waters was cheap and easy. So at the auction, he bid big. For some fields he offered ten times what anyone else did. Many analysts thought Eike had overpaid. Others looked at his team of insiders and saw the aggressive bids as a sign of informed confidence. *What did they know that the rest of the market didn't?*

Eike scheduled the IPO for June 2008, as oil approached a record $145 a barrel. In his road show he called OGX's engineers his "dream team." One of them, Paulo Mendonça, a thirty-four-year Petrobras veteran, had led the department that discovered the pre-salt province. Though Eike's men had yet to examine OGX's fields in situ, they claimed to be sitting on close to five billion barrels of oil. The PowerPoint slides showed OGX pumping more than Oman by 2015. By 2019, they claimed, it would pump 1.9 million barrels a day, about as much as Petrobras now. Eike worked always in superlatives. This time the IPO raised four billion dollars, another record-breaker. Whatever the doubts in the market, the fear of missing out proved stronger. Investors wanted in so bad that they placed orders for ten times the number of shares on offer.

Eike's timing was perfect. Lehman Brothers, the legendary Wall Street firm, went under just three months later. The markets went into free fall; commodity prices collapsed, stocks in São Paulo too.

But they soon rebounded, and Eike surfed the swell of good feeling about Brazil. Though none of his companies had ever turned a profit, their share prices soared in giddy expectation of future profits. A money manager named Chris Palmer summed up the consensus among his peers when he said, "Eike has his finger on the pulse of what is changing the country."

There was a larger plan here. In his jumble of acronyms, Eike envisioned a system of interlinking operations. To supply electricity for the factories at Açu, MPX Energia would burn coal mined in Colombia and natural gas in Brazil owned by OGX Petróleo. To service his oil wells, OSX Brasil would manufacture oil platforms. And OSX would set up at LLX's port. All told, he raised seven billion dollars in his IPOs. I heard traders joke that, other than Bill Gates, no one but Eike made as much money off PowerPoint.

EIKE WASN'T THE ONLY one getting rich in Brazil, but he was the most visible and the most willing to talk, and this created a feedback loop. He gave interviews to CNN and CBS and the BBC. He made himself the official face of his country and its special moment. "In the last sixteen years Brazil has really put our act together," he told one reporter. He told another, "People want to participate in China because of a gigantic consumer market. People like India because it's a gigantic consumer market. The same story goes in Brazil, with one difference for Americans—we're very much like America, you know?" Once he waved at his interviewer. "Helloo! Time for Americans to wake up."

Eike had a lot to say, and he'd speak in perpetual dependent clauses, one idea leading to the next without quite concluding itself, sliding from a grand declaration about his companies (investing forty billion dollars in ten years!) to another about Brazil (we have the size to match China's appetite!), morphing into advice for lesser businessmen (think big but protect the environment!), and so creating these great run-on sentences that would just kind of abruptly halt.

When Eike went on *Charlie Rose* in 2010, Rose asked him to guess at his net worth in ten years. Eike looked at him. Fifty-three then, he'd gotten his eyelids lifted, his crow's-feet smoothed out with Botox, and at that little interview table that seems to float in space, he looked not so much youthful as otherworldly. He emitted a falsetto *hm* and responded calmly, without hesitation, "A hundred billion dollars." That would put him well above Carlos Slim, then the richest man in the world. He started telling people, "Slim had better clean his rearview mirrors because on one side or the other, I'm going to pass him." He even gave himself a deadline, 2013.

Eike didn't just want to get rich, though. He called his projects "transformational." He said, "I want to do away with this Brazilian mania for improvisation, for doing *puxadinhos*"—little add-ons— "instead of building grand projects." He wanted to change Brazil's culture, the culture of *gambiarra,* the jerry-rigged fix when you can't afford a permanent solution. For poor Brazilians, *gambiarra* is a necessity. At its best it's a triumph of resourcefulness over actual resources—when the stove breaks down, say, using a clothes iron balanced upside down to fry sausage. *Gambiarra* can also be a good way to hurt yourself or die. Faced with a round-pegged plug that won't fit into a square-holed socket, a poor Brazilian might use metal wire and a couple of keys in lieu of an adapter. Or you might see a welder using as his welding mask a sheet of newspaper impaled by eyeglasses to protect his eyes from the hot metal spatter. In Eike's vision of Brazil, as in Lula's, this wouldn't happen anymore. He would modernize the country.

Eike perfectly expressed the optimism of the Lula years. Lula liked to exalt Brazil's achievements by starting off with the line, "Never before in the history of this country . . ." and Eike filled in the blanks with his plans. He took old clichés and turned them on their head. Country of the future? "Brazil is the country of the present," he said. "I'm from the generation—my dad taught me that Brazil might not work out. Dictatorship, constant financial problems."

But Eike didn't buy into that old fatalism, *complexo de vira-lata*. He believed in his country.

As the spokesman of Brazil, Eike wanted to reach ordinary citizens too. In 2010 he joined Twitter announcing, "World, I've arrived! I'm going to tweet my thoughts! My disciplines! My values! How to continue making Brazil a Superpower!" (Perhaps because of his half-German upbringing, he often capitalized nouns like that.) He was a hit because when people tweeted at him, he tweeted back. Sometimes they asked for jobs, and he told them to send in their résumé. Once a guy wrote, "Thank you for being Brazilian," and Eike tweeted his thanks in return. He gained thousands of followers each week. Some put Xs in their Twitter handles in homage to him.

Eike spoke to a feeling in the emerging middle class, however tenuous, that *you too could get rich*. This explains why his book was a huge bestseller. The title was *O X da Questão*, which translates roughly as "The Crux of the Matter," with the X as always alluding to wealth multiplication. The subtitle was *The Trajectory of Brazil's Greatest Entrepreneur*. Part memoir, part business self-help book, it unconsciously followed an old American literary tradition that held that wealth sprang from your personal will, from the sheer power of imagining your own success.

When journalists asked Eike how he did it, he cited something he called 360-Degree Vision, which basically involved considering all aspects of a business venture before diving in. There was a diagram of the Vision in his book. It looked a bit like your high school textbook depiction of an atom, with oblong loops connecting dots labeled "financial engineering," "engineering of communication," "engineering of engineering," and so on, surrounded by a wider circle of themes like "stop loss" and "perseverance" and "meritocracy" and even "humility." The 360-Degree Vision, he wrote, "allows you to see the soul of a business." In the middle was an Incan sun meant to conjure supernatural powers. Each of his company logos had this sun too. Eike was open about the importance of luck, but he also believed you could influence luck. Because of this, he inserted the number sixty-three—the number of his boat in many victorious races—wherever he could. All of OGX's bids for oil blocks had ended with sixty-three *centavos*.

EIKE DID HAVE HIS skeptics. My first big story on him, in early 2011, was about the delays in getting his projects off the ground. Dozens of multinationals had agreed to build factories at Açu, but two years after it should have come online, the port still amounted to a ten-mile pier of concrete in shallow sea that needed dredging. MPX Energia had a coal plant firing, and MMX Mineração now mined some ore, but with production just ramping up, both still spent cash much faster than it came in. A year after going public, OSX Brasil hadn't even begun building its shipyard, much less any oil ships. Not that there was any use for them yet. OGX Petróleo had yet to take up a drop of oil from the sea. Eike said the delays didn't matter because the idiot-proof margins on his projects could absorb them. Still, in the months leading up to my story, Eike's companies had lost nearly seven billion dollars in market value.

Between the people who were bearish on Eike and those who were bullish on him, stock prices could swing dramatically. Since his companies were startups, you couldn't measure their progress in hard numbers like profits. What you had were expectations, mainly. To buoy these expectations, Eike's press people released a constant stream of videos with epic movie-trailer music that mixed real photos of the projects under way, confusingly, with shiny computer graphics and archival images—the girders of some kind of factory going up, pipes sucking oil from the seabed, a ship thrusting through waves. The videos played as commercials, not just in Brazil. I remember once at Bloomberg headquarters in New York hearing the soundtrack of an EBX commercial piped into the bathroom and feeling vaguely invaded.

At other companies, Eike said, "you'll see executives promoting the shares, telling only the best stories, so as to push up the value of the stock as soon as possible. Here, we do the opposite. We're conservative, and we're always trying to surprise the shareholder." But he had to know that his talk served as wind in his companies' sails. One day he announced that OGX had discovered natural gas deposits equal to half the reserves of Bolivia, South America's natural gas powerhouse. "I think I have a pact with nature," he said, "because when I drill, I find things." Eike's investor relations people did their part by releasing a constant stream of cheery projections for stock analysts. Every time one of OGX's drill rigs struck oil, an otherwise banal event in an exploration campaign, the company filed a statement with the local securities and exchange commission, announcing the find with confident phrases like "excellent geological conditions" and "high-quality carbon reserves" and hinting always at low costs, high volumes, and extensive deposits of crude. Interpreting these filings as signs of progress, analysts usually came up with stock price forecasts that endorsed Eike's vision: those Power-Point arrows pointing powerfully up and up. OGX's campaign appeared so successful that when at last it turned up a dud well, Eike said, "Good thing it was dry, because no one could believe anymore that we just keep striking oil." Part of the reason Eike did so much press was that his products were invisible to the public eye, and he could stand in for them—becoming, in a way, the product himself. Who else could say something like "OGX is *zero* percent speculation," as he did?

OGX's exploration campaign was ambitious. It exceeded that of all the foreign oil giants combined offshore of Brazil. But its scope was also a liability, because it steadily drained the cash raised in the IPO. To bring in fresh money, Eike had spent much of 2010 trying to sell a stake in OGX's fields to Total in France or Statoil in Norway. Rumors swirled for months. Eike let slip that one of China's state oil companies would make an offer. But in the end no one bit, at least not at the price Eike wanted. This made some investors nervous—what had the French and the Norwegians and the Chinese seen that they didn't like?

For every investor who said Eike had "the Midas touch," there was another who compared him with Donald Trump, more talk than substance. You could see this dynamic at play in April 2011, when Eike made a grand announcement: According to a report from De-Golyer & MacNaughton, a top Houston oil consultancy, OGX's fields held nearly eleven billion barrels of oil, more than double previous estimates. This sounded like cause for celebration. But Eike downplayed the bad news: that D&M labeled most of the reserves "prospective" rather than "contingent"—jargon that meant that it was still hard to say how much of the oil could in fact be profitably extracted. Having hoped for something more concrete, a few analysts cut their stock recommendations from "buy" to "hold," and OGX's stock price plunged by seventeen percent in a single day. Others deemed the selloff overdone, though, and kept their large targets. And the price crept back up again.

Eike knew what some people said about him. A feisty interviewer, Diogo Mainardi, laid into him once on live TV. "I have the feeling your companies are like a prayer to Saint Anthony on the stock exchange," Mainardi said. "Do they in fact exist? Does any of them generate revenue? Do they turn a profit? Do they have any real function?"

Smiling with barely contained umbrage, Eike talked about his first gold mine. He said he'd developed eight more around the world, creating twenty billion dollars in value for his shareholders by the year 2000. Gesticulating with one hand, palm downward as though rearranging invisible stacks of poker chips, he said the story had never been told "because we had a kidnapping problem in Brazil." His dad, a public man, had told him not to expose himself. "But eventually I got tired of being the son of *doutor* Eliezer and the husband of Luma de Oliveira, and I had two sons, so I said, 'Hey, I'm going to open up my kimono. I like Brazil.'"

EIKE'S RESPONSE SHUT DIOGO up. Few questioned his precious metals expertise, and this was a testament to Eike's storytelling prowess. In his book, he called his gold company, TVX, "the vehicle for one of the most successful mining-industry trajectories of all time." He often repeated that twenty-billion-dollar figure. But I could never figure out where it came from. Digging into his early business history, I came to see how he smoothed out the rough edges of his rise—a bit like Macedo, actually. I also noticed patterns that seemed to be repeating themselves once again.

The part of the story Eike told was that, in the early eighties, he had teamed up with some Canadian investors and put his gold concessions into a Toronto-listed shell company, Treasure Valley Explorations, which he renamed TVX (ah, that first X). At first his appetite for risk spooked his own partners. When he identified a rich mine in Chile, they refused to go along because the mine was paralyzed by dozens of lawsuits from locals who claimed to own the rights to the land. Also, it was a hundred miles from any source of water or power. So he went it alone. He spent fifteen million dollars of his own money to buy up all the legal claims, then negotiated the purchase of the mine on TVX's behalf. The risk paid off, and his feat earned him respect in the provincial world of gold.

As TVX's chairman and chief executive, Eike stayed aggressive. And with the price of gold hovering near a healthy four hundred dollars an ounce, his style paid off. In 1996 the company's market value hit $1.8 billion. In his book, though, he skipped over what came next. He got cocky. Betting the house on a new complex of mines in Greece, he promised to double TVX's output in just a few years. "If not," he declared, "you shareholders can shoot me." But Greeks living near the mine, fearing environmental fallout, began to picket the project. They sued to block development. Then archaeologists found ancient ruins at the site. Greek courts repeatedly froze the project. Eike, convinced he would overcome it all, kept pouring in cash—a quarter-billion dollars in the end. At the same time, he poured cash into another ill-fated mine in Russia. He did this as gold prices slowly but steadily declined to a two-decade low. Eventually he bled TVX dry. If you had bought a hundred dollars' worth of TVX shares at its peak in 1996, you would have just a few dollars when Eike stepped down in 2001. After that, TVX sold itself to a larger competitor, and its Greek subsidiary filed for bankruptcy.

A few things confused me about this story. One was that Eike thought no one would notice if he covered up an episode thoroughly reported by the Canadian business press. Another was that he seemed to be right, because journalists almost never brought it up. Also confusing was that he hid the collapse of TVX while admitting to other errors along the way. "I have my failures to prove that I'm not infallible," he wrote. There was the jeep factory he started in the nineties. He sank thirty million dollars into that one. He sank another ten million into the cosmetics firm he started for Luma. Then there was a voice pagers venture. When the e-commerce craze hit, he bought up package delivery companies to compete against Brazil's postal service. But he couldn't make the logistics work. "Jeff Bezos did something like this," he said later—implying that, if he hadn't been thwarted by some unnamed local condition, he would have founded another Amazon.com.

As a serial entrepreneur, Eike was unrepentant, displaying the zeal of the newly in love each time. In the late nineties, when he dipped into industrial water supply, he proclaimed, "Gold is a jurassic industry. Water is the industry of the twenty-first century." He liked to say he read "the newspaper of tomorrow." Even now, trying to get five public companies up and running—it wasn't enough. Paulo Mendonça, the OGX exec, told a story about how Eike stayed home sick from work once. He spent the day in bed. The next day when he showed up at the office, he said, "You're all fucked. I didn't sleep well, and I wrote up twenty-seven new business ideas that we need to get cracking on right away."

Eike had endless side ventures. He opened an upscale Hong

Kong–style restaurant in Rio, Mr. Lam, and brought over a chef from his favorite restaurant in New York. He sponsored a new volleyball team, RJX. He started a private clinic, MD.X. He opened a catering business, NRX-Newrest. He had hotels and an office building. For his new girlfriend, a perpetually tan lawyer named Flávia Sampaio, he opened a beauty clinic, Beaux, where you could sip champagne while getting your nails done. Eike's entertainment business, IMX, brought Cirque du Soleil to Brazil and organized Ultimate Fighting Championship matches. He was thinking of getting into coffee, that nineteenth-century boom crop. He looked at getting into television, but the Marinho brothers talked him out of it. Still, he was looking ahead—planning to build electric cars! Asked if he planned to invest in tech, he said, "I'll be dedicating resources to that too. I've got so many—my plate is pretty full, no?"

Despite his nationalistic ambitions, Eike spoke about entrepreneurship in American, not Brazilian, terms. He lamented that in Brazil *failure* was a bad word. "I'm glad to have had failures," he said. "In the United States, failure is the basis for doing something better afterward. There you can go to the market and raise capital again and everything's okay. I think failure should be seen more as a learning experience." If you didn't fail, after all, you weren't taking risks, and in Brazil success without risks meant doing business with the government on sweetheart terms. "Everyone got used to receiving a contract," Eike said. He loved to criticize *empreiteiros,* construction tycoons like those who ran Camargo Corrêa and Odebrecht. "When I ask my good friends the *empreiteiros* if they have the appetite to invest in drilling for oil, you know what they say? 'You mean I'm going to spend eighty million dollars and I might not find anything? I don't have the stomach for that.' This is very Brazilian." What Eike wanted to convey was that, in a nation of rent seekers, who sought to control the economic pie rather than make it larger, he put his own capital on the line—all to make Brazil a better place.

So if Eike was unabashed about his failures, why did he frame TVX as a success? Perhaps he truly believed that it was a success, somehow overlooking all that happened in the end. Or perhaps he believed that its failure had nothing to do with his abilities as an entrepreneur. On the rare occasions he spoke about it, he blamed the Greek government for failing to fulfill its contract with him. He didn't blame himself for betting the house on an uncertain prospect. With Eike I would learn that the line between deception and self-deception often blurred.

Whatever his reverence for the American business tradition, Eike didn't feel the need to flatter its greatest exemplars. When a reporter asked what he thought of Bill Gates and Warren Buffett, he scoffed and said the difference between him and them was that Gates built just one company and Buffett acquired other people's companies on the cheap. "I create things from zero," Eike said. He knew that some people thought he was a megalomaniac. "That doesn't bother me," he wrote in his book. "In the right proportion, a bit of megalomania or daring is recommended. No successful entrepreneur doesn't have at least a little. When the business proves viable, its creator is no longer a megalomaniac. He becomes a visionary."

And then in January 2012 his vision looked vindicated. After all the delays, OGX's first well started pumping at last. Webcams livestreamed the moment the underwater valves opened. It was a triumphant moment, not just for Eike but for his country—the first time a private Brazilian company had ever produced oil. A reporter asked Eike how he planned to celebrate, and he said, "I have a cellar with magnums of champagne from vintages going from 1956 to 1980. We're going to open one of these bottles." The accompanying photo showed Eike smiling in a dark suit and black T-shirt, splayed on top of his desk in a pose worthy of Luma, his Playmate ex. Through the windows behind him, Sugarloaf Mountain rose proudly from the sea.

THE FIRST TIME I spoke to Eike was right before the launch of the Bloomberg Billionaires Index in March 2012. I got all sorts of reactions when calculating net worths. Some billionaires, concerned about accuracy, directed their press people and private bankers to confirm the details of their assets. Plenty of others said they could not care less what we published. The spokesman for a guy in the top five suggested we'd valued him too high. Eike, meanwhile, took a special interest in the process. His people sent a detailed breakdown of his assets, some with photos. There was the 115-foot Pershing yacht, the *Spirit of Brazil VII,* worth forty-two million dollars. There were three jets: a Gulfstream G550 (sixty million dollars), an Embraer Legacy 600 (fourteen million), and an Embraer Phenom 300 (ten million). More than a hundred million dollars of real estate just in Rio.

As we prepared to launch the index, Eike's fortune hovered around thirty billion dollars, exactly where *Forbes* had put him in 2011. On our list he would rank tenth, enormously rich. With his net worth he could pay off the entire foreign debt of Bangladesh with enough left over to settle Belize, and still never work again. But according to his own yardstick, he'd made little progress. He'd been talking about overtaking Carlos Slim as the world's richest man for a couple of years now. According to one report, he'd even challenged Slim face-to-face. Every year there's a secretive meeting of Latin billionaires and their heirs, and during a panel discussion with Carlos Slim Jr., Eike called out to Carlos Slim Sr. in Spanish from the stage. "*Te voy a pasar,*" he said—I'm going to pass you. The rotund old Mexican looked baffled in the audience. He was still more than twice as rich as Eike.

Eike's people fought with me to try and juice his net worth. As with most billionaires, his fortune existed mainly on paper: the number of shares he owned in his five public companies multiplied by their prices in the stock market. But he also had all these side ventures for which no objective value existed. The main sticking point was a company called AUX. According to its last audited report, AUX sat on three and a half million ounces of gold in Colombia, all of which remained under the earth—waiting, like so much else of value in the world, to be extracted by Eike. Despite this, he said AUX was worth five billion dollars. According to our models, based on the value of similar companies, it was worth less than a billion.

This did not please Eike. The index would go live on a Sunday night. On the Friday afternoon beforehand, one of Eike's press people called me up and patched him through. He wanted to set the record straight personally.

"They're telling me that you've been using some wrong numbers," he said in a tone of excessive amusement. This morphed into outrage. "The problem is that the mine had three and a half million ounces, and it has nine today. You know you can't do what you've done. I mean, it's going to look ridiculous, because in a few months we're going to have the audited reserves come out"—proving that they had uncovered all this new gold. "Listen, Alex, I'm going to make you look very foolish. I'm going to say you're giving out wrong information. I'm going to tweet it, actually!"

He went on like this for a while. In his excitement, he tripped over his words. My heart was beating hard. I couldn't help feeling out of my element in this land of many zeroes. But I wanted something quotable for a story about his quest to surpass Carlos Slim, so after a while I cut in to see if I could ask a question.

"Go ahead," he replied, "because listen, we're not understanding each other—so what do you want to ask me."

Eike had pushed back his deadline for becoming number one. Now he said 2015 instead of his previous 2013. Did he regret making his challenge in the first place?

"Jesus, Alex, you're very primitive," he said. Then he caught himself, switched to pitch mode: "This year is a major turnaround for the group. We're estimating close to a billion dollars in cash generation this year, it will double for next year, and then it triples for 2014, and then we're running like—what's the name of this Jamaican guy? Bolt, Usain Bolt." He was referring to the Olympic runner. His point was that the delays were over; at last the profits would roll in. Altogether, he said he was sitting on a trillion and a half dollars in assets—the equivalent of more than sixty percent of Brazil's GDP. At times it seemed like numbers became purely abstract for Eike, and billions might as well be gazillions. He pointed to his climb up the *Forbes* list—"I was in position one-sixty-three, then eighty, then thirty, and then eight . . . so I do not regret it. Absolutely not. Next question."

Why did he care so much about ranking high on some rich list?

Right away he responded, "For me it means that I can help my country. I'm going to invest in universities, you know, schools, hospitals for my country. That's what it means." This wasn't just talk. In his short time on the wealth rankings, Eike had already given away far more money than most of his fellow Brazilian billionaires. He donated twelve million dollars to clean up the polluted lagoon overlooked by his mansion. He chipped in another twelve million to Rio's successful campaign for the 2016 Olympics. For Rio's favela pacification units, the UPPs, he spent ten million a year buying police equipment and vehicles. He gave fifteen million for a new children's cardiac hospital. For a mining museum in his native Minas Gerais, he donated another fifteen million.

Eike's point was that he wasn't just making himself rich; he was contributing to the nation. Asked once if he was embarrassed to be so rich in a country this poor, he answered by talking about the jobs he created, the taxes he paid, and the oil and mining royalties he would generate for the government. His money wasn't in the bank earning interest, he said; it was productive capital helping the country move forward. EBX might not turn a profit yet, but it employed twenty thousand people. This gave him great satisfaction. In his book he pictured the life of one of his workers: "I imagine his children, where he lives, what he wears or eats, what he does during his time off," he wrote. "I think of his children at school. I can glimpse that family sitting together at the dinner table, and the father or mother who just hours before was clocking out after a day's work at one of my companies. It's great to think that I influence the life of these people, that I make it possible for a man to provide a better life for his family."

But the fact of being ranked relative to other billionaires, I asked—did that in itself help him in this quest?

Eike started up, "Listen, I'm competitive, you know. It's Brazil's time to become number one." His anger had given way to the usual ebullience. "I want my country to compete openly with the international companies—Exxon, Shell." And he wanted more. He wanted to change the way people understood wealth in Brazil. "I want a young generation of Brazilians not to be shy of showing off their wealth, assuming it's made with transparency and honesty. The thing is, Brazilians admire soccer players or singers and don't mind seeing them running around in a Ferrari. The millions of honest entrepreneurs in Brazil who have earned their money honestly, with fair competition—they should be proud."

Eike repeated the word *honest* three times for a reason. When Brazilians think of the rich, many think of Paulo Maluf, Sebastião Camargo, the shady backroom deals that allow old oligarchies to thrive at everyone else's expense. As a businessman in Brazil, you run the risk of kidnapping, but you also run the risk people will assume you're a crook. The same went for Eike. His fortune had engorged so fast that many assumed he'd pulled off some *malandro* trick. Often when his name came up in bar conversation, someone would say to me in a confidential tone, "You know his dad gave him a map of Brazil's best mining sites, don't you?" The fact was that Eike's first successes in gold had come when Eliezer Batista still led Vale, the state mining giant. In the mid-nineties, one of Eike's former business associates claimed that Vale had passed Eike inside info on promising gold deposits, but investigations went nowhere. Eike's one real scrape with the law came in 2008, when police raided his offices and his mansion, looking for evidence he'd evaded taxes on gold exports and fixed the bidding on a railway contract. Again no charges were filed. Given the way justice works, though, that didn't prove to Brazilians that Eike was clean. If the map story persisted in the public imagination, it may have been precisely because it was unprovable.

What Eike wanted was to redefine wealth in Brazil as a measure of success that needs no other justification, as in the United States. In this version, his conspicuous consumption—his jets, his yachts, the McLaren in his living room—was an act of idealism, bravery even. More than a symbol of wealth, he was an apostle of wealth. He contributed to society, and his luxuries were the just rewards.

"Brazilians have always admired the American Dream," Eike told me. "What's happening in Brazil is the Brazilian Dream, and I happen to be the example."

CHAPTER 7

HELPING HANDS

THOR'S CRASH, EIKE'S PRIORS, AND A STUMBLE

"I want to build an empire that will last centuries."
—VISCOUNT OF MAUÁ (115,000 *CONTOS DE RÉIS*)

"Since I haven't sold a single share, I haven't lost anything!"
—EIKE BATISTA ($20 BILLION)

TWO WEEKS AFTER MY CONVERSATION WITH EIKE, HIS SON THOR ran over Wanderson Pereira dos Santos on the highway between Petrópolis and Rio. It was not a big story for Bloomberg, but the way Eike reacted revealed much about the way he approached the world.

He turned first to his one million Twitter followers in his son's defense. The day after the crash, he tweeted that he "deeply lamented" the accident but maintained it wasn't Thor's fault. He wrote: "I'm mega proud that he provided assistance + a handwritten declaration + Breathalyzer of 0.0%! You've got to have a lot of courage and manliness [to do that]! He was educated to be this way! He fulfilled all the laws and rules! Proud." By "assistance" Eike meant that his son had tried to help the victim, which he hadn't.

Eike's fans offered their support. One asked about Thor's "psychological state," and Eike replied, "One never comes out of a tragedy like this well!" Those who criticized his son, Eike called "ignorant and envious." Someone tweeted, "You started out well, building things. Your son started out destroying . . ." and Eike said: "Wrong! The imprudence wasn't his! It could happen to you!" It was low-hanging fruit for Internet trolls. As they provoked him, Eike only doubled down. "The cyclist's imprudence could have killed three people!" he tweeted—by which he meant that, apart from causing his own death, Wanderson could have killed Thor and Thor's friend too. One woman suggested that Eike's press people needed to shut him up. He replied, "Dragons breathe fire, *senhorita*!"

At least one person close to Eike did try to stop his campaign on Twitter. Alessandro Corona, the Italian renowned for Eike's second scalp, told me he had privately tried to persuade Eike to quit calling the dead man imprudent. "This is a human being we're talking about," Alessandro told him. "But I am a father," Eike replied. Eike wouldn't listen. He could only support his son.

Eike pointed users to a Twitter account Thor had created to relay his version of the crash. It repeated much of what he'd told police: "I was driving in the left-hand lane very carefully, without even speaking to my passenger, [when] suddenly a cyclist crossed from the right-hand shoulder into the middle of the left-hand lane." Thor said he always drove with one foot on the gas and one on the brakes so he could react as quickly as possible, but that night he had no time. Over the days that followed, Thor posted news that reflected well on his case. When an autopsy revealed alcohol in Wanderson's blood, Thor tweeted a link to the story and added: "almost three times the maximum allowed by Brazilian law." (He had no comment when it emerged that he'd also struck an old man the previous year.)

Thor seemed convinced he had no responsibility for Wanderson's death, but just the same he planned to help those Wanderson had left behind. "I will not leave the family unassisted under ANY HYPOTHESIS," he wrote. "I would like to give a hug to Vicentina"—Wanderson's aunt, who'd raised him. And indeed, a few days later, the press reported that he had met with Vicentina and Wanderson's widow at their lawyer's office. "They cried, embraced, and conversed," the lawyer said. It was the first step toward talks about compensation.

In one interview Eike said, "The victim is obviously the person who passed away. But Thor is a victim too, isn't he?" Thor posted photos of his injuries on Twitter. One showed his twenty-year-old face with tiny scattered scabs from shards of windshield. In another, red scratches streaked his biceps. It didn't look too bad. Actually, it looked like he was flexing. This would be hard to imagine if it were anyone else. But Thor was open about his fixation on his looks. "If I'm not satisfied with my body I can't think straight," he told the magazine *Veja Rio* once. He was six foot three; his biceps measured eighteen inches in diameter; he worked out every day and possessed four percent body fat, he said. He put pictures of himself on Instagram doing curls, too-tan veins all poppy, lips pursed, dyed-blond hair darkened with sweat. He said he used the steroid DHEA and took blood tests every ten days to monitor his hormones. "Endocrinology tip of the day," he tweeted once, "monitor the prolactin levels in your blood, antagonist of DOPAMINE, the lower they are, the higher your DOPAMINE."

Even in the face of tragedy, Thor seemed often to be posing. At the Church of the Resurrection, a Catholic church in Ipanema, he and his mom held a seventh-day Mass for Wanderson, arriving in a convoy of polished pickups escorted by bodyguards. Someone tipped off the press, and photographers shot the whole affair from outside through the church's glass doors. They registered Thor as he took a seat in one of the pews. Expressionless, his face settled into a full-lipped pout like his mom's. He wore fashionably torn jeans and an army-green stretch-tight Armani Jeans T-shirt. His girlfriend, a beautiful college student, sat beside him in a white blazer. A sound system played "*Nossa Senhora*" (Our Lady) by the crooner Roberto Carlos. A few of the fifty or so guests approached Luma to give her a hug. She looked aged compared to her *Playboy* days, heavier arms emerging from a conservative dress. No one from Wanderson's family came.

If Thor felt the need to pose, it's because Eike and Luma's celebrity extended to him. Whenever he showed up at a *shopping* with a new girlfriend, paparazzi indiscreetly snapped pictures. Not that he hid from them. He often took friends by private jet to São Paulo just for a night of partying. He'd rent one of the club's *camarotes,* VIP booths with table service of Dom Perignon—his favorite drink, he said—and ice buckets loaded with sweating cans of Red Bull and bottles of Grey Goose. "We have a life of luxury, sure, but I don't throw money away," Thor said. "I know people who blow sixty thousand *reais* in a night"—about thirty thousand dollars then. "I spend six thousand max." Still, Thor liked to treat his friends. On the day of the fatal crash, he'd bought lunch for several of them at a steakhouse in Petrópolis.

Growing up rich wasn't all easy. Thor's brother Olin, four years his junior, used to respond to admirers on a Q&A website called Formspring. Asked if he'd ever been depressed, Olin said sure: "Everyone has their moments of depression, no matter how well off they are. Obviously someone better off is less likely to get depressed, but it's unavoidable!" Dudes asked Olin to gift them money; girls asked him to screw them (*"ME COMEEEEEEEEEEEEEEEEEEEEEEEEEEE"*). Someone asked whether it was true that Olin farted coins. "And I crap hundred-*real* bills," Olin replied. Did he ever get tired of gold diggers hoping to get pregnant by him? Yes.

Olin was fourteen when he started throwing parties on the *Pink Fleet,* the 177-foot yacht his dad kept in Guanabara Bay. At seventeen he took up deejaying, and his dad's Phenom 300 jet took him to shows at nightclubs across Brazil. Reportedly it cost more to fly him to the gigs than he earned playing at them. When he did giant bashes at one of his parents' adjacent mansions in Rio, random girls would line up outside because security guards let the hottest ones in. But even then it was hard to get to Olin, because he would mount a VIP *camarote* inside his own home. The night of the accident, Thor and his friend had planned to hit up a party Olin was throwing at their dad's.

Olin didn't seem to mind when people called him a playboy. But Thor wanted to prove himself. In his interview with *Veja Rio*, Thor named two role models, Arnold Schwarzenegger and his dad. At the launch of his dad's book, in a bookstore at Rio's chic Shopping Leblon, Thor told reporters it was the first book he'd ever read from start to finish. And he read it twice. He also admired Steve Jobs and Bill Gates, he said, "not because of the wealth they created, which I think is kind of futile, but because of the great things they've done in life."

Thor complained that the media didn't portray "the real Thor," who didn't just work out but worked. He tried to emulate his dad. Following the financial news, he traded stocks on his own account and bragged that he'd used his own trading profits to buy an Aston Martin. He had one of those Bloomberg terminals that cost twenty-four thousand dollars a year. It was hard to say how much he used it, though. On the terminal, when a user is active, there's a little green dot next to their name. Whenever I visited Thor's profile, the dot was yellow, for "idle."

Thor had dropped out of a top Rio business school in his freshman year because it was too tough, he said. Eike, a college dropout himself, didn't seem to mind. At investor conferences he presented Thor as his heir apparent. He'd included Thor in the business from early on. At nine years old, Thor accompanied his dad on a trip to Chile to sell a gold mine. Now he attended regular board meetings at Eike's companies. But he didn't quite share his dad's entrepreneurial instinct. He'd made a stab once, teaming up with a Rio socialite to open a franchise of the Ibiza nightclub Pacha, but it never got off the ground even with Eike's money backing them. So Eike gave Thor something else to manage, SGX, a security firm.

"I grew up hearing my dad say that a man's greatest source of pride is to see his son surpass him," Thor said. "I would always dry-swallow when he said that. Doing more than him is almost impossible."

Thor also mimicked his dad's love of speed, though here too he failed to match up. In May, two months after his crash, he took his bright red Ferrari 458 Italia to a legal closed-circuit drag race near São Paulo. He got it up to 192 miles per hour and came in ninth place. He didn't seem to fear what the outside world might think of this. Nor did he seem to worry about proving he followed the law. In Rio the next evening, police stopped him at a drunk-driving checkpoint because the car had no license plate in front. There was no slot for it, Thor explained, because in the Italy of Ferrari, you need only the one in back. He was sober, but they impounded it anyway.

It was a few days later that police released their report calculating his speed on the night he ran over Wanderson—83 miles per hour, well above the speed limit. Thor's lawyers called it "science fiction" that caused "indignation." They'd commissioned their own forensic analysis that put the McLaren comfortably below the limit. But prosecutors were unmoved. They indicted Thor for involuntary manslaughter that same day. A court ordered him to hand over his driver's license—which should have been taken away before the accident ever happened, because of all his speeding tickets. When he arrived at the offices of Rio's department of motor vehicles, photographers shot him marching into the building, his shirt unbuttoned halfway down his hairless chest.

EIKE HAD HIS OWN father drama. He never tried too hard to hide it. When a reporter asked him if it was hard growing up with such an important dad, he replied, "No, because my mom raised me. Up until I was twenty, I practically never saw my father." The reporter asked if they had affection for each other—if they embraced—and Eike said, "We *ended up* having it, but it's funny, that only came later." As a kid he'd suffered from asthma, and it was his late German mother, Jutta, who helped him overcome it. She's the one who pushed him to swim as a twelve-year-old in a pool on cold European days. She also pushed him to make something of himself, laying down a challenge like the one Eike would later suggest to Thor: Each of her children had to outdo their father. What brought Eike and Eliezer together in the end? "It was my mother's death," Eike said, "and the growth of my business. Now he's an adviser of mine."

Given the importance of family ties in defining one's place in Brazil, reporters often asked Eike how his famous father had contributed to his success. But Eike rejected the idea that Eliezer had ever helped him at all. He said the greatest benefit he got from his parents was a good education, though he didn't finish it. Sometimes he talked about how, when he dropped out of college to go to the Amazon, Eliezer had disapproved of his plans. Pounding his fist on the table, he had said Eike deserved an "idiot's diploma." This may explain why Eike prided himself on finding "idiot-proof" assets.

Eike claimed that he didn't reconnect with his father till he was thirty and already a successful gold tycoon, and the press—local and foreign—mostly swallowed this version. But it was another case where Eike smeared the outlines of the truth. In 2014, two different books about Eike by local journalists would reveal how Eliezer had helped him along. When Eike got his start in the gold trade, the military regime still held power, and though Eliezer was a technocrat who'd never served in the armed forces, he had a lot of pull. As head of Vale, the state mining giant, he was in charge of one of the government's largest investments, a complex of mines called Carajás. It's the project that Eliezer Batista is most famous for.

A geologist had discovered the Carajás deposits in the sixties. Flying over the Amazon, his helicopter hit a patch of fog and made an emergency landing on a mineral-rich bald patch in otherwise tree-blanketed hills. Everyone assumed it was too isolated to make for a viable mine. But the ore was high quality, and Eliezer calculated that a large enough mine connected via rail to a large enough port could compete with the Australian firms that ruled the flourishing iron ore market in Japan. His innovation was to rethink a daunting *physical distance* as a surmountable *economic distance*. And it worked. When Carajás came online in 1982, it was one of the largest mining projects in the world; it still is.

Eliezer liked to say that a mine was actually a logistics business, and two decades after Carajás started up, his son made that insight his own. Eike structured MMX Mineração according to this exact logic. Likewise, he championed the port of Açu as a "mega-logistics complex." And yet even as he praised his dad's contributions to Brazil, helped to finance a documentary about him, and proudly appointed him to multiple corporate boards, Eike criticized his lack of vision. "My father doesn't believe in taking risks," he said—because his dad never left government to be an entrepreneur. "God gave him every talent but one: the talent for making money. That one He gave to me."

Eike always laughed off the rumor that his dad had given him a map of Brazil's best mineral deposits. In 2008, he claimed, Eliezer had reacted with surprise when he sold one of MMX's projects to the South African mining giant Anglo American for five and a half billion dollars. "Where did that come from?" Eliezer asked him. And Eike replied, "É, Brazil is big indeed." For all the fuss about the map, though, what we know about his help from Dad is less exciting. Being the son of Eliezer Batista opened doors. At twenty-one, after he borrowed a half-million dollars to get his start in the gold trade, his first partner screwed him out of the money. But he convinced those jewelers in Rio to lend him another half-million. How? In his book he said they believed in his "capacity for execution." In an interview he gave later, though, he conceded that the jewelers knew how important his dad was. According to the book about Eike by the journalist Malu Gaspar, Eike secretly mortgaged the family apartment in Brussels to raise the money. Either way, family was key.

Though he had ridiculed Eike's plans, Eliezer didn't try to block them. On the contrary, he often lent a hand. When an employee at Eike's trading firm was caught at the airport in Rio with undeclared gold, it was Eliezer who got them out of trouble. Eike told the story of his first mine, the mechanized alluvial gold project, as one of personal perseverance, but later it would emerge that he'd gone broke trying to set it up. Eliezer prevailed upon a friend, the owner of a major mining company, to buy it from him, saving him from a loss. For Eike's second mine, Eliezer set up a partnership with the son of another former mining minister and a wealthy heir named Olavo Monteiro de Carvalho. I met Olavo once, and he told me Eliezer wanted him to manage the project because Eike was better at finding assets than at bringing them to fruition. Even then they ran into money problems. So Eliezer got another friend, a rich Japanese businessman, to put more cash in.

Eliezer Batista was an invisible hand in Eike's rise. Eike liked to say he'd left TVX, his failed Toronto-listed gold venture, with a billion dollars in the bank—but other sources, and my own math from digging through his financial history, suggested he was broke by the time he set his sights on Brazil. His father helped him make his comeback. In 2000, as blackouts rolled across Brazil, the government announced an emergency plan to build power plants, offering cheap credit and guaranteed profits to attract investors. Eliezer connected Eike with the governor of the northeastern state of Ceará, who awarded him the contract for a natural gas plant. It was a great deal. In the end he never even had to turn the plant on, and he still got paid. The company that built it grew into MPX Energia.

This power plant became famous for another reason. Eike then was still married to Luma de Oliveira. At an event with Eike, President Fernando Henrique Cardoso, and Ceará's governor, photographers delighted as she fought the Ceará winds to keep her yellow dress down. The press dubbed the plant Termoluma in her honor.

AS THE STANDARD-BEARER OF a new Brazilian Dream, Eike was supposed to be an American-style entrepreneur, a meritocratic risk taker—the opposite of Brazil's "cordial man," who leaned on connections to get ahead. But there was more that didn't square with his self-image. Like the construction tycoons he disparaged, he pulled every lever he could to make sure the risks played out in his favor. His projects required licenses and financing, so he sought the government's backing in the usual way. In Rio, where most of his projects were based, he generously financed the governor, Sérgio Cabral. He donated four hundred thousand dollars to his reelection campaign, falling short only of Camargo Corrêa and two other construction firms. Eike also gave Cabral unlimited access to his Legacy jet for trips personal and official. And sure enough, the favors came back to him. Cabral gave his companies tens of millions of dollars in tax credits and fast-tracked permits for his port.

The same pragmatic logic led Eike to Lula. As late as 2002, the year Lula was elected president, Eike had given an interview saying that the labor leader would be a *retrocesso*, a step backward. But four years later, for Lula's reelection campaign, Eike gave half a million dollars, one of the largest individual donations. Like most of his fellows in business, he was willing to bury his old skepticism for the prospect of favors from a powerful state. Still, it took a while for the old autoworker to come around to the playboy.

It was a chapter in Eike's father drama that brought them closer together. In 2009 Eike wanted to take over Vale, whose shares had gotten cheap thanks to the financial crash. He'd missed the chance to invest when Vale was privatized in the nineties, because Eliezer had kept him away to avoid the perception of a conflict of interest. But with his dad now retired, Eike sensed an opportunity. Lula was upset that Vale had laid off workers during the crisis. So Eike sought him out and promised maximum employment. Speaking the language of "developmentalism," he also promised to invest in steel plants, adding value to Vale's main product rather than just exporting the ore raw. To take over Vale wasn't a mere personal ambition; Eike called himself a "soldier of Brazil." Lula liked what he heard and gave his blessing for the takeover. Though the bid ultimately failed, Eike had won Lula's ear.

The two began meeting to talk business, and it turned out that their visions overlapped. Lula wanted to bring the nation not so much into the twenty-first century, with tech and high finance, but into the twentieth, with ports, dams, and big, basic Brazilian companies like Eike's. His idea was to take advantage of the windfall from the commodities boom to create national champions that could compete on the world stage.

The state development bank was at the center of this strategy. Lula appointed a die-hard developmentalist named Luciano Coutinho as its president, and during the financial crisis, the BNDES rescued a few major companies facing bankruptcy by financing mergers with their main competitors. Thus was born BRF, the world's top poultry producer, and Fibria, the world's top maker of pulp, the main ingredient in paper. The bank also backed a push abroad, and a company known as JBS became the world's top beef producer after it took over two major U.S. meatpackers. In 2009 the BNDES lent out seventy-six billion dollars, more than the World Bank lent out in the entire world. The next year, though the crisis was waning, it lent even more.

The BNDES was controversial. Born under President Getúlio Vargas in the fifties, it granted long-term financing when private-sector banks were unwilling to risk their capital, and for this it won praise from economic nationalists. Others accused it of political favoritism, worried how much it was costing public coffers, and feared that it would keep the private sector from ever learning to finance itself. But business leaders were just about unanimous in seeking BNDES support, whatever their ideological convictions. In a country where the average bank charged thirty percent a year on loans, it was the only lender that offered interest rates in the single digits. For Eike, the lure was obvious.

What Lula and Luciano Coutinho saw in Eike, in turn, was many national champions in one. And so the BNDES would approve five billion dollars in loans for Eike's projects—one of the largest packages awarded to any group in Brazil. Though he sneered at the supremacy of public money in Brazilian business, Eike had no problem taking government loans himself; he called the BNDES "the best bank in the world." When a Twitter user called him out on this contradiction, Eike replied that all governments finance "Projects of National Interest" and cited the example of NASA (never mind that NASA is not a private enterprise). Also, he owed it to shareholders to find the cheapest financing possible (never mind that the largest shareholder was Eike himself).

As BNDES funds rolled in, Eike paid little favors in return. On top of his campaign donations, he gave half a million dollars to fund the gushy biopic *Lula: Son of Brazil*. That night in 2010 when he made headlines for his newly pouffy hair, he was sitting next to Lula's wife at a charity auction in São Paulo, and he spent a quarter-million dollars to buy the suit Lula had worn to his inauguration. Eike liked to call himself "apolitical," but he also said of Lula, "I'm certain that his name has already entered the ranks of the great statesmen of our history."

Eike's generosity didn't go unnoticed. Asked about his campaign donations at a televised round table in 2010, Eike said, "My concept is very simple. We have chosen democracy. To keep democracy on its feet, I have to help it sustain itself." Then he contradicted himself. One of the journalists said that some businessmen ponied up out of fear of retaliation if they didn't. "Yes, of course," Eike replied. "We have projects in various states, and they won't get held up because of political issues." He believed in democracy, in other words, but also believed you needed to grease the wheels to keep elected officials on your side.

Throughout the round table, the journalists pressed Eike on his ties to Lula. After skirting their questions for over an hour, he finally replied in a defensive tone: "My relationship to the government is zero. I don't have any government contracts"—apparently forgetting his government loans. "I don't need to go to Brasília. If the president of the country calls me, then as a citizen, Eike Batista, I go. Obviously, it's the government that awards my concessions. But they're open and transparent. I go invest my billions, and I make things happen, so I don't need any kind of government ties, okay? I think this is very important. And I'm proud of this. This is what I tell my investors, I don't need to go to the minister of ports. I got the license to build my port. I don't need anyone. I'm self-sufficient."

Eike danced an awkward dance. One day he was reveling in his closeness to the state; the next he was denying a state role in his rise. But even in preparing for Thor's trial, Eike's actions betrayed his true feelings about the value of government connections. Putting together the defense team, he brought on Márcio Thomaz Bastos, a criminal lawyer who had served as Lula's justice minister (and previously defended Edir Macedo from charges of charlatanism). Replying to yet more heckling on Twitter, Eike wrote, "I only hire the best, there a problem with that?"

I SOMETIMES HEARD EIKE compared to Irineu Evangelista de Sousa, the Viscount of Mauá. Though Eike called himself Brazil's greatest entrepreneur—ever—the reality is that Mauá exceeded him. In the nineteenth century, Mauá constructed an empire of proportions seen few times in the history of any country. He owned eight of the ten largest companies in Brazil at his peak: banks, railroads, utilities, ports. At 115,000 *contos de réis*—around sixty million dollars then—their assets exceeded the imperial government's entire annual revenue. He was one of the richest men in the world; *The New York Times* called him the Rothschild of South America. Part of the economic canon in Brazil, Mauá's story offered up warnings for Eike, not that he would have heard of them. A journalist once asked Eike his favorite business book, and he said, "I don't read business books. My life is a book."

As the biographer Jorge Caldeira tells it, Mauá was early in sensing a point of inflection in Brazil. Well into the nineteenth century, the country had an antebellum South–style economy with no industry to speak of. But in 1850 Emperor Pedro II bowed to pressure from England and enforced a ban on the transatlantic slave trade, Brazil's most profitable business. Forced to liquidate their affairs, Rio's slave traffickers found themselves with a lot of idle cash on their hands. And Mauá was ready to leap on the opportunity. A prosperous Rio merchant, he had recently wound down his import-export firm and raised European capital to invest in ventures that few Brazilians had ever tried before. The most important among them was a bank, Banco do Brasil, for which he held a mega-IPO, selling shares to ex-slavers and imperial senators.

A century and a half before Eike, Mauá saw himself as the vanguard of a great transformation. Inspired by a trip to England, where thousands of miles of railroads crept across the country and factories burped the smoke of progress, Mauá hoped to finance Brazil's industrial awakening. Addressing his new shareholders at Banco do Brasil, he said, "The establishment of which you form part opens a path that, over time, will become a broad highway to public prosperity." He wasn't shy about his ambitions; in a letter to a friend, he wrote, "I want to build an empire that will last centuries." Also like Eike, he wanted to build it fast—so he leveraged up. He took loans from Banco do Brasil using his own shares in the bank as collateral, and invested the money in a slew of startups. Using English engineers, he built Brazil's first railroad from Rio's Guanabara Bay north through Petrópolis, Pedro II's summer home. He built an Amazon ferry service and a gas lighting utility. He put money into a foundry and shipyard. Then he reused the shares in his startups as collateral for even more loans from Banco do Brasil. The structure was dangerously close to a pyramid scheme.

With Banco do Brasil up and running, money flowed more freely in Brazil than it ever had, sparking a brief kind of gilded age. Emerging from cushioned cabriolets on the streets of Rio, men sported black top hats that trapped the tropical heat on their scalps. Most of them lived off their accumulated capital, profits from the slave trade, or incomes from the imperial court. Mauá stood out because he worked to grow his money, tirelessly. As much as possible in those days, he was self-made. Though his family owned land down south, they'd sent him to work at a Rio trading firm when he was just nine years old, and he'd risen the ranks by his own wit and effort. He was no aristocrat. Pedro II named him baron only after his first railroad came online, viscount after he built the first underwater cable linking Brazil to Europe.

Much as Eike touted an American culture of risk, Mauá held up the Anglo-Saxon line that self-interest was the engine of progress, and in this way too he went against the grain. The standard economic text in those days, the Viscount of Cairu's *Princípios de Economia Política,* was supposed to be an adaptation of *The Wealth of Nations,* but Cairu jettisoned whatever concepts didn't jibe with facts on the ground. Forget the invisible hand: "The sovereign of each nation must be considered the chief or head of a vast family, and thus care for all those therein like his children, cooperating for the greater good." It was a "cordial man" approach to economic policy, *state capitalism* before the term ever existed. The problem, of course, was that the "greater good" didn't always extend past the sovereign's circle of friends.

Mauá's ambition caused a backlash. Feeling the center of power shifting away from them, the old plantation owners accused him of pursuing personal profit over their parochial idea of the greater good. Conservative senators denounced Banco do Brasil's iffy finances, sparking a run on the bank. When Pedro II made a takeover offer, Mauá had no choice but to accept. Under state ownership, Banco do Brasil tightened the spigots of credit, directing the flow to friends of the court.

This episode gave rise to a legend of Mauá as the lonely economic liberal in a nation run top down. A quote is often attributed to him, probably apocryphal, but in line with other statements he made: "A government's best economic program is not to get in the way of those who produce, invest, save, employ, work, and consume." Like Eike, meanwhile, Mauá believed in the free market with great conviction— but selectively. His ventures all depended on government contracts, subsidies, and protective tariffs. His foundry's first orders came because of a contract he won through a politician friend to route water to Rio from a nearby river. At the government's request, he financed a proxy war against Argentina, and his foundry supplied Paraguayan forces with warships and cannons. When he created his Amazon ferry service, it was because the government wanted to assert its claim to the territory, fearing incursion by the United States. Later he was elected to the lower house of Congress, where he openly defended his own business interests.

As an entrepreneur, Mauá was ahead of his time in Brazil—big-thinking, adept at accounting, and smart at delegating authority. But his success, like Eike's, came in importing ideas that had already worked elsewhere. And whatever his self-image, he depended on the state to carry them out. Except that the state didn't always stand by him. This, combined with leverage, proved to be his undoing. By the 1860s he had become the largest creditor to the tiny nation of Uruguay. When Pedro II threatened to invade to protect the interests of Brazilian cattle ranchers in the country, Mauá lobbied to prevent war but failed. The conflict threw Uruguay's economy into chaos, bankrupting the government, which now had no way to pay him back. Then in a railroad project in São Paulo, he got into a costly legal battle with his European partners. A fire destroyed his shipyard, and he poured in money to rebuild it even as essential tariffs expired. A double-edged crisis hit when Brazil invaded Paraguay just as the American Civil War sapped demand for coffee. When a global panic struck in 1873, he didn't have the cash to cover a run on his bank. He appealed to the government for an emergency loan, but Pedro II balked at bailing him out. Mauá had no choice but to declare bankruptcy.

Forgetting his laissez-faire ideals, he blamed the government for his collapse. All he'd needed, he said, was a bridge loan to get through the crisis. As the historian Raymundo Faoro put it in his treatise on Brazil's particular form of capitalism, *patrimonialismo,* "Businessmen wish for two ideals: at the top, state support; at the company level, free enterprise." In other words, they wanted the best of both worlds.

Mauá ended up all right, though. Once he'd settled the last of his debts, he had enough money left over that he remained one of Brazil's richest men. He lived out the rest of his days at a luxurious rural estate near Rio. And he left a legacy. Banco do Brasil still exists. Still owned by the government, it's one of Brazil's top lenders.

I'D SEEN MAUÁ'S NAME many times before bothering to wonder who he was. He had a square named after him across the street from the old Bloomberg office in Rio. In those days it was hemmed in by construction boarding whose bright paint announced Rio as an Olympic city, modernizing for 2016. Mauá usually had a statue there, but workers had hauled it away for a makeover of the old port area.

I passed by Praça Mauá the first time I visited Eike's headquarters, not long after Thor's crash. I was going to meet with one of Eike's top guys, a low-profile executive who agreed to speak with me on the condition I never print his name—so I'll call him Wagner here. Turning left out of the Bloomberg office, I walked away from Praça Mauá down Rio Branco Avenue. I passed newsstands and *botecos* in the shade of century-old buildings with ornate facades stained blackish by the sea air. Rio's downtown, like São Paulo's, bustles during the day but gets sketchy at night. It slipped into decline when Brasília became the nation's capital in 1960, and most of the moneyed bureaucrats picked up and left.

Rio's run-down state was one more Brazilian shortcoming that Eike planned to correct. He had adopted the city as his home and now styled himself its patron. On top of the twelve million dollars he donated for Rio's Olympic bid, he was investing tens of millions more in downtown real estate. He was fixing up classic but decrepit buildings like the seaside Hotel Glória, which he aimed to make one of the world's top hotels in time for the World Cup in 2014. At the cost of yet more tens of millions, he was revamping a nearby old marina too. In ten or fifteen years, Eike predicted that Rio would embody the best of Houston, New York, and California. (Unlike São Paulo, where New York threw up on L.A.)

Rio Branco Avenue ends at a square where the bay curves in to reveal the sea again. Turning back, I saw a rounded twenty-three-story tower bulging from the city. Known as the Edifício Serrador, it was an art deco icon from 1944 with cream-colored stone studded by aquamarine windows. After a thirty-million-dollar remodel, it now played home to Eike's empire. It was the most prominent symbol of his efforts to remake downtown Rio.

I walked through a gaping stone mouth and past a wall of dark glass, and an EBX person met me in an atrium whose ceiling rose several person-lengths high. She swiped me through the electronic turnstiles that clicked with comers and goers in well-cut suits. Thirteen hundred people worked in the building, all for Eike: managers, geologists, dozens of PR people. My guide punched in the number of a high floor, and we filed into a "smart" elevator, one of the features Eike had requested in his remodel. When he arrived at work in the morning, an elevator already awaited him and his four security guards and sometimes his German shepherd, Eric, who hung out at the office with him.

Wagner and I were going to discuss Eike's favorite topic, his wealth—which had grown. Eike had just announced a major deal, selling a two-billion-dollar piece of his empire to the United Arab Emirates. It was an unusual transaction. Rather than invest in any single company, the Emirates, through one of their so-called sovereign wealth funds, were acquiring 5.63 percent of EBX as a whole (always with the sixty-three). It took a while for me to unravel it, but this meant they were buying into not just his public companies, but his even airier private ventures—and also into the ideas that had yet to fully hatch but merely rattled around Eike's subconscious, waiting to enter the world. I got to speak to Eike again when he called me to celebrate the deal. He sounded a lot jollier than he had earlier in the month, when we parried over the exact size of his fortune. Already he was in talks to sell another stake in EBX to a different sovereign wealth fund. What was he going to do with the money? Just then he was hammering out a partnership with Foxconn, the Taiwanese manufacturer, to make iPhones in Brazil at "civilized prices" at the port of Açu. "It will be the Brazilian Silicon Valley," he said. (In Eike's Silicon Valley, ideas would be copied from abroad—much as Mauá had done.)

I asked what the Emirates' investment did for his quest to become the world's richest man. Like the speedboat racer he was, Eike said, "Imagine me getting my engine and adding another turbocharger." And indeed, if you did the math, the deal implied a valuation for his empire substantially higher than the one you could see on the stock exchange. At Bloomberg we recalculated his net worth: $34.5 billion. On our daily ranking he leaped to eighth place, above the American Koch brothers. It was a new high for Eike.

Wagner received me in a chilly little conference room. Typical of the men who formed Eike's inner circle, he was a Rio native and spoke with flawless, nonchalant conviction. He had a strong hint of the *malandro* to him. He said things like "People are knocking down our doors to give us money." He told me how the Emirates' sovereign wealth fund, the Mubadala Development Company, had sent a hundred and fifty people to analyze EBX's projects. "They spent a year going through our books, doing due diligence," he said. "Really clever guys, young guys from Harvard and Yale."

From the windows I could see a view of afternoon Rio: thrusting mountains, dark blue sea, distant oil tankers. Wagner shut the blinds. He planned to make use of a whiteboard. Despite Eike's surge on our index, Wagner thought he could get him higher. As before, the point of contention was AUX. Drawing diagrams with colored markers, speaking in mining jargon he knew I didn't understand, Wagner explained in detail how they'd found five, six million ounces of new gold at their properties in Colombia. When I mentioned that AUX's deposits lay next to a mine recently shut down by the Colombian government, which feared it would contaminate the local water supply—raising the specter of a TVX-like debacle—Wagner waved those worries away. They'd already thought of that. "We're professionals," he said. "We've been doing this for a long time." It occurred to me that I was witnessing firsthand how Eike created wealth "from zero." It seemed to involve will and persuasion as much as work and investment. Then again, what did I know about gold?

I imagined Eike somewhere in the building, probably on the floor above, doing deals over the phone while receiving a vitamin cocktail intravenously, as he was known to do. The first time we spoke, he told me he was going to make me look foolish. Queasily I wondered now if my skepticism was misplaced. Soon it would emerge that the Qataris were in talks to buy half of AUX for two billion dollars. That would value it at more than four times what we estimated.

Wagner had another quibble with our net worth estimate: "Are you going to subtract the value of the McLaren?" This was supposed to be a joke. He meant the car that Thor was driving when he hit Wanderson. The car cost 1.2 million euros; Eike's fortune fluctuated by many times that amount from one second to the next.

EIKE AND WAGNER BOTH touted Mubadala's investment as a "seal of approval" from a nation that knows oil. Talking to people in the market, though, I heard another interpretation of the deal. The Emirates had a lot of money on their hands, a trillion dollars in accumulated oil profits, and with U.S. interest rates near zero, it wasn't easy to put two billion in one place and make a decent return. The sheikhs weren't the only ones facing this problem. In the wake of the 2008 crisis, the U.S. Federal Reserve had flooded the financial industry with newly printed money. The hope was to drive investment in the American economy, but lots of those dollars made their way abroad, where returns looked higher. With all this liquidity sloshing around, it was a seller's market—and Eike was selling.

Eike rode the wave of a new Brazil, but he also rode a wave of cheap money. He benefited from it in each of his IPOs, and he benefited again in 2011. After failing to sell a piece of OGX Petróleo to one of the global oil giants, he still needed to raise money for the company's exploration campaign. So he turned to the bond market, effectively borrowing money from a large pool of investors. Apparently he was violating an oil industry maxim, "never drill with debt," which is to say, don't leverage up till you're producing something. Moody's and Fitch Ratings, which are supposed to tell you how safe an investment is, labeled the bonds "speculative grade," a polite term for what everyone else in the market calls "junk." But investors like Pimco, the world's largest mutual fund company, piled in anyway. They needed to deliver returns, and Eike offered a juicy yield, so he had no trouble selling the entire $2.563 billion bond issue. A year later, with OGX barely pumping oil, he went back to the bond market and raised another $1.063 billion.

Investors took Eike's obsession with the number sixty-three as a funny quirk of his. But his insistence on financing his company based on a superstition might have hinted at the squishiness of his business plan. The appended sixty-threes in just these two bond deals amounted to $126 million, not an irrelevant chunk of cash. Though of course, there was an even larger issue that went equally ignored: $3.6 billion was a lot of fresh debt for a company with almost no revenue. Eike would have to hit all his ambitious production targets to pay it back on time.

Eike seemed to believe that, in backing him, the market was doing its job: financing a risky venture for the promise of long-term reward. But the truth was that for many investors, it didn't matter if his companies ever made a profit at all. What mattered was the prices they bought and sold at. OGX's earliest backers, like the billionaire Ziff brothers and Gávea Investimentos, had bought shares on the cheap before the company went public—then got out with a healthy profit as the shares soared. They had no stake in whatever came next. Short-term investors like these played a key role in getting Eike off the ground. They were speculators; at Bloomberg I heard them called *smart money*.

———

THE EMIRATES, SOME BELIEVED, were dumb money. Having missed out on the early phase of the Brazil fever, they were now playing catch-up. Only they arrived late to the party. The Brazil of 2012 wasn't quite the Brazil of the Lula years. To power through the financial crisis, Lula had thrown open the spigots of credit and never tightened them. Hoping to stimulate new consumers, he pushed banks to offer payroll loans, and his emerging middle class began to look American in an alarming way, taking on debt to buy cars and plasma TVs and smartphones. It wasn't just the nouveau riche spending with abandon now. The average Brazilian family spent a fifth of its income on interest payments, twice as much as the average American family. Partly this is because banks in Brazil offer exorbitant rates. Credit cards charge three hundred percent a year or more.

The bill would come due under Dilma Rousseff, Lula's hand-picked successor. She faced two major problems when she took office in 2011. At home, a hot economy and quickening inflation. Abroad, a slowdown in China that brought down commodity prices. So she mixed austerity and stimulus. Interest rates went up, then they went down again. She made big cuts to the budget, then offered big tax cuts to manufacturers. But the confusion went deeper. She and Lula shared Workers Party backgrounds, and both had dabbled with socialism, but where Lula embraced the market, Dilma accepted it only begrudgingly. An adherent of the *desenvolvimentista* school, she pursued a top-down idea of development—and having studied economics, she put great faith in her own formulas. She capped prices for gasoline and electricity with massive subsidies, and the BNDES lent out more than ever before to established corporations. But her measures failed to stoke the economy, and the national debt ballooned.

Dilma seemed surprised that businessmen didn't return her support. Unlike Lula, though, she tried to avoid actually receiving them in Brasília. In fact, back in her days as government minister, I heard she'd kicked Eike out of her office once. Now, however, even as much of the business class turned against her, she drew closer to Eike. In April, a month after the Emirates deal, she took part in a ceremony at the port of Açu, up the coast from Rio. She flew in by helicopter. From up there she would have seen the pier, that ten-mile L of concrete in green water, future "highway to China" from which giant ships would carry Brazilian goods eastward. She would have seen the rich brown of freshly moved earth where one day factories would manufacture cement and steel and cars. Eike received Dilma when she touched down. He guided her around two unfinished terminals, and she posed for photos in a hard hat with some of his five thousand port workers. Once it was up and running, the port would employ fifty thousand workers, he said. He planned to build a whole city, Cidade X, for their families.

Why did Dilma Rousseff, the onetime Marxist guerrilla, buy in to Eike Batista, Brazil's foremost capitalist? When she ran for president, of course he backed her as he'd backed Lula, with campaign cash. But more important was that he shared her nationalist vision. Dilma was one of the strongest voices behind a new Brazilian version of Herbert Hoover's "Buy American Act" requiring companies with oil concessions to use equipment made by Brazilian firms. Eike's OSX Brasil, which was building its shipyard at Açu, fit into this idea. Rather than purchase oil platforms abroad, it would manufacture them at home. Eike hoped one day to supply Petrobras too. And he got special encouragement from Dilma on her visit.

In a temporary auditorium at the port, a big screen announced the delivery of OGX's first cargo of oil. After the national anthem played, with Eike uncertainly mouthing along, Governor Sérgio Cabral stepped up to a podium to introduce his faithful campaign donor. He praised Eike's "Fordist vision." Perhaps concerned people wouldn't get the reference, he then praised Eike's "Steve Jobsian vision." He said, "You're continuing the work of a great Brazilian, your father, just like Dilma is continuing the work of a great Brazilian, Lula." Behind Cabral on stage, Eliezer sat beaming next to his son. Thor, the dutiful heir, was there too—three generations of Batistas.

Dilma spoke next. "Eike is our standard, our hope, and above all the pride of Brazil," she declared. "He truly understands the interests of his country." Then she hinted at the possibility of state support for his oil company, the only one of his major ventures that didn't win BNDES funds. "Between Petrobras and OGX, there isn't and there mustn't be any spirit of competition," she said. "Both would have much to gain from a partnership." This even though Eike had raided the company for engineers.

After her speech, Dilma donned the bright orange jacket of OGX's rig workers, specially decorated with black handprints of faux crude. Eike wore one too, unzipped low enough to reveal a pink tie. He gave her a miniature barrel of oil as a memento. As they stood side by side onstage, he raised both hands in Vs of victory. Then he crossed his forearms to form an X, his wide smile revealing bright white teeth.

DILMA COULDN'T HAVE KNOWN IT THEN, but she had consecrated Eike as national champion just in time for his first major stumble. Even as she visited Açu, his dream team had run into problems. Pressure was falling in OGX's first well, and to keep up the flow of oil, they might have to inject water into the reservoir—unusual at this stage. In March, two months after it came online, Eike had told me the well was pumping fifteen thousand barrels a day, but this wasn't true. The number had dipped below ten thousand by then.

Hoping this shortfall was a fluke, Eike decided against making it public until the second well started pumping. But the second well didn't work any better, and it dawned on his engineers that they'd misread the geology in OGX's main field. It didn't contain one uninterrupted reservoir but many separate pockets of oil. This meant the company would need more wells to slurp it all up, drastically increasing costs. And OGX was already spending more to extract the oil than it earned selling it.

Eike stalled as long as he could, and for a while he maintained the appearance that everything was proceeding according to plan. He announced an investment in the Rock in Rio music festival, posing with an electric guitar as he beamed for the cameras. He stopped by São Paulo's stock exchange to launch a new spinoff, CCX Carvão, which would develop coal deposits in Colombia. Following the Emirates' lead, General Electric then announced a three-hundred-million-dollar investment in EBX. GE's chairman and chief executive, Jeffrey Immelt, called Eike the world's—not just Brazil's—greatest entrepreneur.

Behind the scenes at OGX, though, too many people knew what was going on, and as information leaked out, OGX's stock price slumped. Traders mounted bets against the company by executing "short sales"—borrowing shares, selling them in the open market, and buying them back later at a lower price—an operation that itself can push the price down. Finally, Eike had no choice but to release news of the problems to the public. And so on June 26, after the markets closed, the company filed a statement whose bland language was like cold water after the bullishness of filings past. OGX's first two oil wells, it said, were each pumping just five thousand barrels a day.

This was a massive disappointment. Just months earlier Eike had trumpeted the potential for each well to pump *twenty* thousand barrels a day. But the problem was not just that Eike had pitched the next Petrobras. It was that he had borrowed money accordingly. Now it didn't look like OGX would bring in cash fast enough to pay back its debts when they came due. At this rate, even the interest payments might be a problem. Eike had priced everything to perfection, as finance people say, and fallen short of perfection. It threw all his PowerPoint projections into doubt.

The reaction was immediate. When markets opened the next morning, OGX's shares plunged by twenty-five percent, wiping out a quarter of the company's market value in a single day. Eike's grand vision, the interconnectedness of his empire, now became a liability. His oil company wasn't the only one losing money on its sales. Eike had bid aggressively for contracts he couldn't yet fulfill. MMX, Eike's mining company, had agreed to ship iron ore to Korean and Chinese buyers, but with its port unfinished and production capacity lacking, it had to buy the ore from rival firms and ship through rival ports. To meet its contracts with utilities, MPX, Eike's energy company, had to buy electricity at a premium from rival power companies. OSX Brasil, the oil services company, still hadn't built its shipyard, so to supply OGX Petróleo, it had to buy an oil platform from Singapore. The port of Açu likewise remained a construction site. And Eike had piled leverage separately onto each of these companies. Adding it all up, his empire carried around fifteen billion dollars in debt, more than the entire nation of Panama. Even the bad news was nation-size with Eike.

Startups are supposed to lose money at first. But Eike was in the commodities business, and with China's economy slowing, commodity prices were coming down. More urgently for the spokesman of Brazil, Brazil fever was waning. Previously willing to forgive his delays for the prospect of fat profit margins, investors now lost their patience. "I just don't know what I can believe anymore," one fund manager told me, sounding like someone whose spouse had cheated on him one too many times. With all this dammed-up skepticism over the years, OGX's letdown served as the *gota d'água*—the drop of water that makes the reservoir overflow.

Eike set up an emergency conference call to convince investors that OGX remained a viable enterprise. He reminded them that the company still sat on several billion dollars in cash and a big portfolio of offshore prospects. "We're going to produce lots of oil," he insisted. Then he invoked his past: "I would like to stress that throughout my career I have taken a lot of risks in developing a lot of projects. The only risk I have never taken is the financial risk of not being able to execute my projects."

This wasn't true, as the collapse of TVX had shown, but no one called him out on it. Not that they believed him. The day after the conference call, OGX's stock price tanked again. In just two trading sessions, the company lost nearly half its market value. Like dominoes, his other companies' share prices tumbled too—and four billion dollars disappeared from Eike's net worth in that same span. Rushing to cover every new development, the Bloomberg newsroom in São Paulo worked itself into a frenzy, and the stress of it all mingled with a kind of disbelieving glee. Improbable as Eike's wealth had always seemed, I was stunned to see how fast it evaporated. In just the three months since the Emirates deal, it dropped from $34.5 billion to around $20 billion. And yet he rejected the idea he was down at all. "My fortune is in my assets," he tweeted. "Since I haven't sold a single share, I haven't lost anything!"

IN HIS BLUSTER, EIKE made an unintentional point about the nature of a net worth estimate. If never having sold a share meant he'd never lost anything, it also meant he'd never really gained those thirty billion dollars and change. Since his companies made no profits, he earned no dividends. Over the years he'd earned cash from selling pieces of his empire, but he put almost all of it back in, buying shares in his own IPOs or starting new side ventures. His wealth existed mostly on paper, in the form of stock certificates. You could calculate their value by the prices on the exchange, but even that was subjective, because if Eike were to try and sell all his shares at once, there wouldn't be enough demand to absorb them; the price would collapse.

After the deal with the Emirates, when Bloomberg raised his net worth estimate to $34.5 billion, it reflected an even vaguer concept of value. We turned a single investor's bet, albeit a big one, into an objective measure of worth. The whole ranking enterprise was in fact inherently subjective. We created models, we consulted with analysts, but if we tweaked one assumption in our cash calculator, it might raise or lower someone's net worth by hundreds of millions of dollars. It was a system of educated guesses. Since we appraised AUX by comparing it to other gold companies, the value likewise fluctuated wildly depending on which ones we picked.

The list itself also became a tool for Eike's own PR efforts. But it was a double-edged sword. Eike's fixation on rich lists wasn't just about ego. His credibility in the marketplace fed off the size of his fortune, which in turn fed off his credibility in the marketplace, and this meant his image was as much an asset as the oil and iron ore he sat on. By saying he wasn't quite so rich after all, we threw a wrench in his perpetual-motion machine.

As Eike's net worth deflated, Brazilians on social networks called him *bolhonário,* a play on the Portuguese words for bubble *(bolha)* and billionaire *(bilionário).* His celebrity was the kind that shares a border with schadenfreude. The press delighted in his decline, making it constant front-page news. Former associates emerged saying they'd known all along he was a fraud. One was J. C. Cavalcanti, a mining tycoon who'd worked with Eike on an iron ore project that became part of MMX. He said, "The only thing Eike really produces these days is a very good noodle dish at Mr. Lam, a Chinese restaurant he opened, where they also serve wonderful shrimp."

A billionaire himself, J.C. invited me to meet him in the lobby of a São Paulo hotel he partly owned. I was curious to see what sort of people Eike had struck deals with before his rise to fame. The man showed up in a caravan of black SUVs driven by bodyguards. Short but portly, he had white hair and a white beard and wore all black. He spoke of himself like a ring announcer introducing a boxer: "J.C., the sniffer of minerals, the pointer, the hunting dog . . ." These days he was developing rare-earth deposits in northeastern Brazil that he claimed to be worth eight billion dollars. He told me how, when he was visiting Beijing and strolling through Tiananmen Square, a bunch of Chinese lined up to get his autograph. At first he assumed they thought he was George Lucas. Except that one kid in line told him no, they all knew who he was, the king of mining. (Either that or his translator had decided to flatter him.) As J.C. spoke, he sometimes closed his eyes for a minute at a time. I noticed that his beard had left dandruff on his shirt.

Much of what J.C. said made sense, though. The market had failed to predict OGX's problems, he said, because stock analysts are not geologists. They understand numbers but rarely how mining or oil extraction works. Of course, Eike had led even some experts astray. After acquiring a piece of MMX in 2008, Anglo American, the South African mining giant, had spent billions to get it up and running but hit untold logistical complications. "Anglo was *engambelado*," J.C. said—seduced, coaxed, deceived. "They fell for Eike's blue eyes."

It was remarkable to see how the same global investing class that had very recently thronged to Eike now backed away, herd style. The Nissan car company and China's Wuhan Iron & Steel both canceled plans for factories at Açu, and others followed suit. They had signed "memorandums of understanding" to set up there, but these clearly meant little. The consensus was emerging that Eike had oversold everything. And yet in press interviews he insisted otherwise. Once he had thirty wells pumping, he said, no one would care if two of them produced just five thousand barrels a day.

Eike needed to show the market he was doing something. So he fired Paulo Mendonça, OGX's chief executive, and replaced him with another of his poached Petrobras veterans. He fired other top execs too, but people in the market just chattered about "rearranging the deck chairs on the Titanic." To some of his associates, he appeared manic depressive. He would stay home for days at a time and then show up at the office with mysterious bandages on his face, full of moon-shot ideas—like somehow raising enough money to buy back all his companies' shares on the exchange. "If the market doesn't want me, I want me," he started saying.

In October Eike made a more modest announcement. It was still pretty ballsy by most standards. He signed a contract promising that if OGX ran out of capital, he would put a billion dollars of his own money in. Hoping to send the message that the company was undervalued after the sell-off, and that he still believed in its future, he promised to buy new shares at a hefty premium to their current market price. He made similar promises for MMX and OSX, and his big talk inspired enough confidence to give the shares a little bounce.

Despite his ups and downs, Eike hadn't lost his sense of humor yet. On a visit to Bloomberg's office in New York, he joked, "You guys could publish that list only on the days I'm up, you know." Truth was, even as the foundations of his empire trembled, he had reasons for optimism. Dilma still stood by him. In November, the government would announce a partnership between Eike, the BNDES, and IBM to build a microchip factory. In typical fashion, Eike called it a future Brazilian Intel.

He had another important ally. Lula, even as ex-president, remained a power broker. And lately he'd been visiting Eike at the Serrador building. I started hearing whispers that, if things got bad enough, the government would bail Eike out.

CHAPTER 8

THE PROFIT MOTIVE

A NEW RICHEST MAN, MERITOCRACY, AND THE VALUE OF MONEY

"Money in and of itself isn't what fascinates me."
—JORGE PAULO LEMANN ($20 BILLION)

"Jorge Paulo created a whole management culture
in Brazil that is extraordinary."
—EIKE BATISTA ($13 BILLION)

DESPITE HIS EFFORTS TO STANCH THE BLEEDING, EIKE'S WEALTH continued to shrink. In November 2012, his net worth slipped below nineteen billion dollars, and suddenly, for the first time in three years, he was not the richest person in Brazil. When I asked his people for comment, though, they sent this oddly upbeat statement from him: "Brazil deserves to have more Brazilians on this list. May all businessmen continue investing and creating jobs, like we do at EBX!" After that Eike went silent for a while, retreating from Twitter and TV as he worked to save his empire.

A buyout tycoon named Jorge Paulo Lemann took Eike's place as Brazil's richest man. I asked his people for comment about his new title, but he had none. Throughout his seventy-three years, he had mostly avoided press. Few had heard of him, in Brazil or abroad, even though he and his partners at 3G Capital had acquired two of

America's top consumer brands, Budweiser and Burger King. And they were working on yet another. With Warren Buffett backing them, they would soon announce the takeover of H. J. Heinz, the Pittsburgh ketchup company. Valued at twenty-eight billion dollars, it was the largest acquisition in the history of the food industry—but not the largest in Lemann's history. In 2008 he got control of Anheuser-Busch by orchestrating a fifty-two-billion-dollar merger with Belgium's InBev. The company that emerged was responsible for brewing one in every five beers drunk on earth.

I ended up profiling Lemann after the Heinz deal. I wasn't too thrilled about the assignment at first. Next to Eike, he felt boring. He struck me as one of those high school overachiever types you want to dislike but can't because they're too nice. He's a tennis pro who played Wimbledon and the Davis Cup as a young man. He funds scholarships at American universities for smart young Brazilians. Also, it was hard to get people to talk about him. When I called up his friends and business associates, some said he'd asked them not to speak about him with journalists. A few did agree to speak on the record, and several others off the record, but the praise was just about unanimous. One source I spoke to was an economist named Arminio Fraga. He worked under Lemann in the eighties, later advised George Soros, and then served as president of the central bank before setting up his own investment fund—Gávea, one of the initial investors in OGX. "Lemann carried out a revolution in the way people think about business," he said.

Mostly unknown to the public at large, Lemann is a legend in the world of money. He's seen as the man who brought meritocracy to Brazil, proof the American Dream can flourish in this nepotistic soil. Eike might proclaim these same values, but Lemann symbolized something very different. One article called him the "anti–Eike Batista." He appealed to a discreeter slice of the elite who found Eike crass and gaudy, a seller of unlikely dreams and a self-promoter. I spoke to a management consultant named Vicente Falconi, who'd worked with Lemann since the nineties, and in his description, Lemann simply took intellectual pleasure in his pursuits. His net worth had hit twenty billion dollars, but money per se didn't matter to him; the challenge of it mattered.

Reporting the profile, I got sort of starry-eyed myself. Lemann's drive for perpetual improvement, in business and in tennis, made me think of a quote from *Infinite Jest,* the novel by David Foster Wallace: "Tennis's beauty's infinite roots are self-competitive. You compete with your own limits to transcend the self in imagination and execution." Maybe it's a coincidence, but while reporting on Lemann, I got some kind of entrepreneurial itch and started to think about quitting my job to write this book.

LEMANN'S STORY IS IMPORTANT for what it reveals about the values of the business world, in Brazil and beyond. Hero of meritocracy, he was self-made but not the rags-to-riches kind. His dad, scion of a family of cheese makers from Emmental, Switzerland, moved to Brazil and opened a dairy company known as Leco, a brand you still see on shelves here. His mom was the daughter of Swiss immigrants who exported cocoa from northeastern Brazil. He attended the American School of Rio de Janeiro, where students voted him most likely to succeed, even though he spent most of his time surfing and playing tennis. His dad died when he was a teenager, and it was his mom who encouraged him to apply to Harvard.

He once spoke about his Harvard years to a group of students in São Paulo. Wearing a gray suit that looked overlarge on his wiry frame, under auditorium lights that made his white hair glow, he said he didn't take to it at first. He hated the cold and missed the waves back in Rio. So he made up a system to get his bachelor's in just three years. Before signing up for a class, he interviewed the professor and students who'd already taken it. He also discovered that the library archived previous years' finals, and that they varied little from semester to semester, allowing for easy cramming. Harvard mainly was worthwhile, he said, because it made him get creative to finish early.

One thing Lemann and Eike shared was an appetite for adventure. Lemann told the students about a trip home on summer vacation from Harvard. A powerful storm was making waves that broke perilously late, right on the beach. They were more than thirty feet tall, he claimed. Used to ten-foot waves, he decided to surf them anyway. "I took the wave and felt the blood go to my feet," he said, a smile spreading across his wrinkled face. "It was a lot faster than I was used to, and a lot taller, but I went for it, and I managed to get out before it crashed. My adrenaline was at the maximum." At key moments in his career, he went on, "I thought back to that wave I surfed in Copacabana far more than I thought about the things I learned in college. It gave me a certain self-confidence when it came to taking risks."

After graduating with an economics degree, Lemann juggled his tennis career with a series of jobs in the financial industry, which was effervescent in the miracle years of the military regime. In 1971 he teamed up with some fellow traders to take over a Rio brokerage called Garantia. Lemann had heard about Goldman Sachs's partnership model at Harvard, and he liked the idea of giving managers a stake in the business—"skin in the game," as finance people say—to align their incentives with the boss's. At Garantia he and his partners instituted the Goldman model on steroids. Instead of giving away shares once a year for a job well done, he let the best performers use *two* annual bonuses to *buy* shares. Because Garantia offered lower salaries than the competition, becoming a partner was a risk and a sacrifice. Owning shares might make you rich on paper, but you had to forgo the fancy new car for now. Seniority carried little weight, and for top performers to win a larger share of the bonus pool, the laggards got crowded out. Some called the system Darwinian.

In the early days of Garantia, fancy cars were frowned upon anyway. Lemann set the example of austerity by driving a ten-year-old Passat. He didn't use designer watches or even a tie. He wore khaki pants and rolled-up shirtsleeves, setting a casual style that still reigns among Rio financial types. He scoffed at the cushy standards of Brazil's corporate scene. Everyone in middle management then had his own personal secretary, but Lemann shared one with several partners. He knocked down the walls between offices and sat with everyone else in an open pit. This had a practical end, because his talent was to listen to everyone's ideas and synthesize them. He was a strategist; he oversaw and delegated.

Multinational corporations used to offer the best jobs in Brazil, but by the eighties Garantia was one of the most sought-after employers for smart young Brazilian men. (Even today there are few women in Lemann's world.) Résumés didn't matter as much as *faca no dente e brilho no olho,* sharp teeth and bright eyes. Candidates had to go through a gauntlet of interviews with Lemann and eight or ten other partners. The partners came up with an acronym for the profile they sought: PSD, for "poor, smart, deep desire to get rich." Sometimes the partners posed odd or offensive questions just to throw you off balance. One guy I talked to remembered being asked whether he had sex with his girlfriend. Others had their sexuality questioned outright. If you made it through, no one held your hand on the job. No one gave you a task; you had to figure out for yourself how to contribute. The first person to go home for the day would receive ironic applause. The words *fanático* and *obsessivo* were considered compliments.

Lemann's current outfit, 3G Capital, is so named because its three main partners came from Garantia. Lemann is one; the other two clawed their way to the top of the Garantia system. They were prototypical PSDs. Marcel Telles first joined Garantia as a glorified *office boy*—an English phrase Brazilians use to describe someone who gets coffee and runs errands. Carlos Alberto Sicupira had started and sold his first brokerage by the time he was eighteen. He joined Garantia after he met Lemann practicing a sport known as underwater fishing, which involves spearing your prey. Once he caught a 664-pound blue marlin, a world record. Telles and Sicupira are now billionaires too.

———

WHEN THE TAKEOVER OF Heinz became public in February 2013, the American financial press called out Warren Buffett for teaming up with Lemann. 3G was known as a private-equity firm, and Buffett had long criticized this style of investing. When private-equity firms take over a company, he said, they load it up with debt, strip it down, and fire people to free up cash and pay themselves dividends. Then they resell whatever's left over. But Lemann takes a different approach, more in line with Buffett's own, because he and his partners aim to hold on to their biggest takeovers forever. Of course, they do follow one part of the private-equity playbook. Sicupira has a saying: "Costs are like fingernails: You have to cut them constantly."

I knew a few foreign entrepreneurs in São Paulo, and even they got a shine in their eye when Lemann came up. Much of the fascination, I realized, was practical: *How did he do it?* In many ways he embodied the style of John D. Rockefeller, "daring in design, cautious in execution," in the words of the biographer Ron Chernow. The few times he ever spoke about the reasons for his success, though, Lemann minimized his own talent. In 1989, when he bought the Brahma beer company, he explained the move by saying he looked around Latin America and noticed that the richest families all owned breweries. "These guys couldn't all be geniuses," he said. "It's the business that must be good." He used to hand out a list of maxims to Garantia employees, and one was "Innovations that create value are useful, but copying what works well is more practical."

When Lemann started taking over companies in the real economy—first a retailer known as Lojas Americanas, later Brahma—he put Sicupira and Telles in charge of making them more profitable. They put Lemann's maxim into practice. From Sam Walton, the founder of Walmart, they learned about squeezing suppliers to deliver low prices to customers. From Jack Welch, the longtime CEO of General Electric, they adopted the twenty-seventy-ten rule: Promote the top twenty percent of your employees, maintain the seventy in the middle, and fire the rest. Mixing and matching the best from all over, their constant ingredients were ruthless cost-cutting and Garantia-style incentives. They got rid of executive perks like dedicated elevators and business-class flights and gave large stock bonuses to the best performers. It worked so well that Telles once referred to their operation, with self-deprecating humor, as a "one-trick pony." The trick was a formula for making money.

Lemann did have his personal failures. His dedication to work, for instance, was slightly insane. In 1999 a driver was taking the three young children from his second marriage to school when two cars blocked the street. Would-be kidnappers opened fire. Wounded, the driver still managed to get the children to safety. Lemann soon would move his family to Switzerland, but on the day of the shooting, his children didn't miss school. Nor did Lemann miss any meetings. To his business associates, the only sign of something wrong was that he arrived late.

As it had done since his surfing days, Lemann's intensity went beyond work. Even while overseeing mergers and acquisitions and a full-service investment bank, he still played tennis most mornings at six-thirty and competed in, and sometimes won, world championships for "veterans" (middle-aged dudes). Eventually the adrenaline took its toll. At fifty-four he had a heart attack. He was forced to take a year off just as Garantia reached its peak. In a sign of its clout, the bank managed to bring Margaret Thatcher to Brazil for a meeting with local businessmen in 1994. And that year Garantia cleared a billion dollars in profit. Pioneers of risky American-style financial bets, its traders got cocky. They sold tons of insurance on Brazilian government bonds without properly hedging their bets, and when the Asian financial crisis exploded in 1997, sending interest rates soaring in emerging markets, Garantia lost hundreds of millions of dollars. Telles would later explain the disaster by blaming Lemann's absence and the fact that he himself, along with Sicupira, were busy with their outside takeovers. Whatever the truth, Lemann and his partners decided to sell the bank to Credit Suisse. They got

$675 million, a good deal less than they would have a couple of years earlier.

Like Eike, Lemann knew that failure is just part of entrepreneurship. The sale of Garantia was a blow to Lemann, the end of an era, but it left him with cash to invest. So he bought a stake in Gillette, the razor manufacturer, and won a seat on the board. He probably did it just to spend time with Buffett, who also owned a piece of the company. In board meetings he impressed Buffett with his quiet, thoughtful style, and they became friends. It was this friendship that would lead to their joint offer for Heinz in 2013.

GRADUALLY I REALIZED THAT Lemann's business-class appeal went beyond the nuts and bolts of his empire building. I couldn't help but think of *Roots of Brazil,* the book my girlfriend had recommended to me. In it Sérgio Buarque de Holanda came up with two archetypes: the worker and the adventurer. He believed that it was the methodical worker who colonized New England, while the precocious adventurer colonized Brazil. The Portuguese came for quick profits to send back home, he wrote, not for any lasting project of civilization—"riches that come at the cost of daring, not riches that come at the cost of work."

Buarque made a common lament, that the Protestant ethic was not a thing in Brazil. In the nineteenth century, an English traveler named Thomas Ewbank wrote about meeting the heir of a wealthy Brazilian family fallen on hard times and suggesting he find a job. The young Brazilian replied with horror, "Work! Work! We have blacks to do that." In colonial Brazil the idea of effort was so abhorrent that, according to the historian Gilberto Freyre, you'd see velvet-laden lords in rural parts being carried about by their slaves in palanquins. For a wealthy landowner's son, educated in Portugal and settled in Rio, the only acceptable jobs were in law or civil service, which afforded you a title and a place in the imperial machine but kept actual work to a minimum.

When the ruling class brought over Europeans to whiten the racial mix in the nineteenth century, their hope was for Germanic immigrants to offset the indolence of the Portuguese. Northern Europeans, they thought, were a race that could build a modern society. The idea lives on. Even today I'll hear Brazilians say they wish the Dutch, who ruled a piece of northeastern Brazil for a few decades in the seventeenth century, had colonized the whole country. In this light it's easier to understand the fascination of Lemann. One magazine profile said his Swiss dad's "greatest legacy" was the Protestant work ethic. In Buarque's taxonomy, Lemann is a worker.

If one applies Buarque's categories in the billionaire world, it's obvious who the adventurer is. In his haste to erect the greatest business empire Brazil had ever seen, Eike Batista acted as if he could skip the steps in between, as if just concocting the idea was enough. He didn't yearn to build the empire so much as arrive at its pinnacle. He loved the phrase *unlocking value,* which for him meant identifying an opportunity, buying the asset cheap, doing some groundwork, and selling for a quick profit. But Eike also clung to the ideal of the Protestant ethic. Once he tweeted: "I was born middle class! In my case, once middle class always middle class! I didn't change!! I continue to work like before and I haven't lost my Humility!" True to Brazil's racial mythology, he credited his German mother for instilling in him the value of work.

Of course, Eike's claim to humble beginnings was hard to swallow, given how he leaned on his dad's connections to build his fortune. Lemann, on the other hand, despite his well-heeled upbringing, had made a reputation as someone who genuinely rose through simple hard work and individual merit. Fernando Henrique Cardoso met Lemann when he was president of Brazil in the nineties, and they became friends; when news of the Anheuser-Busch InBev merger first leaked in 2008, they were on vacation together with their wives in the Gobi desert. When I asked him about Lemann's path to success, he told me, "Lemann's approach to business is the opposite of those who live under the umbrella of the state banks, expecting to receive subsidies and favorable interest rates. I have never seen him ask for any benefit or favor from the government."

I put this quote in the first draft of my *Bloomberg Businessweek* profile of Lemann, but my editor deemed it too fawning to include. I realized I might have swallowed some of the Kool-Aid when he said I made Lemann sound like The Most Interesting Man in the World, a debonair character from a beer ad campaign who carried out impossible feats without losing his cool—spearfishing, giant wave surfing, Wimbledon playing, all while buying up famous American brands.

The other problem with Cardoso's statement was that it wasn't exactly true. Lemann may not need the state banks' umbrella, but he receives it just the same. In the past decade, the BNDES has lent more than four billion dollars at taxpayer-subsidized rates to Lemann's companies in Brazil, even though he has ample access to cheap credit abroad.

There were other chinks in the myth of Lemann. Like most other businessmen, he leaned on his connections when he needed to. In 1976, he reached a tentative agreement to combine Garantia into a joint venture with JPMorgan in Brazil. He came to regret his decision, fearing he would lose control of his baby, but could see no way to back out without losing face with one of the greats of Wall Street. So, according to a book about him by the journalist Cristiane Correa, he turned to his contacts at the central bank and asked them to impose a condition for approval of the deal: that he must hold fifty-one percent of the new venture. When JPMorgan learned of this condition, it withdrew from the negotiations. The move might have been deft, but it belonged more to Buarque's "cordial man" than to any ideal of laissez-faire.

Another episode took place when Cardoso was president. In 1999 Lemann and his partners merged the Brahma beer company with its main local competitor, creating AmBev. Since AmBev would control nearly three-quarters of Brazil's beer sales, Lemann deployed a team of advisers to lobby officials at the antitrust agency. They framed the tie-up as a matter of economic sovereignty, for it would create a national champion too large to be taken over by foreign beer giants. There's no sign Cardoso pulled any strings to help him, but Lemann's crew played at least one sneaky trick to ensure swift approval. On the eve of approval, a court ordered a freeze on the proceedings. To keep the order from reaching the antitrust agency, according to Correa's book, his people tied up all its fax lines by sending hours of darkened pages. That allowed the proceedings to continue while Lemann's lawyers obtained a reversal of the freeze. Late that same night, the antitrust agency approved the deal with a few minor restrictions.

Once a business gets big enough, dealings with the government are inevitable. But the way Lemann approaches these dealings doesn't fit with his free market symbolism. AmBev is one of Brazil's top campaign donors. When I asked Lemann's PR reps what those donations are supposed to achieve, I got an official statement with the standard line that they "strengthen the democratic debate." When I followed up asking how strengthening the debate serves AmBev's shareholders, Lemann's people refused to answer. With Lemann's ruthless approach to costs, though, that can't be money wasted. So what is he buying? In a conference call with investors in 2014, AmBev's CEO credited the company's "dialogue" with the government for getting a tax increase on beer postponed. He framed it as a "win-win" that would protect jobs and investment. And maybe it was. But the interests of billionaires may not always mesh with the interests of ordinary citizens, no matter how much the Odebrechts, the Marinhos, and Lemann too might believe it.

Tráfico de influência—"influence peddling"—is illegal in Brazil. But while lobbying occupies a legal gray area, most "dialogue" between campaign donors and elected officials is considered kosher. And yet Lemann hasn't always played by the rules. In 2005 Brazil's securities and exchange commission, the CVM, accused him and his partners of abusing their control of AmBev to enrich themselves at minority shareholders' expense. Ahead of the company's merger with Interbrew in Belgium, they had sold nonvoting shares in AmBev and used stock options to buy voting shares. This proved profitable once the merger was announced, because, thanks to the way they had structured the deal, the price of the nonvoting shares sank while that of the voting shares soared. In 2009 the three men settled for just two and a half million dollars each, a fraction of their allegedly improper gains. As usual in these cases, they didn't have to admit any wrongdoing.

After my profile of Lemann came out, one of his press people called me to complain that I'd included this episode in the story. She didn't see why I had to talk about it. No one in Lemann's world talked about his contradictions. But either Lemann is more Brazilian than his admirers think, or countries with a Protestant ethic, like the United States, are more *malandro* than people think. Looking at it this way, lobbying—a hallowed American tradition—is the essence of "cordial man."

LEMANN'S FANS MAKE A big deal of his personal austerity and scoff at the ostentation of Eike. But this too may be wishful thinking. In the nineties Lemann used to drive his old Passat in Rio, but after he moved to São Paulo he acquired a $7.5 million EC-155 helicopter for his buyout firm. A luxury real estate broker (the same one who showed me the penthouse with the butterfly wall in Rio) told me Lemann kept an outwardly discreet but inwardly lavish, sprawling apartment near the beach in Leblon. This is nothing crazy for someone worth twenty billion dollars, but also nothing like his friend Warren Buffett, who's lived in the same modest Omaha home for six decades. Personal austerity also has a practical end: freeing up money to reinvest in the business.

In a way, Eike in his flashiness was just more honest, more transparent about the power he wielded. People who know Lemann told me he hates seeing his name on rich lists, but this seemed to me an aversion more to publicity than to riches. If nothing else, Lemann sees the utility of money as a marker of his own success. "Money in and of itself isn't what fascinates me," he said once. "It's simply a way of measuring if the business is going well or not." Hinting at the scale of his ambition, he told a tennis magazine that he decided to dedicate himself to business after realizing he'd never be one of the world's ten best tennis players. "I saw that I would never be an *astro,*" he said—a star.

Despite his outward modesty, Lemann never made a secret of his philanthropy. He has a foundation that carries his name. Over the years he's funded fifteen hundred scholarships for Brazilians to study abroad and made generous gifts to Harvard, Stanford, and UCLA. He spends money to improve Brazilian public education too. These are good causes. If you add it all up, though, it appears to be less than what his beer empire spends on lobbying and political campaigns in the United States and Brazil. One of Lemann's largest gifts, a fourteen-million-dollar donation to the University of Illinois, amounted to less than 0.1 percent of his wealth. For someone with a net worth of a hundred thousand dollars, an equivalent donation would be less than a hundred dollars. When I asked Lemann's people what was bigger—his charitable giving, or the taxes he avoids by putting 3G's funds in the Cayman Islands—they refused to answer.

Working at Bloomberg, I saw how polarizing philanthropy can be. For every person who believes that it fills in where government falls short, there's another who finds it deeply annoying. I never got so many inflamed comments as when I wrote about the Giving Pledge. Warren Buffett teamed up with Bill Gates to create the pledge in 2010, and whenever a new batch of billionaires signed up to give away at least half their wealth, I got a flood of emails from readers calling them fakes and narcissists. I heard their charity called legal tax evasion. There's something to this. In Brazil, where inheritance taxes top out at four percent in most states, philanthropy is rare.

But there's more to charity than keeping your money from the taxman. Eike donated millions of dollars to national parks while fighting fines from environmental regulators. Why? When I visited

EBX headquarters, Wagner spoke of Eike's gifts as if they were investments, meant to win over government officials and the public at large. Lemann's charity doesn't appear entirely pure either. In 1995, one of his foundations awarded a scholarship to a young woman whose dad, José Serra, then served as health minister—an important man to have on your side when you own a beer company.

Eike, though, sought glory too. He didn't want to be just the world's richest man, he said, but the world's greatest philanthropist. This way he could inscribe his name in history like Carnegie, Rockefeller. Even when the desire to help is genuine, this is the dream of an empire builder. Take Bill Gates, who reclaimed his spot as the world's richest man in 2013. First he created the world's largest software company, then he created the world's largest private foundation. Whatever the benefits his philanthropy has brought—and there are many—the fact is that he hopped from one world-size conquest to another.

Billionaires never put their giving in these terms. Gates says he wants to "give back." He implies he owes something to society, and maybe he does. His money comes from Microsoft, and like other tech companies, Microsoft keeps billions of dollars offshore to avoid paying taxes at home. For years, to maintain its dominance of the market, he also engaged in anticompetitive practices that brought government lawsuits from the United States and the European Union. What did Gates's monopoly cost us? It's hard to calculate the size of that debt.

Buffett has his contradictions too. He became a hero to social progressives by calling for higher taxes on billionaires, without offering to pay them unilaterally. Until tax laws change, he prefers to choose how his surplus cash is distributed. This reasoning is nothing new. Buffett reportedly gave Gates a copy of Andrew Carnegie's *Gospel of Wealth*, first published in 1889. In his essay, Carnegie declared that it's the duty of the rich to give away their fortunes. Nobly, he said his accumulated profits belonged not to him but to society.

He just didn't trust society to allocate them on his behalf. The rich man, he said, should act as "agent and trustee for his poorer brethren, bringing to their service his superior wisdom, experience, and ability to administer, doing for them better than they would or could do for themselves."

As the greatest philanthropist of his day, Carnegie managed to remake history. Still surrounded by the libraries and music halls he funded, most people forgot how he amassed his fortune to begin with: by taking illegal kickbacks as a railroad executive, leveraging them into a steel empire protected by government tariffs, colluding with his fellow steel makers to fix prices, and busting unions to keep work hours long and wages low. According to the biographer David Nasaw, Carnegie believed all the while that his philanthropic ends justified the brutal means he used to build his wealth. Though not a religious man, he conceived a kind of divine order that placed him at the top. He held up the writings of Herbert Spencer, a philosopher who saw Carnegie and his fellow tycoons as harbingers of a natural march toward prosperity and perfection.

It makes sense, in this light, that the billionaires who oppose higher taxes often philanthropize the most—like Stephen Schwarzman of Blackstone, the private-equity giant. They too want to *give back,* just on their own terms. Governments are not efficient, the thinking goes; businessmen are. Take this vision to its logical end, and it's public policy privatized. Philanthropy can do real good, and government can make bad spending decisions, but as the German shipping magnate Peter Kramer put it, "These guys have so much power through their wealth that they, instead of the government elected by the people, can decide what's good and what should be promoted and subsidized." He was talking about the people who signed the Giving Pledge.

Whatever the contradictions, Lemann hasn't signed the Giving Pledge. For all his meritocratic symbolism, he apparently plans to leave most of his fortune to his six children. Along with Telles's and

Sicupira's heirs, they've received training from a young age in the art of managing great inheritances.

LEMANN COMMENTED RECENTLY ON the inequality debate. "Brazil is full of people who think equality is great," he said. "I think equality is great too, just that it doesn't work. Equality of opportunity, yes. But equality for equality's sake . . . People are not equal."

Meritocracy, like any word, loses its meaning if you repeat it often enough. I started to feel this, immersed in Lemannland. As a concept it's hard to argue with, but as it travels, it gets diluted. Among well-to-do Brazilians, *meritocracia* became an incantation against the mediocrity of government and those who survive on its teat. That book by the Globo exec—*We Are Not Racists,* which called affirmative action unfair—was one example. Once I met a twentysomething named Beth who complained about Bolsa Família, the welfare program; she had attended private school, still lived with her parents, and worked at her father's textile company. My dentist shared Beth's disdain. "Some of us, like you and me, have to work," she told me once while poking an instrument in my mouth. "But we have these people who do nothing and get to live the good life." When I asked her if she puts her money into CDBs—high-interest certificates of deposit—she said yes. She was surprised when I pointed out that this too was a public subsidy, a much larger one, since the government pays huge sums for banks to hold its bonds. I should have mentioned that three-quarters of the adults on Bolsa Família also work for a living.

There's a confusion here about personal effort and public assistance, how we achieve prosperity and who deserves a piece of it. Until recently, Eike's Brazilian Dream—something like the Horatio Alger myth that anyone who works hard enough, no matter how poor, can get rich—never found much traction among ordinary Brazilians. The poor believed the game was rigged against them. That sounds fatalistic, but they had plenty of reasons. I met a few people in the favela—like Rene Silva, founder of the *Voz da Comunidade* newspaper—with the wit and will to succeed but without the structure or starting capital. Even Andrew Carnegie credited his success not so much to his own personal genius as to America's environment of opportunity, a common creation of the nation's civic culture. The myth of Lemann, the myth of pure meritocracy, can be dangerous: a wishful justification for an unequal status quo.

I should probably put the lens on myself. Some people admired my guts in quitting my job in New York and moving to South America to become a reporter. But I usually left out the fact that my grandparents gave me ten thousand dollars when I graduated college, and I had this to sustain me as I learned the ropes of reporting, and along the way my parents gave me a few thousand more. Even if I ran out of money and Bloomberg hadn't offered me a job, I could have moved back to my parents' place in Albuquerque to regain my footing. All this also made it easier to consider quitting to write this book. It's easier to scratch the entrepreneurial itch when you have something to fall back on.

ONE SOURCE I SPOKE to about Lemann was a businesswoman from São Paulo who's known him for over a decade. When I questioned the myth of Lemann, she said, "But don't people need myths? Can't myths be a good thing?" Maybe she's right. And yet I wondered what exactly he represents, even without his inconsistencies. The irony of Lemann and his fellow billionaires is that they insist they don't do what they do for the money; yet they equally insist, with few exceptions, on the imperative to maximize profits above all else. Businessmen tout Lemann's success because they measure it in terms of money. With ever larger takeovers, he and his partners extract great economies of scale, widening the profit margins of the giant companies they combine. Since they merged Anheuser-Busch with InBev in 2008, the stock has far outperformed all the benchmark indexes. The company pays out juicy dividends, returning more value to investors than ever. And as the largest shareholders, Lemann, Telles, and Sicupira have gotten richest of all. So by the metric of money, they are clearly successful.

There are other metrics, though. At AB InBev, Lemann's execs turned to cheaper suppliers, and many consumers found the new hops inferior. In the United States, a few even filed a lawsuit claiming that the company watered down its beer. This is something Lemann wouldn't notice or care about. A teetotaler who prefers a bottle of water and a salad, he personally has no use for the products he sells. He acquired Burger King before he'd ever eaten a Whopper, and when he tried one, he said he found it too big. For Lemann, the appeal of these companies was abstract: He liked how they generated cash. His longtime adviser Vicente Falconi summed up their thinking like this: "People say the customer comes first and all that, but actually it's cash."

Following this logic, Lemann is unsentimental about jobs, a line on an earnings statement. To pull off the AB InBev merger, he raised fifty-four billion dollars in debt, equivalent to the entire foreign debt of Peru. (In this way, Lemann is like Eike: the product of a world with lots of speculative cash in it.) To make sure they could pay the debt back, Lemann's crew made the usual cuts, getting rid of free beer for workers, free BlackBerrys for managers. They also fired fourteen hundred employees in the depths of the financial crisis. They repeated the formula at Burger King, firing four hundred more. At Heinz, another seven thousand workers would lose their jobs. Among those who remained, some relished the new Darwinian system where a PSD could speed up the corporate ladder. But plenty of others found the new work-life balance screwy. In anonymous reviews at Glassdoor.com, longtime employees used words like *cutthroat* to describe the new office environment. Most people don't care to work twelve-hour days to make ketchup.

Those who know Lemann say one of his greatest motivations is to give smart young people a chance to succeed. But with money as the measure of progress, the best and brightest end up increasing profit margins on Whoppers. Lemann has said that if he'd been born later, he would have gotten into tech, and this makes sense. In Silicon Valley, where great innovations have sometimes birthed industries, scores of ambitious kids now spend their days disrupting logistical bottlenecks in restaurant delivery, taxi services, and laundry. This is where the money is, but does it count as progess?

The 3G guys have a saying: "Any organization, to be successful, must grow." But once they've streamlined away a company's inefficiencies and possibly diluted its product, and there's nothing left to trim, they can only keep expanding through acquisitions. And then by making more cuts. And the cycle repeats. In 2015 Lemann and Buffett would team up again to take over another American brand, Kraft. Then AB InBev swallowed up SABMiller, the world's second-largest beer maker. All told, Lemann and his partners already control companies with a combined market value larger than that of Berkshire Hathaway, Facebook, or Exxon. Still, rumor held that Pepsi might be next, or maybe Diageo, the company that makes Smirnoff and Johnnie Walker. What's the point for Lemann— accumulation for its own sake?

Warren Buffett speaks highly of Lemann's efficiency, and this makes sense, because he's a shareholder in Heinz. When I asked Lemann's PR reps how his efficiency helps society as a whole, I got this official response: "It is efficiency that allows the world to evolve, new things to be created, and more people to be employed. It is this efficiency that allows these companies to survive in the long term, feeds their growth, and drives constant job creation." It's a standard Econ 101 answer—one that equates profit with progress. And yet it's not quite that simple. Anheuser-Busch InBev now employs more than a hundred and fifty thousand people, but that's not because Lemann created these jobs; it's because AB InBev keeps swallowing up its rivals in takeovers. Despite Lemann's synergies, meanwhile, beer prices are no lower. So by firing people, Lemann may not be eliminating costs at all but shifting them onto the rest of society.

When I asked Lemann's people to name a "new thing" he's created, they didn't respond. A recent Heinz investor presentation touted innovations that included yellow mustard and hot sauces. It's like creative destruction without the creative part.

Lemann said once that he hopes to build companies of "lasting greatness." He said he wants his model of corporate management to outlive him. To put this another way, he wants to build an empire and to leave his mark on history. But in the end, his corporate alchemy struck me as a sophisticated form of rent seeking: claiming a piece of the economic pie rather than making the pie larger. In the long run, this may prove counterproductive even for him. Take Lemann's efficiency to its logical end, and few consumers will be able to afford his beer. Henry Ford had a similar insight in 1914, when he doubled wages so that his workers could afford a Model T. Higher profits don't always translate into more investment or more jobs. In recent years, corporations have spent less on research and development than on buying their own shares on the exchange, thus inflating the price. This is good for shareholders and for executives with stock options, but not so useful for society as a whole.

The pride of Brazil's business class, Lemann ultimately seems to be a man without a nation, and not just because of his Swiss heritage. He keeps homes in Rio and in a village near Zurich, he controls companies in Brazil and the United States and Mexico and China, his buyout firm has its offices in New York but keeps its funds in the Caribbean, and no one but his closest associates knows where he'll physically be on any given day. When he took over American symbols like Budweiser and Heinz, it struck me that he wasn't really planting the green, yellow, and blue Brazilian flag in St. Louis and Pittsburgh. He was planting the obscure banner of a new rootless class of global billionaires.

MY STORIES ON BILLIONAIRES elicited all sorts of reactions. On *Businessweek*'s website, several readers of my Lemann profile said they had a new reason not to drink Budweiser or eat at Burger King. One reader lamented the American jobs lost, while another was inspired to write that "wealth is an absolute good," font of society's advances. "You're welcome for the industrial revolution," he said.

Once a reader accused me of prejudice against entrepreneurs. Wondering about this, I looked for counternarratives to the stories I'd been pursuing. I wanted to find someone who'd gotten rich by innovating. I wouldn't find this person in beer. Brazil's only tech billionaire is Eduardo Saverin, who got rich because of his lucky decision to put money into Facebook before anyone else. As far as I could tell, the only Brazilian billionaire who ever created anything new was Walther Moreira Salles. Already rich as a banker in the sixties, he backed an American venture to extract a rare element known as niobium from a deposit in Minas Gerais. There wasn't even a market for this stuff yet, but studies indicated it made steel stronger and more flexible, and the venture, CBMM, developed the technology to apply it at the industrial level. Niobium now is widely used, and after buying out their American partner, Walther's sons control most of the world market for it.

In the end, though, this exercise struck me as unfair to Brazil. Of the four hundred richest Americans according to *Forbes,* more than a quarter inherited their money. Of the self-made among them, more made money from money, through investments, than from tech. And even in tech, most didn't come up with the main innovations behind their companies. Before Microsoft or the Macintosh came Xerox's Palo Alto Research Center. Before Facebook, Friendster, and MySpace. Before the iPhone, U.S. government agencies developed GPS, touchscreens, and voice recognition. Bill Gates himself recently noted that private companies could never have created the Internet. The main genius of Gates and Steve Jobs and Mark Zuckerberg was to build teams, marshal resources, and streamline and mass-market the innovations of others. All three played key roles in the advancement of technology, but in none of these cases did the inventors reap the greatest rewards.

It turns out that even some billionaires are skeptical of the contributions of their class. One is Guilherme Leal, the cofounder of Natura Cosméticos, an Avon-like company that sells perfumes and soaps made with ingredients from the Amazon. It's considered one of the world's most environmentally friendly companies. I went to meet Leal at his office in São Paulo, and in the spirit of sustainability, I fast-walked there from home on a muggy day, expecting air conditioning on my arrival. But of course he had none, so I sweated a lot for the first fifteen minutes or so.

Leal has gray hair and a slight paunch and wore a dark suit and stylish thick-rimmed glasses. Unlike Lemann, he believes financial profit shouldn't be our only measure of success. He believes that the future of the planet depends on it. "There must be other *bottom lines*," he told me, using the phrase in English. "These bottom lines will have to be richer; they'll have to consider social and environmental questions. These are cultural questions, questions of values. The definition of happiness, the definition of success in business—both have to change." He spoke excitedly of so-called benefit corporations, which are for-profit but put social and environmental goals in their bylaws. One example is Warby Parker, which for each pair of hipster glasses it sells distributes another pair to someone in the developing world.

The irony of Leal's vision is that he pursues it in much the same way his fellow billionaires pursue theirs. To spread his ideas, he gives money to political campaigns in Brazil and funds nonprofits like the B Team, which also has Richard Branson as a backer. He complains about the "cult of the private entrepreneur," about the "omnipotent visions" of Eike Batista, but he also talks about how to end poverty at the World Economic Forum in Davos, where the entrepreneur is held up as the nexus of all progress. Leal is a contradictory figure. When I asked him how he felt about being so rich in a country as poor as Brazil, he was the first billionaire I could think of who didn't launch into a defense of his wealth. "It makes me uncomfortable," he said. "I think the happiest societies are the least unequal, where everyone can have a pretty decent, pretty reasonable quality of life. If I had to give up a significant piece of my wealth, thirty percent, forty percent, to higher taxes, but at the same time got to live in a country with less inequality, I would be happier. I wouldn't miss that thirty or forty percent." He said this, and yet in 2013 Brazil's tax agency ordered Natura to pay three hundred million dollars in unpaid taxes, interest, and fines. (In his defense he explained, "Here in Brazil, if you don't try to deal intelligently with the tax burden, you'll go broke.")

I wondered if I would ever find a billionaire fit to be a hero. And then I wondered if billionaires need to be heroes. If we take them as people rather than symbols, it may be easier to weigh their contributions.

EIKE OFTEN SPOKE THE New Age language of Leal. Though his fortune derived from old, dirty industries, he prided himself on using clean coal technologies in his power plants. He touted a solar panel project even though it produced enough electricity to supply just fifteen hundred families. "I think fifty years into the future," he said. But when a journalist asked him why he didn't bet bigger on renewable energy, he replied that it just wasn't financially viable yet. Despite his love of risk, this was a risk he wasn't willing to take. Eike belonged to the Lemann camp. Like most of his fellows in the business world, he saw profit as a simple force of nature. It was immutable, something to be harnessed: galvanizer of wills. Even on its own terms, though, the profit motive can backfire. Eike's story is proof of this.

"Jorge Paulo created a whole management culture in Brazil that is extraordinary," Eike said once, praising Lemann. And he followed a similar model of remuneration. To lure the best people in oil and mining, he offered stock incentives that dwarfed the salaries they earned at Petrobras or Vale. The system worked like this: After a few years at one of his companies, management could buy shares from him for just pennies each. As at Garantia, the idea was to push them to increase the company's value, aligning their interests with his. It seemed to work for a while. Share prices rose, shareholders were happy, Eike's executives got rich. At least ten of them made more than twenty million dollars, according to one report.

Eike only liked Lemann's approach to compensation, though, not to costs. While Lemann believed that little luxuries ate up money better distributed to shareholders, Eike's guys got first-class flights and top hotels on the company dime. OGX employees took to calling the company OGChic (which rhymes in Portuguese because the X is pronounced *sheesh*). Their office even boasted a mini-cellar for wine and champagne. There was so much money floating around, the feeling was *why not*? Eike's public companies footed the bill for his three private jets too.

Another problem: Eike didn't understand that the "skin in the game" concept doesn't always work both ways. During the financial crisis, he asked his execs to put some of their own money back into MMX Mineração, as he'd done, to help keep it afloat. Many refused and quit instead. Many who stayed, meanwhile, found ways to protect themselves from losses—and in so doing made things worse. Because new stock grants vested once a year, some stayed just long enough to exercise their options, sell the shares, take their "fuck-you money" (as they termed it), and quit. This meant that, until they could cash out, they had an incentive to withhold information that could hurt the share price. In the months before June 2012, when OGX revealed how little its wells were producing, several of Eike's guys found a bank willing to pay them up front at a discount for yet-to-be-vested shares. Selling desperately this way, they sent a clear but nonpublic sign that the company was in trouble. Coincidentally or not, one of that bank's funds then mounted huge bets against OGX, selling its shares short in the market. The fund made a killing. In this way, the profit motive appeared to work against Eike.

The perverse incentives were many. In each of his IPOs, Eike had offered investment banks a sliding fee based on how high they could push the offering price. In theory, a "Chinese wall" separates the arm of a bank that takes companies public, promoting the stock to anyone who will listen, from the arm that gives clients advice, ostensibly objective, on which stocks to buy. In practice, analysts work to boost the IPOs their banks are peddling. Eike made sure of this. When analysts questioned his rosy projections, he'd call their bosses to demand a correction. If an analyst slapped an Eike stock with a "sell" recommendation, Eike might shut the underwriting side of the bank out of his next deal. And a single deal could mean tens of millions of dollars in fees. Pumping up the stock, meanwhile, could bring you rewards. Eike ended up hiring a bullish Credit Suisse analyst as chief executive of MMX. Right up until the eve of OGX's June letdown, almost every major analyst had a "buy" recommendation on the company's shares.

In his interview with Charlie Rose, Eike had bragged about his management system. To stay on top of his web of companies, he said he consulted with his top guys every day. And he said, "I read people better than I read books." A different picture emerged, though, as people jumped ship and started talking to the press. Eike cultivated an environment where bringing bad news got you sidelined. If you cast doubt on a project's chances of success, he called you *calça-curta*, "short pants," which is to say, a little boy. "How many billions of dollars have *you* made?" he would say. Or: "Why don't you tell that to Luciano Coutinho?"—the president of the BNDES, which lent all those billions to Eike's companies. All the press attention only seemed to reinforce Eike's self-confidence.

In anonymous interviews, onetime Eike men made a poker reference in English, "all in all the time," to describe the attitude that got you promoted. Eike himself said that, in that pivotal oil rights auction of 2007, he had ignored the advice of ex-Petrobras guys who advised caution and told them to "think bigger." This is how Paulo Mendonça ended up as OGX's chief executive. Notorious at Petrobras for his unfailing optimism, Mendonça told Eike what he wanted to hear. As his influence grew, Mendonça created his own little fiefdom inside the Serrador, even keeping data from his own colleagues. And Eike let it happen. He gave Mendonça a pet name, Dr. Oil.

Some compared the scene at Serrador to *Big Brother,* the reality TV show popular in Brazil for its juvenile dramas between attention-loving characters all trapped in a house together. After his deal with the Emirates, Eike hired an adviser named Aziz Ben Ammar to scare up fresh cash in the Middle East. A grandson of Tunisia's deposed prime minister, Aziz had met Eike at a nightclub in Saint-Tropez. He favored a Panama hat even during business meetings. After one such meeting, a banker called up someone in EBX's finance department to ask whether it was some kind of practical joke. Eike introduced Aziz around the Serrador as "chief entertainment officer."

Picking the right people, listening, and delegating: These are essential qualities in a successful mogul. Even Steve Jobs, notoriously dictatorial and convinced of his own intuitions, kept himself open to dissent. But Eike commanded his empire like an emperor: arbitrary, infallible, also hereditary. In September of 2012 he named Thor a director at EBX. This didn't inspire much confidence in anyone. The first hearing in Thor's manslaughter trial had come less than a week earlier, and witnesses described Thor zigzagging past them on the highway. The defense's best witness was a truck driver. The McLaren couldn't have been going all that fast, the guy said, because he'd had time to admire it.

AS 2012 DRAGGED TO A CLOSE, Eike and Aziz, his new right-hand man, met with little success raising fresh cash in the Middle East. The sheikhs weren't actually as bullish as Eike had claimed, nor as credulous as his skeptics imagined. At Bloomberg, after piecing together tips from bankers and ex-EBX men, we found out that the Emirates' two-billion-dollar investment carried secret conditions. To protect their sovereign wealth fund from losses, Eike had put up his own shares in his companies as collateral. It was far from a straight-up equity investment and certainly not a gung-ho "seal of approval."

This meant that the deal never implied the frothy valuation we at Bloomberg gave him credit for. Realizing our mistake, we removed the premium we had applied to his net worth estimate, and his fortune fell below thirteen billion dollars. He was now, just like that, the world's seventy-third richest person.

Eike had stopped giving interviews, so when I asked his people for comment, one of his executives called me up and gave me a not-for-attribution scolding. He was furious. He told me I was biased, that we had no right to do this, and he had a point. Not about my bias, because even if—I admit—I took some pleasure in taking Eike down a notch, the decision wasn't mine alone to make. He had a point about our right to do what we did. Demoting Eike on our index was just as arbitrary as bumping him up to eighth place in the world just nine months earlier. In a way, ours was an Eikean undertaking: assigning a theoretical value to something and making it true just by repeating it.

Eike, though, had reached the limit of his power to shape facts with words. The first time we'd spoken, he told me his companies would earn a billion dollars in 2012. They ended the year with more than a billion in losses. With operations behind schedule, revenues below target, and spending over budget, they just kept burning through cash. He needed to shock the market into believing him again. So finally he did something out of character. He deigned to share the limelight. In March 2013 he announced a deal with André Esteves, the billionaire head of a Brazilian investment bank known as BTG Pactual, to turn his companies around. People called Esteves a prodigy because he became a billionaire before his fortieth birthday. He did this by selling Pactual to UBS, the Swiss bank, for three billion dollars in 2006. Three years later he famously bought it back, much enlarged, for just two and a half billion.

In signing on with Esteves, Eike was signing on to the legacy of Lemann. A magazine once referred to Pactual as "Garantia's rib" because it was founded by one of Garantia's first partners, Luiz Cezar Fernandes. Esteves stood out from the start as the ideal PSD, sharp-toothed and bright-eyed. He wasn't born with a silver spoon in his mouth. His mom, a university professor, raised him on Rio's working-class north side, and he started at Pactual in 1989 while studying for a math degree. He needed the job to repay the loan on his car, which got stolen on his first day at work. No matter: He rose quickly from IT guy to trader to head of a whole new asset-management division. Luiz Cezar took him under his wing, mentored him. But in the late nineties, when Luiz Cezar got into debt, Esteves saw an opportunity to increase his stake in the bank. So he led Pactual's junior partners in a kind of mutiny, demanding Luiz Cezar hand over his shares for emergency loans. Luiz Cezar had no choice but to accept. He later said Esteves "would sell his own mother to gain power."

Esteves intrigued me because he both celebrated and censured the profit motive. I had interviewed him a few months earlier, when *Bloomberg Markets* magazine put him on its list of the world's most influential people in finance. With EBX foundering, Esteves took Eike's place as the list's only Brazilian. We met in a conference room at BTG Pactual's headquarters in São Paulo, and he showed up an hour late wearing a rumpled button-up shirt coming untucked from his suit pants. Despite his reputation for cunning, I found myself disarmed by his boyish face and toothy smile. As he shook my hand, he effusively thanked me as if I personally had anything to do with the list. Then he launched straight into an attack on his own industry. He blamed his fellow bankers in the United States and Europe for the financial crisis. "The money people were making on Wall Street didn't make sense," he said. "It was too easy. Obviously the risk/return was imperfect. A guy would make millions and millions of dollars without running any personal risk. He would screw everything up, switch jobs, and not lose a thing. It can't be like this." What he described was Eike's system, meritocracy gone amok, on a much grander scale.

I wondered how much of Esteves's criticism was just arrogance. BTG officially stood for Banking and Trading Group, but unofficially it stood for Better Than Goldman—as in Goldman Sachs, the most profitable firm on Wall Street. And yet while he cited Lemann as a mentor, Esteves uttered free market blasphemy. He called for more regulation, more conservative capital requirements, and tougher fines for misconduct. "The world has become overly financialized," he said. "We can't forget that the financial system's function, broadly speaking, is to transform savings into investment." Proudly he spoke of all the capital he invested directly in the real economy—pharmacies, Internet providers, ports. Of course, Esteves had also helped to make Eike possible. Pactual underwrote all of Eike's stock offerings since MMX in 2006. (And later, when crisis struck, it would engulf Esteves too.)

Eike and Esteves hadn't always gotten along. Eike once called up Esteves to yell at him when one of his analysts wrote a negative report on OGX. More recently, Eike believed that Esteves's traders had been short-selling OGX's shares. But he was desperate, and the investing class loved Esteves. The first thing Esteves did was to announce a billion-dollar credit line for EBX, a sign of his confidence in Eike's empire. The markets reacted as hoped. OGX's stock price jumped sixteen percent in a single day. Reportedly, Eike went around the office saying, in English, "The magic Eike is back!"

Esteves's competitors, though, seemed to take the deal as a sign they wouldn't be first in line for future fees—and thus had less of an incentive to hedge their criticism. Within days, analysts at multiple banks downgraded OGX, recommending belatedly that clients sell the stock. Without the lure of short-term profits, it got easier to see Eike's empire for what it was.

CHAPTER 9

THE BACKLASH

PROTESTS, COLLAPSE, AND ACCUSATIONS

"I always acted in good faith, and I always will."
—EIKE BATISTA ($200 MILLION)

WAS SITTING AT HOME ON A SUNDAY NIGHT WHEN MY TWITTER feed filled up with posts from @eikebatista, and I realized how much I'd missed them. It had been many months since his last public statement. "Read the interview with André Esteves in *Estadão*!" Eike wrote. "BTG is my creditor and it knows me inside out!" Esteves had just given an interview to this São Paulo newspaper, talking up the quality of Eike's assets. He said he planned to sell off large stakes to raise cash for Eike and spread his risk among outside partners.

No sooner had Eike breached the dam of silence than a flood of tweets burst forth. He assailed his enemies. "Rumors and Gossip are the Weapons of short sellers!" he said—who would be "caught with their pants down" when share prices rebounded. "Unique Projects always prevail!!!"

By "Rumors and Gossip," Eike meant all the bad news about his empire that abounded in the early months of 2013. Shortly after he struck his partnership with Esteves, a colleague of mine uncovered more secret guarantees behind EBX. As with the Emirates, Eike had pledged his own shares as collateral for loans to his companies from local banks. Certain of his vision, he put leverage on top of leverage, much as the Viscount of Mauá had done. As long as his share prices rose, this wasn't a problem. Now they were falling, and the banks demanded he put up more collateral. If he didn't, they could take his shares as if foreclosing on a house.

Few knew for sure how much debt Eike had piled on, but the chance of him paying it all back seemed increasingly distant. After my colleague's story came out, OGX Petróleo's bonds took a big hit in the market. Having traded at ninety cents on the dollar just weeks earlier, the bonds' price now sank below eighty cents, a clear sign that investor confidence was disappearing.

Still, for those who thought his silence implied surrender, Eike wanted to send a message. He planned to hoist his empire up from the abyss. On Twitter he said he needed just five more years to erect his empire and, in so doing, remake the nation. "My Plans," he declared, "are to build a mega-efficient Brazil." As he lashed out at his critics, he also riled up his base. Users sent dozens of tweets of support, which he retweeted and responded to. One fan said, "The problem with this country is that people don't like those who are successful and have money"—and Eike replied, "Great Truth!" Another told him not to give up, and he said, "I won't stop! Thank you." And: "I don't get tired of believing in Brazil."

Esteves's first coup came less than a week after Eike's tweet storm, with the sale of a majority stake in MPX Energia to a German power company. The deal would put close to eight hundred million dollars of much-needed cash in Eike's pocket. But the Esteves bump didn't last long. Eike's name had grown so corrosive that Esteves's bank began to suffer in the stock market too. Investors worried about how much money Pactual had on the line with EBX. A low-level freak-out bubbled in the market. People began to talk of *systemic risk*. If Eike's empire collapsed, some feared it could cause huge losses in the financial sector. To minimize the contagion, Esteves's partners gave off-the-record interviews underplaying Pactual's exposure to Eike's companies.

Pactual's people were supposed to be turning Eike's companies around. Under the terms of their agreement, Esteves's fee would depend on how much Eike's share prices bounced back. On the surface, it seemed like a formula for success, but once again, Eike might have misjudged the incentives. Some in the market believed Esteves had swooped in not to rescue Eike but to make sure Pactual would be first in line to recoup its loans. Despite his goofy exterior, Esteves was, after all, famous for ousting his own mentor. He had barely extended his billion-dollar credit line to Eike, but he soon quietly withdrew it.

If the private sector increasingly doubted Eike, it still looked as if he could count on the government. President Dilma had made at least one important phone call abroad, exhorting the prime minister of Malaysia to consider an investment in OGX. And in January, Dilma received Eike in Brasília. Together with three of her ministers, they discussed installing a Petrobras terminal at the port of Açu to make up for the foreign tenants that had bailed. Eike was Brazil's national champion, and Dilma's administration feared that his failure could hurt the national image. He wasn't the only one whose success relied on appearances. The Brazilian economy had lost steam and piled on debt. If foreign investors believed it wasn't going to bounce back, they would take their capital and go elsewhere. Foreign banks would charge more to lend money to Dilma's government. And the pessimism would self-fulfill.

Lula, still influential as ex-president, worked to find solutions for Eike too. Meeting with Dimitry Medvedev, the prime minister of Russia, he suggested an alliance between OGX and Lukoil, the Russian oil giant. Then in March it emerged that Lula had visited Açu. In the photo you could see him walking on a windy tarmac to what appeared to be one of Eike's private jets. Chatting and gesticulating alongside him, Eike wore sneakers and jeans and a denim shirt, a uniform nothing like his usual getup for the press. Though the port remained a construction site, Lula liked Eike's pitch. He liked the idea of a future "mega-logistics complex" employing thousands of Brazilian workers. Eike just needed some tenants beyond his own companies. So while Dilma looked into the possibilities with Petrobras, Lula called in favors in Brasília to pressure a private Singaporean firm, then planning a shipyard in the neighboring state of Espírito Santo, to bring its project down the coast to Açu.

The story caused a minor scandal when it came out. The problem was that, by attempting to lend a hand to Eike, Lula fueled the impression that the government meddled too much in the economy—and even worse, to help its friends. The governor of Espírito Santo was especially outraged. So Lula distanced himself from the bad publicity, and Eike lost the Singaporeans.

Amid the uproar, Eike maintained that he'd done nothing improper. Just the opposite. "President Lula's visit as a great Brazilian citizen filled me with Pride," he tweeted. "He knows Brazil Deeply and can identify transformational projects." Then he echoed that line I'd heard from Blairo Maggi. Açu, he wrote, "is not Eike's project [but] a Project of National Interest. . . . Obviously the State can and should participate in the Investment!" Still, while he was open to government assistance, he bristled at the idea he needed a bailout. In one tweet he said: "I'm not the one clamoring for Help, Brazil is." Playing up the nationalist angle, Eike retweeted a comment from his most reliable booster, a guy who went by the handle @Gilson_Perlla_X: "Does *Veja* want businessmen investing outside of Brazil? Does it want the Gov against things that will bring efficiency to Brazil? #Sad."

Probably no person as rich as Eike ever interacted so much with ordinary citizens. He would argue with anyone who tweeted at him, as if he could convince all of Brazil, person by person, that his empire wasn't going under, that his intentions were noble, that his interests were their interests too. But there were always new doubts to assuage. In early April, analysts at Standard & Poor's warned that OGX Petróleo could run out of cash by 2014. This caused a fresh selloff. If you had bought a share for eighteen *reais* after OGX started pumping oil, you would have less than two *reais* in your pocket just over a year later. Worth twenty billion dollars when it went public, the company was now valued at a mere four billion. One user asked what Eike had to say to those who'd believed in him and lost money, and he wrote, "I didn't sell my shares! I'm just as disappointed as you and working to change this reality with new discipline."

Of course, not everyone was losing money on Eike. Every day brought a fresh reason to buy or sell his companies. Rumors mingled with real news, and his share prices oscillated wildly. It was a feast for speculators. First came news that Malaysia's state oil company, heeding Dilma's request, had agreed to buy a stake in one of OGX's oil fields. This was true. Then came news that Lukoil, heeding Lula's request, would invest in OGX also. This was false. Eike himself added to the volatility. You got the impression he couldn't decide whether to scale back or double down. To conserve cash at OGX, his new chief executive initially curbed its ambitious exploration campaign. Then, even though OGX couldn't get its own wells producing yet, he spent several hundred million dollars on new oil blocks.

Through it all, the surest bet was on Eike's decline. So many people were shorting OGX that, to meet demand from traders, the São Paulo exchange twice raised the limit on how much of a company's stock could be lent out at any given time—first to thirty percent of the total outstanding, and later to a whopping fifty percent.

As Eike's net worth slipped below eight billion dollars, he looked increasingly desperate. He sought help everywhere. Rumor had it that he'd even hired an "esoteric consultant" recommended by Sérgio Cabral, Rio's governor. Dressed all in white, the wizened old lady wandered the halls of the Serrador building looking for signs. Finally she located the problem. The Incan sun in his company logos shone the wrong way. I didn't quite believe the story when it first leaked out, but soon I saw that on company websites and email signatures, the stylized licks of solar flame had been reversed. They now twirled counterclockwise.

EIKE STILL HAD HIS SUPPORTERS, but public opinion was turning definitively against him. For those who'd listened to the hype, put money into his companies, and lost it, this made sense. But something else was going on too. You could feel a new unease in Brazil.

After years of hearing Eike and Lula claim that Brazil's long-promised future was on the cusp of arriving, people couldn't help noticing how distant that future remained. For the working class, material life had improved; they had flat-screen TVs, smartphones, and cars bought on high-interest installment plans, and in this way they resembled an American middle class. In other important ways, they didn't. The constitution guarantees free public healthcare and education, but if you lacked private insurance, you might wait all day in the emergency room when dengue fever broke out in São Paulo. If you couldn't afford private school, your kids stood little chance of making it into a free, high-quality public university. Without private security, you faced one of the world's highest crime rates—fifty thousand murdered each year. More than half the population had Internet access, but fewer than half had sewage lines. Unemployment remained near record lows, but now inflation was spiraling out of control.

The first protest against Eike came in late April. It was small, a few hundred people marching against what they called the privatization of Rio's Maracanã soccer stadium. In advance of the World Cup in 2014, Eike had partnered up with Odebrecht to buy the rights to run the Maracanã for the next thirty-five years. Though he had just a five percent stake in the partnership, he became a target because he was a lot more famous than anyone in the complex family tree of Odebrecht shareholders. Outside the stadium, protesters chanted "Eike, you thief, leave the 'Maraca' for the people!"

Eike used to sneer at those who latched on to the government nipple, but now here he was with Odebrecht, the company with more public contracts than any other in Brazil. And this deal blurred the line between public and private in typical fashion. Governor Cabral, Eike's friend, decided to lease the Maracanã based on a proposal from IMX, Eike's entertainment venture. Cabral then hired IMX to carry out the viability study that would define the bidding rules. And

IMX and Odebrecht ultimately won the bidding. Public prosecutors at first blocked the lease, claiming that IMX had unfairly benefited from inside information. But Cabral's administration appealed and got the block lifted. Under his watch, the state had already paid half a billion dollars for Odebrecht and another firm to fix up the stadium to the standards of FIFA, the notoriously corrupt organization that puts on the World Cup. Protesters chanted: "FIFA, Cabral, and Eike are a construction racket!"

People were outraged because the Maracanã is part of national history. It went up just in time for the World Cup of 1950, the last time Brazil hosted soccer's great event. Befitting the country-of-the-future feeling of those years, it was built with the first cement ever made in Brazil. It was here that the Brazilian national team, the Seleção, after dispatching all its opponents with poetic ease, lost to Uruguay in the final match. After the final whistle blew, all you could hear among the stadium's two hundred thousand fans were scattered sobs. The millions of fans huddling around radios across Brazil wept with them. The legendary striker Pelé, then just a boy, remembers feeling as if Brazil had lost a war. "What happened on July 16, 1950, deserves a collective monument, like the Tomb of the Unknown Soldier," the journalist Carlos Heitor Cony wrote. Paulo Perdigão called it "a Waterloo of the tropics and its history our Götterdämmerung." Nelson Rodrigues said, "It was our Hiroshima."

The defeat left a scar on the nation. It seemed that Brazil had missed the chance to prove itself a serious country. Nelson Rodrigues had coined the term *complexo de vira-lata* to describe this feeling. Now this historic site had been turned over to a man who was supposed to rescue Brazil from its old inferiority complex. Instead, Eike seemed to be repeating the Seleção's performance six decades earlier: grand hopes, then a letdown.

Eike had said he would be the world's richest man by this point. Instead he was rushing to get rid of whatever he could to raise cash: his hotels, his marina, even some of his toys. In May he put his Legacy 600 jet on sale for fourteen million dollars. He offered up the party boat *Pink Fleet,* where his son Olin used to throw parties. He also put his philanthropy on hold. He canceled his donations to the favela pacification program, to the Rio lagoon cleanup, to the Jutta Batista children's hospital, named for his mother. He needed every cent now. Even as creditors hounded him for more collateral, he had to make good on promises to put fresh money into OSX and MMX to keep them afloat.

The first round of layoffs came in May, when Eike fired thirteen hundred workers building OSX's shipyard at the port of Açu. Still he couldn't stanch the bleeding fast enough. Each day his companies consumed tens of millions of dollars.

THE TRIAL OF THOR BATISTA fed into the national unease. It had been dragging along for a year now. In December, for his second hearing, Thor's bodyguards had driven him to the courthouse in Rio's working-class *subúrbio.* This was not Thor's natural habitat. It was a run-down sprawl of dull red cinderblock mixed with pollution-stained storefronts, motorcycles threading past lurching buses, and sidewalks packed with harried-looking people hoisting bundles. The dingy whitish courthouse blended in with the overcast sky. Across the street, crude banners offered cut-rate legal advice under laundry-flapping balconies and windows hung with hammocks.

Thor emerged from a silver sedan wearing an adolescent beard and a white T-shirt that clung to his monumental trapeziuses. He was accompanied by his mom, Luma. Their bodyguards cleared a path through the press. No reporters were allowed inside the court-room, but I visited later, and it was so tiny that it barely fit the judge and a half-dozen plastic chairs. Trials here usually involved working-class people no one cared to observe.

The hearing opened with testimony from Hélio Martins Júnior, the forensic analyst who produced the evidence at the heart of the case. Once he'd explained his speed calculations, a member of Thor's defense team—Celso Vilardi, a top lawyer who also worked for Camargo Corrêa—made an objection. Martins, he complained, had introduced new material. He wasn't contesting the science of Martins's analysis; his complaint was procedural. He said that Martins's full report hadn't been shared with the defense.

The judge, Daniela Assumpção, agreed to a brief recess for the defense to huddle. When they reconvened, she called Thor to testify. But he just kept quiet during her questions. He sat there impassive, refusing to answer. This went on for ten or fifteen minutes. Then the fluorescent lights blinked out. The power had gone in the entire building, and no one knew when it would come back. Assistants lit candles as Assumpção brought the hearing to a close. *"Só no Brasil,"* I heard someone comment afterward—Only in Brazil—a frequent phrase.

With his phalanx of bodyguards, Thor filed out without speaking to the press, ducking into one of the identical silver sedans waiting curbside. Vilardi addressed reporters with theatrical lawyerly indignation. "A new document was presented," he said, "the official forensic report. It seems the prosecution has had this for some time, but it hadn't been filed with the court. We were always requesting access to the speed calculations, but we never got them." And why hadn't Thor testified? "Thor remained silent because we didn't agree with the fact this document was presented only now."

After the hearing, Thor's lawyers demanded to suspend the trial on the grounds that his right to a full and fair rebuttal of the evidence had been violated. The holidays passed, and in early January a magistrate sided with them. He put the trial on hold until the procedural lapse could be analyzed. Arguing that it relied on inadmissible evidence, Thor's lawyers now demanded the case be shelved entirely.

For a few weeks it looked like Thor would get off on a technicality. Though the case ultimately went ahead, Assumpção met the defense halfway, throwing out the forensic report—a major coup for Thor. By making improper contact with Martins, she found, the prosecution had raised doubts about the impartiality of his findings.

The old analysis put Thor's speed at 83 miles per hour; a new analysis pegged it between 62 and 72 miles per hour. The speed limit was 68. Assumpção called Thor back to testify in March, but his lawyers brought a doctor's note saying he had come down with an undisclosed illness. In Brazil you can apparently call in sick to your own manslaughter trial.

When at last Thor returned to the courthouse in April, he showed up with his hair trimmed close, wearing jeans and running shoes and a light green button-down shirt with radii of sweat expanding from his armpits. Luma, all in black with dark sunglasses, held his hand as they walked down the hall to the courtroom. This time he consented to testify. The session lasted just forty minutes. Mostly he repeated the defense he'd made on Twitter: "The accident was impossible to avoid." He'd been following the speed limit, he said. He'd only learned about his speeding tickets from the papers and suspected his bodyguards had racked them up, since they often drove him around at night when he was tired. As evidence of his contrition and goodwill, he said he'd given the equivalent of three hundred thousand dollars to Wanderson's aunt and widow. He'd done this, he said, despite his own family's "financial difficulties."

His arguments didn't win over Assumpção. Wanderson might have been drinking, but investigators calculated that Thor should have noticed any crossers from thirty or forty meters up the road. His McLaren, well-made car that it was, could brake from sixty miles per hour to zero in three seconds. All this, together with the testimony of witnesses who'd seen him frenetically zigzag before the crash, led Assumpção to believe that Thor had been driving at "extremely high speed," despite the findings of the new forensic report. And so on June 5 she handed down her verdict, convicting him of involuntary manslaughter.

Struggling to save his empire, Eike didn't comment on the ruling. But Luma was appalled. On Facebook she wrote, "It's clear that my son was judged based on his economic and social condition," as if wealth were a tragic disease. Beyond the bad press, though, Thor didn't have much to worry about. Assumpção sentenced him to two years' community service and fined him a half-million dollars. Thor's lawyers immediately filed for appeal, and in the meantime, he would be free to drive. For now he could forget about the community service too. The fine, if ever enforced, would cost him less than a new McLaren.

THE UNEASE GREW. When Sérgio Cabral officially handed the Maracanã to the Eike-Odebrecht consortium in May 2013, protesters returned to the stadium wearing masks of the governor and his billionaire ally. In São Paulo, another movement emerged when the city raised bus and subway fares by twenty *centavos,* to 3.20 *reais.* The day after Thor's conviction, a lefty group known as the Free Pass Movement called a march. They'd been organizing protests for years without much success, but this time they drew five thousand people. Their banners read SE A TARIFA NÃO BAIXAR A CIDADE VAI PARAR—If the fare doesn't come down, the city will shut down. Demonstrators blocked roads with burning tires, broke bank-office windows, and smashed up bus stops. Downtown traffic came to a standstill. The protest appeared unrelated to Eike, but the two movements would soon coalesce.

The demonstrations spread to Rio, where fares had gone up the previous year. The press was unanimous in its disapproval. On its front page, *O Globo* ran a headline reading REBELLION AND VANDALISM; THE MARCH OF SENSELESSNESS and a photo of a half-dozen college kids being led to jail, their wrists tied together with plastic bracelets. Meanwhile *R7,* Bishop Macedo's news site, reported that protesters had thrown rocks at a church. At first, most Brazilians seemed just as appalled. But then on June 13, a police officer pointed his shotgun at a twenty-six-year-old newspaper reporter on her way home after covering a protest in São Paulo. She was on a side street distant from the action, and she wore a press badge around her neck, but he shot her in the face with a rubber bullet anyway. She was photographed crumpled on the ground, blood streaming from her right eye, the skin around it distended and split. She was lucky she didn't lose her eye. It was just one of many examples of police truculence that night.

As this image and others like it made the rounds of social media, public opinion abruptly shifted. The violence awakened something hard to define, a latent discontent. With all the crime in Brazil, it often seemed like police just took their cut from the drug trade and looked the other way—and now here they were beating up on defenseless young women? Ever more cars clogged the roads, buses with bad shocks puttered overloaded with commuters, packed sweaty trains broke down every other week—and now, people asked, they want to charge us more for this?

The weekend passed. On the Monday following, two hundred thousand people gathered in São Paulo. Though the Free Pass people had called the protest, they no longer led it. The movement had ballooned from a few thousand hardcore kids with a simple, concrete goal to a messy coalition with dozens of grievances, organized by no one. Commuting home from Bloomberg that evening, I became stuck in a long line of buses paralyzed by the protest, so I got out and walked. I entered the crowd streaming down Faria Lima Avenue. Students carried signs decrying the fare hike while others championed gay rights. I also saw older Brazilians with conservative banners calling for sixteen-year-olds to be tried as adults. Most people looked middle class but I saw working-class people too; one girl held a sign reading I MAY BE POOR BUT I'M NO SUCKER. *"Vem pra rua!"* people chanted—Come to the street!—and as the march crept down Faria Lima, even the bankers observing from high floors took the elevator down and joined in, because they were sick of government corruption. The confusion that night was jolly. Tens of thousands marched in Rio and Brasília too.

Scared I might get hurt, my editors in New York asked me to work from home for a while. But I was too curious not to check out the protests once work was over. So the next night I went downtown.

After a standoff with police at the city council building, masked pro-testers had scattered through the area smashing up shops. Oppor-tunists took to looting. Later I found myself on Rua Augusta, where the bars and whorehouses had drawn down their metal shutters. Fifty yards up the street from me, policemen in chunky black body armor and black helmets tightened into a wall of Plexiglas riot shields, each with the word CHOQUE written on it. A deep explosion thundered in the sky, followed by a bright flash of white light, and another—*bombas de efeito moral,* flashbangs. I stood at the corner of a still-open gas station, watching as kids with covered faces scat-tered down a side street where flames danced up from a pile of gar-bage. Police had dispersed so much tear gas that even after the clouds wafted away, my eyes watered and my nose and throat felt peppery. The taste passed through a neural pathway that recalled the fire-works I'd set off as a child on the Fourth of July.

Another boom and flash filled the sky. A black semitruck screeched up, another detachment of riot police filed out, closed ranks. Some raised truncheons above their shields, ready to strike. I began to panic as I realized I now stood in a no-man's-land between two lines of shock troops armed with shotguns that fired rubber bullets. As one row of cops advanced toward the gas station, marching shoulder to shoulder, closing in, I retreated into the area behind the filling pumps where some bystanders had taken refuge. One guy shouted to the police, *"Aqui só tem trabalhador!"*—Nobody but honest working folk here! But the shock troops weren't after us. They swept down the side street after protesters who'd run off that way.

I knew it was big news when Globo canceled its telenovelas to broadcast the protests live in the nights that followed. Marking a careful line, anchors celebrated the "peaceful majority" of protesters while condemning the "violent minority" who resorted to vandal-ism. The vandals responded with black graffiti that read VIOLÊNCIA É CORRUPÇÃO, which means that the real violence is corruption. The Marinho brothers wanted to be on the right side of history, to ride the wave of discontent, even though they were among the rich and powerful who fueled the discontent. Protesters mobbed Globo's headquarters in Rio and revived a chant from the eighties, *"O povo não é bobo, abaixo a Rede Globo!"*—The people aren't stupid, down with TV Globo! On social media, references to Eike's family surfaced also. "Hooray for impunity!" went one tweet. "These protests are also an homage to the playboy Thor Batista! Murderer!" And another: "Just imagine, Thor Batista at a protest fighting for the right to drive his Ferrari in a bike lane?"

Hoping to head off further protest, authorities in São Paulo and Rio reversed the fare increases. Just the same, on June 20, in the absence of any concrete cause at all, more than a million people marched in hundreds of cities across the country. It was easily the biggest protest movement since 1992, when Brazilians marched for the impeachment of Fernando Collor. *"O gigante acordoooouuuu,"* people chanted—The giant has awakened. The giant was the Brazilian people. In Brasília that night, protesters crossed the moat surrounding the foreign ministry and tried to break in. They tossed Molotov cocktails, trying to set the building on fire. Watching these images live, I worried that this furious mass, protesting everything, could turn into an accidental government overthrow. But the police held them at bay, extinguished the flames.

The explosion of protests took everyone by surprise, perhaps most of all Brazilians themselves, who usually resigned themselves to griping about the waste, mismanagement, corruption, crappy public services, and inflation—with the eternal caveat *"Fazer o quê?"*— What are you gonna do? I saw placards reading IT'S NOT JUST ABOUT THE TWENTY CENTAVOS ANYMORE. But what was it about? On the radio, the journalist Ricardo Boechat said, "I think the feeling is: 'I've had enough.' I've had enough of political parties, I've had enough of politicians, I've had enough of representatives, senators, ministers, authorities. I've had enough of the Brazilian state, of what it's transformed itself into—the private and exclusive property of those who occupy the administration and the houses of Congress. . . . You want to go to the streets and ask what's the purpose of all

this? . . . You're asking an atomic bomb after it explodes to ratio-
nally direct its fantastic energy before it flows to wherever it wants
to. What we're seeing here is this energy that exploded within the
Brazilian people, within Brazilian society, flowing to wherever it
wants to, without an owner, without logic, without direction."

ALL ANYONE TALKED ABOUT was the protests, at bars, on Facebook, at the water cooler. It was a heady time, and strange. In the
confusion, everyone—lefties, conservatives, anarchists, Workers
Party people—tried to claim the voice of the protests for themselves.

When Dilma addressed the nation on TV, she spoke as though the
protests weren't aimed at her government too. She interpreted them
as a fresh mandate for change and promised twenty-five billion dollars for new transportation projects. She promised to import Cuban
doctors to serve rural areas and to put all the royalties from Petrobras's pre-salt fields into education. "As president, I have the obligation to listen to the voice of the streets," she said. But she added, "All
within the limits of law and order . . . Government and society can-
not allow a violent, authoritarian minority to destroy public and private property, attack temples, set cars on fire, throw rocks at buses,
and try to bring chaos to our main urban centers." The onetime rebel
no longer countenanced rebellion. "Dilma, what happened to the
guerrilla fighter?" one protest chant went.

Terrified of what the protests might bring, the rest of Brasília
joined her in a show of action. In two weeks, Congress passed more
laws than anyone could remember getting passed in two years. One
law redefined corruption as a "heinous" crime. This put it in the
same category as rape and murder and doubled the minimum sentence to four years. The difficulty of convicting and sentencing the
corrupt remained, but the Supreme Court made a symbolic gesture,
ordering the imprisonment of a sitting congressman for the first time
since the military dictatorship. Later in the year, twenty people convicted in the *mensalão* scandal of 2005—when Workers Party opera-

tors were caught buying votes in Congress—would at last go to prison too. For so many rich and powerful people to actually serve their punishments was unprecedented in Brazil.

Some foreign journalists compared the protests to those of Occupy Wall Street two years prior in New York. I resisted the idea at first, despite the Guy Fawkes masks I saw, despite how people used social media to organize—superficial similarities. For one thing, Occupy never had anywhere near as much popular support. But the two movements shared a thread. Just a month earlier, protesters had brought Istanbul to a halt too. In all three countries—America, Turkey, and Brazil—people were expressing the feeling that their governments failed to serve them and instead served someone else. Who?

The shock of this moment of upheaval mingled with an old skepticism. You could gauge the latter by the millions of YouTube views chalked up on a sketch by the comedy troupe Porta dos Fundos (Back Door). Titled "Emergency Meeting," it takes place in the presidential palace. A fake Dilma gravely tells her cabinet, "We're going to have to steal less." One of her ministers laughs, but when they realize she's serious, they react with shock. "This isn't right!" says one. "I didn't say stop stealing," Dilma says, "just slow it down a bit." Another minister says, "I've got all this money committed for the World Cup! What am I going to tell the *empreiteiros*"—construction tycoons—"who are depending on this money?" After much shouting, they acquiesce, but only on the condition that they can later steal "retroactively" to make up for lost time.

Amid the confusion of the protests, the World Cup emerged as the unifying cause. Partly this was an accident of timing. The upheaval coincided with the Confederations Cup, a warm-up for the big event in 2014. With the international press in attendance, protesters seized on the games as a media opportunity, burning tires and clashing with police outside stadiums. But there was more to it than that. When Lula won the rights to hold the World Cup back in 2007, he wanted to show off. Brazil's economy was booming then, as the developed world began to stall. Best of all, much like the Belo Monte mega-dam, the event looked like a political jackpot—with contracts for campaign donors and pork for politicians in twelve host cities. For ordinary Brazilians, meanwhile, it offered a chance to redeem the defeat of 1950.

It's hard to overstate the importance of soccer here. Brazilians believe their soccer style expresses something inherent to Brazil, something other nations lack—"surprise, craftiness, shrewdness, readiness, and I shall say individual brilliance and spontaneity," in Gilberto Freyre's words. These are the qualities of the *malandro*, that archetypal Brazilian hustler. In a country that fought its last war in the 1860s (against Paraguay), soccer generated emotions that otherwise came from the battlefield. The national team was Brazil's victorious army, and from early on politicians hitched their wagons to it. Fernando Henrique Cardoso credited some of the success of his anti-inflation plan to the optimism that gushed forth after Brazil's fourth World Cup win in 1994.

True to his discourse of national development, Lula pitched the World Cup as an excuse to build modern airports, subways, monorails, and even a bullet train between Rio and São Paulo. But it took three years for his government to design its package of public works. Now, with the World Cup just a year away, only one of the forty-four transportation projects was complete. Ten projects, the bullet train among them, had been scrapped altogether. In its defense, the government said that improvements not ready in time for the event would still get done afterward. But then why did it need the World Cup as an excuse to build them?

As useful projects languished, twelve fancy new stadiums went ahead. Lula's ministers had promised they'd need no public money at all, but the construction giants—expected to run the stadiums afterward—balked at investing in cities like Manaus, off in the middle of the Amazon, where soccer games tend to draw a couple of thousand fans. So the BNDES offered subsidized loans. Some cities offered tax credits, others guaranteed revenues. With time short and international pressure mounting, costs ballooned. Of the World Cup's eleven-billion-dollar budget, four billion would go to stadiums. No other country had ever spent so much on its World Cup arenas. Even within the government, auditors warned that some of them would end up as "white elephants," never to earn back their investments. Grasping for a solution, one official suggested turning Manaus's stadium into an open-air prison afterward.

To make room for World Cup projects, meanwhile, the government evicted thousands of people from their homes, mostly in favelas. As compensation, *favelados* sometimes got to move into affordable housing projects, but far from their old neighborhoods; other times they won a cash subsidy, but not enough to cover soaring rents. At the Maracanã, the stadium Eike and Odebrecht were acquiring, police in riot gear cracked down on Indians protesting the demolition of the adjacent Museu do Índio, which they had been using as a sanctuary since it fell into disuse years earlier. On top of all this, most World Cup tickets would cost way too much for working-class Brazilians. And FIFA would pay no taxes on its revenues. The whole thing looked like your typical boondoggle, where most Brazilians get screwed and a few well-connected people get rich. As usual, the companies that spent the most on political campaigns secured the richest contracts. Odebrecht got to work on four of the stadiums; Camargo Corrêa won transportation bids. A recurring graffiti tag asked, COPA PRA QUEM?—basically, Who's this Cup for, anyway?

Eventually it felt silly to write about anything else, so I asked to cover the protests. At one march I reported on, a protester told me his dream was to see Paulo Maluf behind bars. But one sign in particular stuck with me. It read, THE $ FOR HEALTHCARE WENT TO ODEBRECHT / THE $ FOR EDUCATION WENT TO OAS. The message was simple yet accurate. Budgets are limited, so if the government loans out billions of dollars for stadiums, it will have less to spend on subways, daycare centers, sewage lines. Economists call this an opportunity cost. Brazilians had always loathed the incestuous ties between government and its allies in business, but they rarely made the connection so openly.

I realized I had a chance to combine the billionaire beat with my protest coverage. I decided to do a story outing OAS's owner, Cesar Mata Pires, as a "hidden billionaire." I'd been watching him for a while now. In the nineties, OAS had colluded with Paulo Maluf to inflate costs on Roberto Marinho Avenue. In more recent years, it had worked on the Belo Monte mega-dam. It was one of Brazil's top construction firms, though it had emerged later than Camargo Corrêa and Odebrecht, toward the end of the military dictatorship. People jokingly referred to the company as "Obrigado, Amigo Sogro"—Thanks, Friendly Father-in-law—because Mata Pires married the daughter of the governor of Bahia, who funneled him contracts. Now he had interests in World Cup stadiums, São Paulo's international airport, and a subway line in Rio. Looking into his financial statements, I saw that Rio's fare hike had added some fifteen million dollars in revenues to one of his companies.

At Bloomberg we calculated Mata Pires's net worth at $4.7 billion. Despite his wealth, he kept a low profile, like most of his fellow public works tycoons. I found just a few photos of him; he was jowly and heavy-lidded, with slicked-back gray hair. He refused to speak with me, so instead I met with Diego Barreto, his director of investor relations. Mentioning that I'd seen OAS's name on a protest sign, I asked what he thought of the idea that the company prospered at taxpayer expense. Diego labeled the idea "ignorant and simplistic." OAS had won its stadium contracts fair and square, he said, and it was the government's decision, not OAS's, to build them.

"Did campaign donations influence that decision?" I asked.

He replied, "It's a sweet illusion that we can force the government's hand."

But OAS had given more than ten million dollars to the Workers

Party for the regional elections of 2012. That was three percent of all the money the party received that year. I had a fellow reporter with me in the interview, and he insisted: "Why donate so much?"

Diego responded with a typical line: "The company finances campaigns of all parties so they can each bring their best discourse to the street, and may the best discourse win, so that this nation can happen."

AT THE HEIGHT OF the protests, one of Eike's Twitter followers asked him, "If you could go out anonymously, like any common citizen, would you take to the streets along with the youth?" and Eike replied, "I would with Pleasure!" As the spokesman of Brazil, he may have believed—as Dilma and the Marinho brothers and everyone else seemed to—that the protests represented him. But they probably sealed his downfall. Just when he needed the government most, politicians needed as never before not to look beholden to special interests. And given his stadium deal with Odebrecht, Eike was especially toxic. The protests against him crescendoed at the final match of the Confederations Cup, which took place at the Maracanã. The signs read, NO TO PRIVATIZATION and THE MARACANÃ IS OURS, NOT EIKE BATISTA'S and EIKE-CABRAL GET OUT! To defend the stadium, Governor Cabral deployed six thousand riot police, and they dispersed the protesters the usual way, with clubs and rubber bullets. You could taste the tear gas inside the stadium.

As the tear gas floated away, prospects of an Eike bailout faded too. In Brasília, the ministers who had met with Eike to find a solution to his problems just months earlier now distanced themselves. Drily they told reporters that he didn't need their help.

Eike's Mauá moment had arrived. His empire was unraveling. He'd tried to hold it together with the usual bluster—but failed. Toward the end of May, an Internet troll had tweeted at him, "OGX IS GOING BANKRUPT! GOING BANKRUPT!" and Eike responded, "What a fool! One more who doesn't have the Patience to wait!" Another user wrote, "What's the deal, lately your companies only post losses?" and Eike: "Investment isn't a Loss! *Ufa!* Can you make bread before the Bakery is ready?" New oil wells would come online, production would increase, and share prices would "hockey stick," he said, surging back to previous highs. "Look at the story of Google, Facebook, Tesla, electric cars take 10 years until the [first] Profit! We're doing it in much less!" Someone else asked, "How will you pay OGX's debt, and the interest on the debt, and maintain investments?" And Eike wrote: "We're going to present a business plan soon! Tied to the good older projects and to new areas and Partnerships! . . . Rumor Radio won't prevail!"

Eike's last claim to credibility was that he had held on to his investments in his shaky startups. Even as he wrote these words, though, he was selling shares in OGX for the first time ever. The disclosure emerged quietly in a regulatory filing a week and a half later. Over just a few days, he'd unloaded sixty million dollars' worth of stock, the equivalent of two percent of the company.

He still held a majority interest, but the sale raised a red flag. The previous year, to demonstrate his confidence in a turnaround, he had promised to put a billion dollars into OGX at more than six *reais* a share. But now he'd sold at less than two *reais* a share. Why would he sell low today only to buy high later? Though he released a statement promising not to sell anymore, the implication was clear: Eike no longer planned to put fresh capital into the company. Without that guarantee, it would run out of money much sooner than investors had been banking on. OGX's shares soon plunged below one *real*. Eike's flagship business had become a penny stock. In the debt market, meanwhile, investors were paying less than fifty cents on the dollar for OGX's bonds. When bonds trade at this level, it's usually because bankruptcy is not far off.

Eike's share sales also gave the impression that, as chairman and controlling shareholder, he might know something the rest of the market didn't. The impression seemed to be confirmed on July 1. That day, OGX announced a complete halt to production. "The company has concluded that, at this moment, no technology exists for economically viable development of the Tiger Shark, Cat Shark, and Sand Shark fields," the release read, referring to the company's main areas. In other words, after spending five billion dollars to drill more than a hundred wells offshore of Brazil, Eike's dream team had determined there was no way to turn a profit from the reserves he had announced as some of the richest in the world. In his book, Eike had cited a quote attributed to John D. Rockefeller: "The best business in the world is a well run oil company. The second best business in the world is a badly run oil company." Eike was proving Rockefeller wrong. As his share prices once again plummeted, his net worth slipped to four billion dollars.

With Eike's companies going under, a lot of people wanted to know why the BNDES had lent so much money to them. It became a political issue, symbol of a Workers Party policy of "picking winners." Called to testify before Congress, the bank's president, Luciano Coutinho, minimized the risk to public coffers. Though the BNDES had approved a total of five billion dollars for Eike's companies, it actually had only three billion dollars on the line with him, Coutinho said, because when EBX's troubles emerged in 2012, the bank had refrained from disbursing the other two billion. That was still a large chunk of the bank's capital, but Coutinho insisted that Eike had offered guarantees that protected taxpayer money.

What Coutinho didn't say was why the bank had kept its concerns to itself. He also ignored the question of opportunity costs. Even if the BNDES didn't lose money, what could Brazil have gained if it had put the money elsewhere? And perhaps most important: Did Eike, with his talent for raising private investment, really need government help?

Coutinho had spoken candidly about the guarantees, however. Through a freedom of information request, one of my colleagues discovered that Eike had put up a billion dollars in personal assets as collateral for the BNDES's loans. To cover the rest, he had acquired letters of guarantee from private banks. We knew Eike had piled on leverage, but this revelation meant he was swimming in it. And more debts would soon emerge. It turned out that the Emirates were calling in their investment, and even after handing over what little he still had of value, Eike owed one and a half billion dollars to their sovereign wealth fund. Adding up all the liabilities we now knew about, and subtracting them from the value of his much-depreciated assets, his net worth stood at around two hundred million dollars.

EIKE BATISTA HAD CEASED to be a billionaire. When we announced it in a story on July 25, every media outlet in Brazil picked it up. The national icon of wealth had lost just about everything—thirty-four billion dollars—in sixteen months. It felt like the end of an era. The news went beyond the business pages. It was the stuff of small talk with taxi drivers. An Eike reference even made it into one of Globo's telenovelas. "I made some bad investments," a character named Guto tells his ex-wife. "I put all my money and some clients' money into shares of that billionaire who went broke. The guy went broke, and I went broke along with him, baby. My money went up in smoke."

A running joke sprang up on social media. "Eike's so poor . . ." it would start, followed by one of the daily indignities that ordinary Brazilians endure. "Eike's so poor that he was seen waiting in line to recharge his Bilhete Único [public transit card]. . . . Eike's so poor that he started drying his clothes behind the fridge. . . . Eike's so poor that he took to the streets to shout that it's not about the twenty *centavos* anymore."

I happened to be in New York for a team meeting when Eike lost his billionairehood. It was a big story for us too. Bloomberg TV producers asked me to comment three times that day. I'd done live linkups from São Paulo a few times, but going on TV still felt surreal. The only way I could overcome my fear of public performance was by acting as if it were theater, with me playing the role of a financial journalist. This felt no less strange for being my actual profession. That day I managed to ad-lib with apparent confidence, but in the heat of improvisation, I said something I now regret. The anchor Tom Keene asked me whether, in the United States, Eike could ever have risen as he had. Without time to think, I blurted, "Well, it could not have played out as it has"—and explained that our regulators took a stricter approach to grandiose forecasts like Eike's.

This might technically be true, but only technically. American capitalism has created its share of bubbles. Writing about the railroad tycoons of the 1800s, the historian Richard White speaks of the "utilitarian fictions of capitalism" that they spun to sell impossible projects to investors. Railroad bubbles popped and reinflated a few times in those years, jerking the world economy from growth into depression and back again. A century later a slew of Silicon Valley men raised money for startups even airier than Eike's, and when the dot-com bubble popped in 2000, trillions of dollars' worth of market value was destroyed. Many who lost their savings rebuilt them in the next bubble, and when the subprime mortgage market collapsed, many trillions more evaporated, and the economy all but seized up entirely. In the end, Eike wouldn't take down the BNDES, but his bubble was different from those only in its scale, not in its essence. What he offered was an old kind of gimmick: great rewards and negligible risks—impossible every time.

AFTER HIS TRIUMPHAL RETURN, Eike was staying off Twitter again. He had gone silent after the protests. Instead he published an op-ed in *Valor Econômico,* Brazil's leading financial newspaper (co-owned by the Marinhos). Long, circular, and repetitive, showing few signs of outside editing, it was his defense before the court of public opinion. He vowed to pay back his creditors. He knew he had let people down and spoke of his frustration at failing to deliver what he'd hoped. "I always acted in good faith, and I always will," he wrote. He'd hired the best people in the oil industry, and they fed him nothing but good news, he said. And the Big Three credit rating agencies had never noticed anything amiss.

"Obviously, I was in ecstasy over the information I was receiving," Eike wrote. "Could I have kept it to myself? No, I was the controller of a publicly traded company, and what I did was to share all of that splendor and respective challenges with the market, as well as"—this aside like a pharmaceutical warning label—"all of the involved risks and chances of success in this very high-risk business."

Eike's memory, at least in the op-ed, was selective. He reminded his readers that world-class auditors, DeGolyer & MacNaughton, had estimated OGX's reserves at nearly eleven billion barrels back in 2011. What he didn't say was that D&M's vice-president had written a letter privately complaining that Eike had distorted its report. According to the letter, later made public, OGX's press releases lumped together mostly uncertain reserve estimates with more probable ones in a way that violated international standards. Eike apologized to D&M's people but never issued a public correction.

"I ask myself where I went wrong," Eike went on, then offered an explanation that contradicted itself: "Maybe I put too much trust in people who didn't deserve that trust, even if the ultimate responsibility is all mine."

A lot of ordinary Brazilians had in turn put too much trust in Eike. The local press started running interviews with people who, like the guy in the Globo novela, bet their money on him and lost it all. Many had bought into OGX at its peak in 2010, when Eike made his trillion-dollar pitch in that Web video for a local brokerage. One middle-aged Brazilian, João, had put his life savings into OGX. When the stock price tanked, João said that Eike's defiant tweets gave him the courage to double down. He sold land he'd inherited from his dad to buy even more shares. By now he'd lost eighty thousand dollars, money he'd meant to use as down payment on a new apartment. When a Bloomberg reporter spoke to him, João asked to omit his last name; he'd yet to tell his wife.

Eike knew João's pain. "The one who lost the most with the destruction of OGX's value was one shareholder: Eike Batista," he wrote. "No one lost as much as I did."

———

THE NEXT TIME I went to Rio, I passed in front of the Serrador building, and tall, flimsy boards surrounded it. During a series of teachers' protests, demonstrators had thrown rocks through the high glass panes at the entrance. The glass now appeared to be melting in the heat. The dark-tint film that covered it acted as a sack for the shattered fragments, and this sack sagged gradually earthward like a painting by Dalí. Eike's employees used a side entrance for a while. But Eike could no longer afford the rent, more than a million dollars a month, and his staff just kept shrinking. So he moved back into a building he used to occupy on Flamengo Beach. He seemed to have resigned himself to winding down his affairs in orderly fashion.

Just months after forging their partnership, Eike had fallen out with André Esteves. There was no evidence he'd worked to undermine Eike, but he hadn't succeeded in saving EBX, either. So in August 2013, Eike scaled back his agreement with Pactual and hired a restructuring expert instead. "Restructuring" is what happens when big companies fail, a euphemism for liquidation. With luck, something would be left over for Eike at the end of it.

Piece by piece, the empire of Eike, Brazil's national champion, was being hawked off to foreigners. He'd already sold MPX Energia. In August he agreed to hand over control of LLX, the company building Açu, to a U.S. investment fund. The fund paid half a billion dollars, a fraction of the money Eike had spent trying to build it. With China's growth flagging, iron ore prices fell so low that MMX Mineração looked hopeless. But Eike managed to sell its port to the Emirates and a Dutch commodities trading firm. Negotiating from a position of weakness, Eike earned far less with his deals than he might have before. Privately he complained that he'd sold MMX's port *a preço de banana,* for the price of a banana. He had reportedly broken into tears after selling Açu, his favorite project. But he freed himself from the companies' debts, and this was his most urgent task.

Eike still had to deal with his oil company and the venture meant to service it with oil platforms. No one wanted to touch these. Despite his promise not to sell any more shares in OGX Petróleo, between late August and early September he sold more anyway. Bankruptcy seemed a question not of if but when. OGX's suppliers complained about overdue bills, and in October the company missed an interest payment on its bonds. What happened next would come to haunt Eike. Fearing lawsuits from shareholders down the road, OGX's management formally asked Eike to make good on his promise to put money into the company. This was OGX's last hope to stay afloat. But Eike refused. He invoked a clause in the contract that allowed him to back out if the company's business plan changed— and halting operations, of course, counted as a radical change. This clause had been kept secret up till now.

On the last day of October, OGX, with more than five billion dollars in debt, had no choice but to file for bankruptcy protection. It was the largest corporate bankruptcy Latin America had ever seen. OGX's sister company, OSX Brasil, filed a week and a half later. Meant to service an oil giant that never materialized, it had little reason to exist anymore. On the stock exchange, the companies were now nearly worthless. Their bonds traded for pennies on the dollar.

The Xs that once stood for wealth multiplication came to look like a curse. OGX soon changed its name to the merely descriptive Óleo & Gas Participações. The American investment fund that took over LLX renamed it Prumo. The German power company that bought MPX renamed it Eneva, and people in the market joked it was short for Eike Never Again. No one wanted to be associated with Eike Batista anymore.

JUST WHEN IT SEEMED Eike's life couldn't get any worse, the accusations came. Brazil's securities and exchange commission, the CVM, tends to take years to pursue investigations. After opening its probe into Jorge Paulo Lemann, it took four years to reach a settlement.

But public pressure now was intense. Minority shareholders had sued the agency, claiming that its poor oversight had allowed Eike to swindle them. They had grounds to believe this. When Eike took OGX public in 2008, the offering prospectus had cited oil reserve estimates based not on any physical study but on extrapolations from nearby fields—data that, in the United States, regulators deem too uncertain for a public company to release at all.

The CVM apparently failed to enforce its own rules too. Based on guidelines from Brazil's National Oil Agency, even when a well begins pumping, initial measurements are too iffy for use in estimating future production. Eike released these estimates as soon as the oil gushed forth, and regulators said nothing.

In its defense, the CVM had minimal staff and a tiny budget. A friend of mine joined the agency out of a sincere hope to crack down on fraud in the market, but spoke with resigned chagrin about how little he could do. Sometimes they couldn't even afford toner for their printers. But they moved now with rare speed, forwarding their findings to public prosecutors in Rio and São Paulo, who joined them in poring over securities filings, examining the minutes of board meetings, interviewing former executives.

Over the course of 2014, prosecutors would produce three separate indictments, charging Eike with manipulating the market, false representation, misleading investors, conspiracy, and three counts of insider trading. Some of the accusations were leveled at his former executives too. On top of all this, Brazil's internal revenue service fined Eike eighty-five million dollars for allegedly evading capital gains taxes.

The charges centered on OGX Petróleo. To prove that Eike had misled investors, prosecutors described how he and his men had exaggerated the company's prospects in fifty-five *fatos relevantes*— regulatory jargon for vital company information. Every time they found a trace of oil, OGX announced it using confident phrases that projected low costs and abundant reserves. Since most investors don't know the oil industry, and most stock analysts aren't geologists, these filings were interpreted as signs of progress, that Eike's vision would be fulfilled. Doubling as press releases, they often led OGX's share price to jump in the next trading session.

In his op-ed, Eike claimed he was just sharing the good news. But prosecutors said he'd released only the most optimistic interpretations of OGX's data, hiding anything that could hurt the share price. As early as 2011, Eike's own engineers found indications that the oil in OGX's main fields was divided into too many separate pockets to be extracted for a profit. Early drilling also detected what's known in the industry as death gas, which makes it prohibitively expensive to pump oil without killing your platform crew.

The most blatant omission came after the bombshell announcement of June 2012, when the company revealed that its first two wells were producing just a fraction of what they were supposed to. Eike had replaced Dr. Oil with a new CEO named Luiz Carneiro, and one of the first things Carneiro did was to hire Schlumberger, the Houston oil services giant, to carry out an independent analysis of OGX's reserves. Schlumberger calculated that of the eleven billion barrels of oil Eike proclaimed, only a few hundred million could be taken up and sold at a profit.

The report was ready by September of that year, and according to securities law, prosecutors said Eike should have disclosed the findings to the public immediately, because they drastically changed the outlook for the company. Instead he sat on them. But not only that. It was a month *after* the Schlumberger report that he promised to put a billion dollars of his own money into OGX if it ran out of cash. Prosecutors believed that the contract's hidden escape clause proved that Eike had never intended to fulfill this promise. It was a manipulation, they said, to boost the stock price.

One count of insider trading aimed at Eike's first sale of OGX stock, when he dumped shares even while tweeting that the company was going to make a comeback. If he'd waited to sell till after July 1, when OGX announced it was shutting down its fields, he would have earned less than half as much. Adding in the other two counts, for similar maneuvers, Eike avoided losses of around a hundred million dollars. This sounds small when you compare it to the thirty-billion-dollar fortune he once held. But all that paper money had vanished, and creditors were breathing down his neck, and every million mattered now.

If convicted on all charges, Eike could go to prison for as long as thirteen years. As a college dropout, he might even end up locked away with common prisoners, since according to Brazil's penal code, only university graduates enjoy the right to a special cell, no matter how rich they are. It would be the first time someone had ever served time for financial crimes in Brazil—though of course, insider trading became a crime here only in 2001, a fitting delay in the land of the cordial man. As with his son, few believed someone like Eike could ever go to jail. But the case against him was much better than the one against Thor for manslaughter. And Brazilians wanted to see someone rich and powerful get his due.

CHAPTER 10

TOO BIG TO FAIL

DEBT, CRISIS, AND A COMEBACK

"When you've done the right thing, you just keep on going."

—EIKE BATISTA (NEGATIVE $1 BILLION)

WHEN I FIRST STARTED REPORTING ON BILLIONAIRES, I assumed I'd speak to Eike all the time. It was only later that I realized I didn't fully believe my own skepticism of him, and some large part of me imagined he'd just stay on top forever. But then his empire began to sink, and he stopped giving the press the generous access he used to. Later, complaining about the media's coverage of him, he would single out Bloomberg for its focus on his obliterated fortune. As he headed toward zero, the net worth obsession lost its fun.

After I quit my job to write this book, I tried to talk to Eike again. I tried all throughout 2014 and into 2015. He had winnowed his press army to just one person, and she kept dangling the possibility of an interview, never saying no, never saying yes. Speaking with her, I made the argument journalists often make, that it would be better *for him* to share his point of view with me, to help shape the narrative. But we both knew the truth, that the interview was for me. I'd only ever talked to Eike on the phone, and having lived with him at the front of my brain for a few years, I desperately wanted to meet him face-to-face. I wanted to throw my ideas at him and see what stuck.

As the indictments rolled in, Eike fought to stay above water. His companies reported stunning losses for 2013—ten billion dollars all told. Most of the twenty thousand workers he once bragged about had been laid off. In February a group of bondholders took over his oil company. Money was so tight now that management even sold off office equipment. They held an auction for desks and computers and coffee mugs that carried the OGX logo with its spinning Incan sun. Eike's third and fourth bankruptcies, of MMX and MPX, would come later in the year.

Eike's net worth soon fell below zero on Bloomberg's ranking. The memes about him seemed real when he was spotted at Rio's international airport with Flávia Sampaio—by now the mother of his third son, born amid the protests of June 2013. (They named him after another Norse god, Balder, he who radiates light.) The paparazzi used to shoot them jogging around the Rodrigo de Freitas Lagoon, he looking trim and vigorous in his Nike shorts, she in a halter top that showed off a bronzed six-pack. Now it looked like Brazil's onetime richest man couldn't afford to pay for a private jet. He was seeing her off before she checked in on a commercial flight to Miami. At one point, as one of their staff tended the baby stroller, Eike draped his arm over Flávia's shoulders as though he needed support. He wore his double-denim outfit, blue jeans and a wrinkly blue shirt with the sleeves rolled up. He didn't smile, he looked tired.

Brazilians knew what it was like to go into debt. Under Lula and Dilma, millions had used credit for the first time in their lives. But they weren't used to it, and many took on too much at too-high rates and found themselves on bad credit lists, receiving phone calls and text messages from banks and retailers, now friendly, now cajoling, urging them to pay up. Globo ran frequent specials on consumers swimming in past-due bills. And they did what you do, cut back on expenses, made payment plans.

It was different for Eike, though. There's a quote attributed to the late American billionaire J. Paul Getty: "If you owe the bank a hundred dollars, that's your problem. If you owe the bank a hundred million dollars, that's the bank's problem." Since Eike's debts were backed by the assets he still owned, creditors had an interest in seeing him prosper. This explains why the Emirates' sovereign wealth fund paid him a salary of five million dollars a year to keep his office running.

The memes about Eike were just wishful thinking. If anything, he was billionaire-poor. He and Flávia now flew commercial when they went abroad, but not in coach, and for domestic trips he chartered his own plane. A rumor circulated that he'd sold his Lamborghini, but then he was seen driving a Ferrari around Rio. A few nights before OGX filed for bankruptcy protection, his son Olin hit up an electronic-music club called Zozô. He reserved multiple camarotes—VIP booths—and ran up a tab of around seven thousand dollars. Now eighteen, Olin still deejayed at clubs around Brazil, gold-plated headphones around his neck. A gossip reporter interviewed his girlfriend, Babi Rossi, who came to fame as a scantily clad dancer on one of the Sunday variety shows that are a staple of Brazilian TV. "I don't ask about the crisis," she said. "I don't really know what's happening, but nothing changed. His standard of living hasn't fallen."

Thor, now twenty-two, would later say that he became depressed in those days and took heavy meds to get to sleep. Privately, he worried about "ending up poor." But life on the outside looked the same as always. On his Facebook page, he posted a selfie with his latest girlfriend in the cockpit of a helicopter. As he smiled wide, a silver necklace dangling into his V-neck, she pursed her lips in a smile-approximation that avoided wrinkles. In another photo they posed on the deck of a yacht, Thor in Speedo, Lunara in a leopard-print bikini top and high-arcing G string. Thor kept doing what he loved. He sculpted his body into the perfect array of muscle. On Instagram he posted a photo of himself in his personal gym, arms crossed, every fiber flexed, biceps like oversize shot put balls with veins, as he pursed his lips and made a mean look past the camera. He said he now weighed 230 pounds. (One of his lady followers commented, "He's going to explode!")

When Thor was spotted driving his Aston Martin, journalists called one of his lawyers for comment. The lawyer confirmed that, yes, Thor had been convicted for vehicular manslaughter—"but that doesn't mean he won't be acquitted" on appeal. The conviction had changed nothing for Thor. In one Facebook post, he recorded a video showing a close-up of a sports car dashboard. Embossed in the steering wheel was a backward E that shared its spine with a B, for Eike Batista. With a flip-flop-clad foot visible at the bottom of the frame, Thor revved the engine, and the tachometer's needle repeatedly flicked, registering the car's power.

But none of this caused much outrage anymore. Just months after the explosion of June 2013, the reaction was a collective *"Fazer o quê?"*—What are you gonna do?

I HAD GOTTEN USED to the protests. For a while they became a weirdly normal feature of life: *Sorry I'm late—protesters blocked Paulista Avenue. . . .* I would meet sources for stories about billionaires, and we'd small-talk about the protests as you small-talk about the weather. But after the show of action in Brasília, the protest movement ebbed. Most Brazilians put down their placards and returned to normal life. Now you couldn't organize anything without the "black blocs" showing up, kids in masks who believed breaking shit was a political message, and they scared off the mom-and-pop protesters. Bankers no longer came down from their offices to join the crowd. The story became less of a story, so fewer reporters showed up too. All this made it easier for the police to crack down again. The giant had awakened, then gone back to sleep, even though the national unease only grew.

Brazilians still talked about the protests. "June" gained a kind of mythical significance. Just that no one could figure out what it all meant. People grasped for connections in unrelated events, like when teenagers from the poor *periferia* started gathering en masse at malls. In December, six thousand teens filled the vast parking lot around Shopping Metrô Itaquera, a mall tucked beside a train station on São Paulo's working-class east side. They formed dance circles. Boys strutted in neon Adidas and board shorts and flat-brimmed baseball caps, some bare-chested, some wearing faux-gold chains draped over T-shirts with logos large enough to read on the screens of the smart-phones capturing it all on video. There was Quiksilver, Hollister, Abercrombie & Fitch. There were girls in halter tops and purposely torn jean-shorts. They called their meet-up a *rolezinho* or "little stroll."

Soon enough an SUV rolled up, lights flashing. A security guard hopped out and said something that was hard to hear over the racket but could have been nothing other than an order to disperse. A couple of guys who'd been dancing got in his face, thrusting their chests out; one pushed him. As more security guards arrived, the teens streamed into the mall. Loudly they swept through the food court, where fluorescent bulbs lit up table after table of trays filled with fast food from Bob's Burgers and Habib's. Diners looked up from their fries and falafel with nervous curiosity. Some kids smoked joints and drank hard liquor from the bottle. When a few of them broke into a run, others joined them without even knowing why, and this morphed into near-panic. Cops showed up, shopkeepers brought down their shutters, the mall closed early; slowly everyone left.

More little strolls followed at malls elsewhere on the outskirts of São Paulo. With each event the tensions rose. Police felt their authority challenged. The whole thing peaked in mid-January when three thousand teens descended on Shopping Itaquera, the site of the first little stroll. Riot police showed up. In the parking lot, they shot rubber bullets and tear gas canisters into the crowd. Reporters saw cops, unprovoked, clubbing and kicking the teens as they dispersed. Meanwhile, to protect chic *shoppings* in the city center, security guards at the doors demanded ID from anyone of color.

The tension of "June" clung to the air, but now the collective upset turned away from the rich and powerful and found an outlet in old social differences instead. On the SBT network an anchor named Rachel Sheherazade declared, "Malls became popular in Brazil because they provided a place for shopping and leisure for those who sought *security*"—she drew out the word, *se-gu-ran-ça.* "And now even this refuge has been violated!" On YouTube videos of the little strolls, commenters went further: "You give them Bolsa Família and create this bunch of useless bums . . . they just want to steal and make children . . . bunch of trash." And: "These *favelados* don't deserve a mall." And: "Today they're packing the malls, tomorrow they'll pack the prisons." On its editorial page, *O Globo* lamented above all the losses to commerce that these gatherings caused.

Perhaps because of the taste of tear gas, some lefties imagined the beginnings of a movement, poor youths asserting their right to public space. It was way less ambitious than that. *Folha de S.Paulo* interviewed a seventeen-year-old named Lucas Lima who organized *rolezinhos* on social media. On Facebook he had more than fifty thousand followers. He was one of several *ídolos*—teen idols with no fame beyond the online fans, mostly girls, who admire the photos where they pose with shiny new sneakers, brand-name T-shirts, and crisp baseball caps. *Folha* ran a picture of Lucas Lima wearing an Ultimate Fighting Championship tank top with a loose gold chain laid over it. His close-cropped mohawk perfectly gelled, he crossed his arms to display a knock-off Invicta watch and smiled boyishly with perfect white teeth. He said he bought everything *parcelado,* on high-interest installment plans. He told *Folha* he'd kissed sixteen or seventeen girls at the last two *rolezinhos.*

The strolls briefly spread to Rio, then petered out. These kids didn't want to protest; they wanted to belong. While at Bloomberg, I'd started teaching English once a month in the favela of Real Parque across the Pinheiros River. When I asked my students, mostly in their late teens, if any of them had joined the protests of June, they scoffed like *what does that have to do with us?* The *rolezinho* was anti-political. It was about kissing and commerce. The strolling youths listened to *funk ostentação,* a gaudy variation on the favela-born rap *baile funk.* Here's a typical line from MC Guimê, a tattoo-covered dude who looks too scrawny to stand under the weight of his giant watches and heavy gold chains: "Counting up hundred-*real* notes inside a Citroën / we invite the girls because we know they'll get in."

The message of *funk ostentação* overlapped with the message of Eike, and with Lula's. It was a message about how you measure success in life, how you measure progress. Later I taught in another favela, João XXIII. There a sixteen year old kid named Bruno said to me, "You can be in the United States. Why do you choose here?" Because I like the people, I said, which is true. Later, when I asked the class how the United States was different from Brazil, Bruno was quick to volunteer, "Cars are a lot less expensive there." I'd heard the same sort of comment from rich Brazilians in Miami. Bruno got to school on a crappy motorcycle, and he hoped to purchase something nicer. He loved English, he applied himself, and he aimed for a solid job one day, but I wondered what he was after—and what he could really hope for.

This was the youth of the Workers Party years, the new generation of an emerging middle class. In the United States you'd call them poor, though they were not poor by Brazilian standards. They ate well, they dressed well, they owned things; they were better off than their parents had ever dreamed. But their status as citizens remained incomplete. A short walk from Shopping Itaquera, I visited a favela known as Paz and hung out in homes that had Internet connections but leaned precariously over a shit-smelling foamy black creek full of trash. The *ídolos* and their fans might have flat-screen TVs, but they sleep in a room with four people. They might have smartphones— LGs and Nokias in blinged-out cases—but they have no family doctor. If there was a Brazilian Dream, as Eike claimed, these kids grasped its shallowest outlines.

Three months after he first made national news, the *ídolo* Lucas

Lima again appeared in the newspaper. He had been killed during a fight at a *baile funk* party. His family buried him at Itaquera cemetery, one of the east side's few stretches of green.

SOON ENOUGH, EIKE AND "June" and the *rolezinhos* all faded into the background. It was 2014, and no one could pay attention to anything but the World Cup, just a few months away. The nation dragged itself to an improvised finish. Airport expansions were still under way, so construction firms threw up temporary terminals to receive tourists. With light-rail and express-bus lines unfinished, cities declared holidays to ease traffic for the matches. I watched the first game at a friend's house, and on TV you could see that São Paulo's half-billion-dollar Arena Corinthians wasn't quite complete yet either. The roof's support beams lacked glass covering on two sides. Odebrecht had promised to deliver the stadium by the end of 2013, but in November a giant crane swooned and collapsed, dropping a four-hundred-ton section of the roof and crushing two workers to death. Another worker died in March when he fell from a high row of bleachers he was installing. This meant the temporary seating for twenty thousand of the sixty thousand fans now in the stadium had never been fully tested.

In the event, though, nothing collapsed on live TV. And the Seleção beat Croatia three–one. And that night, despite the general ill will, Brazilians all around the country celebrated the win, and much *cachaça* and beer was consumed with varying degrees of cognitive dissonance.

Normally, weeks in advance of the World Cup, people would hang the Brazilian flag from their windows and paint their streets green and yellow. This time São Paulo looked as it usually does, beige. A lot of Brazilians had decided to root against the national team. A friend of mine, Vinícius, put it like this: "The thing is that if we win, people are going to say it was all somehow worth it." The day after the opening match, though, Brazil's green and yellow fluttered from balconies across the city. Drivers encased their side-view mirrors in elastic flag-koozies. Soon all anyone talked about was *futebol*. With no job to go to—I'd left Bloomberg several months earlier—I let myself get carried away in the game-watching too. For each Brazil match, companies let their employees off early, banks and government offices closed, and the country ground to a halt, an old World Cup tradition. Everyone decided to forget for a time why they'd been protesting. They forgot Eike's sketchy stadium deal. They got swept up in the tingly prospect of a sixth World Cup title, an older Brazilian dream.

This made the defeat all the more painful. I watched the semifinals amid a sea of canary-yellow jerseys overflowing from a bar near my home. When the Germans scored an early goal, my friend Pedro comforted himself saying, "Wait, it's still early." But then the second goal came just a few minutes later. Around me groans of disappointment mixed with shouts of encouragement for players who couldn't hear them. The third goal came so quick, some thought it was an instant replay. I had never seen anyone, much less a group of people, cycle through emotions so quickly. On the fourth goal, I heard mutters of distraught shock. By the fifth: disgust. Brazil was down five–zero on its home turf, in the semifinals of the World Cup, not just missing the chance to atone for the loss of 1950 but making a mockery of it, mocking soccer, the Brazilian sport. When the Germans scored their sixth goal, a guy next to me held his plastic cup in his teeth and tore his Seleção jersey in half, leaving intact only the green hem at the bottom, releasing his hairy beer-belly into the evening air. "*Que vergonha!*" he shouted—Shame! But plenty of others ironically cheered the goal. Pedro blew his vuvuzela. The embarrassment gave way to a giddy, unreal feeling. That tragedy-farce thing. By the seventh goal, people were laughing. Brazil's last-minute goal, bringing the score to seven–one, only inspired eye-rolls—like, *Where were you ninety minutes ago?*

The next day on newsstands the front pages in giant letters blared MASSACRE; HUMILIATION AT HOME; THE GREATEST FIASCO IN HISTORY; DEFEAT OF DEFEATS. Photographs showed Brazilians in their yellow jerseys sobbing. Some had burned the Brazilian flag. For a couple of years now people had joked, whenever the country's basic infrastructure fell short, *"Imagina na Copa!"* Or in other words, If you think this is bad, just wait for the chaos of a million tourists here for the World Cup. Brazilians had imagined any kind of disaster but this one. One much-shared tweet proclaimed that the defeat had officially resurrected the *complexo de vira-lata,* that old inferiority complex. On Facebook an old colleague of mine from the São Paulo newsroom wondered, "How will this affect my children?"

The stock market rallied on the defeat because investors bet that it would hurt Dilma's reelection chances later in the year. Paradoxically, though, the defeat drew attention away from questions about how public money should be spent. On the whole, Brazilians now seemed more concerned about the legacy of a lost soccer match than about the four billion dollars sunk into shiny stadiums. They had expected such a mess from the organization that when none of the stadiums collapsed, it felt like success, and when Dilma claimed victory for Brazil off the field, it seemed believable.

The problem was that the cost of this victory went even beyond the stadiums. My personal GDP fell during the month of games, and I wasn't alone. What with all the half-days for matches of the Seleção, and the general *carnaval* atmosphere of the days in between, the World Cup cut into factory shifts and kept shoppers at home. The economy, already suffering from the drop in commodity prices, dipped into recession. Capital flowed out of the country, and the *real,* which had soared in value during the Lula years, now weakened against the dollar. This would make those trips to Miami more expensive, but more urgently, it raised the cost of imported goods in Brazil. With the cost of living up and actual production down, some analysts diagnosed stagflation.

———

AFTER THE WORLD CUP, Eike's indictments resurfaced in the news cycle. By now local journalists had published two books on him, with another on the way, and none of them were flattering. So his lawyers set up a round of interviews for him to present his defense. I was—agonizingly—left out, but when the interviews were published in local papers in September, I devoured them like someone breaking a fast. Eike hadn't made any public statement since that op-ed a year earlier. He didn't allow photos, but two different reporters described his hair as grayer than before. One said he looked to be on the verge of tears. "I never intended to trick any investor," Eike said. "I didn't run away. I'm here honoring my commitments."

Down as he was, Eike remained Eike. Did he have regrets? Sure, he regretted using the stock market to fund his startups. Though he had promised short-term successes, he blamed investors for their short-termism. Also, he regretted having given so many interviews. But his media campaign had been a selfless act. "Without this kind of overexposure, you can't reach the youth," he said. "Deep down I always wanted to send a message to young Brazilians that this country needs to think big." He didn't mention the *rolezinho* kids, though his message had trickled down to them too.

What about the shareholders who lost their savings—did he feel bad for them? "*Poxa*, if minority investors had made money, nobody would be complaining," he said. "Sorry, that's the way this industry is. Oil exploration is a risky business anywhere in the world." In other words, you should have known what you were getting into, even though he proclaimed his projects "idiot-proof." Self-serving as it was, he had a point.

Asked whether his big talk might have inflated hopes for his companies, Eike just ignored the question. He said he'd tweeted on the eve of OGX's collapse because he *still believed in the company*. To justify why he hadn't released the Schlumberger report, which declared his main oil fields to be duds, he said he'd ordered further studies because the findings were inconclusive. "How are you going to announce something you don't know?" he asked. Of course, he'd never been so cautious about data that made OGX look good. But for this he again blamed his executives. His stock options, he now recognized, gave them an incentive to massage the numbers. And then he said this: "Myself, unfortunately, I do not understand oil."

Whenever I spoke to Brazilians about Eike now, they were certain he'd stashed away untold millions in offshore accounts. Eike insisted he'd pledged everything to creditors and still had debts left over. He pegged his net worth at negative one billion dollars—making him, as one Bloomberg headline announced, a negative-billionaire. "Many have told me, 'Eike, what you've gone through a lot of people couldn't endure,'" he said. "I was born as a middle-class kid. To go back to that . . . for me, obviously, it's a big blow to my family."

The idea that Eike had ever been middle class was hard enough to swallow. The idea that he was middle class now inspired a new round of memes. BuzzFeed's Brazilian site published a list of twelve suggestions on how he could save money, given his new economic status. One was: "Look for neighbors with unlocked Wi-Fi networks." Another: "When your detergent gets low, add a bit of water. Shake well. Use normally." But as the accusations moved forward, people got a sense of how rich Eike remained even deep in the hole. Apparently hoping to shield his assets from seizure, he'd transferred two properties to Thor and Olin worth a combined twenty-five million dollars— his beach house in Angra, plus the Rio mansion next to his where they lived with Luma. To Flávia Sampaio he transferred an apartment in Ipanema. He also transferred tens of millions of dollars in cash to them. To make sure there would be something left to seize in case of a conviction, the judge on Eike's case, Flávio Souza, froze $120 million he held in local bank accounts and a bond fund.

For almost every accusation, Eike had an explanation. He addressed the insider trading charges by saying he didn't sell his shares for personal gain but because the creditors to whom he'd pledged them demanded it. He claimed he'd tried to sell as little OGX stock as possible, instead paying his debts with cash or by handing over stakes in private companies. If this was true, though, why did he still have $120 million in the bank? Anyway, as far as prosecutors were concerned, Eike's justifications for selling didn't matter. What mattered was that he'd sold shares with access to nonpublic information, and that he received more money than he would have by selling them later, when the rest of the market knew what he knew.

In each interview, Eike repeated a defense that he seemed to consider his trump card: He had held on to the vast majority of his stake in OGX. If he knew the company was going under, why hadn't he sold more? But Eike's argument had a flaw. It was probably impossible to sell much more than he had. Even at OGX's peak, he'd failed to pawn off a stake to one of the global giants of oil. And the moment he started selling shares in the open market, investors assumed he no longer believed in the future of the enterprise. OGX's promise had always depended on Eike's personal backing—his "skin in the game." If he had attempted to unload his shares earlier, demand in the market would have vanished.

Despite his popular discredit, Eike's claims of good faith got a good reception from some businessmen. Olavo Monteiro de Carvalho, the wealthy industrial heir who worked with Eike in the eighties, told me he believed Eike truly had been misled by his executives. Rubens Menin, a low-income-housing billionaire, chalked up the ill will toward Eike to "anti-business prejudice." Others blamed pathological self-belief, not malice, for Eike's debacle, as if that were better. For a long time, I believed this too. Reading the accusations, though, things got cloudier. When he hid disappointing data, had he fooled himself or had he hoped to fool others? Did he figure that he was in too deep to turn back, that his only chance was to bluff his way through it, praying for a change of fortune down the road?

In her book on Eike's downfall, the journalist Malu Gaspar reveals a telling episode. Before OGX started going south, one of Eike's geologists had brought him bad news on a new well in a promising area: A dangerous gas leak had forced them to shut it down before they could estimate how much oil it held. "But can't you even speculate?" Eike asked. The geologist said it would be a wild guess at best. "Give me a hypothetical value, a range," Eike insisted. His employee hesitated but said that if they managed to reopen the well without any new leaks, it might hold between a hundred and fifty and six hundred million barrels of oil. "Great!" Eike said. "Six hundred million!" And the number only grew from there. By the time it was leaked to the press, it had somehow risen to two billion barrels.

In the end, deception and self-deception probably mingled in Eike—and fed each other. Prosecutors may be able to prove when he *knew* OGX was going under, but proving when he *believed* it will be harder.

TOWARD THE END OF 2014, I told Eike's PR person that I'd be in Rio one last time before I finished the reporting for my book, and that this would be Eike's last chance to speak with me. She responded with three emojis: a thumbs-up, a winking face, a kissy face. I took this to mean *Okay; I get you; goodbye!*

In November, though, I got to see him in person at last. Flávio Souza, the judge on his case, had called the first hearing in his trial for the charges levied by Rio prosecutors. The courthouse was downtown, not far from the Serrador. I got there early and took the elevator to the top floor. It was a beautiful *carioca* day, the sky rich blue. As I walked down the hall to the courtroom, Christ the Redeemer flashed through the windows.

Inside, the courtroom resembled a small college auditorium. Reporters milled about as photographers and cameramen set up at one side. I heard that Eike had entered the building through a back entrance and come up in a VIP elevator. When he walked in, we all went quiet, but the silence filled with the cascading clicks of two dozen cameras. He wore a gray pin-striped suit that looked ill-fitting, and he had traded the usual pink tie for a sedate blue one. I could detect a paunch. He sat in the front row. We all wanted to talk to him, but lawyers and court security formed a loose cordon around him.

I walked around to the front of the room, entering the photographers' frame, and stood as close as I could to him. I stared at him for a while. He appeared tired, his eyes squinty. Otherwise his face was expressionless. He didn't look at the cameras; he acted as though a hundred eyes weren't on him now. I could see his scalp peeking from under thin gray hair, and I wondered whether he'd stopped visiting Alessandro for his monthly maintenance. Eventually I started feeling like a gawker at a car accident, so I went back to my seat in the press area a few rows back.

Eike took out his phone, a Samsung. His hands looked small, his fingers very white and delicate, as he fiddled with the big screen. A photographer positioned himself behind me and snapped pictures of Eike's phone with a zoom lens. I asked to see the photos. In one, Eike scrolled through his news feed on Facebook—billionaires use Facebook. In another, he chatted with *"Flávia Linda e encrenqueira"*—Flávia the beautiful troublemaker. "Everything's going to turn out all right, my love," she wrote. "I wish I could be by your side. My heart is. We love you." He responded, "You're the best, my love. Thank you for your infinite affection. I'll be thinking of you and Balder"—their son, now seventeen months old.

Eike wasn't slated to testify today, so he just sat and listened. His lawyers demanded that the judge kick the reporters out of the room and hold the hearings in secret. Their argument was that they couldn't make a full defense without revealing Eike's personal financial details and thus violating his privacy. (So now Eike was modest about his wealth.) The judge overruled them. "We're being smothered here!" one of the lawyers said while miming self-strangulation. "With all due respect," he added. It was not a jury trial—a single judge would deliver a verdict—so the grandstanding seemed more for our benefit than anything else.

As the prosecution called up witnesses who rehashed the accusations, Eike sometimes scoffed and murmured something to a bald old lawyer at his side. He had a lot of lawyers. At one point a butler no more than five feet tall came by with a tray and handed Eike a little cup of coffee. As he sipped it, the cameras whirred and clicked. They whirred and clicked every time Eike shifted his weight or made a face or put a finger to his chin.

I was sitting next to an old Bloomberg colleague when we noticed a sudden commotion. Eike had slunk out of the room. We rushed out after him, ran down the hall joining a stampede of reporters and photographers, but a security guard stopped us and said Eike was just going to the bathroom. Instead of returning to our seats, though, we waited for him to emerge. We chuckled at ourselves, business journalists acting like paparazzi. When Eike came out of the bathroom he made a pained smile of forced composure and walked briskly by, giving a few nods to acknowledge our presence as the cameras shot him rapid fire.

We edged in on him, half-blocking his passage as some shouted questions, and I saw a look of vague panic on his face. The look maybe reflected the fear that we wanted to eat him alive. He was, after all, our sustenance. I myself had made something of a career out of his downfall. For perhaps the first time, I felt bad for him.

FLÁVIO SOUZA WAS DETERMINED to make an example of Eike. After adjourning the hearing, he spoke to reporters in the hall. Rotund in his judge's robe, his face flushed as we scrummed around him shoving microphones in his face. He seemed to have prepared his message. He held up the case as a historic moment for Brazil, the first time someone of Eike's power and renown would face such a trial. Then he went further: "Eike was always the poster boy for his own companies, with the megalomaniacal dream of becoming the world's richest man." Even in Brazil, where judges often fancy themselves a superior class of citizen, it wasn't normal for a judge to talk to the press like this. Eike's lawyers leaped on the comments, petitioning to have Souza removed from the case for what sounded like judicial bias.

As usual, the case was delayed by bureaucracy. To consolidate the charges against Eike from prosecutors in São Paulo, Souza put the trial on hold, promising to resume early in the new year. In the meantime, he seized more of Eike's assets, arguing that it was necessary to secure payment for fines in case of a conviction. Police showed up at Eike's mansion in February 2015 and hauled off a piano, a computer, a smartphone, sixteen watches, two speedboat motors, thirty thousand dollars in cash (of various currencies), and a Fabergé egg that turned out to be fake. They also loaded six cars onto tow trucks, including a Lamborghini Aventador LP 700-4. A week later they showed up at Eike's beach home in Angra dos Reis and took three Jet Skis. They wanted to take his yacht too—the *Spirit of Brazil VII*, his 115-foot Pershing—but they had nowhere to keep it so they just declared it "seized" and left. Then they went to Luma de Oliveira's mansion, next door to Eike's. Even though she'd divorced him more than a decade earlier, police took her two Toyotas and a BMW.

There was little precedent for this. Usually the rich and powerful in Brazil, even when convicted, got to hold on to their assets and skip jail too. On its Sunday news show, *Fantástico*, Globo ran a special on the seizures. The images were satisfying because they were like upside-down luxury: voyeurism of loss, not of gain. A reporter interviewed Souza, who said that on top of everything, Eike had several unpaid traffic tickets and was late on his vehicle taxes too. "Why didn't he sell the Lamborghini to pay debts?" Souza asked. He mentioned Thor and Olin, who had just spent New Year's in St. Barths. "They've kept up with a level of ostentation that makes no sense for someone with multibillion-dollar debts." He sounded moralistic and vengeful, an appealing tone for anyone who felt wronged by Eike, though maybe not the right tone for a judge who is supposed to be impartial.

Something was off about the thoroughness of the seizures. Eike hadn't been convicted of anything yet, but even as his lawyers' petition to remove Souza awaited decision, the judge set a date to auction off Eike's assets. And then two days before the auction, something weird happened. One of Thor's friends happened to live in the same apartment building as Souza, and he spotted what looked like Eike's white Porsche Cayenne in the garage. The friend tipped off Thor's family, and the license plate was the same. He snapped pictures. Someone else photographed Souza driving the Porsche to work that day. A reporter got Souza on the phone, and the judge claimed he'd taken the Porsche home because he didn't want it damaged by rain and sun in the impound lot. There was no legal provision for this, obviously. Soon it emerged that he'd taken another of Eike's cars home too. He'd taken Eike's piano and put it in a neighbor's apartment.

A Rio court postponed the auction and started investigating. Within a couple of weeks, Souza confessed to stealing three hundred thousand dollars he had ordered seized in an unrelated drug-trafficking case. He was taken off Eike's trial, and the auction was canceled. Eike's $120 million in cash remained frozen, but he and Luma soon got their stuff back.

Souza had pulled off an impressive feat: He made Eike look like a victim. He had hoped to take Eike down a peg, but by abusing his power, he granted Eike a victory. What's more, he reinforced the old feeling that the justice system just doesn't work in Brazil. When a different judge absolved Thor of his manslaughter conviction, saying the evidence was "contaminated by doubts," the popular reaction now resembled that of Germany's seventh goal against the Seleção—resigned, bitter hilarity. On the satirical website Sensacionalista, a headline captured the feeling: COURT ORDERS DEAD CYCLIST TO FIX THOR BATISTA'S WINDSHIELD.

AS TIME PASSED, EIKE'S collapse gained a curious meaning in Brazil. Though he had raised billions of dollars from private investors, it became popular to attribute his rise solely to the largesse of the Workers Party. His flagship company, OGX Petróleo, didn't receive any state money, but just like his other ventures, it became the symbol of a failed policy of "picking winners." "Eike could never do what he did without the generous support of Lula," a right-leaning Brazilian declared to me once. This selective blame was symptomatic of a larger confusion.

To be fair, there was good reason to be upset about state help for billionaires. For Dilma to dole out tax breaks and cheap loans for beer producers and soccer stadiums, the government had to take on a lot of debt at high rates. And even after hundreds of billions of dollars in corporate subsidies, there seemed to be little to show for it. Economists on the right and the left believed that businessmen had largely pocketed the windfall rather than boosting investments. Meanwhile, what Dilma now spent in one year on interest payments— money transferred to banks and wealthy families—exceeded twelve years of spending on the Bolsa Família welfare program.

All the contradictions became hard to take. As Brazil headed into its worst recession in decades, Dilma even lost her own base on the left. She had won reelection in 2014 by promising to avoid the austerity her opponents said was inevitable, but after running campaign videos in which evil bankers stole the food right off a family's table, she then put a banker in the finance ministry. She hoped to lure back investors, so she slashed spending, and the deepest cuts came in the education budget. She removed caps on gas and electricity prices, and the cost of living spiked. All this even as unemployment and pension benefits were scaled back.

Despite Dilma's self-image as champion of the poor, austerity weighed heaviest on the lower ninety-nine percent of the income pyramid. After twelve years in power, she and Lula never implemented party planks like a wealth tax, which would have rubbed their allies in business the wrong way. Believing they could use billionaires as tools of economic policy, they had struck generous deals without asking much in return. Now, as taxes on day-to-day consumption went up, taxes on dividends stayed at zero. Interest rates soared, and while people with money in the bank fared just fine, businesses were forced to cut back. Across the country, public works stalled as money dried up. More than a million jobs vanished—for the Workers Party, an existential failure.

The grand Workers Party bargain for progress was blowing up. But the failures weren't just economic. Believing it was the only way to govern, Lula and Dilma had allied themselves with Brazil's entrenched interests, and somewhere along the way that old compromise, *rouba mas faz*—"he steals, but he gets things done"—spun out of control. The extent of their pragmatism became exorbitantly clear in a corruption scandal that emerged during Dilma's reelection campaign. The press called it the largest corruption case in the history of Brazil, and that's saying a lot. It involved the same construction giants who once embodied Lula's vision of lifting up workers by lifting up their employers.

The investigation was dubbed Lava-Jato—Carwash—because some of the money was laundered through a Brasília gas station. At the heart of the scheme was a cartel allegedly formed by Odebrecht, Camargo Corrêa, OAS, and a few of their would-be competitors. For years, investigators said, these firms had colluded to divvy up all the major contracts from Petrobras, the state oil company. At least two billion dollars in bribes were funneled to Petrobras officials, government ministers, and two dozen members of Congress, mostly from Dilma's coalition, many from the Workers Party. With all the inflated costs, a refinery in Lula's home state of Pernambuco, originally budgeted at $2.4 billion, saw its price soar to $18.5 billion in a decade. This looked especially bad for Dilma because she had served as Petrobras's chairwoman when Lula was president. She didn't appear to have any personal role in the scheme, but for years, she had either failed to notice the corruption or failed to act.

The scandal gained momentum as Dilma's austerity measures began to sink in, early in her second term. I was at my apartment when she went on TV one Sunday to explain the cutbacks, which she called "adjustments." I heard a din from the city outside, pots and pans clanging from balconies all around me. It was a *panelaço*, an old Latin American form of protest. It wasn't long before Brazilians took to the streets again. In March 2015, more than two hundred thousand people gathered on Paulista Avenue, with thousands more marching in cities across Brazil. This time was different from the protests of June 2013, though, less diverse. The crowd was mostly well-to-do, conservative, white. And they had a concrete cause: impeach Dilma. Their banners decried corruption, but as I spoke to them, I heard just as much about economic grievances, and it occurred to me that corruption is truly an issue in Brazil only when inflation gets out of control. That's why Collor fell in 1992, but Lula didn't fall in 2005. The Brazilian people are pragmatists too.

Corruption was just the surface outrage of a deeper unease. Lula's conciliation of right and left, business and labor, depended on boom times. Under Dilma the economy soured, and the pacts fell apart. Once pacified by cheap credit and tax cuts, the business class now agitated for her ouster. With less pork to spread around Brasília, the Workers Party's former political allies rebelled against Dilma in Congress. Lacking the political capital to get new taxes approved—and, in a vestige of ideological consistency, hesitant to cut too much from social programs—Dilma's austerity push failed even to win back the confidence of the market. In September 2015, Standard & Poor's became the first ratings agency to strip Brazil of its investment-grade credit rating.

The boom that had begun under Lula was over. If I had put a hundred dollars in the stock market when I arrived in 2010, I would be left with less than thirty dollars now. Petrobras, that symbol of the nation's economic prowess, had lost more than eighty percent of its value in that time. The plunge in the *real* affected the wealth rankings too. Dozens of freshly minted billionaires saw their fortunes dip back into the hundreds of millions—at least in dollar terms. Though of course, none of them faced hardship like that of the middle and lower classes.

Despite the affluent scene on Paulista, the discontent spread far beyond the upper echelons of Brazilian society. Even those who'd risen to some measure of prosperity in recent years, the *classe C* that Dilma liked to call a middle class, turned against her. Though they'd benefited from a higher minimum wage, subsidies for private college, and affordable housing projects, surveys showed that they overwhelmingly attributed their success to their own effort, not to government policy. After all, they'd worked hard and dealt with grueling commutes and dangerous streets. Now they feared that all they had achieved was fading away.

Worst of all for the Workers Party, Dilma finally lost support among her most loyal voters, the poor who benefited from Bolsa Família. Maria, my cleaning lady, told me she'd voted for Dilma in 2010 and 2014 but now wanted her impeached. Her utility bills had jumped by forty percent, and this is hard to bear when you make just a few hundred dollars a month.

What Maria had in common with the protesters on Paulista was that few had much clue what would happen if Dilma was forced out. Few understood the legal basis for impeachment, or cared that no evidence linked Dilma directly to the Petrobras scheme. Few knew who would gain power afterward or worried about how clean they were. They just wanted Dilma gone. The energy of June 2013—desperate, confused, but somehow optimistic too—had devolved into a feeling near nihilism. Some even clamored for a military coup.

Brazil had rarely been so polarized. Each side latched on to narratives that just obscured the scope of the dilemma. Less than a year after the World Cup, protesters took aim at Workers Party bribe-taking but left the construction giants off their placards, ignoring the other side of the equation, as if politicians were the sole root of corruption here. This was the same selective logic that made Eike's rise and fall only the fault of Lula. Curiously, this logic fit well with the contractors' own defense. Cristiano Kok, the owner of a firm known as Engevix, claimed he'd been "extorted" into paying bribes, as if he were a favela bar owner and not a business leader who could denounce it to the press. It was a new version of extortion where the victim made billion-dollar profits.

On the left of the polictical spectrum, the Workers Party tied itself into knots just as confused. At one point reporters asked Dilma about plea-bargain testimony from a construction tycoon who said he'd funneled bribes into her reelection campaign. "I don't respect informers," she replied. "Partly because I was imprisoned in the dictatorship and I know what that is. They tried to turn me into an informer." In other speeches, she rightly praised the Carwash probe as a sign of institutional progress, pointing to scandals from the nineties that had ended in *pizza*. The Petrobras scheme itself had started before Lula ever came into office. But Dilma refused to accept any responsibility for the sheer scale of corruption under the Workers Party. And rather than turn on her campaign donors, she warned that punishing the accused firms would kill jobs, paralyze public works, and allow foreigners to dominate the economy. A couple of construction firms, since Petrobras halted payments and banks now balked at lending to them, had already filed for bankruptcy protection. One was OAS, whose owner I had outed as a hidden billionaire. Though Cesar Mata Pires himself didn't face charges, some of his top executives would be convicted of bribery and money laundering.

Following Dilma's lead, many of her remaining supporters blamed the investigation of corruption, not the corruption itself, for hurting the economy—and the media for reporting on it. In another plea bargain, the CEO of Camargo Corrêa confessed to participating in what came to be called *o clube da propina*—the bribe club—which turned out to extend far beyond Petrobras. Just for Camargo's piece of the Belo Monte mega-dam, he said the company paid ten million dollars in kickbacks. And yet rather than target Camargo Corrêa, pro-government websites demonized Sergio Moro, the judge in charge of Carwash. They framed him as a right-wing crusader because he'd accepted *O Globo*'s Difference Maker prize from João Roberto Marinho. After Judge Moro ordered the arrest of Marcelo Odebrecht, the heir who now led the family empire, one well-known blogger even wrote that tycoons like him deserved to be treated not just as citizens but as national institutions.

An antitrust official compared Dilma's Faustian logic to the one that prevailed in the United States in 2008, according to which some banks were "too big to fail," regardless of what they'd done wrong. Brazil's "bribe club" was responsible for the country's most important public works—including the projects for the Olympic Games in Rio. If Camargo Corrêa and Odebrecht went under, the country could face international embarrassment in 2016, and the economy truly would suffer. So the government offered leniency deals. In return for immunity from prosecution, Camargo Corrêa agreed to cooperate with investigators and pay a two-hundred-million-dollar fine. It was a historic amount—but just three percent of the conglomerate's annual revenues. Which raises the question: Will it be enough to prevent relapses in the future? Prosecutors hope the deal with Camargo will help bring down a decades-old cartel and clean up Brasília. It remains to be seen whether their gamble will pay off.

AMID ALL THE SCANDALS, Lula had long seemed invincible. But thanks to his paid talks for construction giants and efforts to promote them abroad after his presidency, he would end up under investigation for influence peddling. This sparked the usual polarized confusion. His supporters chalked it all up to Globo-orchestrated political persecution, downplaying the fourteen million dollars he'd earned. *Época* magazine, owned by the Marinho family, didn't hesitate to brand him the country's "lobbyist in chief." And yet his critics failed to realize that, if Lula had broken the law with these activities, then a whole system of officially sanctioned influence—based on money flowing between private interests and political campaigns—should quite possibly also be considered criminal.

Straight-up graft—as in a quid pro quo bribe—is one way to wrangle special favors from public servants, but not the only one. After Congress opened its own inquiry into the corruption at Petrobras, Marcelo Odebrecht was called to testify. Though he was suspected of corruption on a grand scale, in Brasília now he was greeted with politeness that verged on kowtowing. At one point Marcelo mentioned his dad, Emílio, and a congressman from the main opposition party, the PSDB, said, "Kudos, I too am very proud of my father." Later, when Marcelo declined to answer a question, another PSDB congressman said, "You don't have to apologize, because it's your right." A congressman from the Workers Party asked, "Do you, sir, consider your arrest appropriate and just, given that you have always made yourself available to investigators?" And Marcelo responded: "Thank you very much for your questions, because they would be my answers." None of these lawmakers were alleged to have received bribes from the Petrobras scheme, but Odebrecht generously funded their parties through legal means, and that secured their loyalty.

Odebrecht is just one of many players in this system. It goes beyond the Workers Party and beyond the construction industry. A single family-owned company, the meatpacking giant JBS, spent one hundred and eighty million dollars on the 2014 elections—seven percent of *all* donations that year. If every politician who had received JBS money formed a party, it would be the largest in Congress. Of course, there's some overlap with other donors—Odebrecht funds many of the same politicians—but then again, Odebrecht has many of the same interests. One of them is a generous BNDES. Another is low taxes on capital. There's also the power to finance elections.

Two weeks after Odebrecht's hearing, the Supreme Court decided a case that had dragged on since 2013, ruling that campaign donations by companies are unconstitutional because they undermine political equality. The ruling matched up with public opinion—three-quarters of Brazilians say they're against such donations—but congressmen responded by showing where their loyalties lie. The Chamber of Deputies immediately approved a constitutional amendment that would make the donations legal again. As of this writing, the amendment awaited a vote in the Senate. In the meantime, individuals are still allowed to give ten percent of their income to political campaigns. The ruling put an effective cap on donations by billionaires—an important advance—but it still leaves ordinary citizens at a disadvantage. And it may yet be undone.

THE CARWASH PROBE ENDED up touching Eike. In plea-bargain testimony, a lobbyist said he had paid a million dollars to a friend of Lula in hopes of winning Petrobras platform contracts for OSX Brasil, Eike's shipbuilder. OSX never actually won the contracts, though. Called to testify before Congress about the BNDES's lending policies, Eike denied having hired the lobbyist at all—and as of this writing, it didn't look like the claim would lead to charges. Eike's trial for financial crimes, meanwhile, ground to a halt. In administrative proceedings, regulators at the CVM fined him four hundred thousand dollars and banned him from public companies for five years—but during his appeal, as usual, these penalties were suspended.

Eike, in any case, isn't dwelling on the past. During his post–World Cup round of interviews, two different reporters asked if he still hoped to become the world's richest man. He didn't say yes; he also didn't say no.

Eike is already planning his comeback. It started in 2015 with a PR campaign called #EikeTudoPeloBrasil, which means "Eike: Everything for Brazil." The website offers T-shirts signed by Eike and lists his contributions in business and philanthropy. It also features interviews with friends and associates and random celebrities. One is with Jordan Belfort, the real-life Wolf of Wall Street. "The fact that Eike is going through a crisis doesn't diminish him for me," he said. "He's capable of achieving things that others can't. . . . I hope he can get through this."

Eike claimed that the campaign, despite its slick design, constant updates, and habit of posting EBX press releases, was a spontaneous initiative by his fans. Whatever the truth, he does still have admirers.

Ten thousand people have liked the Facebook page, and they flood it with praise every day. They thank him for helping to develop the country, creating jobs. They call him a Mauá of the twenty-first century. They call him a visionary.

On the website, Eike also responds to his fans' questions. Asked why he doesn't leave the country and live the good life in Miami, he replied, "My duty as a patriot, as a soldier of Brazil, is to make Brazil better, to make things here work better. If all the good Brazilians who know how to do something, who know how to create great projects, leave . . . what will happen to Brazil?"

Eike couldn't stay away from the limelight for long. In June 2015, he gave his first TV interview since his empire started going south. He wore a gray pin-striped suit and a pale pink shirt, and his shiny pink tie was back. Fifty-eight now, he looked older, his sideburns whitish, thinning. But this wasn't the teary-eyed man of the previous year. The show opened with a clip from the movie *Terminator 2* where Arnold Schwarzenegger says, "I'll be back." The interviewer, Mariana Godoy, asked if that summed up Eike's plans. He replied, in English, "I'm back."

Eike brought good news. He no longer had any debt. He'd convinced his creditors to take his collateral and give him a new chance. In just a short time, he claimed, he got himself off the hook for around twenty-five billion dollars in personal liabilities. Ever superlative, he seemed proud now even of the scale of his rise and fall. "It was the craziest, fastest wealth creation ever, and it was the fastest to disappear, but it's also the fastest anyone ever zeroed their debts," he said, smiling wide as he thrust his hands up and down to illustrate his points. Godoy suggested a parallel with Donald Trump—who went through four corporate bankruptcies. "Don't compare me to him, please," Eike replied. "All he does is buildings." Eike preferred to think of himself as an innovator like Elon Musk, the founder of the electric car company Tesla.

Eike was willing now to admit mistakes—"I expanded too fast"—

but he complained bitterly about his treatment in the press. Asked if he felt like a victim of unfair criticism, he nodded gravely. Did it hurt his feelings when people called his companies "PowerPoints"? Again he said yes, but threw his hands up and laughed, "PowerPoint?" The port of Açu, he said, had shipped its first loads of iron ore from the mining company Anglo American. (Never mind that he no longer owned the port, or that new management had drastically scaled it down.) His coal plants, he said, now produced as much electricity as a new Amazonian dam. (Never mind that even under German ownership, they had gone into bankruptcy protection.) "These are real projects that are going to serve your children and mine," he said. "If God took all this wealth from me, what matters are the legacies that will remain." When Godoy asked if Eike felt he'd let down his dad, he said no. "When you've done the right thing, you just keep on going," he said. And what was his net worth now? "Enough."

Eike had hit rock bottom, then crawled back up again, and his self-belief had just solidified. Not only that—he'd found investors who still believed in him. He'd never stopped dreaming up new projects. Even as he renegotiated his debts, he'd flown to South Korea and met with another fallen star, a scientist named Hwang Woo-suk. Once known as the "Pride of Korea," Hwang had lost his job at Seoul National University after he faked a study in which he claimed to have cloned human stem cells. The two men now planned to set up a Brazilian lab to clone cattle and rare animals. Eike was well received in South Korea. He was also teaming up with a South Korean pharmaceuticals company to make generic Viagra that dissolves under your tongue. But he's got more mundane projects too. Working with the energy expert Roberto Hukai, an old friend of his dad's, he's trying to raise money for a biofuels venture and a wind park in Rio. Also, he's been trying to sell solar panels to a chain of Brazilian churches.

Alongside Eike, Thor has his own business ideas. In an interview with the Brazilian edition of *GQ*, he said he'd concocted an energy drink that intensifies your orgasms. His dad had tried it. "Oh, man . . . It's really cool," Eike said.

EIKE CAN'T STOP. EXPANSION is his nature. Expansion is the billionaire nature, and Eike's got the best and worst of it. This drive can be productive. It leads people like him to tackle big projects: railroads, superports, social networks. When they turn out well, these projects grow the economy, provide jobs and tax revenue, and advance technology. Society benefits, and their creators get rich, a win-win. The problem is that even when society doesn't benefit, this symbiotic ideal justifies a system geared toward the interests of our wealthiest citizens. It's an ideal that grows from the heroic stories that billionaires tell us and themselves—stories that often stray from the truth.

Billionaires tend to act as if their wealth were the exclusive product of their own merit, and how else could you live with such rewards? Among those who didn't inherit their fortunes, most bet everything on an intuition at least once and often more than once. Eike himself lost a whole fortune in the nineties before making his meteoric comeback a decade ago. But once an entrepreneur has made it, something funny happens, a narrative forms. A tale with heavy doses of luck and guesswork and help from others morphs retroactively into one of pure individual courage and wisdom. The failures become rites of passage, and the successes seem preordained. We don't hear about the all the people who risk everything, lose everything, and never get rich at all.

Eike's story shows that even a thirty-billion-dollar fortune is not an irrefutable sign of one person's genius. He always had a rare talent for identifying opportunities—and for selling them—but like most of Brazil's billionaires, he was born into serious connections in a country where just getting a good education made you one in a hundred. Someone with equal talent and dedication, but no connections and no starting capital, would have taken much longer to get as rich as he did as a young man, or wouldn't have gotten there at all. Any entrepreneur will tell you the first million is the hardest. After that it gets easier, because wealth acts like a magnet on the world.

Crucially, Eike also had an unusual hunger for risk. And he made the most of his gifts. And then a decade ago he found himself in the right place at the right time (Brazil, the Lula years) with the right message (something like "I am the future") and the capital to take advantage of it all. Someone with equal talent and dedication and connections and capital, but no historic wave to ride, could never have come up with a pitch as ideal, no matter how great a salesman. That's timing. Even Eike recognized his luck in taking OGX public just as oil prices peaked, a few months before the financial crisis erupted. Still, as he hopped from success to success, he allowed his hard work and good fortune to congeal into hubris. And as he leveraged other people's money, his quest to be number one became a liability for the rest of us. In backing his ambitions, the government put the entire country on the hook for Eike's big bets.

IN THIS MESH OF public and private interests, the billionaire traditions of America and Brazil meet. You might rise by latching on to the state, as Sebastião Camargo did. Or you might rise through the financial markets, like Jorge Paulo Lemann. Either way, once at the top, both defended their empires through similar means, putting their money to work in the political system. The curse of the cordial man—patrimonialism—isn't exclusively Brazilian. It's just an extreme version of a common relationship between wealth and political power. When winners emerge in the race for profit, free markets become less free. The winners gain leverage in government, and the line between public and private blurs. In *The Wealth of Nations*, Adam Smith himself warned of this danger—of businessmen as a class "whose interest is never exactly the same with that of the public, who have generally an interest to deceive and even to oppress the public." The same drive for expansion that can help progress along can also make it falter.

Of course, what's even more effective for billionaires is when they frame their quest for personal glory as a quest for society's progress—when they frame special favors for their businesses as preconditions of economic growth—and their arguments trickle down. But the truth is that our empire builders can't build empires without us. Eike didn't inflate the bubble on his own. He needed the press to create a feedback loop of his dreams. He needed the government to make him into a national hero. Book buyers and a million followers on Twitter fawned over him. Bankers had their own incentives to pump him up, and investors hated to miss a fad. Eike had his critics, but if he thought he was infallible, it's partly because people deified him. His messianic vision of himself was contagious. It's not the first time a society hoaxed itself. We believed him. We might believe him again.

AFTER THE CRASH

A S I NEARED THE END OF MY REPORTING FOR THIS BOOK, I flew from my home in São Paulo to Rio, then drove up to Petrópolis. Leaving the city, the highway is hemmed in by big-box construction stores, outlet malls, and "motels"—by-the-hour hotels Brazilians hit up for trysts. Farther north the suburban clutter gives way to rolling hills with the odd tumbledown shack where locals sell snacks or garish textiles. As the hills grow into *serra,* the northbound side splits off and veers right, carving acute switchbacks into mountains too steep for farming or grazing, and so still covered in vegetation, overhung by vines and heavy branches. Drivers on the left sped by my wheezing rental. Past them, through the dense green's gaps, the view plunged into a deep valley and a horizon of scattered bluish peaks.

I stopped in Petrópolis briefly before coming back down toward Rio. This was the route Thor Batista took that night in March 2012. I had examined the crash scene photos enough to recognize the place where he'd pulled his McLaren to a stop after the crash that killed Wanderson Pereira dos Santos. But as I drove by now, it was different. Caution-yellow construction equipment breathed and beeped along the wayside, turning up the earth, preparing to widen the southbound highway. On the shoulder, just a few feet from me, locals pedaled by on their bikes, and it looked way too easy for another tragedy to happen here. Maybe, though, things will improve a little. Once the project is finished, access roads will keep the speeding highway separate from local traffic.

In the time I spent writing this book, I thought a lot about the crash. My instinct was to blame Thor. Not hard. As a character in a novel, he would feel contrived: a parody of a playboy, fake-tanned and muscle-necked, the picture of unearned privilege, self-absorbed, witless—a cliché on wheels, fancy ones, which he liked to drive fast. I resisted acknowledging someone else who deserves blame. When Eike spoke of Wanderson's "imprudence," he showed a lack of decency and class, but was he wrong? Wanderson had been drinking, even though he knew he had to cross a busy highway on his bike. He didn't respect his own life. I had seen this often in Brazil.

The worst injustice, though, went beyond any one person's recklessness. Wanderson might have failed to take care that night, but the threshold for screwing up was much lower for him. He lived in a favela nestled by the highway, and there was no bridge to the supermarket on the other side of the road. Ten other locals had been run over in the same place in as many years—and two of them also died. The society they belonged to never made them a priority. Thor, whatever his faults, became a scapegoat for this injustice, receptacle for the collective guilt. Even if he had served time in prison, it wouldn't have changed the reality of life for people like Wanderson.

WANDERSON'S DEATH WAS THE product of national priorities. Four years later, as Rio prepares to host the Olympics, the priorities look much the same as before. Some public works, such as express bus lines, will improve the city for everyone. But others look like gifts to a well-connected minority. A lot of the Olympic budget is being poured into Barra da Tijuca, a wealthy suburb far from the pedestrian-friendly city center (and farther still from the Complexo do Alemão favela). One project is the billion-dollar Olympic Village that will temporarily house athletes. Odebrecht and a wealthy landowner named Carlos Carvalho won the right to build it, financed as usual by a low-interest government loan. After the games, the village's thirty-one high-rise towers will be converted into luxury apartments that Odebrecht and Carvalho can sell on the open market. None are slated for affordable housing, as London did after the Olympics of 2012. Meanwhile, after promising to invest in Rio's favelas to integrate them with the rest of the city, Mayor Eduardo Paes has instead used the Olympics as a pretense to demolish favelas to make room for projects like this one. It should be no surprise by now that Carlos Carvalho is a major donor to Paes and his party, the PMDB. Odebrecht likewise has given the PMDB millions.

Just months before the Olympics, media around the world filled with images not of Rio in its triumphant moment on the world stage, but of newborn babies with abnormally small heads, apparently caused by prenatal exposure to the Zika virus. When this epidemic struck Brazil, it seemed an almost biblical hardship—a straight-up plague on top of the economic and political crises. But Zika was not a curse from above. For decades, Brazil had suffered from outbreaks of dengue, which is carried by the same mosquito, the *Aedes aegypti*. This mosquito thrives on urban neglect. Because it lays its eggs in stagnant water, it flourishes in neighborhoods where people keep tanks on their roofs for the days when the taps go dry, where sewage lines are lacking, where garbage trucks rarely come through and old tires and discarded bottles pile up. Because the mosquito feeds on human blood, it likes favelas where whole extended families occupy the same narrow shack, with no air-conditioning or even screens on their windows. None of these problems were new. You didn't see images of the wealthy cradling microcephalic infants. The way that Zika spread reflected Brazil's vast gap between rich and poor, but also the failed promise of the boom years in narrowing it.

In the six years I lived in Brazil, I watched a national dream of prosperity approach and then recede. Clearly, the future was never as close as Eike would have had you believe. It's also not as distant as it might look now. This recession may prove to be the worst in a century, but some of Brazil's most important gains appear safe. Even amid the austerity push, there has been no serious attempt to roll

back Bolsa Família, which keeps a quarter of the country's population from going hungry. This is big.

Also important, the Carwash probe shows no signs of slowing
down. Every week, new revelations shake up Brasília. But if this
scandal proves too damaging to brush off as the price of progress,
that might be a good thing for Brazil's democracy. No one as rich and
powerful as Marcelo Odebrecht had ever been forced to await trial in
jail. Amid suspicion that he paid bribes for government deals, André
Esteves, the billionaire investment banker I interviewed, would
briefly end up behind bars too. Both men had allegedly meddled with
investigations—and both, just a few years ago, would have had little
to fear in doing so.

Impunity was dealt another blow when the Supreme Court ruled
that a conviction must be upheld only once before a defendant serves
his sentence, making it harder for high-priced lawyers to put off jail
time with endless appeals. And then in March 2016, Marcelo was
sentenced to nineteen years in prison for corruption, money laundering, and conspiracy. Such a high-profile conviction would have been
unthinkable until very recently.

Something even bigger came to pass around the same time. On
March 4, armed agents showed up at Lula's home in a suburb of São
Paulo and temporarily detained him for questioning. Investigators
had found signs that in the final days of Lula's presidency, Odebrecht
and OAS had paid to fix up two properties linked to him: a ranch he
would later frequent and a seaside apartment that he had an option
to purchase. Though such favors are common for Brazilian politicians, these had allegedly served as compensation for a still-undefined
role that Lula may have played in the Petrobras scheme. Prosecutors
now also believed that his speeches for Odebrecht were a back-door
way to pay him for influencing the BNDES to finance its projects
abroad. This allegation went beyond the mere lobbying of foreign
leaders.

The sight of Lula in the back of a black police truck, just five
years after he stepped down as the most popular president in Brazil's

history, stunned the whole country. Lula's detractors celebrated it as the beginning of the end of a party they saw as irredeemably corrupt. His supporters, as usual, claimed it was nothing more than political persecution. Lost in the middle were complicated questions: Could state policy toward construction giants—long at the center of power in Brazil—really be pinned on one person, rather than a larger system of ideology and influence? And if there was no quid pro quo, had Lula violated the law in taking payments from companies with state business, or did the vague laws about Brazil's political revolving door need to be made clearer? Lula himself denied the allegations, of course. He claimed he had simply served the national interest by promoting construction giants abroad. But even if he wasn't guilty of any crimes, hadn't he violated the spirit of political equality that drove the creation of the Workers Party? By making himself the spokesman of a few billionaire families, hadn't he sold out?

If Lula is ultimately convicted, this could be taken as a sign that the relationship between money and political power in Brazil is finally changing. It remains to be seen, however, if future governments will be subject to the same scrutiny. It's impossible to separate the broad public support for Carwash—vital to its success—from the ill will over the current economic crisis. Left-wing talk of a media conspiracy is overblown, but the fact is that Globo and the rest of the establishment media haven't given the same attention to scandals involving opposition politicians. And to imagine that corruption begins or ends with the Workers Party is a dangerous delusion.

Dilma Rousseff too is teetering on the brink. Two separate cases threaten to remove her from power. The one most likely to succeed, opened by Congress, calls for her impeachment based on the allegation that she violated budget rules, disguising shortfalls in order to spend more than the law allows—and thus helping to fuel the economic crisis. The other case, now before Brazil's electoral court, claims that her reelection campaign received money skimmed from the Petrobras scheme. Given the atmosphere in Brazil, both cases will likely be decided not just on the legal merits but on public opinion. Dilma's base calls them coup attempts—*golpismo*—but they do have a constitutional basis. And they got an additional boost when a Workers Party senator signed a plea-bargain deal implicating Dilma's administration in efforts to obstruct the Carwash investigations. Further provoking her opponents, Dilma even named Lula as her cabinet chief, thus kicking his case up to the overloaded Supreme Court—in an apparent attempt to protect him from Judge Moro. As this book went to press, she looked unlikely to finish her term.

As with the charges against Lula, Dilma's ouster could represent an advance for Brazil's institutions if they mean that future governments will be held to the same rigorous standards. But it could also prove to be a Pyrrhic victory for the anti-corruption movement. If she fails to escape impeachment, Vice President Michel Temer will take office, and unlike Dilma, he has been directly named in the Petrobras scheme, along with many others from his party, the PMDB. Many believe they will try to put a lid on Carwash—seeking a *pizza* of epic proportions. Meanwhile, if the electoral court rules to invalidate her election, Temer could be removed along with her, in which case new elections would be called. But two of the most likely opposition candidates have also been cited in recent scandals.

Brazilians sometimes lament that the protests of June 2013 turned out to be meaningless, an impotent cry for a cure to a vague malaise. Briefly, though, people on the streets put fear into politicians and their campaign donors. Even if tenuous, this may be a sign that pressure from below can weaken the flood of money from above. By the same token, apathy could enable politicians to shore up the old status quo. The Supreme Court's ban on corporate campaign donations opened the door to greater political equality in Brazil, potentially weakening the influence of big money in public policy. But Congress may yet reverse the ruling. Despite the pressure of the Carwash investigations, many observers also fear that companies will keep financing elections with under-the-table payments. Enforcement and public engagement are both key here.

I can't help but think of the United States, my country. As in Brazil, surveys show that a healthy majority of Americans think money has too much influence in politics. And yet Democrats and Republicans are now raising billions of dollars for the 2016 elections. Actual kickbacks are uncommon in Washington, but with all that money changing hands, it's worth wondering what is being bought. We're at a similar kind of crossroads.

LIKE THE DEATH OF Wanderson, Eike's bubble was the product of a whole system of values, privileges, and rules. If he's convicted for his alleged financial crimes, it will serve as more proof that Brazil's justice system can put a rich man in jail. But it won't be enough to keep the next bubble from inflating. Stricter regulation on the way stocks are promoted would help—another small step toward a different set of national priorities. Of course, that's not on the table right now.

As of early 2016, Eike's trial is still on hold. It remains to be seen how long the excesses of Judge Souza will delay the case. In the meantime, Eike isn't letting it slow him down. He's busy laying the foundations for the next of his empires.

I keep thinking of an image from the first hearing in his trial. A quick recess had been called, and I watched Eike in the courtroom as he stood among his lawyers. He was at his lowest point then, detested by the public, facing a mountain of debt and a vindictive judge. And yet in the half hour since the bathroom break when he was mobbed by journalists, his face had changed. His fear had given way to something else. He bounced on his toes. He looked around the courtroom, eyes narrowed. He was smiling.

Acknowledgments

T HIS BOOK WOULDN'T HAVE BEEN POSSIBLE WITHOUT A LOT OF help and input from a lot of people. I owe thanks, first of all, to the Brazilians who welcomed me in their country and shared their thoughts and feelings with me, going back to my first trip in 2005.

Working at Bloomberg News taught me so much about reporting and about business. I'm grateful to the people there who took chances on me, especially Adriana Arai, Matthew G. Miller, and Peter Newcomb.

My agent, Howard Yoon, saw the potential in a jumble of stories and characters and helped me whip them into book shape with unfailing enthusiasm. Just as important, he helped me find my writing voice.

My editor, Chris Jackson, challenged me to "interrogate" my own ideas, and the book wouldn't read half as well without his insights on how to structure it. I'm also grateful for the efforts of the rest of the team at Spiegel & Grau.

I can't thank Gabriel Reilich enough for suggesting the title. Ted Alcorn, Angelina Clarke, Kathleen Cuadros, Nicholas DuBroff, Jake Goodman, Kieran Kaal, Nicolás Llano Linares, and Blake Schmidt were generous enough to read drafts of this book; their smart feedback was invaluable. And Simone Costa's fact-checking helped me avoid some embarrassing errors.

Over the past few years, I've talked about billionaires so much that by this point my friends and family know Eike by his first name too. I thank them for putting up with that. I especially thank my parents, Luis and Kathleen Cuadros, for supporting me in just about everything I've done.

My godfather, David Sullivan, incited me to fall in love with Brazil, and I wish he were around to read this.

Notes

THE FACTS IN THIS BOOK COME FROM FIRSTHAND REPORTING AND interviews, official histories, press reports, books, and academic papers. When I make generalizations about Brazil, they're also based on conversations with all sorts of people while I lived in the country from 2010 to 2016. My understanding of the ultra-rich has additionally been informed by conversations with these tycoons and heirs: Eike Batista, Alexandre Birman, J. C. Cavalcanti, Marcelo Claure, Abilio Diniz, André Esteves, Prakash Hinduja, Guilherme Leal, Blairo Maggi, João Roberto Marinho, Rubens Menin, Jorge Pérez, Otaviano Pivetta, and Stephen A. Schwarzman.

The notes below detail where I got information whose source isn't clear in the text and that wasn't widely reported. For simplicity's sake, I generally converted *reais* into dollars by rounding the average market rate that year to the nearest full number. For any questions about numbers or sources, feel free to email me at alexcuadros@gmail.com.

PROLOGUE: THE CRASH

xi **On a stretch of highway.** Details of Thor's crash are from a forensic analysis by Rio police and reports and photos from local media, plus witness testimony and Thor's own statements on Twitter and to the authorities.

xii **"You just killed that guy."** Hanrrikson de Andrade, "Testemunha diz ter avisado Thor Batista sobre morte de ciclista no Rio," *Universo Online*, March 21, 2012.

xii **"I've never seen the state work so fast."** The lawyer Cleber Carvalho Rumbelsperger, from "Pela Lei de Trânsito, Thor Batista não poderia dirigir," *O Dia*, March 19, 2012.

xiii **One of a dozen of its kind.** Other sources cite smaller numbers, but a September 12, 2008, discussion on the website Portal Mercedes-Benz Brasil notes McLarens that may have been imported irregularly.

xiii **1.2 million euros.** Ronaldo França and Ronaldo Soares, "O Mr. X da Bolsa," *Veja*, June 14, 2008.

xiii   **four thousand dollars.** Eight thousand *reais:* "Filho de Eike Batista atropela e mata ciclista," Mariana Durão, O *Estado de S. Paulo,* March 18, 2012.

xiv   **"Just because he's a billionaire."** José Luiz Datena, on *Brasil Urgente,* March 19, 2012.

xiv   **"poor, old Brazil."** André Forastieri, on his blog at *R7,* April 16, 2012.

xiv   **eighth-richest person.** In 2012, Eike became the world's eighth-richest person on the Bloomberg Billionaires Index, but *Forbes* ranked him seventh that year.

xv   **seventh-largest economy.** In dollar terms, Brazil's GDP was set to fall from seventh place at the end of 2015, but the economy remains the world's seventh-largest in terms of purchasing power, according to the International Monetary Fund.

xvi   **Of the few people.** Brian Solomon, "Billionaire Blow-Ups: Eike Batista Isn't the First to Go Belly-Up," *Forbes,* July 26, 2013.

CHAPTER 1: GOD IS BRAZILIAN

4   **Abilio Diniz.** I first met Abilio on July 16, 2013, along with other Bloomberg journalists. For the details of his life, I relied on an additional conversation with him on October 3, 2013, and his book, *Smart Choices for a Successful Life* (Rio de Janeiro: Campus, 2006), in addition to press articles over the years.

4   **four-billion-dollar fortune.** According to Bloomberg's ranking at the time.

9   **fifth-largest economy.** Alana Gandra, "Brasil pode ser a quinta economia do mundo na próxima década, diz presidente do Ipea," Agência Brasil, May 20, 2010.

11   **photos or video of the birth.** Giovanna Balogh, "Para registrar nascidos em casa, cartórios pedem até foto de parto," *Folha de S.Paulo,* June 24, 2014.

11   **twenty-six hundred man-hours.** World Bank's "Doing Business 2013" report. See www.doingbusiness.org.

11   **"a little Babel."** Manoel Sousa Pinto in *The Brazil Reader: History, Culture, Politics,* edited by Robert M. Levine and John J. Crocitti (Durham, N.C.: Duke University Press, 1999), 110.

14   **"He's no statesman."** "Antônio Ermírio de Moraes," *IstoÉ,* October 30, 2002.

14   **Lula came from the northeast.** Details of Lula's life are from his official biography at the website of Instituto Lula (www.institutolula.org) and statements to the press over the years.

14   **swigged** *cachaça* **on breaks.** *Entreatos* (2004), a documentary directed by the billionaire banking heir João Moreira Salles.

15   **"I worked my whole life."** Video for the website of *CartaCapital* magazine, October 2014.

17   **once or twice a year.** Since that time, *Forbes* has added a daily ranking to its website.

18   **one in seven Miami home purchases.** "Profile of International Home Buyers in Florida 2012," National Association of Realtors, August 2012.

20   **took São Paulo hostage.** Details on the PCC takeover are from William Langewiesche, "City of Fear," *Vanity Fair,* April 2007.

20   **one morning in 1989.** Abilio narrated his kidnapping to *Playboy*'s Brazilian edition, February 1990. When the kidnappers were arrested, police paraded them

before the press in Workers Party shirts. This was later believed to be an effort to influence the upcoming presidential election in which Lula was running against Fernando Collor.

20   **they were beaten.** Ariadne Araújo, "Me sinto traído," *IstoÉ,* May 19, 1999.

21   **I visited Abilio's mansion.** On November 13, 2013.

22   **travelers from Europe chuckled.** *1889,* by Laurentino Gomes (Rio de Janeiro: Nova Fronteira, 2013), 74–75.

23   **"Shirtsleeves to Shirtsleeves."** The Brazilian version of this saying is *"Pai rico, filho nobre, neto pobre"*: Rich father, noble son, poor grandson.

28   **cluttered their mansion in São Paulo.** I saw this during my November 13, 2013, visit.

29   **poured seventy million dollars.** Simon Romero, "A Keeper of a Vast Garden of Art in the Hills of Brazil," *New York Times,* March 9, 2012.

30   **the first hidden billionaires I uncovered.** "Brazil's Beer Baron," *Bloomberg Markets,* June 2012.

CHAPTER 2: THE PRICE OF PROGRESS

31   **Sebastião Camargo ($13 billion).** This net worth estimate applies to his widow, Dirce, when I uncovered her fortune in 2012.

32   **Paulo Maluf.** Details on Maluf are from his authorized biography, *Ele: Maluf, Trajetória da Audácia,* by Tão Gomes Pinto (Rio de Janeiro: Ediouro, 2008), court documents, press reports, and videos on YouTube. I tried repeatedly to interview Maluf for this book, but his spokesman, Adilson Laranjeira, declined to make him available.

32   **one of Brazil's Supreme Court justices.** Ricardo Lewandowski.

33   **Porsche 996.** Roberto Kaz, "Nas curvas com Maluf," *Piauí,* October 2007.

34   **one case from the British island of Jersey.** Most details here are from the November 16, 2012, ruling in Jersey. Though the court determined that Maluf controlled the money, he was not technically a defendant; his holding companies were the defendants.

36   **not-very-long tunnel.** Known as the Ayrton Senna Tunnel, it was originally budgeted at 147 million *reais* and ended up costing 728 million *reais,* according to the 2009 ruling.

36   **cutting the city's budget.** Fernando Lancha, "Maluf cortou US$ 581 milhões da área social," *O Estado de S. Paulo,* January 9, 1994. Maluf was also convicted of "administrative improbity" in 1998, after he issued municipal bonds to pay city debts but illegally redirected the proceeds to public works. But he appealed, and when he turned seventy in 2001, he was absolved because the statute of limitations had expired.

36   **Odebrecht got a slap on the wrist.** The company is appealing this ruling.

36   **applicable only to the subsidiary.** The subsidiary is known as CBPO. Odebrecht denies the charges and is also appealing.

38   **"a good criminal is a dead criminal."** Rogério Pagnan, "Metade do país acha que 'bandido bom é bandido morta,' aponta pesquisa," *Folha de S.Paulo,* October 5, 2015.

38   **a common myth.** Elio Gaspari's four-volume history of the regime (Rio de Janeiro: Intrínseca, 2014 edition) details several corruption cases involving mem-

bers of the armed forces during the military regime. Examples can be found in all four books in the series: *A Ditadura Envergonhada* (42, 136–37, 163, 172, 225, 330, 345), *A Ditadura Escancarada* (58, 162, 373–74, 384), *A Ditadura Derrotada* (86, 267, 449), and *A Ditadura Encurralada* (107, 284, 299, 434). The top brass was well aware of the corruption. In Ronaldo Costa Couto's *História Indiscreta da Ditadura e da Abertura* (Rio de Janeiro: Record, 1999), General Ernesto Geisel, president from 1974 to 1979, is quoted as saying, "Corruption in the Armed Forces is so great that the only solution for Brazil is to carry out the *abertura*"—the *opening* toward democracy that he initiated.

38   **didn't start in the nineties.** Maluf was cited in at least one corruption case in the seventies, when censorship began to ease up. While serving as São Paulo state transportation secretary in 1974, he allegedly wrangled cheap loans from the BNDE (as the state development bank was then known) for a bankrupt company owned by his wife's family.

38   **João Paulo dos Santos.** His account is from Claudio Dantas Sequeira, "O homem da mala da Camargo Corrêa," *IstoÉ,* March 6, 2015. The author of the article surmised that it wasn't a heavy conscience that got Santos talking, but resentment over the promise of a postretirement payment that he said the company had failed to fulfill.

39   **a think tank known as Ipês.** Details on Ipês are from the 2014 report by Brazil's National Truth Commission (2:316ff.) and hearings I attended that year at the commission's São Paulo chapter. Apart from the names I mention in the text, other contributors include Octávio Frias de Oliveira, owner of the *Folha de S.Paulo* newspaper, and Júlio de Mesquita Filho, owner of *O Estado de S. Paulo.* Some companies supported the 1964 coup by providing the military with equipment, including vehicles, batteries, and medicines. According to the commission's report, they include the wood products company Duratex (owned by the billionaire Setubal and Villela families), Eucatex (Paulo Maluf's family business), and foreign companies B. F. Goodrich, Esso (Exxon), Firestone, Goodyear, Johnson & Johnson, Pfizer, Texaco, and Volkswagen.

40   **claiming the Soviets had infiltrated.** Eduardo Gomes Silva, "A *Rede da Democracia* e o golpe de 1964," (master's thesis, Universidade Federal Fluminense, 2008).

40   **suggested Maluf to run a state bank.** Delfim Netto's suggestion is from Maluf's authorized biography, Tão Gomes Pinto, *Ele: Maluf, Trajetória da Audácia* (Rio de Janeiro: Ediouro, 2008), 41. The bank was Caixa Econômica Federal.

40   **Operação Bandeirante.** Details on Oban are from the 2014 report by Brazil's National Truth Commission (2:329ff. and Gaspari, *A Ditadura Escancarada* 61ff.).

40   **Pianola Boilesen.** From the documentary *Cidadão Boilesen* (2009) and Jorge José de Melo, "Boilesen, um empresário da ditadura," (master's thesis, Universidade Federal Fluminense, 2012).

40   **"the tone of a civic project."** Thomas E. Skidmore, *The Politics of Military Rule in Brazil, 1964–1985* (Oxford; New York: Oxford University Press, 1988), 126. According to Gaspari (*A Ditadura Escancarada,* 63), Maluf fixed up Oban's headquarters with fresh asphalt, electrical wiring, and lighting.

41   **joined an underground organization.** Details on Dilma are from Luiz Maklouf Carvalho, "As armas e os varões," *Piauí,* April 2009.

41   **cracked down on protests.** I got good background on student protests from Zuenir Ventura's *1968: O Ano que Não Terminou* (Rio de Janeiro: Nova Fronteira, 1988).

41   **"uterine hemorrhage."** Dilma's quote from the National Truth Commission report, 1:387.

41   **"on the parrot's perch."** Quoted in Sandra Kiefer, "Documentos revelam detalhes da tortura sofrida por Dilma em Minas na ditadura," *Estado de Minas,* June 17, 2012.

42   **The family that founded Ultragaz.** According to the website of the Comissão de Valores Mobiliários (CVM), Brazil's securities and exchange commission, members of the Igel family own a combined 21.5 percent of the stock in Ultragaz's parent company, Ultrapar—a stake worth $2.1 billion in October 2015. When I contacted Ultrapar's press department, the company declined to comment on its involvement with Oban.

42   **"It was either us or them."** Gastão Vidigal of the Banco Mercantil de São Paulo, quoted in Gaspari, *A Ditadura Escancarada,* 64.

42   **Mário Wallace Simonsen.** Details of his downfall are from the National Truth Commission report (2:325) and Áureo Busetto, "Sem aviões da Panair e imagens da TV Excelsior no ar: um episódio sobre a relação regime militar e televisão," in Beatriz Kushnir, ed., *Maços na gaveta: reflexões sobre a mídia* (Niteroi: EDUFF, 2009), 53–63.

42   **One civilian in the military government.** Paulo Egydio Martins. According to the National Truth Commission (2:330), other contributors to Oban include Amador Aguiar, the owner of Banco Bradesco; the newspaper *Folha de S.Paulo;* and the foreign companies Ford, General Electric, General Motors, Mercedes-Benz, Nestlé, and Siemens.

43   **frozen meals. Sebastião's joint venture with Ultragaz was called Supergel.** Camargo Corrêa's head PR person didn't just decline to comment on Sebastião's relationship with Oban; he declined to decline to comment. "Just say we never returned your calls," he said, and asked me not to print his name.

43   **tight with the generals.** In addition to specific citations below, details on Sebastião Camargo are from the Camargo Corrêa website and *Memórias do Brasil Grande* (São Paulo: Saraiva, 2008), by Wilson Quintella, a former Camargo Corrêa CEO.

43   **owned a mansion.** Personal details in this and the following paragraph are from social columns in *Folha* on May 2, 1965, March 18, 1973, November 4, 1973, December 22, 1973, and November 18, 1975, among others; horse auction notices such as "Leilão de cavalo arabe faturou Cr$ 5,5 milhões," *Folha,* February 24, 1978; and "A fortuna de um construtor de estradas," *Folha,* December 15, 1982.

43   **"mysterious, enigmatic."** The friend in question is Miguel Reale, quoted in "Amigos destacam liderança e pioneirismo do empresário," *Estado,* August 28, 1994.

44   **"completely loyal to Brazil."** Quoted in Michael Smith, Sabrina Valle, and Blake Schmidt, "The Betrayal of Brazil," *Bloomberg Markets,* June 2015.

44   **leaned on regime friendships.** For details on the construction industry's ties to the military government, and general background on the regime's infrastructure

drive, Pedro Henrique Pedreira Campos's dissertation, "A Ditadura dos Em- preiteiros: as empresas nacionais de construção pesada, suas formas associativas e o Estado ditatorial brasileiro, 1964–1985" (PhD diss., Universidade Federal Fluminense, 2012), was essential. An article from the magazine *IstoÉ*—"A obra da ditadura," March 24, 2004—also cites an unnamed former executive at Ode- brecht saying that the company's founder, Norberto, forged ties with the regime's hard line to expand his business.

45   **decompression sickness and bone necrosis.** From Campos, "A Ditadura dos Em- preiteiros," 443.

45   **one day having the bomb.** From Campos, "A Ditadura dos Empreiteiros," 476, and Gaspari, *A Ditadura Encurralada,* 129.

46   **the company that built the Big Worm.** Construtora Rabello also worked on the Rio–Niterói Bridge in the consortium led by Camargo Corrêa.

46   **Marco Paulo Rabello.** Some have cited his closeness to former president Juscelino Kubitschek, later discredited by the regime, as the reason for his company's de- cline in the seventies. But Camargo too was close to Kubitschek.

46   **"o homem dos relacionamentos."** From Quintella, *Memórias,* 41.

46   **he grew up poor.** Details in this paragraph are from Quintella, *Memórias,* 41ff, and "Camargo montou um império com o trabalho," *Folha,* August 28, 1994.

47   **conspiring with its political patron.** Caio Prado Jr., "Interessados e parceiros," *Estado,* March 30, 1948.

47   **Limoeiro.** The interview with Otávio Frias Filho appeared in *Folha,* December 2, 1990. Details on the construction itself are from Quintella, *Memórias,* 152ff.

47   **the construction of Brasília.** Details in this paragraph are from Quintella, *Memórias,* 161ff.

48   **"It's you gentlemen who change."** From Campos, "A Ditadura dos Empreiteiros," 89.

48   **"the cordial man."** Sérgio Buarque de Holanda's *Raízes do Brasil* (São Paulo: Companhia das Letras, 1995) is as fresh in many ways today as it was when it first came out in 1936.

49   **assistant to the colony's governor-general.** Henrique Meirelles, "Raízes do (novo) Brasil," *Folha,* March 22, 2015.

49   **first real business elite.** Details on Rio's slave-trafficker aristocracy come from Laurentino Gomes's *1808* (São Paulo: Planeta, 2007) and Jorge Caldeira's *Mauá: Empresário do Império* (São Paulo: Companhia das Letras, 1995).

50   **Raymundo Faoro.** His treatise on Brazilian patrimonialism is *Os Donos do Poder* (São Paulo: Globo, 2001).

50   *caixa dois.* Estimates of undeclared campaign donations come from Sérgio Laz- zarini's *Capitalismo de Laços,* 3rd ed. (Rio de Janeiro: Elsevier, 2011), 46.

51   **shaves more than a percentage point.** Corruption's cost to GDP is from a March 2010 report issued by the Federação das Indústrias do Estado de São Paulo (Fiesp).

51   **"No company can survive."** Quoted in Eduardo Belo, "Empresas não são inocen- tes, diz Odebrecht," in *Folha,* June 26, 1994.

52   **shares in Eucatex.** The value of the Maluf family interest in Eucatex is based on the combined twenty-three-percent stake reported on the website of the CVM. Eucatex's market value hovered around seven hundred million *reais* in 2012.

52   **twelve billion dollars in revenue.** From Camargo Corrêa's 2012 annual report.

52   Sebastião's widow, Dirce. Eight months after my story appeared, Dirce died, leaving the family fortune to her three daughters.

52   "giant without a face." Denize Bacoccina, Flávia Gianni, and Nicholas Vital, "Camargo Corrêa: um gigante sem rosto," IstoÉ Dinheiro, December 23, 2009.

53   golf course. From "O meu campo de golfe," Veja, July 10, 2002.

53   When the story went live. My story was published as "Brazil's Richest Woman Unmasked with $13 Billion Fortune," Bloomberg, August 23, 2012.

53   a bridge built by Camargo. In mid-2015, Camargo Corrêa's toll-road joint venture, CCR, handed over control of the bridge concession.

53   Lula used to advocate. André Singer's Os Sentidos do Lulismo (São Paulo: Companhia das Letras, 2012) provided insights on Lula's transformations.

54   a quarter to half of all donations. For example: Fábio Zanini, "Empreiteira e banco foram os maiores doadores do PT," Folha, May 17, 2007, and "Ranking de doação a partidos é liderado por construtoras," Folha, May 4, 2010.

54   four percent of the total. I calculated Camargo Corrêa's campaign contributions using numbers from the website of Brazil's electoral court, the Tribunal Superior Eleitoral (TSE).

54   nothing new in Brazilian politics. In 1997, congressmen were allegedly paid to amend the constitution to allow Fernando Henrique Cardoso to be reelected as president. "Deputado diz que vendeu seu voto a favor da reeleição por R$200 mil," Fernando Rodrigues, May 13, 1997.

55   "people you'd invite home for dinner." Miterhof told me once that if his goal was to prevent corruption, he would have pursued a different career path. Still, he recognized the importance of regulation and improving controls on corruption.

55   Like the leaders of the military regime. Lula once said that General Ernesto Geisel—military president from 1974 to 1979—had overseen the "last great period of development in this country." Demetrio Magnoli, "Lula celebra Geisel em Belo Monte," Estado, April 29, 2010.

55   win-win for business and labor. In line with his public works program, one of Lula's most important initiatives was an affordable housing program called Minha Casa, Minha Vida—My House, My Life. The program subsidized homes for the poor and also helped to mint at least one billionaire, Rubens Menin, the owner of MRV Engenharia. When I interviewed Menin in May 2011, he told me he was one of the main advisers on the program that benefited him.

55   at the presidential palace in Brasília. This exchange happened on July 4, 2012. Dilma's office declined to grant an interview or discuss her relationships with old allies of the military regime.

56   "What's good for General Motors." This is a misquote of former GM president Charlie Wilson at his hearings to become defense secretary in 1953.

57   talks for private companies. According to investigations by the Conselho de Controle de Atividades Financeiras (COAF), an arm of the finance ministry, Lula earned 27 million reais from speeches from 2011 through 2014. The investigations were leaked to Veja in August 2015 and Época in October 2015.

57   promoted the firms with foreign leaders. In a Folha editorial on April 7, 2013, Marcelo Odebrecht stated proudly that his company paid for Lula to give talks abroad and that Lula advocated for Odebrecht's interests in foreign countries. Lula declined my interview requests for this book, and José Chrispiniano, a

spokesman at his foundation, Instituto Lula, declined to discuss Lula's ties with construction firms. But the foundation has publicly confirmed that Odebrecht and other firms paid Lula to give talks abroad—while denying that Lula's efforts to promote them constitute "lobbying" or influence peddling.

CHAPTER 3: MANIFEST DESTINY

59   **a hundred dollars an acre.** Sue Branford and Oriel Glock, *The Last Frontier* (London: Zed, 1985), 49, and Daniel Popov, "Corrida pela Terra," *Dinheiro Rural*, May 2013.

59   **rubber barons.** Greg Grandin's *Fordlandia* (New York: Metropolitan, 2009) and Charles Gauld's *The Last Titan: Percival Farquhar, American Entrepreneur in Latin America* (Stanford, Calif.: Institute of Hispanic American and Luso-Brazilian Studies, 1964) provide good background on the rubber boom. The Amazon port cities of Manaus and Belém both have world-class opera houses from those days; Manaus's was built with marble from Italy and roofing tiles from Alsace.

59   **Otaviano Pivetta.** I interviewed him on September 11, 2013. Vanguarda's land holdings are from investor filings on its website.

61   **brought soy to Brazil a century ago.** Odilon Guimarães, "Soja 100 anos," *Globo Rural*, August 17, 2015.

61   **government research body.** The Empresa Brasileira de Pesquisa Agropecuária (Embrapa) partnered with the soy tycoon Olacyr de Moraes to breed these new varieties.

62   **Blairo Maggi.** I interviewed him in Brasília on October 1, 2013. His net worth, attributed to his mother, is from Anderson Antunes, "The Richest People in Brazil 2013: The Full List," *Forbes*, September 9, 2013.

62   **"the slightest guilt."** Larry Rohter, "Relentless Foe of the Amazon Jungle: Soybeans," *New York Times*, September 17, 2003.

65   **Forest Code.** Background on this 2012 law is from the website of Instituto Socioambiental (ISA), a nonprofit that focuses on environmental and social issues.

66   **"the Amazon is not their property."** Al Gore, in 1989. Quoted in "Whose Rain Forest Is This, Anyway?", Alexei Barrionuevo, *New York Times*, May 18, 2008.

66   **"I don't want any gringo."** "Meta para reduzir emissões mostra que 'a gente fala menos e faz mais', diz Lula," *G1*, November 26, 2009.

67   **it was a symbol.** Renée Pereira, "Orçado em R$ 16 bilhões, custo da Usina de Belo Monte já supera os R$ 30 bilhões," *O Estado de S. Paulo*, May 11, 2013.

67   **The biggest winners.** The members of the Consórcio Construtor Belo Monte are listed on the consortium's website.

68   **with two billion dollars invested.** The Transamazônica's cost is from "Inaugurada a Rodovia Transamazônica," *Acervo O Globo*, September 23, 2013.

69   **One of Médici's initiatives.** Details on Amazon policy during the military dictatorship are from Branford, *Last Frontier*. Apart from Sebastião Camargo, other big Amazon investors during those days included Volkswagen and Amador Aguiar, the owner of Banco Bradesco, whose daughters are billionaires today.

69   **Indians as foreign elements.** I got good background on Indians from Gilberto Freyre's *The Masters and the Slaves* (New York: Knopf, 1956) and Scott Wallace's *The Unconquered* (New York: Broadway, 2011).

69   **Waimiri-Atroari tribe.** The alleged massacre is from Brazil's National Truth Commission, 2:235.

70   "the Wild West stage." Quoted in Washington Novaes, "30 anos da lei ambiental, que fazer para cumpri-la?", *Estado,* June 17, 2011.

70   The sheriff still hasn't arrived. Eric Nepomuceno's *O Massacre* (São Paulo: Planeta, 2007) provides a complete account of a notorious massacre of peasants in Pará state in 1996.

70   Dorothy Stang. Details of her murder are from Felipe Milanez, "Uma Década sem Dorothy Stang e com Muito Sangue na Terra," *CartaCapital,* February 12, 2015.

71   supposed to install. Details on Norte Energia's commitments are from its Projeto Básico Ambiental, available on its website (www.masterambiental.com.br), and from ISA.

71   New Jersey–size. Belo Monte originally would flood an 18,000-square-kilometer area, according to ISA.

72   Tucuruí. Details on this dam's construction are from Branford, *Last Frontier,* 120.

72   Tuira Kayapó. The video of this confrontation can be found on YouTube. youtu .be/TrIzcBgLM1Q.

72   helped keep it alive. Details on Lopes's career are from Rafael Cariello, "A barragem e a onça," *Piauí,* February 2013.

72   a more palatable version. Details on the new plan are from "A Batalha do Belo Monte," *Folha de S.Paulo,* December 16, 2013.

72   about the same amount of electricity. Tucuruí produces an average of thirty-nine terawatt-hours per year. Though Belo Monte will have a larger generation capacity than Tucuruí, it's expected to produce a similar amount on an annual basis because it won't run at full speed all year round. According to the Empresa de Pesquisa Energética, an arm of the mines and energy ministry, Rio de Janeiro consumed about forty-one terawatt-hours in 2014.

72   just three and a half billion dollars. As late as 2009, the government estimated a cost of as little as seven billion reais, according to "Análise Crítica do Estudo de Impacto Ambiental do Aproveitamento Hidrelétrico de Belo Monte," a report on the dam signed by forty experts on October 29, 2009.

72   outsourced the viability studies. From the May 2009 Relatório de Impacto Ambiental on Norte Energia's website.

73   "gun to our heads." From a letter signed by members of the Munduruku, Juruna, Kayapó, Xipaya, Kuruaya, Asurini, Parakanã, and Arara tribes quoted in André Borges, "Índios ocupam canteiro de obras de Belo Monte," *Valor Econômico,* May 2, 2013.

73   forty experts who issued a report. This is the "Análise Crítica" report cited above.

73   billion-dollar plan. 3.7 billion *reais* according to a September 15, 2014, statement on Norte Energia's website.

77   fortune of six billion dollars. Anderson Antunes, "The Complete List of the 150 Richest People in Brazil," *Forbes,* September 18, 2014.

77   cleaner energy sources like wind. Brazil does invest in wind and solar too, but Amazonian mega-dams have been the Workers Party's main energy priority.

77   "Belo Monte is very important for the country." From "Marcelo Odebrecht fala sobre Belo Monte no Seminário da Tendências Consultoria," April 29, 2010. www.youtube.com/watch?v=jXnA2_2hhkg. Odebrecht has also invested in wind and solar, but much more recently and on a much smaller scale than its investments in hydroelectric power.

78   **"go without electricity?"** Bruno Peres, "'Você preferia ficar sem luz?', diz Dilma sobre impacto de Belo Monte," *Valor Econômico,* August 5, 2014.

78   **rain clouds that make their way southeast.** This is according to Antonio Donato Nobre, a researcher at the government research body Instituto Nacional de Pesquisas Espaciais, among others.

CHAPTER 4: NATION BUILDING

79   **Roberto Marinho ($25 billion).** This net worth estimate applies to his three sons, when I calculated their fortune in 2012.

80   **I didn't get telenovelas.** I got background on novelas from academic papers written by Maria Cristina Palma Mungioli, Jane Aparecida Marques, and Roberta de Almeida e Rebouças.

81   **"why in the world would I want to go to Hollywood?"** "Telenovela 'Avenida Brasil' Speaks to Brazilians," Vincent Bevins, *Los Angeles Times,* February 2, 2013.

81   **raked in a billion dollars.** Anderson Antunes, "Brazilian Telenovela 'Avenida Brasil' Makes Billions By Mirroring Its Viewers' Lives," *Forbes,* October 19, 2012.

81   **more than half of all money spent on TV ads.** Rodrigo Manzano, "Inter-Meios: setor cresce 5,98% em 2012," *meio&mensagem,* March 18, 2013.

81   **six billion dollars a year in revenues.** 12.7 billion *reais* according to financial statements released by Globo Comunicação & Participações.

81   **"institution of power."** From Pedro Bial's authorized biography, *Roberto Marinho* (Rio de Janeiro: Jorge Zahar, 2005), 282. In the sections that follow, details on Roberto Marinho come from Bial's biography; Walter Clark's *O Campeão de Audiência* (São Paulo, Best Seller, 1991); Daniel Herz's *História Secreta da Rede Globo* (Porto Alegre: Tchê!, 1987); José Bonifácio de Oliveira Sobrinho's *O Livro do Boni* (Rio de Janeiro: Casa da Palavra, 2011); Joe Wallach's *Meu Capítulo na TV Globo* (Rio de Janeiro: Topbooks, 2011); the Memória Globo website; and the documentaries *Roberto Marinho: O Senhor do Seu Tempo* (2011) and *Além do Cidadão Kane* (1993). I also consulted a collection of Roberto Marinho's editorials, *Uma Trajetória Liberal* (Rio de Janeiro: Topbooks, 1992). For the most part, I haven't included notes for facts that were reported in more than one of these sources.

82   **anti-Goulart propaganda.** For example, the front-page story "Criou-se um soviete na Marinha de guerra," *O Globo,* March 31, 1964. The activities of Radio Globo are mentioned in the National Truth Commission's 2014 report (2:321) and Eduardo Gomes Silva's master's thesis, "A *Rede da Democracia* e o golpe de 1964" (Universidade Federal Fluminense, 2008). In January 2015 I asked Globo's press people for comment on Roberto Marinho's ties to the dictatorship; they declined to comment.

82   **willing to squelch bad news.** Fernando Morais's biography of Assis Chateaubriand, *Chatô, o Rei do Brasil* (São Paulo: Companhia das Letras, 1994), provides good background on Brazil's media industry. Chateaubriand openly admitted to taking money in return for favorable coverage for politicians. He not only squelched bad news about companies that paid him for ads, he also invented bad news about companies that competed with his own outside interests.

83   **a legendary figure.** I got good background on Getúlio Vargas from Thomas E.

Skidmore's *Politics in Brazil, 1930–1964: An Experiment in Democracy* (New York: Oxford University Press, 2007).

83   **"a state of semi-slavery."** "No Sul, Lula evoca Getúlio e cobra investimentos privados no PAC," *Jornal do Brasil,* August 25, 2007.

84   *O Globo* **actually lent its support to Goulart.** Goulart was initially elected vice president in 1960. When President Jânio Quadros resigned in August 1961, it wasn't clear at first whether Goulart would be allowed to take office as president. *O Globo*'s front page blared, "Serious Warning from the War Minister to the Nation: WE ARE AT A CROSSROADS: DEMOCRACY OR COMMUNISM." The military allowed Goulart to assume the presidency only under an improvised parliamentary system. He still had the authority to grant Marinho the license to run a TV station in Brasília in 1962, while campaigning for a plebiscite to restore his full presidential powers—which *O Globo* appeared to back, calling Goulart a "statesman" in one headline. It's unclear whether this was Marinho's way of repaying Goulart for granting the license, but the firebrand journalist-cum-politician Carlos Lacerda would later accuse Marinho of selling his support for the plebiscite in return for loans from Caixa, the state bank. In any case, Marinho soon turned against Goulart once again.

84   **TV Tupi.** Details on the network, owned by Assis Chateaubriand, are from Morais, *Chatô*.

85   **"When he lowered his voice."** From Bial, *Roberto Marinho,* 24.

85   **"You see the world as an ocean."** From Bial, *Roberto Marinho,* 26.

86   RESSURGE A DEMOCRACIA! *O Globo,* April 2, 1964.

86   **popularly elected head of state.** Goulart was technically not elected president but vice president, and took office when Jânio Quadros resigned.

86   **postpone elections.** In 1965, at a private lunch with General Humberto Castelo Branco, who was then the president, Marinho tried to persuade him to put off presidential elections set for the following year. Marinho relayed the details of this meeting to U.S. ambassador Lincoln Gordon, according to a diplomatic cable dated August 14, 1965, and reported in *Folha de S.Paulo,* May 5, 2014.

87   **front page after front page.** For example: "COSTA E SILVA: O GOVERNO JÁ CUIDA DA VOLTA À DEMOCRACIA," March 26, 1969; "PRESIDENTE AOS EMPRESÁRIOS: ESTAMOS QUASE SAINDO DO REGIME DE EXCEÇÃO," July 11, 1969; and "MÉDICI PROMETE IMPLANTAR A DEMOCRACIA PLENA NO BRASIL," October 8, 1969.

87   **labeled all left-wing militants as terrorists.** This is based on my perusal of *O Globo*'s archives from those years.

87   **when terrorists targeted Marinho.** From Elio Gaspari's *A Ditadura Encurralada* (Rio de Janeiro: Intrínseca, 2014), 274–76.

87   **"President, can you assure me."** From Bial, *Roberto Marinho,* 109.

87   **"Nobody messes with my communists."** Cited in many places, including Bial, *Roberto Marinho,* 219.

87   **"If the communists win."** Bial, *Roberto Marinho,* 300.

87   **"never caused me any kind of problem."** Armando Falcão, quoted in *Além do Cidadão Kane.*

88   **swallowed a loss of half a million dollars.** From Bial, *Roberto Marinho,* 219.

88   **censorship of anyone's torture or disappearance.** According to General Ernesto

Geisel, Roberto Marinho told him, "Censorship is all right when it comes to terrorism." From Elio Gaspari's *A Ditadura Derrotada* (Rio de Janeiro: Intrínseca, 2014), 229.

88   **"deserved attention and special favors."** Marinho was lobbying for a license in the city of João Pessoa in 1978. The minister, Euclides Quandt de Oliveira, relayed the conversation to General Ernesto Geisel, who was then president. This is according to a book based on Geisel's personal archive, *Dossiê Geisel*, edited by Celso Castro and Maria Celina D'Araujo (Rio de Janeiro: FGV, 2002), 153–55.

88   **"a kid in Copacabana saw the buffalo."** Quoted in *Além do Cidadão Kane*.

89   **a military helicopter hovering outside.** Roberto Irineu Marinho is the son who saw this. From Mario Sergio Conti, "Carta a Ali Kamel," *Observatório da Imprensa*, October 4, 2013.

89   **"I'll fight with the pope."** From Bial, *Roberto Marinho*, 315.

90   **ACM would intervene.** Herz, *História Secreta*, 63, 65. According to Herz (68), ACM also got rid of a tax, the Imposto Sobre Serviços de Comunicação, thus making it cheaper for Globo to extend its network.

90   **Marinho gave his family the contract.** Herz, *História Secreta*, 48.

90   **the ex-president got the same deal.** TV Mirante switched from SBT to Globo in 1991: "TV Mirante. Há 20 anos, a Televisão do Maranhão," www.imirante .com, March 14, 2007.

90   **distributed these contracts to congressmen.** Elvira Lobato, "Os Marinho são donos do maior império," *Folha*, June 12, 1994.

90   **pillars of power.** Elvira Lobato, "Políticos controlam 24% das TVs do país," *Folha*, August 6, 2001.

90   **"I use this power."** Alan Riding, "One Man's Political Views Color Brazil's TV Eye," *New York Times*, January 12, 1987.

90   **without a Rosebud.** From *Além do Cidadão Kane*.

91   *Condemned to Success.* The title of his unwritten memoirs is from Bial, *Roberto Marinho*, 12; the details about his anxiety are from Bial, 304.

91   **handsome young politician.** For details on Collor and Globo's support of him, I relied on João Braga Arêas, "Batalhas de *O Globo*" (PhD diss., Universidade Federal Fluminense, 2012).

92   **Collor was a disaster.** But maybe not a *complete* disaster. Some analysts credit him for starting to lower Brazil's barriers to foreign trade and open up the economy.

92   **wide-reaching bribery scheme.** "Pedro Collor conta tudo," *Veja*, May 27, 1992.

92   **students sang a song.** From Bial, *Roberto Marinho*, 284.

92   **he joined Lula's coalition.** Collor became senator in 2007. In 2014, he was absolved of corruption charges by the Supreme Court, some for lack of evidence, some because they had exceeded the statute of limitations.

93   **funneling hundreds of millions of dollars.** Fernando Rodrigues, "TV Globo recebeu R$ 6,2 bilhões de publicidade federal com PT no Planalto," *Universo Online*, June 29, 2015.

93   **I got to meet one of the Globo heirs.** I spoke with João Roberto Marinho on December 7, 2012.

93   **Rupert Murdoch.** At the time, he was worth ten billion dollars on the Bloomberg Billionaires Index.

94   **in apparent breach of environmental laws.** Adriana Brasileiro, "Brazil's Rich

Show No Shame Building Homes in Nature Preserves," *Bloomberg Markets,* April 2012. When left-wing blogs revived this story in 2016, the Marinhos denied owning the mansion.

95   **the next generations.** Details on Globo's new shareholder agreement are from "De acordo," *Veja,* September 22, 2012.

95   **They'll deplore how the state has grown.** For example, "Estado esmaga sociedade, e não apenas pelo custo," *O Globo,* October 25, 2015.

96   **frequent on the Globo network.** One recent example is Fábio Almeida and Giancarlo Barzi, "Fraude no Bolsa Família beneficia estrangeiros e até mortos no RS," *G1,* December 16, 2013, which ran on *Jornal Nacional.* On the network's local newscasts, a few recent examples include "Pessoas que já morreram 'recebem' Bolsa Família no norte do Paraná," December 17, 2015; "Fraudes no Bolsa Família cancelam mais de 7 mil benefícios em Ilhéus," October 15, 2015; "Jacarezinho tem irregularidades no Bolsa Família," January 16, 2015; and "Prefeitura de Montes Claros rescinde contrato de servidor que fraudava Bolsa Família," March 20, 2014. Searching newscasts for stories about Bolsa Família, it's rare to find coverage that portrays the program in a positive light. It's more common to find reports of criticisms, such as "Bolsa Família reduz interesse pelo emprego formal," *Jornal Nacional,* June 15, 2012.

96   **tax evasion.** Brazil loses $280 billion a year to tax evasion, according to "The Cost of Tax Abuse," a November 2011 report by the advocacy group The Tax Justice Network. www.taxjustice.net/2014/04/01/cost-tax-abuse-2011/.

96   **Globo itself is fighting charges.** Bruno Marinoni, "Por que a dívida da Globo não é manchete de jornal?", *CartaCapital,* July 31, 2014.

97   **can't remember which congressman.** Karla Alessandra, "Um terço dos eleitores não se lembra em quem votou," *Rádio Câmara,* October 8, 2014.

97   **poignant stories.** The novela was called *Escalada* (1975).

97   **This is an old tradition.** Details on blacks in telenovelas are from the documentary *A Negação do Brasil* (2000). In January 2015 I asked Globo's press people for comment on the network's role in defining the place of blacks in Brazilian society; they declined to comment.

98   **rice powder.** Bial, *Roberto Marinho,* 253.

98   **his country's traditions.** For broader context on blacks in Brazil, I relied on Thomas E. Skidmore's *Black into White: Race and Nationality in Brazilian Thought* (Durham, N.C.: Duke University Press, 1993) and Gilberto Freyre's *The Masters and the Slaves* (New York: Knopf, 1956).

99   **friendlier than the U.S. version.** Brazilians who watched the movie *12 Years a Slave* expressed relief that slavery hadn't been so cruel in Brazil. Lilia Moritz Schwarcz, "Por que deveríamos nos reconhecer nas cenas de '12 Anos de Escravidão,' " *Folha de S.Paulo,* March 2, 2014.

99   **"a *cordial* kind of racism."** Quote from *Trip* magazine, April 2014.

99   **"service elevators."** This restriction is starting to break down somewhat, but you still see plaques next to elevators reminding you that it's illegal to bar someone from entering based on race.

99   **one in six women.** According to the International Labor Organization.

100   **the hundred and fifty Brazilians.** The number of Brazilians worth at least a billion *reais* is from *Forbes*'s Brazilian edition, August 2014.

101   **Complexo do Alemão.** I visited Complexo do Alemão in July 2014. Details on the November 2010 government takeover, UPPs, and the general security situation come from coverage by Globo and other local press.

103   **"Rio de Janeiro is still beautiful."** Though sung by Tim Maia on the telenovela, the song is by Gilberto Gil.

107   **ninety-four percent of** *favelados.* The survey is from Renato Meirelles and Celso Athayde, *Um País Chamado Favela: A Maior Pesquisa Já Feita sobre a Favela Brasileira* (São Paulo: Gente, 2014).

CHAPTER 5: PROSPERITY GOSPEL

108   **two million followers.** According to the Instituto Brasileiro de Geografia e Estatística (IBGE), 1.9 million Brazilians declared themselves members of the Universal Church in 2010. The church has sometimes cited much higher numbers.

108   **he had a net worth of $1.2 billion.** Based on Bloomberg's calculation in early 2013.

108   **"Which is the largest country in the world."** Macedo gave this sermon on February 24, 2013, and I watched it on the website of the Universal Church.

109   **Angola.** Just in Angola, the Universal Church said in 2013 that it has 230 churches and half a million followers. A single church event in Luanda drew 150,000 people—sixteen of whom died of asphyxiation and trampling: Patrícia Campos Mello, "Angola proíbe operação de igrejas evangélicas do Brasil," *Folha de S.Paulo,* April 27, 2013.

109   **sixty thousand more.** The church cited this number in 2013. See Julie Turkewitz, "Eagerly Awaiting Release of Brazilian Evangelical's Autobiography," *New York Times,* February 17, 2013. For background on church members in the United States, one story is Marlon Bishop, "At Latino Church, Faith as an Investment Strategy," WNYC, July 3, 2014.

110   **private jet.** From Macedo's authorized biography, *O Bispo: A História Revelada de Edir Macedo,* by Douglas Tavolaro (São Paulo: Larousse, 2007), 68.

110   **diplomatic passport.** "Itamaraty renova superpassaporte de Edir Macedo," *Folha,* November 18, 2011.

110   **biggest by far.** The Assemblies of God is the biggest evangelical church in Brazil, but the denomination has no single leader.

110   **"Tithes symbolize your faithfulness."** Also from his sermon in Belo Horizonte.

110   **interest-free loans from the church.** From the January 12, 2011, ruling by Judge Leonel Ferreira of the Tribunal Regional Federal da Terceira Região.

110   **forty-five million dollars.** Tavolaro, *O Bispo,* 154.

110   **declared donations of three-quarters of a billion dollars.** The Universal Church declared 1.5 billion *reais* in donations to Brazil's internal revenue service that year, according to the September 1, 2011, accusation by São Paulo public prosecutor Sílvio Luís Martins de Oliveira.

110   **lewd reality shows.** The televangelist Silas Malafaia, for example, criticizes Macedo for this.

110   **inflated prices.** When I interviewed Malafaia on February 5, 2013, he told me he used to buy time on Record at the market rate in the nineties, until one day the

network raised its price tenfold; now only the Universal Church buys airtime on Record.

111 **dragged on since 2009.** Prosecutor Martins's accusations were initially submitted to a state court that year. When I asked for comment in 2013, the church's press people denied all the accusations against Macedo and his deputies. They declined to respond when I asked for comment again in 2014.

111 **"Sua vida está um cocô!"** I saw this sermon at the Universal Church on Avenida João Dias on February 20, 2013.

111 **he was born.** Details on Macedo's life and the early days of the Universal Church are from the biography by Tavolaro; his three-volume memoir, *Nada a Perder* (São Paulo: Planeta, 2012–2014); and my interview with former Universal Church president João Batista on February 7, 2013.

112 **Oral Roberts.** His revenues are from Keith Schneider, "Oral Roberts, Fiery Preacher, Dies at 91," *New York Times,* December 15, 2009.

114 **"Forget everything."** From Macedo, *Nada a Perder vol.* 2, 141.

114 **the main Universal Church.** Until the Temple of Solomon was completed, the main church in São Paulo was on Avenida João Dias.

114 **The first time I went.** I attended the sermons described in this section in January and February 2013.

115 **"When I have sex."** From Tavolaro, *O Bispo,* 89.

115 **blog post decrying anal sex.** Vera Magalhães, "Edir Macedo e 'um belo jantar a dois no lixão,'" *Veja,* February 23, 2010.

115 **the church bought so many copies.** I always saw Macedo's books on sale at the Universal Church. For the launch of the first volume of his memoirs in the United States in February 2013, the McNally Jackson bookstore in New York handled sales. Javier Molea, a McNally Jackson employee, told me that of the seventy-two thousand copies ordered by the day of the launch, most were bought in bulk by the U.S. branches of the Universal Church. (A "disclosure": The McNally Jackson bookstore is owned by the ex-wife of the editor of this book, Chris Jackson.)

117 **"An offering is an investment."** From Tavolaro, *O Bispo,* 206.

118 **two-week-old baby.** From Tavolaro, *O Bispo,* 93.

118 **half a million dollars in a single day.** These details come from my interview on March 4, 2013, with the former bishop Jorge Coelho da Cunha, who joined the church in the mid-eighties and left in the early 2000s. To expand the church's radio network, he acquired stock in four local radio stations; he later filed a lawsuit against church leaders who, he claims, forged his signature to transfer the shares from his name without his permission. There have been similar cases from former bishops Paulo Roberto Gomes da Conceição and Marcelo Nascentes Pires.

118 **a video from a pastors' retreat.** It can be found on YouTube with the title "Bispo Edir Macedo ensinando como roubar os fiéis." (www.youtube.com/watch?v=c5KGw2tNvWk).

119 **a woman named Darnelle.** The bankruptcy case is *The Universal Church v. Robert L. Geltzer.*

119 **a mentally disabled man.** "Fiéis da Igreja Universal contam que foram pressionados a fazer doações," *G1,* August 16, 2009.

119   "When they have more cash on hand." Quote from Bruno Boghossian, "Lula e Dilma ajudam os pobres, que dão mais dízimo, diz ministro da Pesca," *O Estado de S. Paulo*, March 22, 2013.

119   he ordered his bishops. From my interview with Cunha.

120   acquiring the shares in his name. According to the website of Anatel, Brazil's telecommunications regulator, Macedo owns ninety percent of Record and his wife owns the other ten percent.

120   "spectacle of manipulation." Paulo Sérgio Marqueiro, "Lucro certo no reino da Igreja Universal," *O Globo*, April 29, 1990.

120   repeated some of Macedo's orations verbatim. Tavolaro, *O Bispo*, 214.

120   fancy Italian shoes. "Polícia Federal deve indiciar Edir Macedo," *Estado*, October 16, 1991.

120   police found him driving a BMW. "Bispo depõe sobre carro e responde a novo inquérito," *Estado*, June 29, 1991.

120   two multimillion-dollar apartments. Laura Diniz, "Cheque ao bispo," *Veja*, August 15, 2009.

121   fraud, charlatanism, and *curandeirismo*. Tavolaro, *O Bispo*, 26.

121   a half-million-dollar fee. The lawyer is Márcio Thomaz Bastos. Tavolaro, *O Bispo*, 47.

121   transformation into a commercial network. Details from my interview with João Batista.

121   five million dollars in hard currency. "PF encontra R$ 10 mi com bispo do PFL," *Folha*, July 12, 2005.

122   "incompatible with our faith." From Tavolaro, *O Bispo*, 146.

122   "I Learned How to Extort the People." Mariana Sanches, "Aprendi a extorquir o povo," *Época*, October 2, 2009.

122   "How the Marinho Family Destroys Brazil." "Como a Família Marinho destrói o Brasil," *Folha Universal*, September 21, 2009.

122   "God made the Universal stand out." Macedo, *Nada a Perder vol. 2*, 86.

123   By the Bishop's own count. From Tavolaro, *O Bispo*, 204.

123   the form of tax fines. According to Fernando Rodrigues, "Receita cobra R$ 98,360 mi da Universal," *Folha*, July 6, 1997, Brazil's tax agency fined the Universal Church nearly a hundred million dollars in 1997 and Macedo more than a million in 1995.

123   a slew of private businesses. For details on Macedo's and his pastors' business interests, Elvira Lobato of *Folha de S.Paulo* provided me with a trove of documents she obtained over the years, which she wrote about in her book *Instinto de Repórter* (São Paulo: Publifolha, 2009). I re-reported and expanded on what she found, using the 2011 accusation by Prosecutor Martins, the Junta Comercial de São Paulo company registry, and the website of Anatel.

124   "tricked and exploited by me." From Mário Simas Filho, "O céu e o inferno não são folclore," *IstoÉ*, November 23, 2012.

125   "the dregs of society." From the sermon I attended in São Paulo.

126   three-hundred-million-dollar replica. The price is from Simon Romero, "Temple in Brazil Appeals to a Surge in Evangelicals," *New York Times*, July 24, 2014.

130   soldiers arrived in Rio to wait for land grants. Janice Perlman, *Favela: Four De-*

cades of Living on the Edge in Rio de Janeiro (Oxford; New York: Oxford University Press, 2010), 25.

131 **"Napoleon of Wall Street."** Ron Chernow, *The House of Morgan: An American Banking Dynasty and the Rise of Modern Finance* (New York: Grove Press, 2010), 160.

131 **"God gave me my money."** Ron Chernow, *Titan: The Life of John D. Rockefeller, Sr.* (New York: Vintage, 2004), 54.

CHAPTER 6: VISIONARY

135 **Eike Batista recorded a Web video.** For XP Investimentos.

136 **a million barrels a day.** In 2008, OGX planned to reach this target in five years, according to Malu Gaspar's definitive account of Eike's rise and fall, *Tudo ou Nada: Eike Batista e a Verdadeira História do Grupo X* (Rio de Janeiro: Record, 2014), 168.

138 **"God blessed Brazil with these things."** Quote from Eike's appearance on the Globo program *Conta Corrente*, February 12, 2011.

138 **he even set it down in book form.** Details on Eike's early life and career are from his book, *O X da Questão* (Rio de Janeiro: Primeira Pessoa, 2011) and press interviews over the years.

139 **Eike's bodyguards** Eike recounted this story in a few interviews, including "Mayhem Man," *Canadian Business,* April 9, 1999; Adriana Brasileiro, "Billionaire Eike Batista Keeps SLR McLaren in Rio Living Room," *Bloomberg,* June 13, 2008; and Alexei Barrionuevo, "A Brazilian Magnate Points to Himself for Inspiration," *New York Times,* January 20, 2012.

139 **"not to say I was always brilliant."** From Batista, *O X da Questão*, 46.

139 **"I underestimated the weather."** From his interview with Charlie Rose, February 7, 2010

140 **thirty-eight million tons annually.** From MMX's Prospecto Definitivo (final IPO prospectus), 80. According to the document (120), China consumed 420.5 million tons of iron ore in 2005.

140 **"like the *mulatas.*"** Isa Pessoa, "A bela e a fera," *O Globo,* March 6, 1987.

141 **The little *carioca* elite was scandalized.** Rosângela Honor, "Luma de Oliveira e o prazer de provocar," *IstoÉ,* September 1999.

141 **"the husband of Luma."** Aziz Filho and Eliane Lobato, "O marido da Luma," *IstoÉ,* February 27, 2002.

141 **"It's to show I have an owner."** Rodrigo Vergara, "Cantor atrai até os avessos ao desfile," *Folha de S.Paulo,* February 24, 1998.

141 **"Luma is harmful to democracy."** Quote from the sociologist Heleieth Safiotti in Martha Mendonça and João Luiz Vieira, "Poderosa," *Época,* August 25, 2010.

141 **brought her Ferrero Rocher chocolates.** "Eike é meu infinito particular," *Época Negócios,* May 2008.

141 **she got entangled with a studly young *bombeiro*.** Daniel Pinheiro, "Um casamento em chamas," *Veja,* March 10, 2004.

142 **thirty-seven-thousand-square-foot mansion.** Details on Eike's house are from Ronaldo França and Ronaldo Soares, "O Mr. X da bolsa," *Veja,* June 14, 2008; Darcio Oliveira, "O enigma Eike," *Época Negócios,* April 30, 2008; and Adriana

Brasileiro, "Billionaire Eike Batista Keeps SLR McLaren in Rio Living Room," *Bloomberg*, June 22, 2008.

142   **"the new toupee."** This interaction took place on *Roda Viva*, August 30, 2010.

143   **Alessandro Corona.** I interviewed him on June 19, 2012.

143   **"To Get Rich Is Glorious."** "Eike Xiaoping," *Veja*, January 18, 2012.

144   **four-hundred-thousand-ton Chinamaxes.** From an LLX investor presentation, August 2012.

145   **He called himself "a mega-arbitrageur."** Rodrigo Viga Gaier, "Eike Batista diz que pode participar de leilão de aeroportos," Reuters, August 23, 2011.

145   **the government planned to auction exploration rights.** Details on the auction are from Consuelo Dieguez, "Tesouro submerso," *Piauí*, April 2008.

146   **Eike framed the switch as a blessing.** The advantage of shallow waters was cited in OGX's final IPO prospectus, 20.

146   **ten times what anyone else did.** Antonio Regalado, "Brazil Oil IPO Lures Investors," *Wall Street Journal*, June 12, 2008.

147   **he raised seven billion dollars in his IPOs.** Calculation based on numbers from the offering prospectuses.

147   **"Brazil has really put our act together."** This quote and the "Helloo!" quote are both from his interview with *60 Minutes*, December 9, 2010.

147   **"gigantic consumer market."** From his interview with CNN, October 18, 2010.

147   **investing forty billion dollars in ten years.** EBX press materials in 2012.

147   **we have the size to match China's appetite.** This is a direct quote from his interview with *60 Minutes*.

147   **think big but protect the environment.** On Bloomberg TV, April 30, 2012, he said, "When you develop billion-dollar projects, new businessmen developing projects should take care of the surrounding environment."

148   **gave himself a deadline, 2013.** Back in 2008, he started saying he would be number one in five years. Nilson Brandão Jr. and Márcia Vieira, "Ele quer ser o homem mais rico do mundo," *O Estado de S. Paulo*, January 26, 2008.

148   **"Brazilian mania for improvisation."** Juliana Barros, "Sempre querem me derrubar," *Alfa*, March 14, 2011.

148   **"I'm from the generation."** From his interview with Jô Soares, May 20, 2011.

149   **old American literary tradition.** The prime example is Napoleon Hill's *Think and Grow Rich* (Cleveland, Oh.: The Ralston Society, 1937).

150   **My first big story on him.** "Batista's $7.6 Billion Stock Tumble 'Not a Problem,'" *Bloomberg*, January 27, 2011.

151   **"We're conservative."** "Entrevista exclusiva de Eike Batista: 'Vamos ver quem vai rir por último,'" *IstoÉ Dinheiro*, April 20, 2011.

151   **"pact with nature."** Carla Miranda, "Eike diz que vai ultrapassar o homem mais rico do mundo," *Estado*, May 3, 2011.

151   **"excellent geological conditions" and "high-quality carbon reserves."** Cited in the September 11, 2014, criminal complaint by Rio prosecutors.

151   **"Good thing it was dry."** From his interview on *Roda Viva*, August 30, 2010.

151   **"zero percent speculation."** He said this in an interview with *Forbes* in 2010, according to Keren Blankfeld, "Brazilian Whacks: Eike Batista and Brazil's Unfulfilled Potential," *Forbes*, March 3, 2015.

152   **"the Midas touch."** A portfolio manager named Stacy Steimel said this to me for my first big story on Eike, "Batista's $7.6 Billion Stock Tumble."

152   **compared him with Donald Trump.** A portfolio manager named Ed Kuczma said this to me for Alex Cuadros, Juan Carlo Spinetto, and Cristiane Lucchesi, "Eike Batista, the Man Who Lost $25 Billion in One Year," *Bloomberg Businessweek,* March 28, 2013.

152   **Diogo Mainardi.** This interaction is from *Manhattan Connection,* March 13, 2011.

153   **spent fifteen million dollars of his own money.** Gaspar, *Tudo ou Nada,* 63.

153   **market value hit $1.8 billion.** Numbers in this paragraph are from TVX company filings on the website of Sedar, Canada's securities and exchange commission.

153   **"you shareholders can shoot me."** From "Mayhem Man," cited in Gaspar, *Tudo ou Nada,* 24.

154   **He sank thirty million dollars . . . another ten million.** Both numbers from Consuelo Dieguez, "Mais do que o marido da Luma," *Exame,* October 15, 2002.

154   **voice pagers.** "Eike Batista investirá em voice pagers na AL," *Estado,* April 25, 1997.

154   **"Jeff Bezos did something like this."** The venture was called ebX Express. This quote is from his video interview with *Exame,* March 18, 2010.

154   **"Gold is a jurassic industry."** "Brazil's AMX's Batista on $55 Mln Sale to Azurix," *Bloomberg,* September 14, 1999.

154   **"You're all fucked."** Oliveira, "O enigma Eike."

155   **the Marinho brothers talked him out of it.** Gaspar, *Tudo ou Nada,* 273.

155   **"I'm glad to have had failures."** From his *Exame* video interview.

155   **"Everyone got used to receiving a contract."** From "Eike Batista: 'Ser 1° do mundo é consequência,'" *O Globo,* March 20, 2010.

155   **"ask my good friends the *empreiteiros*."** From his *Roda Viva* interview.

156   **"I create things from zero."** From his *Exame* video interview.

156   **"magnums of champagne."** From Marcio Orsolini, "A prova de Eike," *IstoÉ,* January 27, 2012.

157   **he'd even challenged Slim face-to-face.** Darcio Oliveira, Silvia Balieiro, and David Cohen, "As histórias por trás da história do sumiço do império de Eike Batista," *Época Negócios,* May 2014.

157   **three and a half million ounces.** Before Eike took it over and renamed it, AUX was known as Ventana Gold. This figure is from Ventana company filings.

158   **He wanted to set the record straight.** I first interviewed Eike on March 2, 2012. The interview was in English.

158   **Now he said 2015.** For example, in an interview with Bloomberg in March 2011.

160   **inside info on promising gold deposits.** The allegations came from an engineer at an Eike venture known as Dunbrás. According to the engineer, Vale would start exploring a site and, despite signs the site was rich in minerals, abandon it and return the concession to the government, which would then sell it on to the private sector. Tipped off, Eike would allegedly step up and buy the rights. The guy had previously filed an unsuccessful lawsuit claiming that Eike had stiffed him for engineering work on a gold-prospecting machine. Details in "PF investiga informações privilegiadas da Vale," *Estado,* February 15, 1996.

160   Eike's one real scrape with the law. The raid was part of the so-called Operation Midas Touch.

CHAPTER 7: HELPING HANDS

162   He turned first to his one million Twitter followers. As of late 2015, these tweets were still up on Eike's Twitter account, @eikebatista.

163   a Twitter account Thor had created. The same goes for Thor's account, @Thor631.

163   "They cried, embraced, and conversed." Rodrigo Vianna, "Thor se encontrou com família de ciclista morto no RJ, diz advogado," *G1*, March 23, 2012.

164   "Thor is a victim too." Mônica Bergamo, "Imprudência de ciclista poderia ter matado meu filho, afirma Eike," *Folha de S.Paulo*, March 20, 2012.

164   "If I'm not satisfied with my body." From Sofia Cerqueira, "No reino encantado de Thor," *Veja Rio*, June 1, 2011.

164   he used the steroid DHEA. "Thor Batista chega aos 105kg e assume recorrer a anabolizante rejuvenescedor para ficar fortão: 'Nunca usei drogas,'" *Extra*, December 3, 2014.

165   "sixty thousand *reais* in a night." Cerqueira, "No reino encantado."

165   used to respond to admirers. Priscila Bessa, "A língua afiada do filho de Eike Batista," *iG*, August 29, 2011.

165   cost more to fly him to the gigs. Joana Dale, "Olin Batista, o outro filho de Eike," *Extra*, May 25, 2013.

165   Thor and his friend had planned to hit up a party Olin was throwing. Malu Gaspar, *Tudo ou Nada: Eike Batista e a Verdadeira História do Grupo X* (Rio de Janeiro: Record, 2014), 348.

166   the first book he'd ever read. Flávia Salme, " 'Foi o primeiro livro que li', diz filho de Eike Batista sobre trajetória do pai," *iG*, December 6, 2011.

167   closed-circuit drag race. Luciana Nunes Leal, "Uma Ferrari em Curicica," *O Estado de S. Paulo*, May 12, 2012.

167   "my mom raised me." From Eike's interview with Marília Gabriela, March 14, 2010.

168   Eliezer was a technocrat. The first time Eliezer Batista served as minister of mines and energy and CEO of Vale was under João Goulart. Because he spoke commie Russian, the generals pushed him into exile after Goulart's overthrow in 1964. That's why the Batistas moved to Europe at first. But Eliezer was one of the best in the business, and the generals' pragmatism eventually won out, and so after a few years they asked him to lead Vale's expansion in Europe and finally to return to Brazil as CEO. Years later, Eliezer served as one of Fernando Collor's ministers.

168   A geologist had discovered. Details from Vale's website.

169   finance a documentary about him. *Eliezer Batista: O Engenheiro do Brasil* (2009).

169   "Brazil is big indeed." Darcio Oliveira, Silvia Balieira, and David Cohen, " 'Um enorme erro foi não vender parte da OGX por US$ 7 bi,'" *Valor Econômico*, March 17, 2015.

169   the jewelers knew how important his dad was. Alexei Barrionuevo, "A Brazilian Magnate Points to Himself for Inspiration," *New York Times*, January 20, 2012.

169   secretly mortgaged. Gaspar, *Tudo ou Nada*, 45.

169   he often lent a hand. Details in this paragraph from Gaspar, *Tudo ou Nada*, 46ff., Sérgio Leo's *Ascensão e Queda do Império X* (Rio de Janeiro: Nova Fronteira, 2014) 34ff., and my interview with Olavo Monteiro de Carvalho on July 22, 2014.

170   he was broke by the time he set his sights on Brazil. The other sources are a person at EBX who asked not to be named and Gaspar, *Tudo ou Nada*, 77.

170   Eliezer connected Eike with the governor. Gaspar, *Tudo ou Nada*, 69.

171   donated four hundred thousand dollars. From the website of the Tribunal Superior Eleitoral (TSE).

171   unlimited access to his Legacy jet. When the press discovered these trips, a minor scandal erupted. Eike explained, "I'm free to choose my friendships. I do it all with money from my pocket and I'm proud of that." From Luis Artur Nogueira, "Eike empresta jato a Cabral e diz ser livre para escolher amigos," *Exame*, June 22, 2011.

171   tens of millions of dollars in tax credits. Bernardo Mello Franco, "Eike dá R$ 139 mi para projetos de Cabral," *Folha*, June 26, 2011.

171   the labor leader would be a *retrocesso*. Aziz Filho and Eliane Lobato, "O marido da Luma," *IstoÉ*, February 27, 2002.

171   for Lula's reelection campaign. From the website of the TSE.

171   Eike wanted to take over Vale. Sergio Lazzarini has a good account of this episode, uniting various press reports, in *Capitalismo de Laços* (Rio de Janeiro: Elsevier, 2010), 1ff.

172   seventy-six billion dollars, more than the World Bank. From statements by the banks on their websites.

172   the BNDES would approve five billion dollars. Ten billion *reais* were approved, according to statements by the bank. (Only six billion *reais* were ultimately disbursed.)

172   "the best bank in the world." Samantha Lima, "BNDES 'é o melhor banco do mundo', diz Eike Batista," *Folha*, July 2, 2010.

173   half a million dollars to fund the gushy biopic. From Ricardo Mendonça, " 'Lula, o filho do Brasil' terá o maior orçamento da história do cinema nacional," *Época*, February 19, 2009.

173   "entered the ranks of the great statesmen." Nalu Fernandes, "Em jantar com Lula, Eike Batista elogia 'Brasil novo,' " *O Estado de S. Paulo*, September 22, 2009.

173   at a televised round table. *Roda Viva*, August 30, 2010.

174   Mauá constructed an empire. Details on Mauá are from Jorge Caldeira, *Mauá: Empresário do Império* (São Paulo: Companhia das Letras, 1995) and Carlos Gabriel Guimarães, "Mauá por trás do mito," *Revista de História*, September 21, 2007. Guimarães, an Universidade Federal Fluminense professor, also provided insights in an interview.

176   probably apocryphal. The quote attributed to Mauá (*"o melhor programa econômico de governo é não atrapalhar aqueles que produzem, investem, poupam, empregam, trabalham e consomem"*) is reproduced in *A História do Brasil em 50 Frases* by Jaime Klintowitz (Rio de Janeiro: LeYa, 2014). I figure it's apocryphal because it doesn't show up in Caldeira's *Mauá* or in *Exposição do Visconde de Mauá aos Credores de Mauá & C e ao Público* (Rio de Janeiro:

J. Villeneuve, 1878). In this letter to creditors, Mauá also never once uses the words *atrapalhar* or *investir* or the phrase *programa econômico,* and while he uses the verb *empregar* to refer to deploying capital or his own effort, he doesn't use it to refer to employing workers. When he does use the word *consumo,* he refers only to the consumption of specific resources, not to "consumption" in a general sense as we understand it today, e.g., on Sundays at your local mall; and he never uses the verb *consumir.* That said, the phrase jibes with other statements he made, like this one in his *Exposição:* "People complain that in Brazil everything is expected from the government and individual initiative does not exist! And how could it be any other way . . . if capital runs always into terrible prohibitive laws, and when these are not enough, the undue intervention of a government in its role as tutor?"

179   **thirty-million-dollar remodel.** Details on the Serrador are from Gaspar, *Tudo ou Nada,* 307.

179   **I got to speak to Eike again.** On March 26, 2012.

180   **if you did the math.** Two billion dollars is 5.63 percent of $35.5 billion. Eike's remaining 94.37 percent stake would then be worth $33.5 billion. (On top of that, he had one billion dollars in assets outside EBX.) Since the launch of the Bloomberg Billionaires Index a few weeks earlier, Eike's share prices had slid, and his stakes in his publicly traded companies were worth about $23.5 billion on the stock exchange at the time.

181   **receiving a vitamin cocktail intravenously.** Adriana Brasileiro, "Billionaire Eike Batista Keeps SLR McLaren in Rio Living Room," *Bloomberg,* June 22, 2008.

182   **Ziff brothers and Gávea Investimentos.** From OGX's IPO prospectus.

183   **The average Brazilian family.** This comparison uses numbers from Brazil's central bank and the U.S. Federal Reserve.

185   **The number had dipped below ten thousand by then.** Behind-the-scenes details on OGX are from Gaspar, *Tudo ou Nada,* 356, 359.

185   **many separate pockets of oil.** Analysis of these problems in Wellington Bahnemann, "Problema na OGX, de Eike Batista, não é de tecnologia, dizem geólogos," *Estado,* July 1, 2013.

186   **the world's—not just Brazil's—greatest entrepreneur.** According to an anonymous source at EBX.

187   **his empire carried around fifteen billion dollars in debt.** Around thirty billion *reais,* according to company filings.

188   **he earned no dividends.** The one exception was when MPX Energia posted a small gain on its financial holdings.

188   **he put almost all of it back in.** Based on my tracking of his investments as part of keeping his net worth calculation up to date.

189   **"a very good noodle dish at Mr. Lam."** From *Veja,* July 1, 2012.

189   **a billionaire himself.** *Forbes's* Brazilian edition estimated Cavalcanti's net worth at a billion dollars in 2013.

190   **Once he had thirty wells pumping.** This statement is from "Eike Batista responde ao mercado financeiro," *Exame,* July 6, 2012.

190   **mysterious bandages on his face.** Gaspar, *Tudo ou Nada,* 378.

190   **"If the market doesn't want me, I want me."** Also from "Eike Batista responde."

190   **if OGX ran out of capital.** According to company filings, Eike signed a "put op-

tion" that, if exercised by OGX's management, would require him to buy newly issued shares at 6.30 *reais* a share, no matter what the market price at the time.

191   **similar promises for MMX and OSX.** In company filings, Eike announced that he was buying 1.4 billion *reais* in newly issued MMX shares at above-market prices. He also announced that he would fulfill a provision in OSX's IPO prospectus that required him to buy a billion dollars' worth of new shares if the company couldn't find financing elsewhere.

191   **"You guys could publish that list only on the days I'm up."** Quote relayed to me by a Bloomberg employee in New York.

191   **visiting Eike at the Serrador building.** From "A prova de fogo do X," Malu Gaspar, *Veja*, October 10, 2012.

CHAPTER 8: THE PROFIT MOTIVE

192   **Jorge Paulo Lemann.** Details on Lemann's life and career come from the reporting I did for "Jorge Lemann: He Is . . . the World's Most Interesting Billionaire," *Bloomberg Businessweek*, August 29, 2013. This includes interviews with current and former associates Vicente Falconi, Eduardo Alves, Claudio Galeazzi, Luiz Cezar Fernandes, Arminio Fraga, Claudio Haddad, and Marcos Lisboa. I also relied on Cristiane Correa's book about Lemann and his partners, *Dream Big: How the Brazilian Trio behind 3G Capital—Jorge Paulo Lemann, Marcel Telles and Beto Sicupira—Acquired Anheuser-Busch, Burger King and Heinz* (Rio de Janeiro: Sextante, 2014), and the long profile by Alexandre Teixeira, Camila Hessel, and Darcio Oliveira, "O legado de Lemann," *Época Negócios*, January 20, 2009. (Subsequent citations of *Dream Big* refer to the Portuguese edition, *Sonho Grande*, 2013.)

193   **He's a tennis pro.** A curious side note: The supermarket tycoon Abilio Diniz told me he and Lemann sometimes play tennis together.

193   **"anti–Eike Batista."** Márcio Juliboni, "Por que Jorge Paulo Lemann é o anti-Eike Batista (e vai muito bem)," *IstoÉ Dinheiro*, March 25, 2015.

194   **He once spoke about his Harvard years.** In September 2011.

197   **Buffett had long criticized this style of investing.** For example: "Buffett Says Buyout Funds 'Don't Love the Business,'" *Bloomberg*, November 12, 2010.

197   **"Costs are like fingernails."** From Correa, *Sonho Grande*, 77.

197   **"daring in design, cautious in execution."** From Ron Chernow's *Titan: The Life of John D. Rockefeller, Sr.* (New York: Vintage, 2004), 85.

199   **"Work! Work! We have blacks to do that."** Thomas Ewbank, *Life in Brazil; Or, a Journal of a Visit to the Land of the Cocoa and the Palm* (New York: Harper, 1856), 184, quoted in Jorge Caldeira's *Mauá: Empresário do Império* (São Paulo: Companhia das Letras, 1995), 182.

199   **velvet-laden lords.** From Gilberto Freyre's *The Masters and the Slaves* (New York: Knopf, 1956), 363.

200   **his Swiss dad's "greatest legacy" was the Protestant work ethic.** From Oliveira, "O legado de Lemann."

201   **the BNDES has lent more than four billion dollars.** I calculated the BNDES's lending to Lemann's Brazilian companies Ambev, B2W, and Lojas Americanas based on data from the bank's website going back to 2005.

202   tied up all its fax lines. From *Sonho Grande,* 199.

202   AmBev is one of Brazil's top campaign donors. AmBev's campaign donations can be seen on the website of the Tribunal Superior Eleitoral (TSE). Because the company also contributes through hard-to-track subsidiaries, I also relied on Fernando Torres, "Falta transparência nas doações das SAs," *Valor Econômico,* September 23, 2014. According to the article, AmBev ranked third among campaign donors with 44.2 million *reais* in contributions for elections the following month.

202   AmBev's CEO credited the company's "dialogue." The conference call took place on July 31, 2014.

202   abusing their control of AmBev. Details on the CVM's case against Lemann (No. 21/2005) are available on its website. I also interviewed a CVM official who asked not to be named because he wasn't authorized to speak publicly about the case.

203   EC-155 helicopter. "Um novo sabor global," Lucila Soares, *Veja,* March 10, 2004.

203   "Money in and of itself isn't what fascinates me." From an interview in *HSM Management* (January–February 2008).

204   "I saw that I would never be an *astro.*" From an interview with *Tênis Brasil,* quoted in Oliveira, "O legado de Lemann."

204   Lemann never made a secret of his philanthropy. Lemann's press people provided details on his gifts.

204   3G's funds in the Cayman Islands. Filings with the U.S. Securities and Exchange Commission show 3G Capital's funds domiciled in the Caribbean tax haven.

205   one of his foundations awarded a scholarship. Verônica Serra received a scholarship from Fundação Estudar.

205   calling for higher taxes on billionaires. In Warren E. Buffett, "Stop Coddling the Super-Rich," *New York Times,* August 14, 2011.

205   Andrew Carnegie's *Gospel of Wealth.* Details from David Nasaw, *Andrew Carnegie* (New York: Penguin, 2006), with quote from Carnegie's *The Gospel of Wealth and Other Writings* (New York: Penguin, 2006).

206   "These guys have so much power through their wealth." From Stephanie Strom, "Pledge to Give Away Fortunes Stirs Debate," *New York Times,* November 10, 2010.

207   "equality is great." Maria Cristina Frias and Thais Bilenky, "Lemann diz que polarização política trava avanço do país," *Folha de S.Paulo,* November 21, 2015.

209   before he'd ever eaten a Whopper. From *Sonho Grande,* 228.

209   Lemann is unsentimental about jobs. Layoffs at companies controlled by Lemann and his partners were widely reported in the press. I made a rough calculation of the lack of job growth at AB InBev based on employee numbers from the companies that were absorbed into it. Before their giant 2008 merger, Anheuser-Busch had 34,000 employees, while InBev had 89,000; the Mexican brewer Grupo Modelo had some 35,000 before it was taken over in 2012. That adds up to 158,000 even without considering smaller acquisitions since then—like Goose Island in Chicago or Pivovar Samson in the Czech Republic. As of early 2015, AB InBev had 155,000 employees, showing a probable drop in total jobs (though some may also be the result of divestments). In their official response, Lemann's PR people declined to comment on my estimate but said, "We believe that this

model [of corporate consolidation] is part of a natural movement of the international market." After Lemann and Buffett took over Kraft, news emerged that they would cut a thousand jobs. And they not only got rid of free snacks for employees but canceled health insurance for fifteen thousand retired workers, instead providing them with vouchers to buy their own on an exchange. According to Noah Buhayar and Blake Schmidt, "The Brazilian Dealmaker Who Wowed Warren Buffett Is Reshaping the World," *Bloomberg Markets,* October 2013, Lemann once said he was interested in taking over Coca-Cola—and firing most of its hundred thousand employees. "We could run it with two hundred people," he said, apparently in jest.

210   **combined market value larger than that of Berkshire Hathaway.** Based on market values in late 2015, Lemann and his partners control companies worth more than $400 billion: AB InBev ($190 billion); SABMiller ($100 billion); Kraft Heinz ($95 billion); Restaurant Brands International ($20 billion); and Lojas Americanas ($5 billion). At the time, Berkshire Hathaway was valued at around $340 billion, Facebook at $300 billion, and Exxon at $350 billion.

211   **"lasting greatness."** According to Jim Collins, in his preface to *Sonho Grande,* 8.

211   **spent less on research and development.** Karen Brettell, David Gaffen, and David Rohde, "As stock buybacks reach historic levels, signs that corporate America is undermining itself," Reuters, November 16, 2015. An argument in favor of corporate buybacks is that shareholders will spend the money more wisely than corporations with excess profits. But actual productive investment has declined in recent years. Instead, these payouts may be financing increased luxury consumption and campaign finance by the rich: Justin Fox, "How Rich Investors Use All That Buyback Cash," *Bloomberg View,* November 11, 2015. Also, much of the money is apparently being hoarded—a phenomenon economists refer to as the global savings glut.

212   **CBMM.** Details in Cristiane Lucchesi and Alex Cuadros, "Brazil's Richest Family Forging $13 Billion Niobium Dream," *Bloomberg,* March 13, 2013.

212   **more made money from money, through investments.** In Erin Carlyle, "How Self-Made Forbes 400 Billionaires Earned Their Money," *Forbes,* September 18, 2013.

212   **U.S. government agencies developed GPS.** These points have been highlighted by the economist Mariana Mazzucato.

212   **Bill Gates himself.** Gates commented on the role of government in innovation in a blog post titled "We Need Clean-Energy Innovation, and Lots of It," July 29, 2015. www.gatesnotes.com/Energy/Energy-Innovation.

213   **Guilherme Leal.** I interviewed him on November 4, 2014.

214   **three hundred million dollars in unpaid taxes.** "Natura é autuada pela Receita em R$ 628 mi," *O Estado de S. Paulo,* January 7, 2013.

214   **he replied that it just wasn't financially viable yet.** In his video interview with *Exame,* March 18, 2010.

214   **"Jorge Paulo created a whole management culture."** From Fabiola Moura, "Billionaire Dethrones Kings in Beer to Burgers as Batista Model," *Bloomberg Markets,* November 2011.

214   **model of remuneration.** Eike's stock incentives were listed in IPO prospectuses as one of the pillars of investment in his companies.

215   **At least ten of them made more than twenty million dollars.** According to Maria Luíza Filgueiras, "A história secreta dos milionários de Eike," *Exame,* March 19, 2014.

215   **OGChic.** Details on big spending inside EBX are from Malu Gaspar, *Tudo ou Nada: Eike Batista e a Verdadeira História do Grupo X* (Rio de Janeiro: Record, 2014), 252.

215   **found a bank willing.** Details of these transactions with OGX are from Gaspar, *Tudo ou Nada,* 325.

216   **he'd call their bosses to demand a correction.** Details on Eike's relationship with stock analysts are from an anonymous source at EBX.

216   **Eike might shut the underwriting side of the bank out.** This happened with Merrill Lynch, according to Gaspar, *Tudo ou Nada,* 163ff.

216   **a bullish Credit Suisse analyst.** Roger Downey.

216   **Eike cultivated an environment.** Details on the environment at EBX are from an anonymous source at EBX; "A história por trás do sumiço do império de Eike Batista," *Época Negócios,* May 2014; and Gaspar, *Tudo ou Nada.* The best known of Eike's ex-execs was Rodolfo Landim, a top Petrobras guy who'd joined up for the promise of a one percent stake in EBX. The way Landim told it to *Piauí* (Luiz Maklouf Carvalho, "A baleia branca de Rodolfo Landim," January 2011), they began to chafe around the time that he, rather than Eike, showed up on the cover of a magazine for a story about OGX. When he quit, Eike refused to turn over the stake in EBX, so Landim sued him. Complaining to journalists about Eike's betrayal, Landim even handed out a photocopy of the handwritten promise. Landim lost the suit, not that EBX was worth much by the time he might have won it.

216   **"think bigger."** From Robson Viturino, "A hora da entrega," *Época Negócios,* March 7, 2012.

217   **Even Steve Jobs, notoriously dictatorial.** This characterization is based on Walter Isaacson's biography, *Steve Jobs* (New York: Simon & Schuster, 2011).

217   **the Emirates' two-billion-dollar investment.** Details in Alex Cuadros, Juan Pablo Spinetto, and Cristiane Lucchesi, "Batista Said to Pledge Extra EBX Stake to Back Mubadala Deal," *Bloomberg,* December 12, 2012.

218   **They ended the year with more than a billion in losses.** Two and a half billion *reais,* according to company filings.

218   **"Garantia's rib."** Denise Carvalho, "Mais cariocas que suíços," *Exame,* March 22, 2007. I interviewed Esteves on August 1, 2012. Details on his life are from press reports and reporting for Alex Cuadros and Cristiane Lucchesi, "BTG's Esteves Drives 'Better Than Goldman' Rise in Bank's Clout," *Bloomberg Markets,* September 10, 2012.

219   **"would sell his own mother to gain power."** From Consuelo Dieguez, "De elefante a formiga," *Piauí,* November 2006.

220   **Eike believed that Esteves's traders had been short-selling.** From Gaspar, *Tudo ou Nada,* 395.

220   **"The magic Eike is back!"** From Lauro Jardim, "Auto-confiança máxima," *Veja,* March 10, 2013.

CHAPTER 9: THE BACKLASH

221   Esteves had just given an interview. David Friedlander, Raquel Landim, and Ricardo Grinbaum, " 'É natural que a participação do Eike nas empresas caia de 60% para 30%,' " *O Estado de S. Paulo,* March 23, 2013. People call this newspaper *Estadão* for short.

221   a colleague of mine uncovered more secret guarantees. Cristiane Lucchesi and Juan Pablo Spinetto, "Brazil Billionaire Batista Said to Face Collateral Calls," *Bloomberg,* March 19, 2013.

223   they discussed installing a Petrobras terminal. This meeting is described in Malu Gaspar, *Tudo ou Nada: Eike Batista e a Verdadeira História do Grupo X* (Rio de Janeiro: Record, 2014), 405.

223   he suggested an alliance between OGX and Lukoil. This detail of Lula's meeting with Medvedev is from Gaspar, *Tudo ou Nada,* 419.

223   In the photo you could see him walking. Reproduced in Ricardo Setti, "Vejam como Lula fez papel de lobista em prol dos interesses de Eike Batista," *Veja,* March 29, 2013.

225   "esoteric consultant." From Lauro Jardim, "O sol girando para o lado errado," *Veja,* April 29, 2013.

226   The first protest against Eike. For Eike's involvement in the Maracanã auction and other World Cup spending issues, Christopher Gaffney's blog, *Hunting White Elephants,* was helpful. geostadia.blogspot.com.

227   "the Tomb of the Unknown Soldier." Cony's and Perdigão's quotes are from Alex Bellos's *Futebol: The Brazilian Way of Life* (New York: Bloomsbury, 2002), 54, 57.

231   Free Pass Movement. Piero Locatelli's #*VemPraRua* (São Paulo: Companhia das Letras, 2013) has a good account of this group and of the June 2013 protests in São Paulo.

234   "O povo não é bobo." This chant dates to the eighties, when Roberto Marinho allegedly conspired to distort election results to keep a political enemy, Leonel Brizola, from becoming governor of Rio state.

235   the imprisonment of a sitting congressman. Natan Donadon, convicted of embezzlement and conspiracy.

235   twenty people convicted in the *mensalão.* Twenty-four were convicted, but twenty went to prison that year.

237   hard to overstate the importance of soccer. In addition to Bellos's book, I got good background on soccer in Brazil from David Goldblatt's *Futebol Nation: The Story of Brazil through Soccer* (New York: Nation Books, 2014).

237   Fernando Henrique Cardoso credited some of the success. From Cardoso's English-language memoir, *The Accidental President of Brazil: A Memoir* (New York: PublicAffairs, 2006).

237   the BNDES offered subsidized loans. Four hundred million *reais* for each stadium.

237   Some cities offered tax credits, others guaranteed revenues. São Paulo, for example, offered 420 million *reais* in tax credits. For the stadium in the city of Natal, the state government agreed to pay a monthly minimum revenue to OAS.

238   "white elephants." This analysis is from the Tribunal de Contas da União (TCU).

239   a story outing OAS's owner. Blake Schmidt and Alex Cuadros, "World Cup Billionaire Stirs Brazil Protests Over Stadiums," *Bloomberg,* July 10, 2013.

239   Looking into his financial statements. OAS won its interest in São Paulo's international airport and a Rio subway line through Invepar, a joint venture with three public-employee pension funds. Invepar reported the added revenues from the Rio transport-fare hike in its 2012 financial statements.

239   OAS had given more than ten million dollars. OAS's campaign donations are from the website of the Tribunal Superior Eleitoral (TSE) and the website Às Claras, maintained by the corruption watchdog Transparência Brasil.

242   freedom of information request. Reported in Joshua Goodman and Alex Cuadros, "Batista Pledged Personal Wealth for $1 Billion BNDES Loan," *Bloomberg,* July 3, 2013.

243   "I made some bad investments." From the novela *Amor à Vida.*

244   "utilitarian fictions of capitalism." Richard White's quote is from David Nasaw's *Andrew Carnegie* (New York: Penguin, 2006), 129.

244   he published an op-ed. "Se pudesse voltar atrás, não recorreria ao mercado," *Valor Econômico,* July 19, 2013.

245   D&M's vice-president had written a letter. Published in full in Gaspar, *Tudo ou Nada*'s photo section. Eike's apology to D&M is also from *Tudo ou Nada,* 463.

245   put his life savings into OGX. Juan Pablo Spinetto, Peter Millard, and Ken Wells, "Batista's Losers Shout and Sue as OGX Meltdown Casts Pall," *Bloomberg,* December 31, 2013.

246   could no longer afford the rent. Lauro Jardim, "Aluguel de gente grande," *Veja,* October 2, 2013. The price is from Gaspar, *Tudo ou Nada,* 494.

246   *a preço de banana.* From Lauro Jardim, "Eike inconformado," *Veja,* September 11, 2013.

246   broken into tears. From Gaspar, *Tudo ou Nada,* 480.

247   invoked a clause in the contract. According to Gaspar (*Tudo ou Nada,* 448), Eike delayed signing the actual contract for nine months. He relented only when he was allowed to modify the line that said he could back out if the company's business plan changed. By specifying that the clause applied to the business plan *"nesta data"*—which is to say, at the date the contract was drawn up—it would apparently be easier to argue in court that he had the right to renege on his promise.

248   data that, in the United States. From Maria Luíza Filgueiras, "O que seria da EBX e seus acionistas em Nova York?", *Exame,* August 1, 2013.

248   The CVM apparently failed to enforce its own rules. Details on ANP guidelines are from the CVM's investigation, leaked in Samantha Lima, "CVM processa Eike por excesso de otimismo em comunicados," *Folha de S.Paulo,* August 23, 2014.

248   three separate indictments. One by prosecutors in Rio, on September 11, 2014; and two by prosecutors in São Paulo, on September 11, 2014 and September 23, 2014. The second insider trading charge concerned his second sale of OGX stock. The third has to do with OSX. In April 2013 Eike sold seventeen million dollars' worth of OSX shares four days after a board meeting in which he and the directors decided to wind down the company, halting construction of its shipyard. The decision became public only a month later, and if he'd waited to

sell until then, he would have earned four million dollars less. In his defense before the CVM, Eike claimed he'd sold the shares to fulfill a stock exchange requirement that a quarter of OSX's stock trade freely on the market. But according to the prosecutor, the requirement didn't exempt him from the legal prohibition on buying or selling his company's shares in the period before a so-called material fact had been made public. Eike also told the CVM that he couldn't possibly have sold the shares for personal gain because he was simultaneously putting money back into OSX, in much larger quantities, to fulfill a clause in the company's IPO prospectus that obliged him to inject cash if other financing dried up. The prosecutors said this was irrelevant because it's still illegal to trade on inside information. Regardless of what he did with the money afterward, selling the shares when he did earned him more money than it would have a month later, and these gains allegedly came at the expense of other shareholders.

250 **Eike could go to prison for as long as thirteen years.** According to Judge Flávio Souza, speaking to reporters on November 18, 2014. Souza is now off the case, but his estimate was based on minimum sentences for all the charges against Eike.

CHAPTER 10: TOO BIG TO FAIL

251 **he would single out Bloomberg.** In his interview with Mariana Godoy, June 5, 2015.

252 **stunning losses for 2013.** Twenty-three billion *reais,* according to company filings.

253 **a salary of five million dollars a year.** Made public by Judge Flávio Souza.

253 **an electronic-music club called Zozô.** "Olin Batista pendura conta de R$ 16 mil em boate," *Extra,* October 30, 2013.

253 **"I don't ask about the crisis."** Carol Marques, "Babi Rossi diz que pagaria contas de Olin Batista: 'Na pobreza e na riqueza,'" *Ego,* October 31, 2013.

253 **took heavy meds to get to sleep.** From Thor's interview with *GQ*'s Brazilian edition, June 2015.

253 **"ending up poor."** From Malu Gaspar, *Tudo ou Nada: Eike Batista e a Verdadeira História do Grupo X* (Rio de Janeiro: Record, 2014), 488.

254 **"that doesn't mean he won't be acquitted."** "Thor Batista, depois de condenado pela Justiça, já dirige carrão, e em nova companhia," *Extra,* September 2, 2013.

256 **the losses to commerce.** "Rolezinhos e manipulações," *O Globo,* January 21, 2014.

256 **started teaching English.** I taught English in poor neighborhoods one Saturday a month from mid-2013 until late 2014 through a nonprofit called Cidadão Pró Mundo.

260 **officially resurrected the *complexo de vira-lata*.** The tweet is from Maurício Santoro, @msantoro1978.

261 **"I never intended to trick any investor."** The quotes in this section are from the following stories published between September 17 and 21, 2014: Mônica Ciarelli and Mariana Durão, "Eike Batista diz que foi o maior prejudicado por crise do Grupo X," *O Estado de S. Paulo;* "Acuado pela Justiça, Eike se defende e diz que seus ativos são de credores" and "'Tenho chance de recuperar patrimônio,'"

Valor Econômico; Maria Fernanda Delmas and Glauce Cavalcanti, "Eike Batista: 'Botei do bolso. Levaram todo o meu patrimônio,'" *Extra;* Samantha Lima, "'Voltar à classe média é um baque gigantesco,' afirma Eike Batista," *Folha de S.Paulo;* and Malu Gaspar, "Eike: 'Não sou diferente dos outros acionistas. Perdemos juntos,'" *Veja.*

262   **untold millions in offshore accounts.** According to Gaspar (*Tudo ou Nada,* 484), Eike has tens of millions of dollars stashed away in accounts in Panama and Switzerland.

262   **worth a combined twenty-five million dollars.** Raquel Landim and Renata Agostini, "Eike Batista doa aos filhos casas que têm valor estimado em R$ 50 mi," *Folha,* May 4, 2014.

262   **To Flávia Sampaio he transferred an apartment.** According to a seizure order signed by Judge Flávio Souza.

262   **transferred tens of millions of dollars in cash.** Samantha Lima and Marco Antônio Martins, "Governo quer repatriar dinheiro de Eike Batista," *Folha,* February 11, 2015.

262   **froze $120 million.** Judge Flávio Souza froze 122 million *reais* in Eike's bank accounts in May 2014 and another 117 million *reais* in a bond fund in September 2014.

263   **"anti-business prejudice."** From Menin's blog, March 17, 2015.

263   **reveals a telling episode.** Gaspar, *Tudo ou Nada,* 328.

265   **"We're being smothered here!"** Ary Bergher said this.

265   **a bald old lawyer at his side.** Sergio Bermudes.

266   **judges often fancy themselves a superior class of citizen.** In one famous case, a cop at a drunk-driving checkpoint stopped a judge who had no driver's license and whose Land Rover had no license plates or registration. She ordered the judge's car towed, and amid the judge's protests, stated the obvious: He might be a judge but "he's not God." For disrespecting him, she was later ordered to pay a fine of five thousand *reais.*

269   **Economists on the right and the left.** Economists on the right, such as Arminio Fraga, almost unanimously criticize Dilma's heavy use of the BNDES. Laura Carvalho is one economist on the left who has criticized Dilma's massive supply-side tax cuts. The BNDES maintains that investment would have been lower without its loans.

270   **two billion dollars in bribes.** Petrobras declared to regulators that it had lost six billion *reais* to bribes.

270   **She didn't appear to have any personal role.** In his plea-bargain testimony, the *doleiro* Alberto Youssef speculated that Dilma had to know about the corruption at Petrobras, given its scale, but said he had no evidence. Other than that, as of this writing, nothing has emerged that directly links Dilma to the scheme.

272   **"extorted" into paying bribes.** From David Friedlander, "Aparelharam a Petrobras para achacar empreiteiras, diz empresário," *Folha,* March 19, 2015.

273   **plea-bargain testimony from a construction tycoon.** Ricardo Pessoa, of UTC Engenharia.

273   **scandals from the nineties that had ended in *pizza*.** It's impossible to tally all the corruption scandals that ended without convictions, but Dilma liked to cite several cases that involved her main opposition party, the PSDB: the Sivam affair,

the Pasta Rosa, the congressional vote-buying that allowed Fernando Henrique Cardoso to be reelected as president, the so-called *mensalão tucano,* and the São Paulo train cartel. Details of these cases can be found in Elio Gaspari's column "Todos soltos, todos soltos, até hoje," *Folha,* October 19, 2014.

273 **pro-government websites.** These include Brasil247, Diário do Centro do Mundo, and GGN. The blogger I quote is Paulo Moreira Leite, in "PML: 'República Lava Jató' pode quebrar o país," *Brasil247,* June 19, 2015. Leite also compared pretrial arrests of construction tycoons to the use of the *pau de arara* torture device: "Entre a Constituição e o sangue," *Brasil247,* November 29, 2015.

274 **An antitrust official.** Vinicius Marques de Carvalho, president of the Conselho Administrativo de Defesa Econômica (Cade). Julianna Sofia, "Haverá punição severa se cartel for provado, diz Cade," *Folha,* December 2, 2014.

274 **Camargo Corrêa agreed to cooperate.** The company agreed to pay 700 million *reais* for immunity from prosecution for bribery, and in its 2014 annual report, the company reported 26 billion *reais* in annual revenue.

274 **gamble will pay off.** Judge Moro cites Mani Pulite, the anti-corruption investigations that reshaped politics in Italy in the 1990s.

274 **"lobbyist in chief."** Thiago Bronzatto and Filipe Coutinho, "As suspeitas de tráfico de influência internacional sobre o ex-presidente Lula," *Época,* April 30, 2015. Three months after this story, federal prosecutors opened an investigation to determine whether Lula had engaged in "influence peddling" to help Odebrecht win contracts in Africa and Latin America with financing from the BNDES. According to investigations by the Conselho de Controle de Atividades Financeiras (COAF), an arm of the finance ministry, Lula earned 27 million *reais* from speeches from 2011 through 2014, and much of that money came from Odebrecht. In his defense, Lula's foundation claimed the payments for talks were unrelated to his efforts to promote Odebrecht and other *empreiteiras* abroad.

275 **meatpacking giant JBS.** The company's campaign donations are available on the website of the Tribunal Superior Eleitoral (TSE). It donated 366 million *reais* in 2014, of a total of 5 billion *reais* raised by all campaigns that year.

275 **matched up with public opinion.** A Datafolha poll from July 2015 showed that seventy-four percent of Brazilians are against corporate campaign finance.

278 **investors who still believed in him.** Details on Eike's newest business ventures are from Gaspar, *Tudo ou Nada,* 502; Samantha Pearson, "Eike Batista plots comeback in pharma," *Financial Times,* November 13, 2014; and Vanessa Dezem, "Eike Batista's Comeback Plan: Cow Cloning and Viagra," *Bloomberg,* March 31, 2015.

EPILOGUE: AFTER THE CRASH

282 **As I neared the end.** I took my brief road trip to Petrópolis in November 2014.

283 **Ten other locals had been run over.** Ana Claudia Costa, "BR-040: muitos ciclistas e nenhuma sinalização," *O Globo,* March 22, 2010.

284 **invest in Rio's favelas.** Paes promised to integrate favelas with the rest of the city as part of a program called Morar Carioca, but the money dried up.

284 **Carlos Carvalho is a major donor.** According to the Tribunal Superior Eleitoral (TSE).

285   **sentenced to nineteen years in prison.** As of this writing, Marcelo Odebrecht was reportedly mulling a plea bargain that could lighten his sentence.

287   **a Workers Party senator signed.** The senator's name is Delcídio Amaral.

287   **put a lid on Carwash.** Mônica Bergamo, "Temer já desenha equipe de seu futuro governo caso substitua Dilma," *Folha de S.Paulo,* December 9, 2015; Renata Mendonça, " 'Ainda que haja mudança no cenário político, continuaremos tendo muitos inimigos no poder,' diz Deltan Dallagnol," BBC Brasil, April 15, 2016.

287   **two of the most likely opposition candidates.** The two opposition candidates I'm referring to are both from the PSDB. While not personally implicated in the scandals, Geraldo Alckmin, current governor of São Paulo, has presided over a cartel allegedly created by suppliers of subway trains and a more recent case involving embezzlement in contracts for public school meals. Aécio Neves, a senator who ran against Dilma in 2014, has been cited in multiple plea bargains as the possible recipient of bribes skimmed from the state energy company Furnas. He denies the allegations.

288   **that a healthy majority of Americans.** A June 2015 *New York Times*/CBS poll showed that eighty-four percent of Americans think money has too much influence in politics.

Glossary

ARRASTÃO. Literally "trawling," it's a mass robbery at a restaurant, on a beach, or on a traffic-choked road.

BAILE FUNK. A style of music popular in the favela with beats inherited from Miami Bass, melodies sampled from everywhere, and homespun raps. *Funk ostentação* is a version that focuses on material goods.

BANDIDO. A criminal or suspected criminal.

BOMBEIRO. Fireman.

BOTECO. A neighborhood bar-cum-restaurant.

CACHAÇA. Strong sugarcane-based alcohol.

CAFUNÉ. The act of lovingly stroking someone's hair.

CAIPIRINHA. A cocktail made with *cachaça*, sugar, and fruit, usually lime. With vodka substituted for *cachaça*, it's known as *caipiroska*.

CAIXA DOIS. The undeclared "second cash register" companies keep for bribes and under-the-table donations.

CAMAROTE. VIP area at a nightclub or party.

CARIOCA. A native of the city of Rio de Janeiro.

CARNAVAL. The boozy five-day festival that precedes Lent.

CHIQUE. Chic.

CLASSE C. Brazil's emerging middle class, with household incomes from a few hundred to a few thousand dollars a month.

COMPLEXO DE VIRA-LATA. Literally "mutt complex," an old feeling of national inferiority.

COMUNIDADE. The politically correct term for *favela*.

CORONEL. A regional political boss. The plural is *coronéis*.

CUSTO BRASIL. The mysteriously high price of everything in Brazil.

DESENVOLVIMENTISMO. The idea that it is the state's role to guide economic development.

DESPACHANTE. A profession dedicated to navigating the bureaucracy, mostly by making friends with the right bureaucrats.

DOLEIRO. Black-market currency dealer.

DOUTOR. A Latin American term of respect that implies no medical training or formal education at all.

É. The third-person present conjugation of "to be," also used as an interjection basically meaning "yep."

EMPREITEIRA. A construction firm, usually in public works. An *empreiteiro* is a construction tycoon or executive.

FAVELA. A poor, informal neighborhood built ramshackle by its own residents, sometimes referred to as *favelados*.

FAZENDA. A rural estate or ranch, owned by a *fazendeiro*.

FAZER O QUÊ? A phrase to express resignation: "What are you gonna do?"

FILHO DA PUTA. Son of a bitch.

FUTEBOL. Soccer.

GAMBIARRA. A jerry-rigged fix to some problem.

GOTA D'ÁGUA. The last straw (literally "drop of water").

GRINGO. Foreigner, not necessarily from the United States.

JABUTICABA. A delicious purple fruit. Also refers to something that exists only in Brazil.

JEITINHO. If *jeito* means "way," the diminutive *jeitinho* is the "little way" around society's normal rules.

LARANJA. Front man. Also *testa de ferro*.

MALANDRO. A hustler or crook who practices *malandragem*.

MALUFAR. Derived from Paulo Maluf's name, to misappropriate public funds.

MENSALÃO. A scandal that erupted in 2005, wherein Lula's deputies had been buying votes in Congress.

MILÍCIAS. Paramilitary gangs formed by current and former police officers, known especially for their control of certain Rio *favelas*.

MOTOBOY. Motorcycle messenger.

NOVO RICO. New rich.

PADRINHO POLÍTICO. Literally "political godfather," a powerful person who helps you get ahead with nepotistic favors.

PAI. Father.

PARA INGLÊS VER. Literally "for the English to see," a phrase employed whenever the rules are quietly broken and everyone kind of knows it but nobody says anything.

PARCELADO. Bought in monthly installments.

PATRIMONIALISMO. A system wherein business lives off contracts, capital, and favors from the state.

PAU DE ARARA. Literally "parrot's perch," a pole from which people are hung during torture. The phrase also refers to the kind of open-bed truck that Lula and his family traveled in when they migrated to the southeast.

PAULISTANO. Native of the city of São Paulo. A native of São Paulo state is known as a *paulista*.

PERIFERIA. The city outskirts.

PICHAÇÃO. A runic-looking graffiti native to Brazil.

PIZZA. When a scandal dies out with no one powerful suffering any real penalties.

POXA. An exclamation that roughly translates as "Shoot!"

PROPINA. Bribe.

QUARTO DE EMPREGADA. The tiny, usually windowless maid's room in a Brazilian home.

REAL. Brazil's currency since 1994. The plural is *reais*.

RESSURGE A DEMOCRACIA! This *O Globo* headline from April 2, 1964, literally means "Democracy Resurges!"

ROUBA MAS FAZ. "He steals but he gets things done," an old saying.

SAMBA. A style of music that sprang from black enclaves in the early twentieth century, mashing up African drum rhythms with Portuguese mini-guitars and stirring in ballroom styles like polka. Samba schools are the dance troupes that perform in elaborate processions during *carnaval*.

SAUDADE. Nostalgic longing.

SERRA. Mountain range.

SERTÃO. The arid backlands of the northeast. Someone from that area is known as a *sertanejo*—also the name of a style of country music.

SUBÚRBIO. Usually refers to a poor suburb, not like the orderly American kind.

SUPERFATURAMENTO. The practice of inflating costs on public contracts, especially in infrastructure projects.

TELENOVELA. Soap opera—*novela* for short.

TRÁFICO. Usually refers to drug trafficking. *Tráfico de influência* is influence peddling—a crime that shares a blurry boundary with lobbying in Brazil.

Index

ALEX CUADROS grew up in Albuquerque, New Mexico. After getting a liberal arts degree from Sarah Lawrence College, he spent three years in New York City before moving to Bogotá, Colombia, in 2008. There he worked as a freelance journalist for outlets such as *The Boston Globe, Mother Jones, The Nation, The San Francisco Chronicle,* and *Slate.* In 2010 he moved to São Paulo for a staff job with Bloomberg News, and as the "billionaires reporter" for Latin America, he contributed frequently to *Bloomberg Businessweek.* He recently moved back to New York. This is his first book.

alexcuadros.com

Facebook.com/alex.cuadros

@alexcuadros

ABOUT THE TYPE

This book was set in Sabon, a typeface designed by the
well-known German typographer Jan Tschichold
(1902–74). Sabon's design is based upon the original
letter forms of sixteenth-century French type designer
Claude Garamond and was created specifically to be
used for three sources: foundry type for hand composi-
tion, Linotype, and Monotype. Tschichold named his
typeface for the famous Frankfurt typefounder Jacques
Sabon (c. 1520–80).